Leadership

and
INTERPERSONAL
BEHAVIOR

Leadership

and

INTERPERSONAL

BEHAVIOR

Edited by

LUIGI PETRULLO

BERNARD M. BASS

Holt, Rinehart and Winston, Inc.
New York

We wish to thank the following publishers for permission to reprint tables, figures, and excerpts as noted below:

Harper & Brothers, for Figure 1 in Chapter 1 which appeared in *Leadership, Psychology, and Organizational Behavior* by Bernard M. Bass; and, in Chapter 20, for material taken from pages 219–220 and from Figure 2 on page 221, of *Festschrift: for Gardner Murphy.*

John Wiley & Sons, Inc., for material in Chapter 20 taken from pages 184–186, 187, and 190–193 of *Modern Organization Theory* (M. Haire, Editor), 1959.

American Psychological Association, for the following tables in Chapter 13: Tables 1 and 3 from Volume 71 of the *Psychological Monographs;* and Table 2 from the *Journal of Abnormal and Social Psychology,* 1958, Volume 57.

University of North Carolina Press, for Table 1 in Chapter 9 taken from *The Family and Population Control* (p. 290).

Princeton University Press, for Figures 1, 2, and 3 in Chapter 9 from *Automata Studies* (C. E. Shannon and J. McCarthy, Editors), 1956, in the chapter by J. von Neumann, "Probabilistic Logic and Synthesis of Reliable Organisms from Unreliable Components."

Midwest Administration Center, University of Chicago, for Figure 1 and several paragraphs in Chapter 18 taken from *Administrative Theory in Education* (A. W. Halpin, Editor), Chapter 4.

Industrial Relations Research Organization, for several paragraphs in Chapter 18 taken from *Value Dimensions and Situational Dimensions in Organizational Behavior* by C. L. Shartle published in the *Proceedings of the Tenth Annual Meeting of the Industrial Relations Research Association.*

Row, Peterson & Co., for Table 4b in Chapter 12 taken from Table 10, page 699 of D. Cartwright and A. Zander (Editors), *Group Dynamics,* 2nd ed., 1960.

Preface

1168834

In 1950 the Office of Naval Research sponsored a symposium which brought together the results of ONR-sponsored group and leadership research. Since that time, additional research on leadership has made it advisable once again to take stock of the current status of achievement. The symposium has seemed to be a good device for achieving this purpose. Among its important benefits is the opportunity for a group of experts to examine and discuss current research in a particular area. Where a field is expanding, it is desirable to take periodic panoramic views without sacrificing the minute inspection of details. This is possible where there is ample opportunity for interaction.

The plan of the ONR–LSU symposium on leadership was as follows: Participants were selected from the large panel of psychologists who were known to be conducting research on leadership. An attempt was made to include in the group a variety of approaches and to avoid duplication. While the final group selected could not include all those performing current research, a representative sample of those regarded by their colleagues as the most significant contributors to the field was obtained.

Each participant prepared his paper and distributed it to every other participant before the symposium. At the symposium, the author presented an abstract of his work and it was then discussed by two persons previously designated for this purpose. An invited audience of about fifty was present. After three papers had been presented, the large group broke up into small groups to discuss the papers further. This procedure, lasting a half day, was repeated until abstracts of all papers had been presented, criticized, and discussed in small groups. Each author then revised his paper for final publication. The procedure seemed to work well and aided in the preparation of final copy.

President Troy H. Middleton of Louisiana State University, Lt. Gen. USA (Ret.), opened the symposium with cogent observations on leadership in military and educational organizations. Speaking from broad administrative experience, President Middleton stressed the need for knowledge in this field. Some excerpts from his speech follow:

> Ever since men first began to associate with one another, there have been leaders. The first leader was a kind of medicine man. Then the man of God appeared on the scene, and later, the philosopher. As society became more complex leaders became specialists of a sort, until today we have leaders representing all the myriad interests and activities of this complicated Space Age.
>
> The story of leadership, then, is practically as old as the story of man. This could lead one to conclude that the world should abound with experts on leadership. And perhaps it does, but I suspect that those who are among the best informed on the subject of leadership are not always to be found in positions of great public trust. Why this should be true—if indeed it is—I do not know, unless it is because those who know the most about leadership want no part of it—for which I certainly cannot blame them at times.
>
> As for the leaders themselves, their knowledge of the subject may be likened to that of the "shoemaker's wife who never has shoes," interpreted in this case to mean that leaders are likely to be so occupied with the business of leading that they seldom can find time for even a clinical study of what it is that makes leaders tick.
>
> I spent thirty-two active years in the Army, most of them in the classroom. I have been on duty at LSU for twenty-eight years, twenty-two of them in a civilian capacity. I have had an opportunity to observe many leaders in the military establishment, in education, and in areas outside these fields as well, and I have been exposed to many different kinds of leadership through the years. With this background, I suppose I should know something about the subject. But the fact is that the more I have been exposed to it, the more uncertain and confused I have become. Perhaps I have been overexposed.
>
> I feel certain of this, however: In leadership there are few absolutes. The tools of leadership can be discovered, catalogued, and studied, but don't try to apply them across the board—and don't try to find all of them in every leader.

The reason for this is clear to me. I have yet to find two leaders who are, so to speak, identical twins. None of the leaders I have known have had all the same qualities and none have employed identical methods. Which is to say that there are leaders and there are leaders—in the broadest sense of the word, of course. And apparently it takes all kinds to make a world. . . .

The results of good leadership in education and in the military can be assessed in terms of projects completed, results produced, missions accomplished and victories won. But it is very difficult to dissect the character of the leader responsible for these effects. . . .

General Middleton's comments served to recall the central significance of the interaction of person and situation in understanding the leadership process and its elusiveness. The search for understanding of this process was the common objective of this symposium. What distinguishes this group of experts from most similar groups is their faith in, and use of, the strategy of observation, analysis, and experiment. This volume does not provide final answers to an understanding of the leadership process; it represents instead an introduction to a comparatively new way of examining the subject—a way that adds the current notions of experiment to the older, but certainly not to be discarded, methods of observation, history, and analysis.

To complete an undertaking of this kind requires support and cooperation from many more than can be acknowledged. Among those who are mentioned gratefully are those critics and evaluators who read the first drafts of the chapters and presented their evaluations at the symposium. Some prepared careful critiques which might well have been published. However, since the purpose of the symposium was to generate critical comments for use in revising the manuscripts, and since many of the points brought up were adopted by the authors, it would be redundant to include these critiques. Thus, as often happens, the critics remain unsung and unpraised though their contributions were great. These include all of the authors and the following persons: Paul Baker, Irwin Berg, Eugene L. Gaier, Donald J. Lewis, Brendan A. Maher, Roland B. Pellegrin, Thomas B. Richards, William Sloan, Robert Vidulich, and F. H. Sanford. In addition, an invited audience participated in the small group discussions and not only helped in adding interest to the symposium but undoubtedly assisted the authors in sharpening their ideas.

The administrative support of both the Office of Naval Research and the Louisiana State University is gratefully acknowledged. Louisiana State University president Troy H. Middleton (Lt. Gen. USA Ret.) was a gracious host as well as active participant. Dr. Denzel D. Smith, director of the Psychological Sciences Division attended the symposium; his support, participation, and encouragement have been very evident at every stage from planning the symposium to publication of this volume.

A great debt is acknowledged to the following persons at the Office of Naval Research for their administrative and active support of a broad program in leadership research: the Chief of Naval Research, Rear Admiral Rawson D. Bennett; the Deputy and Assistant Chief, Captain Jacob C. Myers; the Chief Scientist, Dr. Thomas J. Killian; the Assistant Chief for Research, Captain H. E. Ruble; and the Director of the Naval Research Group, Dr. S. Silverman. Grateful acknowledgment is made to Dr. F. Joachim Weyl, ONR's Research Director, for his early encouragement of, and interest in, basic research on leadership.

The editors are grateful to Mrs. Richard Nacewski for her careful preparation of the indexes and to Miss Gladys B. Snyder for her tireless assistance in the preparation of the manuscript.

LUIGI PETRULLO

BERNARD M. BASS

November 1960

Contents

Introduction

Luigi Petrullo

Office of Naval Research

Considering the amount of disagreement there has been about the principles involved, it is surprising to find acts of leadership so often executed successfully. Theories of leadership have ranged all the way from Carlyle's "great man" theory (the history of the world is the history of great men) through Pareto's organizational concepts of the rule of the elite, Spencer's deterministic model with emphasis on environmental order, and finally to theories that see leadership as diffused throughout the group. Each such theory has been buttressed by a wealth of empirical data, and each has had many adherents. These theories were not spun out of thin air, but out of hard facts and events which any man could observe historically or contemporaneously. Each had a very persuasive air about it for the reason that it seemed to explain so many cases.

Each such theory seems to have stressed some factor at the expense of others. In doing so, concepts were developed which are the necessary bases of our current theories. What was at one time the crux of some major theory—that leadership resulted from some personality trait, or was determined situationally, or was dependent upon culture, or arose from interaction of peculiar forces—today seems to be but one of the many items considered in the complicated leadership equation. The road from the obscure simplicities of earlier theories has brought us to the current swamp of multifactorial complexities, through which we seek a heuristic path to clearer ground. Nor are there any short cuts; on the contrary, to the masses of historical and empirical data we are adding new kinds of data resulting from experimental and statistical techniques discovered but recently.

Although we believe that personality factors, cultural forces, situations, and interactions are all important in the understanding of the leadership process, we do not really *know* that they are, nor how. Our experimental work was initiated only recently, and there is as yet no systematic science of leadership. A great many scattered bits of evidence have been accumulated but have not been brought together in any integrated theory. A number of writers—for example, Sanford (1952), C. A. Gibb (1954), Cattell (1957)—have suggested the beginnings of such theories, and experimentalists like Hemphill (1958) and Bass (1960) have fashioned theoretical structures, but so recently that there has been little opportunity to evaluate them.

Heider's (1958, p. 2) blunt statement "if we removed all knowledge of scientific psychology from our world, problems in interpersonal relations might easily be coped with and solved much as before" is most pertinent to leadership: it is fortunate that there is a "naive" psychology of leadership, for there is as yet no scientific psychology of the subject. Because there is no science of leadership, it must not be concluded that there is no art of leadership. There is, but effective practice varies so much from person to person and from situation to situation as to make generalization useless.

The need for experiment and for theory in social psychology has been obvious these last twenty years. Barnard (1938), Stouffer *et al.* (1949), R. L. French (1949), Bruner (1950), Asch (1952), Sanford (1952), Cartwright and Zander (1953), C. A. Gibb (1954), and Heider (1958) are but a few who have called attention to the need for integrative theory. Concerning the lack of theory and experiment on leadership Stouffer and his colleagues say:

> There are few practical problems facing social science more urgent than that of studying leadership experimentally and developing some tested hypotheses to replace the copybook maxims that now fill most manuals on leadership, whether written for the Army, for industry, or for organizations like the YMCA (1949, p. 363).
>
> Moreover, until social psychology has contributed a systematic body of theory from which deductions can be made to practical situations, with reasonable assurance from past experimental research that the predictions will be verified, such programs will be only minimally effective. Here is an area of future research in which concentrated and sustained effort is necessary. Only as a result of many experimental studies can it

be expected that the gap between accepted stereotypes of good leadership behavior and actual practice will be materially narrowed (*ibid.,*
p. 391).

Cartwright and Zander have made a further point (1953, p. 535): "It
has been only in very recent years that research on leadership has attempted
to discover cause-and-effect relations regardless of their immediately practical or ideological significance." It is true that most of the theories of the
past have been developed to explain political, military, or economic
behavior.

We now seem on the verge of developing such a science. The last
twenty years have seen much pertinent data brought together; laboratory
and statistical techniques have been developed to assist in studying leadership problems in a controlled manner; old theories have been re-examined
and re-evaluated and new ones are being formed. Many disciplines—
political science, sociology, anthropology, psychology, psychiatry, education—have contributed their specialized talents to a great pool from which
the investigator can receive assistance and guidance.

It is because of our concern for a scientific psychology of leadership,
because of the need for experiment, field work, and theory that this symposium has taken place. There is a good-sized body of experimental work
on leadership and some up-to-the-minute theories based upon this work
that need expression, discussion, and criticism. To help in understanding
the background of current research on leadership, it would be well to state
some basic assumptions underlying such research and some major trends
evident in the work of the last four or five decades.

BASIC ASSUMPTIONS

Except in two extreme situations—really theoretical limits—we find
leadership as an integral aspect of all interpersonal behavior. Where
people are acting in a purely random manner, and where one person's
behavior is as completely unpredictable as another's—in other words, in
bedlam—there is no interpersonal influence and obviously no leadership.
Such aggregates of people behave somewhat like autumn leaves caught by
passing winds. Conversely, where a group is highly organized, with a
complete set of rules for every conceivable act and no slightest deviation
permitted, no personal leadership is possible. Under such circumstances,
the leader does not decide when to initiate action, for the rules or laws
dictate his behavior. It was with highly structured societies that Aristotle
and Tolstoi were concerned when they wrote that kings have the least
freedom of all, since they must conform to the common expectancy to

play their parts as kings should. In a rigid hierarchy, the interaction is actually between positions; prediction is as accurate as the amount of adherence to the prescribed roles. Jones and Thibaut (1958, p. 155) have called such behavior "noncontingent interaction."

Fortunately, life is not lived in an environment of pure randomness or of rigid mechanism. True, the world does have these appearances—the chance that seems to make anything possible, and the inevitableness that seems to make only one end certain. But the world has sometimes another appearance—where we seem to be guided by a feeling of purpose, where we move as if we had some freedom of action and some chance to exercise choice, some opportunity to influence and to be influenced.

Leadership and Democracy

In the continuum stretching from complete individual freedom to completely structured order, all groups of whatsoever kind take their place. Our place is in a purposeful world where leadership must take account of the free choice of those who are led. In a tightly organized society the people who sit at the top may rule, or dominate, or command, but unless those who follow them have some choice to follow or not follow, there is no personal leadership. As Pigors (1935, p. 20) says, where there is no choice there is domination, the antithesis of leadership.

In this symposium we are concerned with leadership in a democratic society. This requires at least two basic and equally important assumptions. The first is that, *to survive, our society must be productive*. The second is that *the individual cannot be sacrificed in the interest of group welfare*. Of leadership, interpersonal relations, and democracy, Lasswell, a political scientist, says (1948): "Our conception of a democracy is that of a network of congenial and creative interpersonal relations" (p. 110). "Leadership is a complex pattern of congeniality and efficiency" (p. 185). These basic beliefs often appear to be in conflict. Philosophers like Reinhold Niebuhr (1958) and Alfred North Whitehead (1933) have attempted a theological and historical reconciliation. It is one object of our research to reconcile them within a scientific framework.

The importance of these assumptions, as well as the apparent conflict in their application, has been stated many times, and very skillfully, by men in all walks of life—political scientists, industrial executives, sociologists, military careerists, and ordinary citizens—as well as by psychologists. Concerning the relative importance of these two factors, Chester I. Barnard (1938) has said:

> The strategic factor in social integration is the development and selection of leaders. The process is usually unbalanced by excessive emphasis

either upon technological proficiency or upon moral status. In some ages moralities have been cultivated in excess of the technological capacities to support them. In the present age the emphasis is upon technological proficiency which is not adequately guided by the necessities of the co-operative system as a whole (pp. 288–289).

Barnard also made a distinction between effectiveness and efficiency in which he differentiated "accomplishment of the cooperative purpose" (effectiveness) from "satisfaction of individual motives" (efficiency), and suggested that the function of the executive was to administer both. This dichotomy suggests various concepts such as Rank's *love* and *force,* Bronfenbrenner's *support* and *structure,* as well as the concepts of *initiating structure* and *consideration* which have been developed from the results of field and laboratory work on leadership (Halpin and Winer, 1957). Again these psychological terms suggest related military terms, such as *accomplishment of mission* and *duty to subordinates* which some have said are the primary responsibilities of the military leader (for example, Lt. Col. J. H. Carter, 1952). When General S. L. A. Marshall (1957) spoke of the two most important characteristics of the leader as being (1) the *ability to get things done,* and (2) *the willingness to take great risks,* he may have been talking about the same two important factors. The ability to get things done is related to productivity, or the task features of an activity; willingness to take great personal risk shows not only a desire to accomplish an objective but a great consideration for the welfare of those with whom one is associated, since he would even sacrifice himself for them.

Viteles (1958), who has consistently stressed the importance of the two factors of *productivity* and *morale* in the industrial area, says this in one of his latest writings:

> To a large extent, such management development programs have been directed toward enlarging both the *technical* "know-how" of the executive and improving his performance as a "coordinator of human effort" in industry. . . . This has brought . . . acceptance of responsibility for individual and social welfare as a component of business management in the United States.

To some extent this reflects a modification of the philosophy of efficiency in production for its own sake which played a part in industrial and business practices in the late nineteenth and early twentieth centuries. Even if individual and social welfare are accepted primarily because they are "good business," their acceptance is nonetheless significant.

In the light of this emphasis on the personal and productive factors involved in leadership, it is pertinent to quote from General Order 21 of the United States Navy (1958) which calls specific attention to certain cultural values basic to carrying out the Navy's mission:

> By naval leadership is meant the art of accomplishing the Navy's mission through people. It is the sum of those qualities of intellect, of human understanding and of moral character that enable a man to inspire and to manage a group of people successfully. Effective leadership, therefore, is based on personal example, good management practices, and moral responsibility. The term leadership as used in this order shall include all three of these elements.

Leadership and Organization

Nevertheless, the business of getting things done—done well and done quickly—is sometimes in conflict with the principle of consideration for individuals. A constantly recurring model of a leader is that of the person trying to meet the task requirements imposed by top management and the requirement for consideration demanded by subordinates. One interesting solution suggested by various investigators (Sanford, 1952; Berrien and Bash, 1951) has been the possibility that during crises democratic groups will accept authoritarian methods in order to get the job done. T. N. Whitehead, a member of the Elton Mayo group which conducted the classic Western Electric studies (*see* Roethlisberger, 1949), differentiated between the face-to-face leader and the "administrator," and suggested the sharing of leadership responsibility as a way out of the conflicting objectives of individual and organization (Whitehead, 1936). Selznick (1957, p. 154) sees the executive as becoming "a statesman as he makes the transition from administrative management to institutional leadership"—a democratic trend.

Is it true that the basic needs of an individual are in conflict with the needs of the organization, as Argyris (1957) asserts? Is Sanford (1952) correct in saying that the "most urgent need [of followers] may be that of protecting themselves from organizational demands"? Do subordinates "usually want more Consideration rather than Initiating Structure" as Shartle (1956, p. 123) states? Does society, indeed, have a different purpose for the individual than the individual has for himself, as Ross said in 1901? Whatever the answers to these and similar questions, and whatever the point of view concerning organizational and individual objectives—whether the individual's welfare is paramount, or the group's—there is now general agreement that neither value can be neglected.

Our beliefs concerning the instrumentality of the group in furthering individual development lead to the acceptance of two additional concepts about leadership. The first is the *concept of the leader, whether selected from above or below, as a freely followed person who is concerned with fulfilling the purposes of the group and the needs of the individuals in it.* Such a leader is in contrast to a "head man" who is appointed to carry out the objectives of those above him by directing or commanding. Gibb (1954, p. 882) says that there is almost general agreement in the literature of the last few years that leadership is to be distinguished, by definition, from domination or headship; in this we concur. The second important concept is that of the *follower as an aspiring and creative individual, seeking and seeing, in the leader, a means of accomplishing his own purpose.*

Leadership and Authority

The question of the source from which the leader derives his authority is an important one. Authority, as Easton (1958) points out, is not coercion; this is related to our assertion that leadership is not domination. Wolpert (1950) has called attention to the fact that the varieties of leaders cannot be understood without an understanding of the problem of authority. Weber has described three kinds of authority—charismatic (emergent-inspiring), traditional (justified by tradition), and rational-legal (justified by reason) (*see* Gouldner, pp. 53–66). Homans (1950) has made a useful differentiation between authority in terms of leader conformity and social control in terms of norms conformity that may help to define the problem of authority more clearly. Perhaps the most potent advocate of authority as being delegated to an elite class was the sociologist Pareto (1935). But to those of us who live in democracies, it seems natural that the leader's authority for leading should come from the people.

The Follower

Our concept of leadership is inextricably tied up with the aspirations of all persons—followers as well as leaders—in a democratic society. Sociologists have long shown a concern for the study of the follower. Cooley seems to have shown a trend from his position on leadership as expressed in 1902 in *Human Nature and the Social Order* to a greater concern with followers as shown in his 1909 volume on *Social Organization* (Cooley, 1956). He tended to explain the leader in terms of "salient initiative," but among the many followers, he said "there may well be increments of initiative which though not salient are yet momentous as a whole" (p. 135). Going even further, Kimball Young (1944) suggested and made a case for the importance of follower–follower relations (possible competitiveness for leader's favor) in the leader–follower relation.

Krout, in his social psychology text (1942), felt followership to be so important that he devoted a whole chapter to it, in addition to a chapter on leadership. Fillmore Sanford (1950) has been one of the more recent experimenters who has consistently stressed the study of the follower. It is interesting that in 1930 Nafe defined dynamic leadership as a "leadership wherein the follower sets off a force within the led which demands action toward a specific goal, a force which is similar to, although not necessarily identical with that which activates the leader toward the same goal," and that Page in 1935 had concluded from a study of leadership at West Point that "effective leadership must always be a proper fraction, of which the denominator, seldom common to two situations, is not the leader, but the led."

The need for furthering individual ends while achieving corporate objectives, and the democratic reaction against domination by an elite class, are important factors underlying our research on leadership. The follower as well as the leader, the interpersonal interaction as well as the person, the situation as well as the interaction, the environment as well as the cultural and historic forces—somehow all of these must be given their proper value in the leadership equation. The object of our research is not to prove the relative superiority of leader or follower, or of group or individual objectives, but rather to discover the principles of leadership.

MAJOR TRENDS

At this point it would be well to examine some major trends concerning leadership concepts and research during the last forty years. Excellent summaries have appeared in various books: Shartle (1956), Fox, Scott, Kirchner, and Mahoney (1955), Andrews (1955), Hare, Borgatta, and Bales (1955), C. A. Gibb (1954), Ruch (1953), Cartwright and Zander (1953), Sanford (1952), Guetzkow (1951), Freeman and Taylor (1950), Gouldner (1950), R. L. French (1949), Stogdill (1948), Eaton (1947), and Jenkins (1947). In addition, many texts in social psychology deal with this topic at length (for example, Bird (1940), Krout (1942), Young (1944, 2nd ed.), Hartley and Hartley (1952). Writers of various chapters in the *Annual Review of Psychology* are also beginning to pay more attention to this subject; this is in contrast with the earlier volumes, where practically nothing was reported. Recently, Browne and Cohn (1958) edited a book of readings in leadership devoted mainly to field and laboratory work of the last twenty years. Thus, there is no dearth of books and articles on leadership, and a complete review is not necessary at this time. It may be worth while, however, to present some of the highlights and show what the status of leadership research was when the Office of Naval Research began contract support of leadership research in 1946.

Experimental History—1900 to 1928

Although sociologists had long been concerned with the problem of groups and leaders, and every major sociologist had written on the subject, psychologists came on the scene comparatively recently, first through child psychology, then industry, and finally, with a tremendous spurt, the military. Very early, Binet (1900) and Terman (1904) had performed an interesting experiment relating to leadership among children, and for some time this remained the classic experiment in the field (Terman's experiment was partly a replication of Binet's). Work with children was the order of the day for several decades although Gowin in 1915 published some interesting material on the physical characteristics of leaders, and sociologists like E. Mumford (1906) had brought together a considerable amount of anthropological and sociological material on leaders— material of great use to psychologists.

World War I, with its great need for the speedy identification and development of potential leaders, gave impetus to the scientific study of leadership. In a world torn by conflict, it was probably very natural to question the accepted principles of leadership behavior and begin the search for superior principles to replace outdated ones. Major A. H. Miller, the writer of a military text on leadership in 1920, voiced this concern when he said: "Before the great test of the World War came, the subject of leadership as a definite study, aside from its tactical application, was given but slight consideration. In the schooling of officers no course was included nor lectures given in leadership as a human science or in its relation to military success as a morale factor in peace or war. . . . The holding of a commission does not make an officer a leader."

Industry expanding at a great rate, also, began to feel the need for new methods for selecting and training leaders—executives as well as first-line supervisors. By 1927 when the Taylor Society and the Personnel Research Federation called a conference on leadership (see *Moore,* 1927), the most important conclusions reported were agreement that leadership concepts were changing and that there was need for experimental work on leadership. That same year, Craig (1927) reported that "no quantitative measures of morale and leadership have been undertaken anywhere on any satisfactory scale except by J. D. Houser of Chicago." [1] Perhaps the most

---

[1] For Houser's work *see* Moore, B. V. The May conference on leadership. *Personnel Journal,* 1927, 6, 124–128.

interesting thing about the May 1927 Conference on Leadership, as we look back, was that though the group sensed changes in the wind, the kind of research they recommended was on (1) questionnaires and interviews, (2) analysis of leadership abilities, and (3) training individuals in leadership techniques. The focus of interest of people like Ordway Tead, W. V. Bingham, L. J. O'Rourke, L. L. Thurstone, J. H. Willits, S. H. Slichter, W. H. Tukey, General M. B. Stewart (West Point Military Academy Superintendent), and A. H. Young was clearly upon the individual leader and his abilities, and hardly at all on the environment, or interaction, or situation. It is quite likely that his conference stimulated many psychologists to search, with methods current at the time, for the "traits" which make for successful leadership, with the result that, by 1948, Stogdill was able to report a fairly general dissatisfaction with the trait approach. A number of interesting studies followed the May 1927 Conference on Leadership and then several exceptionally good books appeared in quick succession. Even though, as mentioned earlier, Binet and Terman had actually performed a laboratory-type leadership experiment, it is odd that their lead was not followed; most of the studies up to World War II used field observation, personality testing, and correlational techniques.

Experimental History—1928 to 1938

Cowley (1928), Seward (1929), Nafe (1930), Westburgh (1931), Parten (1933), and Page (1935) are typical of sociological, psychological, psychiatric, and pedagogical articles of this period. In view of our current concern with groups, situations, followers, and validities in our study of leadership, it is interesting to note that as a result of his research, Page asked whether the proper approach might not be to study leadership as an expression of the group rather than of the individual. He also suggested that those led should be studied as thoroughly as those leading, and tried to show that there was a need for verification of current ideas for the selection and training of leaders.

By 1938 a number of books had appeared citing the need for experimental work on leadership. Ordway Tead, in his book on *The Art of Leadership* (1935) said that he could not wait to write a book on leadership until he could cite "support from controlled scientific experiments." (It is interesting that fifteen years later, Stouffer *et al.* voiced almost precisely the same complaint: ". . . if a book [on leadership] were to wait upon such formal scientific corroboration, none would appear, perhaps for another decade.") Pigors (1935), T. N. Whitehead (1936), and Barnard (1938) also wrote extremely insightful books on leadership during this

period, all of them aware that there was a need for experimental validation. In the meantime, the sociometric movement had started and Jennings
had published an excellent study on leadership in 1937. That the subject
of leadership was now of world-wide concern is illustrated by the various
nationalistic revolutions, each with its insatiable appetite for duces,
fuehrers, and caudillos. It is said that the small German army of post-
World War I days finally developed into an elite corps, each man trained
in leadership techniques so as to maximize the potential strength of the
corps.

Experimental History—1938 to 1960

A converging of major trends began to appear by the time of World
War II, a convergence made inevitable by the failure of "trait" oriented
and "situationally" oriented research to produce results of a positive nature. One kind of research effort had followed the course of the aptitude-
test movement in the tradition of Galton, Binet, and Cattell. Reinforcement for this kind of research came from the success which intelligence
tests had achieved since World War I (Bingham, 1937). The basic technique of such research was the correlation of aptitude-test data with some
criterion measure of performance. Stogdill (1948) and Gibb (1954) have
performed a thorough job of examining the results of such work, and the
conclusion, as stated by Gibb, "that numerous studies of personalities of
leaders have failed to find any consistent pattern of traits which characterize leaders" (p. 889) is generally agreed upon. Nevertheless, as
Gibb is quick to point out, the fact that no relation has been established
between personality and leadership does not necessarily mean that none
exists. There is, for instance, a great deal of work that shows some small
but consistent validities for certain tests used with certain groups in certain
situations. One of the more interesting studies performed recently which
gives a new look at the "trait" approach is the work reported by Crutchfield, Woodworth, and Albrecht (1958) where relationships were found
among perceptual tests, personality tests, and effective leadership. Whether
these validities will stand up under replication is problematical, but that
superior tests are being constructed and experimental methodology improved is not questioned, as the current work in all the military services
(for example, research on officer effectiveness assessment by Donald W.
MacKinnon at the University of California) and such civilian agencies as
the United States Civil Service Commission can attest to. A recent conclusion from the Guilford laboratories is worth quoting: "We are almost
forced to agree with the numerous reports . . . which view leadership
from a behavioral and situational point of view. . . . In essence, this view

means that leadership is a function of the situation and its requirements and of the followers and their expectations as well as of qualities of the leader." (Marks, Guilford, and Merrifield, 1959, p. 23.)

The above approach is an example of the "correlational psychology" which Cronbach (1957) discusses in terms of "variance among organisms" and contrasts with experimental psychology with its emphasis on "variance among treatments." If we are to get anywhere, Cronbach says, we will not only study both of these, but also concern ourselves with the "neglected interactions between organismic and treatment variables." The behavior of the organism-in-situation is the proper subject of study.

The second approach which leadership researchers have followed has come close to the kind of research Cronbach advocates. In its original form, the emphasis of such studies was on observing the individual in a variety of situations. Although this model was not followed in a laboratory where treatments could be systematically controlled, but in nature itself, the better studies made up for the lack of laboratory controls by searching for a sufficient variety in nature.

It may seem a bit strange to toss together in this stream the early Lewinian studies on leadership—Lewin and Lippitt (1938), Lippitt (1939, 1940), Lippitt and White (1947), Bavelas (1942)—with those of the sociometrically oriented Jennings (1937, 1943) and the early work in Germany, England, the OSS, and the United States Army on situational tests of leadership (OSS, 1948). The common element in these studies was the observation of the emergence, or transformation, of leadership as the situation varied, that is, from authoritarian to democratic (Lewinian), from isolation to centrality (sociometric), from various structures even to leaderlessness (situational). A large part of such work was done under the shadow of the early sociological thinkers—Spencer, Tarde, LeBon, Weber, Ross, Cooley, Durkheim, Simmel—and of such studies as Mumford's (1906) and Pareto's (1935). These men were accustomed to thinking in terms of environments and groups. In such research on leadership, detailed observations were made of leadership climates and circumstances. Leadership was viewed as emerging from specific sets of environmental, cultural, and group determinants.

The psychological orientation of these investigators, however, compelled a certain preoccupation with the differences demonstrated by individuals. Consequently, such research showed a somewhat schizoid tendency to focus now on the variance in situations and then on the variance in individuals. The present-day, small-group laboratory where many leadership experiments are now being conducted stems directly from this work and comes very close to providing a setting for experiments of the type

Cronbach has recommended, that is, experiments combining the study of variance among individuals and variance among treatments by concentrating on the behavior of individuals-in-situations.

When World War II started there was a great flurry of activity and research to try to complete quickly some techniques for the valid selection and training of leaders. The fact was, however, that the military services did not have any kind of psychological organization to carry on such work. It is true that between 1940 and 1942 the services did set up research groups to conduct psychological research: the Personnel Research Section of the Army was established in 1940 (Levine, 1959); an aviation psychology branch was started by the Bureau of Medicine and Surgery in the Navy in 1940 (Trumbull and MacCorquodale, 1951); the Army Air Surgeon set up a psychological branch in 1941 (Flanagan, 1948); and the Bureau of Naval Personnel set up a section of research and training in 1942 (Stuit, 1947). But these organizations were not only too recently founded to have research results available for use: they were literally swamped by the need for developing selection techniques. Another important psychological group set up in 1942—the Applied Psychology Panel of the National Defense Research Committee—also confronted with a mammoth job, found leadership research not feasible during the war. Bray (1948), in his history of the panel, has said: "The global approach [to leadership and 'officer qualities'], tentatively tried out by the Panel during the war, led to a recommendation that a detailed, first-hand study of the officer in combat be made. Such a study would have provided at least the first step toward a job analysis of the officer in combat. Since the study was not made possible, the Panel believed that there was little point in continuing its work on combat leadership."

Nevertheless, some material on leadership was accumulated during the early war days and appeared in print. Thus there appeared books such as *Civilian Morale* (edited by G. Watson, 1942, and, among other work, reporting the results of some Lewinian studies); textbook treatments such as Pennington, Hough, and Case's *Psychology of Military Leadership* (1943), and Meier's *Military Psychology* (1943); and pamphlets reporting correlational data between officer performance and individual characteristics (for example, Woods, Brouha, and Seltzer, 1943). Jennings' fine book on *Leadership and Isolation* also appeared in 1943.

The most important wartime work on leadership is reported in the following sources: Jenkins (1947), Stuit (1947), Crannell and Mollenkopf (1947), Bray (1948), OSS Assessment Staff (1948), Stouffer *et al.* (1949), R. L. French (1949), Freeman and Taylor (1950). Primary research emphasis during the war was on (1) developing aptitude tests for commissioned and non-commissioned officers, (2) developing situational tests of leadership, and (3) trying to find some satisfactory criterion of leader performance. Though the results did not appear in published form until after the war, the work was well known to naval psychologists by the time ONR was established in 1946.

By the end of World War II psychologists interested in leadership research (1) had become acutely aware of the need for experimental research on leadership; (2) had started to experiment on leadership "traits," as well as on situational factors in leadership; (3) were becoming aware that situational as well as interpersonal and intrapersonal factors all had to be dealt with before any research answers on leadership could be provided; and (4) since there was no dearth of "theory" and so little experiment, had not yet realized what a modern leadership theory required.

NAVY PARTICIPATION

In the spring of 1946 an intra-Navy Personnel Committee had recommended the establishment of an advisory panel in psychology. By August 1946, when the Office of Naval Research, established by Act of Congress, took over the functions of the former United States Navy Office of Research and Inventions, plans had been made for a meeting of the panel. On October 3 and 4 the first meeting took place under the chairmanship of E. Lowell Kelly and under the auspices of ONR. In addition to psychology, there were representatives for anthropology, economics, political science, sociology, and psychiatry. John G. Darley was the only member of the original panel at this symposium; John W. Macmillan was the ONR psychologist at that time responsible for the human relations program.

The panel had been created to make recommendations to ONR concerning a program in human relations. Among the areas recommended for research support was leadership. Macmillan (1948) reported this recommendation as follows:

> Just as all individuals at some time must operate, within a group, so these groups operate under various forms of leadership. Whether the leader is selected by higher authority, elected from within the group, or emerges spontaneously under pressure of combat or immediate crisis, his contribution is often a determining factor in the group's effectiveness. Research in this area must be aimed at:
> (a) Analysis of different types of leadership—for example, does the conference or administrative leader face different problems than the combat or action group leader?
> (b) Determination of criteria of good and bad leadership.

(c) Analysis of the characteristics of the leader, to provide for more effective training of leaders.

(d) Analysis of the process of leadership to provide for more effective training of leaders.

(e) Analysis of what conditions of group life will ensure that appropriate leadership will develop at the appropriate time.

Almost immediately contracts were written for the initiation of research on leadership problems. Since Carroll L. Shartle had begun a ten-year leadership project at Ohio State University in 1943, this seemed a desirable place to start. Within a few years, additional contractors were added and an important step had been taken by ONR in accelerating the movement, started during World War II, for controlled experimental work on leadership problems. The results of the first five years of ONR-sponsored research on leadership are reported in one section of the volume on *Groups, Leadership and Men,* edited by Harold Guetzkow, and published in 1951. Included in it are reports of research on leadership by Cattell at the University of Illinois; Katz, Kahn, Jacobson, and Morse at the University of Michigan; Shartle and Stogdill at Ohio State University; Carter at the University of Rochester; and Sanford at the Institute for Research in Human Relations. The steady flow of contributions to leadership research by these investigators and their colleagues is now well known.

A large number of publications have resulted from ONR-sponsored research on leadership. Some of this was summarized in a brochure prepared by Richard E. Andrews of the United States Civil Service Commission in 1955. This was the result of "an attempt to relate social science research to supervision in administrative settings and . . . to stimulate a greater understanding of, and sensitivity to, those social factors, frequently unrecognized, that influence supervisory effectiveness." The resulting publication was based to a large extent on material which had been prepared by ONR contractors.

Additional reports on leadership studies supported by ONR may be found listed in the *Bibliography of Unclassified Research Reports in Group Psychology,* Office of Naval Research, 1957 and 1959. The present symposium papers will be, of course, the source for the more up-to-date summaries and bibliographies, and consequently no attempt will be made in this introduction to review the recent work. The trends which had emerged by 1951 seem even more pronounced now.

Recently the United States Navy has taken steps to strengthen the applied aspects of its leadership program. General Order 21, issued in May 1958 (cited earlier) made the Chief of Naval Personnel responsible for all leadership training. The following schedule for 1958–60, as described by Captain John R. Leeds (1958), the Assistant Chief for Education and Training, is evidence of the vigor of the new program:

> The Chief of Naval Personnel is strengthening the leadership content in all curricula, and is emphasizing the teaching methods that require individual participation. Important among the concepts are those allied to the requirements of General Order 21—inspirational, managerial, and moral—and important among the methods are those that attempt to simulate on-the-job conditions—case studies, role playing, and problem solving.
>
> In 1958–59 (for the first time at the U. S. Naval Academy) leadership classes will be supported at the same level as academic department classes . . . further expansion, if approved, would be phased into the course in 1960–61.
>
> NROTC curriculum will be modified to include a three-semester hour course of General Psychology, and a three-semester hour course in Principles and Problems of Leadership (this course already exists, but will be strengthened).
>
> The time devoted to leadership training in OCS is being increased to 45 contact hours (equivalent to three semester hours). This change will be implemented in the fall of 1958.

Other measures reported by Captain Leeds include (1) emphasis on "followership" aspects of the naval service for recruit training; (2) expansion of leadership curricula in technical-training schools and petty officer schools; (3) preparation of new books, such as a revision of the current volume on Naval Leadership (1949), preparation of correspondence course brochures, and so on. In addition, a Special Assistant for Leadership has been assigned and "is preparing a series of guided discussions . . . for use by ships and stations on an in-service training basis."

In October 1958 a civilian counterpart of this program was started for use with civilian employees.

THE PRESENT CONCERN

From what has been reported above, it should be obvious that there is a tremendous concern with leadership in both the applied and research areas. In addition to the psychologists who have wrestled with the problem, there have been many writers in other fields who have found leadership a provocative topic. Many studies are found in fields such as political science, economics, sociology, history, anthropology, and biology. Outside the social and biological sciences there are perhaps even more writers than in these sciences. *Everybody* has thought and written about leadership: military men, journalists, politicians, novelists, dramatists, poets, feminists, financiers, physical scientists—everyone, for indeed leadership, as a ubiquitous aspect of interpersonal behavior, is the concern of every man and woman. It is found everywhere—in democratic as well as totalitarian societies, among primitive as well as civilized people, among children, and even among animals.

With so much written on the subject, why this symposium and why another book on leadership?

The present symposium follows logically from the first one held in 1950. At that time, John G. Darley, in the Introduction to *Groups, Leadership and Men,* said that "the idea of a working conference of contractors emerged as a unanimously accepted and desirable method of integrating and accelerating the Navy's program in the areas under consideration" (p. 3). This idea and hope for "integrating and accelerating" a program of research is followed again in this symposium on leadership and interpersonal behavior, and is indeed the primary reason for it.

We believe that since 1950 we have come a long way and that there is now a great deal of experimental work that needs to be brought together and many ideas that must be discussed. It is just possible that we may know more about the subject than we think we know, and that by pooling our results and examining them critically we may be able to integrate them in some useful manner. We have this hope, I believe, because we are now well aware that the problem is a very difficult one and will yield to no single attack. We now know there are many factors relevant to leadership. There is no prospect that some simple battery of personality tests is going to validly select potential leaders in a miraculous way. We are now convinced, and this humility represents a step forward in the progress of a science of leadership, that we must do more than merely catalogue the characteristics of successful leaders: we must expand the scope of our studies of situational aspects in performance; we must know something about the behavior of groups and of organizations; we must know how cultural influences affect the leadership act; we must invent new ways to perceive, relate, and integrate large quantities of pertinent data.

All the participants in this symposium have made significant contributions to the study of leadership. Likert, Argyris, Shartle, Hemphill, and the Pepinskys have persistently attacked the problem of organization and leadership. Hemphill, Berrien, and Bass have developed theories which require further experiment. Flanagan and Havron have long been concerned with situational factors. Bronfenbrenner, Schutz, and Fiedler have emphasized the personal element in leadership. Roby, Guetzkow, Back, J. Gibb, Criswell, and Hollander have shown concern with intragroup processes. Such mention is cited only as examples of their work and not as their only contributions. In addition, every participant is of course indebted to many whose work influenced the development of what is presented here. C. A. Gibb (1954), for instance, has developed an important outline of a theory of leadership in which analysis of situations, social interaction, and perception of individual differences are primary ingredients which has helped in the development of current ideas. The large variety of investigations show that we require understanding of group tasks and goals, group structure, attitudes and needs of followers, group norms and aspirations, and many other factors—perhaps the whole gamut of variables studied in current small-group research.

Such is the contemporary picture of leadership research, a picture which the contributors to this volume are striving to improve. Though the subject of leadership is old, this book represents a pioneering venture, for in contrast to the great bulk of writing on leadership, it deals with systematic experimental developments—something fairly new in this field, and, it is hoped, of great potential value.

References

ANDREWS, R. E. *Leadership and supervision.* Washington: Government Printing Office, Personnel Management Series No. 9, December 1955.

Annual review of psychology. Palo Alto: Annual Reviews, Inc., Volumes 1–10, 1950–1959.

ARGYRIS, C. *Personality and organization.* New York: Harper, 1957.

ASCH, S. E. *Social psychology.* New York: Prentice-Hall, 1952.

BARNARD, C. I. *The functions of the executive.* Cambridge, Mass., Harvard, 1938.

BASS, B. M. *Leadership, psychology, and organizational behavior.* New York: Harper, 1960.

BAVELAS, A. *Morale and the training of leaders.* In G. WATSON (Ed.), *Civilian Morale.* Boston: Houghton, 1942, 143–165.

BERRIEN, F. K. and BASH, W. H. *Human relations.* New York: Harper, 1957.

Bibliography of unclassified research reports in group psychology. Washington: Office of Naval Research, ONR Report ACR–22, 1957; supplement No. 1, 1959.

BINET, A. *La suggestibilité.* Paris: Libraire C. Reinwald, Schleicher Freres, Editeurs, 1900.

BINGHAM, W. V. *Aptitudes and aptitude testing.* New York: Harper, 1937.

BIRD, C. *Social psychology.* New York: Appleton, 1940.

BRAY, C. W. *Psychology and military proficiency.* Princeton, N. J.: Princeton, 1948.

BROWNE, C. G. and COHN, T. S. (Eds.) *The study of leadership.* Danville, Ill.: The Interstate Printers and Publishers, Inc., 1958.

BRUNER, J. S. Social psyschology and group process. In C. P. STONE and D. W. TAYLOR, (Eds.), *Annual review of psychology*. Palo Alto: Annual Reviews, Inc., Vol. I, 1950.

CARTER, J. H. (Lt. Col.). Military leadership. *Military Review,* 1952, 32, 14–18.

CARTWRIGHT, D. and ZANDER, A. (Eds.) *Group dynamics.* Evanston, Ill.: Row, Peterson, 1953.

CATTELL, R. B. A mathematical model for the leadership role and other personality-role relations. In M. SHERIF and M. O. WILSON (Eds.), *Emerging problems in social psychology*. Norman: Univ. of Oklahoma, 1957.

COOLEY, C. H. *Social Organization.* New York: Scribner's, 1909.

CRAIG, D. R. Measuring morale and leadership ability. *Personnel journal,* 1927, 6, 155–160.

CRANNELL, C. W., and MOLLENKOPF, W. G. Combat leadership. In F. WICKERT, (Ed.) *Psychological research on problems of redistribution*. Washington: Government Printing Office, AAF Av. Psychol. Program Research Report No. 14, 1947.

CRONBACH, L. J. The two disciplines of scientific psychology. *American Psychologist,* 1957, 12, 671–684.

CRUTCHFIELD, R. S., WOODWORTH, D. G. and ALBRECHT, RUTH E. *Perceptual performance and the effective person.* Lackland AFB, Texas: Personnel Laboratory, April, 1958.

EASTON, D. The perception of authority and political change. In C. J. FRIEDRICH (Ed.), *Authority.* Cambridge, Mass.: Harvard, 1958.

EATON, J. W. Is scientific leadership possible? In A. W. GOULDNER (Ed.), *Studies in leadership.* New York: Harper, 1950, 615–643.

FLANAGAN, J. C. (Ed.) *The aviation psychology program in the Army Air Forces, Report No. 1.* Washington: Government Printing Office, 1948.

FOX, H. G., SCOTT, W. D., KIRCHNER, W. K., and MAHONEY, T. A. *Selected annotated bibliography on leadership and executive development.* San Antonio: Lackland AFB, Air Force Personnel & Training Research Center, AFPTRC-TN-55-67, December 1955.

FREEMAN, G. L. and TAYLOR, E. K. *How to pick leaders.* New York: Funk & Wagnalls, 1950.

FRENCH, R. L. Morale and leadership. In *Human factors in undersea warfare.* Prepared by the Panel on Psychology and Physiology for the Office of Naval Research. Washington: Nat. Res. Council, 1949, 463–488.

GIBB, C. A. Leadership. In G. LINDZEY (Ed.), *Handbook of social psychology.* Cambridge, Mass.: Addison-Wesley, 1954.

GOULDNER, A. W. (Ed.) *Studies in leadership.* New York: Harper, 1950.

GOWIN, E. B. *The executive and his control of men.* New York: Macmillan, 1915.

GUETZKOW, H. (Ed.) *Groups, leadership and men.* Pittsburgh: Carnegie Institute of Technology, 1951.

HALPIN, A. W. and WINER, B. J. A factorial description of the leader behavior descriptions. In R. M. STOGDILL and A. E. COONS (Eds.), *Leader behavior: its description and measurement.* Columbus: Ohio State Univ., 1957, 39–51.

HARE, A. P., BORGATTA, E. F. and BALES, R. F. (Eds.) *Small groups.* New York: Knopf, 1955.

HARTLEY, E. L. and HARTLEY, RUTH E. *Fundamentals of social psychology.* New York: Knopf, 1952.

HEIDER, F. *The psychology of interpersonal relations.* New York: Wiley, 1958.

HEMPHILL, J. Administration as problem solving. In A. W. HALPIN (Ed.), *Administrative theory in education.* Danville, Ill.: Interstate Printers and Publishers, 1958, 89–118.

HOMANS, G. C. *The human group.* New York: Harcourt, 1950.

JENKINS, W. O. A review of leadership studies with particular reference to military problems. *Psychological Bulletin,* 1947, 44, 54–79.

JENNINGS, HELEN H. *Leadership and isolation.* New York: Longmans, 1943.

JENNINGS, HELEN H. Structure of leadership. *Sociometry,* 1937, 1, 99–143.

JONES, E. E. and THIBAUT, J. W. Interaction goals as bases of inference in interpersonal perception. In R. TAGIURI and L. PETRULLO (Eds.), *Person perception and interpersonal behavior.* Stanford, Calif.: Stanford Univ., 1958.

KROUT, M. H. *Introduction to social psychology.* New York: Harper, 1942.

LASSWELL, H. D. *Power and personality.* New York: Norton, 1948.

LEBON, G. *The crowd: a study of the popular mind.* London: T. F. Unwin, LTD., 1922.

LEEDS, J. R. (Capt. USN) Training for leadership. In *Naval Training Bulletin.* Washington: Bureau of Naval Personnel, Summer, 1958, 5–7.

LEVINE, M. *The Personnel Research Branch.* Personnel Research and Procedures Division, The Adjutant General's Office, Dept. of the Army, March, 1959.

LEWIN, K. and LIPPITT, R. An experimental approach to the study of autocracy and democracy. *Sociometry,* 1938, 1, 292–300.

LIPPITT, R. Field theory and experiment in social psychology: autocratic and democratic group atmospheres. *Amer. J. Psychol.,* 1939, 45, 26–49.

LIPPITT, R. An experimental study of authoritarian and democratic group atmospheres. Univ. Ia. Stud., 1940, 16, (3), 43–198.

LIPPITT, R. and WHITE, R. K. An experimental study of leadership and group life. In G. E. SWANSON, T. M. NEWCOMB, E. L. HARTLEY, *et al. Readings in social psychology,* New York: Holt, Rinehart and Winston, 1952, 340–355.

MACMILLAN, J. W. Pioneers in human relations. *Monthly Research Report,* 1 April 1948, Washington: Office of Naval Research, 26–32.

MARKS, A., GUILFORD, J. P. and MERRIFIELD, P. R. *A study of military leadership in relation to selected intellectual factors.* Report No. 21 of the Psychological Laboratory of the Univ. of S. Calif., Los Angeles. November, 1959.

MARSHALL, S. L. A. (Brig. Gen.) Combat leadership. In *Symposium on preventive and social psychiatry, 15–17 April 1957.* Washington: Walter Reed Army Institute of Research, 303–307.

MILLER, A. H. (Major) *Leadership.* New York: Putnam, 1920.

MOORE, B. V. The May conference on leadership, *Personnel J.,* 1927, **6,** 124–128.

MUMFORD, E. The origins of leadership. *Amer. j. Sociol.,* 1906–1907, **12,** 216–240, 367–397, 500–531.

NAFE, R. W. A psychological description of leadership. *J. soc. Psychol.,* 1930, **1,** 248–266.

NIEBUHR, R. *Pious and secular America.* New York: Scribner, 1958.

OSS Assessment Staff. *The assessment of men—selection of men for the Office of Strategic Services.* New York: Holt, Rinehart and Winston, 1948.

PAGE, D. D. Measurement and prediction of leadership. *Amer. j. Sociol.,* 1935, **41,** 31–43.

PARETO, V. *The mind and society.* (4 volumes, edited by A. LIVINGSTON) New York: Harcourt, 1935.

PENNINGTON, L. A., HOUGH, R. B., and CASE, H. W. *The psychology of military leadership.* New York: Prentice-Hall, 1943.

PIGORS, P. *Leadership or domination.* Boston: Houghton, 1935.

ROETHLISBERGER, F. J., DICKSON, W. J., and WRIGHT, H. A. *Management and the worker.* Cambridge, Mass.: Harvard, 1949 (1st printing in 1939).

ROSS, E. A. *Social control.* New York: Macmillan, 1901.

RUCH, F. L. (Principal Investigator) *Bibliography on military leadership.* Annotations of selected studies from scientific, technical, and related publications. Maxwell AFB, Alabama: Human Resources Research Institute, June, 1953.

SANFORD, F. H. *Authoritarianism and leadership.* Philadelphia: Institute for Research in Human Relations, 1950.

SANFORD, F. H. Research on military leadership. In *Current trends, psychology in the world emergency.* Pittsburgh: Univ. of Pittsburgh, 1952.

SELZNICK, P. *Leadership in administration.* Evanston, Ill.: Row, Peterson, 1957.

SHARTLE, C. L. *Executive performance and leadership.* Englewood Cliffs, N. J.: Prentice-Hall, 1956.

STOGDILL, R. M. Personal factors associated with leadership: a survey of the literature. *J. Psychol.,* 1948, **25,** 35–71.

STOUFFER, S. A., SUCHMAN, E. A., DEVINNEY, L. C., STAR, S. A., and WILLIAMS, R. M., JR. *The American soldier: adjustment during army life.* Princeton, N. J.: Princeton, 1949, Vol. I, 362–429.

STUIT, D. B. (Ed.) *Personnel research and test development in the Bureau of Naval Personnel.* Princeton, N. J.: Princeton, 1947.

TERMAN, L. M. A preliminary study in the psychology and pedagogy of leadership. *Pedagogical Seminary,* 1904, 11, 413–451.

TRUMBULL, R. and MACCORQUODALE, K. *A history of aviation psychology at NAS, Pensacola, Part I (1939–1946); revised by* R. TRUMBULL, *1 Oct., 1951.* Pensacola, Fla.: U. S. School of Aviation Medicine, Naval Air Station, 1951.

U. S. Navy. General Order 21. 17 May 1958.

VITELES, M. S. Evolution of a program of humanistic studies for executives. *Saertrykk av Bedriftsøkonomen.* NR. 1A., February 1958.

WATSON, G. (Ed.) *Civilian morale.* New York: Houghton, 1942.

WHITEHEAD, A. N. *Adventures of ideas.* New York: Mentor Books, 1955 (originally Macmillan, 1933).

WHITEHEAD, T. N. *Leadership in a free society.* Cambridge, Mass.: Harvard, 1936.

WOLPERT, J. F. *Toward a sociology of authority.* In A. W. GOULDNER (Ed.), *Studies in leadership.* New York: Harper, 1950, 679–701.

WOODS, W. L., BROUHA, L., and SELTZER, C. C. *Selection of officer candidates.* Cambridge, Mass.: Harvard, 1943.

YOUNG, K. *Social psychology* (2d ed.). New York: Appleton, 1944.

Current Psychological Theories of Leadership and Interpersonal Behavior

1

Some Observations About
A General Theory
of Leadership
and Interpersonal Behavior

Bernard M. Bass

Louisiana State University

THE GENERAL THEORY [1]

A general theory has been constructed to provide a broad framework for connecting various aspects of interpersonal behavior. It will only be possible here to review it briefly and follow with some relevant observations about the theory as a whole.

This leadership theory may be organized conveniently into three divisions: the purpose of groups, who shall lead, and factors which determine change in group behavior. A complete presentation of the system of definitions, postulates, and theorems cannot be attempted here, but it is possible to state the most important and visualize how they relate to each other by using Figure 1. This figure portrays the framework of the theory. Such a sketch cannot indicate the rationale involved, as such, but it may serve to guide the reader through the statement that follows.

---

[1] For detailed study of this theory, the reader is referred to the author's work: *Leadership, psychology, and organizational behavior*, 1960.

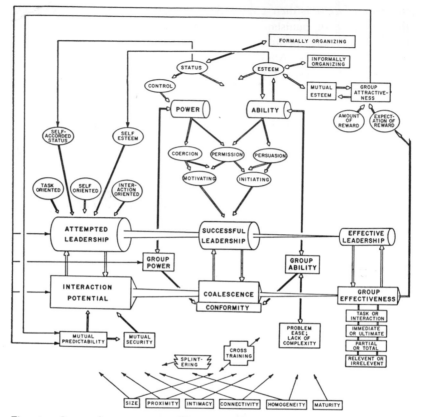

Fig. 1. SOME ASSUMED AND DEDUCED RELATIONS OF THE THEORY OF LEADERSHIP AND GROUP BEHAVIOR. (*From* Bass, 1960, p. 448. Reproduced with the permission of Harper & Brothers.)

Definitions and deductions in the theory imply that a group is an attractive collection. When anticipated rewards for membership in the collection disappear, the group ceases to be a group and becomes a mere collection which will disband when stimulation or motivation to do so is applied. Logically, it follows that an attractive or potentially effective group is "more of a group" than a somewhat less rewarding group, but this particular implication is not fruitful empirically.

Why Groups?

Individuals group together for reward or to avoid punishment. The more reward or reinforcement they anticipate from grouping together, the more *attracted* they are to their group. The more reward they actually earn, the more *effective* is their group. Attracted by the promise of reward (or the avoidance of punishment), if barriers block such attainment, some members will attempt to change the behavior of others. This effort is *attempted* leadership. When the other members actually change, this creation of change in others is *successful* leadership. If the other members are reinforced or rewarded for changing their behavior, this evoked achievement is *effective* leadership. Paralleling our observation of attempted, successful, and effective leadership by individuals is our observation at the group level of the total attempted leadership (or *interaction potential*), the total successful leadership (or *coalescence* of the group), and the total *effectiveness* of the group. The amount of attempted, successful, and effective leadership or the amount of interaction potential, coalescence, and group effectiveness are functions of mutual esteem and group attractiveness.

Who Leads?

Who attempts leadership? The individual who has successfully led earlier. Who succeeds? The previously effective member. Who is effective? The person who has the ability to cope with the group's problems.

Attempts to lead depend also upon whether the individual is task-, interaction-, or self-oriented. Attempts to lead also are greater for members with higher self-esteem and self-accorded status. Moreover, attempts to lead will depend on whether a member views the current situation as similar to one in which he was successful or effective earlier.

Success as a leader likewise depends on numerous factors. One cannot succeed unless he attempts to lead. Whether or not leadership succeeds will depend on the perception by other members of the similarity of this situation to ones in which the would-be leader was effective earlier; or on his *power* to *coerce* other members by being in a position to reward or punish them, or on the *ability* of the would-be leader to *persuade* other members because of his superior ability to cope with the group's problems.

The coercive or persuasive reinforcements are usually secondary rather than dependent on primary drives. The typical older child, adolescent, or adult has already learned characteristic ways of retaining and responding to the verbal appeals and instruction of others. Without this history of prior reinforcement among those to be influenced, the would-be leader's efforts in any given situation would prove most difficult. As noted in *Psychology for the Fighting Man* (Boring and Van de Water, 1943, p. 366) "You can't even boss a dog unless the dog has been trained to obey and has formed habits of responding to commands."

A member's power and ability may derive from his *status*—the value of his position to the group—or they may come from his *esteem,* his value to the group regardless of his position. Both the ability to know when to impose restrictions and the power to do so are required by the would-be *permissive* leader who also can make use of the group's power to increase coalescence of the members and his own success as a leader.

Why Change?

Members of smaller, more proximate, more intimate, better connected, homogeneous, and mature groups are more likely to interact. When obstacles bar goal attainment, higher interaction potential should produce more effectiveness, all other things being equal. Where interaction potential is lacking naturally, because of a group's large size, geographic dispersion, heterogeneity of membership, or immaturity, groups may splinter, formally organize, cross-train, improve connectivity, and introduce other procedures in order to increase group effectiveness by increasing interaction potential within the group.

PHENOMENOLOGY OR BEHAVIORISM?

In dealing with interpersonal behavior, two kinds of data must be examined: data based on observations of the behavior of members and groups, metered either by instrument or human observer, and data based on the participants' verbal reports. It would be foolhardy to attempt to exclude one type at the expense of the other, for it is clear that the behavior of participants in interaction is dependent on their perception of the situation as well as the realities of the situation. Often, the reality of the circumstance, or the stimulating conditions imposed by the experimenter are irrelevant to an understanding of the behavior of subjects in comparison to the subjects' stated interpretation and evaluation of the situation. Conversely, we are all familiar with the erroneous prediction and understanding that may emerge if we depend solely on phenomenological data. Indeed, the actual behavior of participants may differ considerably from what they themselves say they did. What is obvious to an observer may be denied by a participant. Whether we rely on behavioral or phenomenological data depends on the relative significance and weight of each in helping us better to understand, predict, and control the phenomena in which we are interested. For this reason, in the general theory, *both* kinds of conceptualizations are used, and most important of all they are related to each other.

For example, interaction potential, coalescence, and group effectiveness are behavioral concepts; mutual esteem and group attractiveness are phenomenological. The "expectation of reward" is a phenomenological description; "achieving reward" is a behavioral account. Throughout the development of this theory, one sees an admixture of the two types of discourse. However, even the arch-behaviorist Watson resorted to use of "verbal report" which operationally is all that needs to be measured in order to empirically examine any of the seemingly phenomenological relations proposed. Projective devices, free association techniques, and other phenomenological tools still reduce to verbal reports as the basic data for analysis by the scientist studying the phenomenon.

Suppose we deduce that observed attempts to lead will be greater among subjects of high self-esteem. We can measure the attempted leadership behavior directly (Bass, Pryer *et al,* 1958); but we usually must rely on self-reports to gauge self-esteem. In both cases, we eventually must justify the validity of our operations and show how they relate to the constructs, self-esteem, and attempted leadership; but once we have done so we have satisfied the demands of a logical positivistic approach.

An individual perceives the stimulating world around him, and his complex reactions to it can be metered or observed. But, whether we study what is perceived or whether we study behavior, as such, depends on what laboratory operations we decide to conduct. If we restrict the experimental stimulus and observe what particular behavior is evoked by the stimulus, we can make inferences about behavior, per se, from the experiment. If we introduce several stimulating conditions and restrict the possible responses to permit each response to identify for us what the individual is perceiving, we can make inferences on what is being perceived by the organism. Thus, in a typical *learning* experiment, we observe how much and in what ways behavior is modified by a particular stimulating treatment. In a typical *perceptual* or *discrimination* experiment we observe how different stimuli such as black cards, striped cards, and white cards evoke different responses from human subjects—"dark," "grey," or "bright"; or how these varying stimuli tend to cause white rats to turn left, right, or return to a starting box. If the differential response occurs, we infer that the subjects, rats or humans, *perceived* differences in the black, striped, and white cards. The problem bears analogy to the situation in physics where sometimes it is profitable to regard light as a stream of particles, and at other times, as a wave.

NEED FOR A GENERAL THEORY

In the chapters that follow, a variety of theories will be presented each covering some domain of behavior in groups. For example, Berrien will concern himself with homeostatic phenomena; Gibb, with defensiveness; Torrance, with stress; Hollander, with the followers; Roby, with executive decision-making; Back, with influence summation; Schutz, with introjection; Criswell, with sociometric approaches. Then, later in this book, we shall see summaries of empirical investigations, first in small groups, work groups and task groups; and then within the larger military or industrial organization. These final chapters will be brief summaries of literally scores of original experiments and surveys. These new data will add to the several thousand articles and books which have been published since the turn of the century.

Early theoretical efforts by such scholars as Brown (1936), Freud (1922), Pigors (1935), and Znaniecki (1925) to organize the growing body of information took the form of general proposals. A few concepts and some analogies to gestalt psychology, psychoanalytic theory, or the functioning of organisms usually were sufficient to produce a general theory when facts were few and speculations many. The discourse was based mainly on personal observation and induction.

More recently, theorists have increased greatly the rigor of their arguments, but to do this they have had to sharply reduce the range of the phenomena encompassed by their miniature systems. The past decade has seen the development of several useful "small" theories concerned with such aspects of interpersonal behavior as compliance (Festinger, 1950); cooperation (Deutsch, 1949); compatibility, (Schutz, 1953); and small group leadership (French, 1956). These theories are rigorous, precise, but restricted to one or a few aspects of interpersonal behavior. What I have offered is a more general theory integrating by deduction a wider diversity of interrelationships found when group behavior is examined empirically. The plenitude of facts now available made such an effort feasible. It was possible to assemble a larger number of rationally related constructs anchored to the observables of survey, field, and laboratory by constructing a general theory with specified operations defining the relations between observables and constructs; and with constructs related by a few acceptable postulates and derived theorems.

Although this general theory may have a short career, it will have served its purpose if it clarifies for us to some extent the communalities of what heretofore have been regarded often as rather independent domains of social and individual behavior. Further, it is hoped that it may provide a useful framework for displaying what has been done in the area of interpersonal behavior and a definition of what still needs to be done.

SUMMARY

This chapter has outlined a general theory of leadership and interpersonal behavior based on assumptions about reinforcement and the definition of a group as a reinforcing collection of individuals. Some constructs of the theory are phenomenological, others behavioral, but it is seen that there is no conflict in using both approaches and, therefore, a general theory encompassing both domains of study serves a useful purpose.

REFERENCES

Bass, B. M. *Leadership, psychology, and organizational behavior.* New York: Harper, 1960.

Bass, B. M., Pryer, M. W., Gaier, E. L., and Flint, A. W. Interacting effects of control, motivation, group practice and problem difficulty on attempted leadership. *J. abnorm. soc. Psychol.,* 1958, *56,* 352–356.

Boring, E. G. and Van de Water, M. (Eds.) *Psychology for the fighting man.* Washington: The Infantry Journal, 1943.

Brown, J. F. *Psychology and the social order.* New York: McGraw-Hill, 1936.

Deutsch, M. A theory of co-operation and competition. *Hum. Relat.,* 1949, *2,* 129–152.

Festinger, L. Informal social communication. *Psychol. Rev.,* 1950, *57,* 271–282.

French, J. R. P., Jr. A formal theory of social power. *Psychol. Rev.,* 1956, *63,* 181–194.

Freud, S. *Group psychology and the analysis of the ego.* London: International Psychoanalytical Press, 1922.

Pigors, P. J. W. *Leadership or domination.* Boston and New York: Houghton, 1935.

Schutz, W. C. Studies in group behavior. I. Construction of high productivity groups. Systems Res. Lab., Tufts College, Medford, Mass., 1953.

Znaniecki, F. *The laws of social psychology.* Chicago: Univ. of Chicago, 1925.

2

The Sociometric Study of Leadership

Joan H. Criswell

Office of Naval Research

Sociometry was originally developed by a psychiatrist for the therapeutic treatment of groups. For this reason its strongest emphases and most extensive contributions have been in the applied areas of group therapy, educational method, and personnel training and selection. It has been presented simultaneously as a theory of social interaction and a means of dealing with fundamental research problems. However, the intrusion of practical problems has tended to limit theory to a conceptualization of social structure in terms of therapeutic interaction. A prominent casualty of such an orientation is the study of leadership, which must include status differentiations and other formal restrictions not always of great interest to therapists. The sociometric approach may seem, then, to be of little value for leadership study.

It can be shown, however, that sociometry provides a basis for a broad approach to group behavior, covering the full spectrum of structures from informal to formal. A consideration of the development of sociometric leadership study may indicate the nature of its previous retardation and of its promise for future basic research.

THE BACKGROUND FOR SOCIOMETRIC LEADERSHIP STUDY

As originally stated by Moreno (1934) and since amplified in the second edition of his book, *Who Shall Survive* (1953), the sociometric approach provides an orientation of particular interest to social psychologists. The social group is recognized as a milieu that should satisfy not only motivations directly involved in task accomplishment but also basic needs indirectly related to the group goal. It is considered essential that the participant in any activity be assisted in maintaining a feeling of ease, self-respect, security, and successful self-expression. These feelings are assumed to be an important function of congenial social relations. Thus interpersonal experiences are seen partly as a means to an end, the accomplishment of the common task or goal, and partly as ends in themselves, satisfactory companionships appropriate to the task situation. One of Moreno's most important theses is that appropriate interpersonal relations within the task situation are necessary for maintaining members' creativity in the face of the increasing crystallization of structure which characterizes a group over a period of time. Thus the sociometric methods are unusual as psychological instruments in that they are predicated on creativity and the need for self-expression as experimentally approachable characteristics of behavior, and attempt to provide techniques that preserve objectivity without doing violence to this premise. If the approach here presented is followed to its logical conclusion, sociometric methods will necessarily include objective measurement of both task and personal relations, since the latter are seen as operating in close conjunction with task accomplishment.

The measurement technique of chief theoretical interest is the *sociometric test* (Moreno, 1953, p. 92) in which each subject chooses one or more associates to share with him an activity important to his group, such as studying, eating lunch, doing some form of work, or employing periods of leisure time. This activity can be performed either in the laboratory or in field situations. For example, the form of the question "With whom would you prefer to read proof?" closely ties preference to possible activities which would be facilitated by the associates selected.

The process through which facilitation occurs can be clarified not only through use of a variety of criteria but also through use of an auxiliary technique, the *role-playing test* (Moreno, 1953, p. 348). In this method, each participant plays out spontaneously a social situation of significance to him, for example, a job interview or a family conversation. He often chooses his fellow players, and a participative audience is present. The role-playing situation has been developed chiefly as an aid to training or group therapy. For research purposes, it is valuable as an adjunct to preference methods, enlarging the picture of given interpersonal relationships. By setting up situations that bring out different types of interaction and by comparing the role playing of nonreciprocal and reciprocal pairs, sources of friction or attraction (Moreno, 1953, p. 349) and changes in creativity (Jennings, 1953, p. 356) have been determined. Hypotheses based on such findings can be tested through further modification of preference questions.

The role-playing test illustrates the necessarily close relationship between formal and informal elements in sociometric theory, since it calls for the spontaneous enactment of responses to cultural requirements such as job duties or familial relations. The operation of creativity in a restricting milieu is again important. Probably because role playing is an auxiliary rather than a central method in basic sociometric research, its use has not shown a continuing pattern of development, as has that of preference methods. Nor does it promise to progress in a manner different from that which can be brought out for choice procedures. For this reason, extended discussions of role playing will be omitted from the present paper.

The preference structure revealed by choices can be charted in the sociogram in which all group members are symbolized and connected by lines representing attraction or rejection (Moreno, 1953, p. 95). Since the original presentation of the sociogram by Moreno, the pattern of choices has been presented in more mathematically manageable form in the sociomatrix (Forsyth and Katz, 1946) and the directed graph (Harary and Norman, 1953).

According to Moreno, the necessary final stage of the sociometric experiment is the experimenter's reorganization of the group on the basis of the obtained sociogram. As stated, this is done by strict methods of maximizing choice satisfaction (Moreno and Jennings, 1944, p. 402). In practice, however, other considerations enter, so that a problem individual may be placed with those chosen persons most likely to benefit him rather than automatically with the persons he is most strongly bound to by choices (Moreno, 1953, p. 377). Sociometric methods of prediction of group adjustment may also be combined with psychometric data on vocational ability (Moreno, 1941, p. 388). Thus there is some recognition that no unique assignment pattern can be indicated and that a combination of sociometric and other data must be employed.

Although reassignment is a practical problem, it operates as a part of the stimulus situation even in laboratory or basically oriented sociometric experiments. Whether or not reassignment is to be carried out, subjects choose as if it were going to happen and a connection between response and later action is thus established as part of the stimulus. The reorganization problem also relates to basic investigations in another way, through raising fundamental questions of interpersonal compatibility involved in optimal group assignment. It functions as a payoff unusually close to the underlying research.

The methods described recommend themselves to the scientist through their promise of objectivity and precision in dealing with the difficult variables involved in interpersonal attraction. The use of an activity criterion rather than a request for a general statement of friendship or liking is intended to reveal the specific basis on which a selection is made so that an operational definition of interpersonal attraction can be formulated (Jennings, 1950, p. 284). The input (criteria of choice) and the output (actual choice) can be clearly defined and concepts of intervening variables can be constructed through comparison of results from inputs varied according to a rationale. Such intervening variables would be the needs and perceptions that form the basis of choice.

The advantage of the preference approach rests not only in its objectivity but in the fact that its findings can be generalized from the laboratory to the field. In another paper (Criswell, 1958), the writer has discussed the necessity that the laboratory produce generalizable findings, not through an over-all similarity to field situations but through the identification of subject perceptions that are essentially similar in both settings. To be adequately identified in laboratory and field, perceptions must include the subject's concept of his role in relation to that of the experimenter. The sociometric experiment provides such a perceptual link, since it recognizes the role of the experimenter and creates for him and his subjects a frame of reference that also occurs in the field situation where group findings are applied. The experimenter occupies the role of a person in authority over the subjects but cooperating with them, obtaining choices that he can implement for their benefit. This is his group position, even though implementations may not occur. Moreover, the activity criteria can be generalized, since they can relate to group functions that are important and action-connected in the eyes of the subjects, whether performed in artificial or natural settings. This link between basic and applied research has a special reference to leadership, since it takes into account the leadership role, which the experimenter or practitioner often cannot avoid.

The relevance of the sociometric orientation to structural analysis can be seen in definitions derived from current group studies. Thus a group has been defined by Newcomb as necessarily involving shared norms and a system of interlocking roles (1951, p. 38). A role, according to Levinson, can be defined in three alternative ways: "(1) the *structurally given demands* (norms, expectations, taboos, responsibilities, and the like) associated with a given social position; (2) the member's *orientation or conception* of the part he is to play in the organization; (3) the ways in which members of a position act (with or without conscious intention) *in accord with or in violation of a given set of organizational norms"*

(1959). Leadership roles involve acts which, according to Hemphill, initiate the *structure-in-interaction* of the group; that is, the "consistency in behavior occurring during interaction that permits the prediction of behavior that will occur in future interaction" (1958, p. 96). Hemphill distinguishes between *successful* leadership, which results in acts that are carried out by group members but are not necessarily instrumental in accomplishing the task, and *effective* leadership which leads directly to goal accomplishment (pp. 105–106). Glaser (1956, p. 2) further differentiates leadership acts into those facilitating either the *task process* or the *social process* related to maintenance of basic need satisfactions. These definitions will be considered later in relation to past and possible future contributions of sociometry to the understanding of leadership.

The sociometric approach can be summarized as contributing to leadership study an objective and generalizable experimental method which takes account of the creative and therapeutic interaction along with the task functions of group members. This method makes it possible to attack those problems of research which relate to the patterns of interpersonal preference between leaders and followers; clarification of these problems is based on a more precise definition of the choice stimulus as an index of interpersonal perceptions basic to preference.

EARLY SOCIOMETRIC DEFINITIONS OF LEADERSHIP

In spite of the promise of sociometry for illuminating the basis of choice, Moreno's own discussions have treated interpersonal relations in rather too global a manner. His speculations, however fertile and provocative, have been stimulated largely by practical problems and therefore are not aimed at disciplined investigation of the related basic concepts. Although his treatment of creativity as a reducer of group rigidities requires some systematic method of relating informal to formal behavior, he seems to indicate that if we can just facilitate spontaneity and warmth of attraction, formal relationships will automatically fall into place. The result is that the possibilities of the method for elucidating the choice perception are not realized, and relationships as conceptualized tend to revert to the vague, friendshiplike associations which the use of a specific criterion is supposed to avoid. Disregarding the basis of choice leads to a somewhat mystical attitude toward interpersonal relationships.

In view of the fact that preference has not been systematically explored by Moreno, his definitions of leadership are restricted to patterns of relationships as avenues of influence transmission without regard to the type of influence conveyed. The leader is either chosen by a large number of persons (1953, p. 322) or selected by a frequently chosen person (1953, pp. 323–324).

The first of the two definitions has proved to be of considerable value for the development of leadership theory, although its completeness has been frequently questioned. The weakness of the second definition has been brought out by Jennings (1947, pp. 26–27) who points out that, because of the two-way nature of the channels of influence, a person forming the apex of a large network is not for this reason a leader. He may in fact be merely a tool of the highly chosen persons who select him. Most researchers appear to have agreed with Jennings in that they have paid little attention to the "power behind the throne." So far the best resolution of the two definitions is provided by Katz's mathematical formulation, which measures sociometric status not only by choices immediately received by a person but by the choices accorded his choosers, the choices given the choosers of his choosers, and so on, each more remote level of choice receiving less weight (1953).

The preceding definitions contain the important concept of the leader's position as a center from which influence may follow channels of interpersonal acceptance. According to the sociometric philosophy, the kind of influence transmitted is such as to facilitate the social process. Thus a highly chosen person might be expected to have in unusual degree the social growth-promoting functions assumed to be resident in each group member.

It is apparent that additional research is necessary in order to test and refine this hypothesis concerning the function of the sociometrically accepted person. The first attempt to attack these problems was carried out by Jennings through her use of the sociopsyche continuum of preference.

SOCIOPSYCHE CRITERIA IN THE STUDY OF LEADERSHIP

In the use of the sociopsyche method Jennings systematically varied the criterion so as to tap at different points the continuum extending from formally prescribed group task activity to loosely organized leisure time association (1947, 1950, 1953). For a training school for delinquent girls, the criteria used were working together on school vocational projects, living together in cottages, and using leisure time in any way desired. Structures elicited by the three criteria followed an orderly progression, those produced by the task criterion being larger in size, more complex in pattern, and lower in mutuality (1947, p. 5). Under task criteria there was more differentiation of status, with some individuals receiving many more choices than others (1953, pp. 340–341). The more formal task structure was designated by Jennings as a sociogroup; the informal type of structure she called the psychegroup. By utilizing auxiliary data on the behavior of the girls in group living, Jennings was able to obtain a great number of insights into the function of highly chosen or "overchosen" persons.

This work is the only major attempt to develop a sociometric theory of leadership. The experiment demonstrates that for sociogroups, typically there are to be found in the overchosen category persons who exhibit leadership behavior in the sense that they have concern for the welfare of the group as a whole and improvise methods of increasing the participation of members, reducing isolation, and making interaction more rewarding. In the psychegroup, overchosen persons are probably not appropriately designated as leaders (1950, p. 266) because they are personally rather than group oriented. Relationships in the psychegroup are intimate and emotionally supportive but not closely related to the common group life; mutuality rather than hierarchy is emphasized (p. 265).

The view of leadership here presented is a peculiarly sociometric one, since it attempts to keep close to behavior implementing specific interpersonal relations and carries into structure-in-interaction the concept of individual ability to facilitate spontaneity in others. The leader is not simply a more frequent pairer; a new element is born in the form of a relationship which involves more than two people at a time. It turns out, then, that the social growth-promoting functions discussed by Moreno may relate either to individuals or to the group as a whole. The two types of function have some relationship, as shown by correlations of .43 and .52 between socio- and psyche-choice status (p. 252). Thus the socioleader must have also a certain amount of acceptance in the psychegroup. The exploration of relationships between socio- and psyche-structures promises to be worth further attention. Numerous ideas for more detailed work can be derived from Jennings' discussion of the two structures in *Leadership and Isolation* (1950).

The concept of the socioleader is frankly stated in terms of social process. Auxiliary behavior data obtained from peers or house mothers, rather than from work supervisors, were not such as to distinguish clearly between task and social functions. Thus it is probable that, although all socioleaders seemed to be highly accepted for influencing the group's social process, some may have been less well accepted in the task process area. Such a discrepancy would explain Gibb's results (1950) which, although his temporary groups were not very similar to Jennings' long-standing ones, indicate a positive but not perfect correlation between overchosen persons and individuals recognized by associates as task leaders. Gibb's findings do support Jennings' discovery of a significant relationship between psyche- and sociostructures, although he seems to believe that his results diverge from hers in this respect (1950, p. 228).

The most light is thrown on Jennings' findings by Fiedler's work (1958) on a variety of long-standing natural work groups. He found that successful leadership as reflected in overchosenness under a co-worker criterion is necessary but not sufficient for the exercise of effective task leadership. Socioleadership was not synonymous with task leadership; but an otherwise able individual could not exercise task leadership without sociometric channels of acceptance of his influence. Fiedler also found that good task leadership requires a certain social distance between leader and followers. This suggests a curvilinear relationship between psychestatus and sociostatus: too high a position in psyche structure might handicap a socioleader in task functions.

Use of a sociopsyche preference continuum shows how systematic differentiation of criteria can aid in solving the fundamental problem of the meaning of the stimulus to leadership choice. Questions left unanswered relate particularly to the relationship between the social-process and task-process leader functions. However, the type of criterion required for analyzing the task aspect must be modified to take into account role structure, both formal and informal. Criteria of this sort are already developed, although usually for applied research purposes, and await exploitation in more fundamental experiments.

ROLE CRITERIA IN THE STUDY OF LEADERSHIP

Jennings varied criteria of choice from personal needs at one pole to task accomplishment at the other. The criterion was, however, an activity in which the chooser could cast the chosen person and himself in a variety of ways. The exact nature of the behavior involved could be known only through auxiliary data. To reveal the choice process in more detail, it is necessary to refine the criterion by using as stimulus more specific reference to the acts the chosen person will perform. This differentiation introduces roles or role functions as choice stimuli and thus makes possible a more extensive exploration of formal organizational behavior along with informal interaction.

Role-Designation Criteria

The first role criterion developed was less specific than later ones in that it named the entire role instead of separating out functional elements within it. In the most common formulation the chooser selected a companion as the leader of his group. Uses of this type of question as a peer-rating device in the armed forces and industry are well known. A typical investigation is that of Wherry and Fryer (1949) in which a factor analysis of sociometric leader choices and other measures was carried out, sociometric buddy ratings proving to be different from popularity measures and to be the purest measures of the military leadership factor obtained.

Useful as such studies have been for personnel selection, they have left the role-designation criterion with numerous unexplored possibilities for the measurement of group interaction and structure. One approach, suitable when several formal roles exist, would be to have each person make his own sociogram of the group, assigning a specific role to each member including himself. Different group structures might be compared by having the chooser select associates from a variety of different role positions, identifying himself in turn as leader, assistant leader, follower, or adviser. Or each person might be asked to restructure the group, eliminating and adding roles to suit his taste and placing himself and associates in the new role structure. Interaction patterns derived in this way can be expected to throw light not only on group attributes but also on members' personality characteristics, for example, the authoritarian's hypothesized preference for a more hierarchical, rigidly structured group.

For most successful use, the role-designation criterion requires that positions be recognizable and identifiable by name. In the case of roles not formally recognized, an identification in terms of behavior may be required, as in the next criteria to be described.

Need-Satisfaction Criteria

This type of question is less global than the preceding in that it does not name a complete role. However, it uses a specific behavior as representative of a need-satisfying function such as giving advice, providing prestige, or exercising dominance. With its emphasis on basic personal motivations and informal behavior, it should reveal the social-process functions of leaders or perhaps the presence of persons in specialized social-process-leader roles.

Gardner and Thompson's extensive analysis of choice in fraternities has most successfully introduced the need concept into sociometric technique (1956). They selected several basic needs from the Murray list, including achievement-recognition, succorance, affiliation, and playmirth. Each one was reflected in a representative criterion question. For example, for achievement-recognition, the student was to judge fellow fraternity members as possible companions in this situation: "Let us suppose that you have received an invitation for yourself and a male friend to attend a formal reception and ball at one of the embassies in Washington, D. C.

You feel strongly that it is important for you and your companion to make a good impression" (1956, p. 36). Fraternity brothers arranged all other members on a man-to-man scale adapted by Gardner and Thompson in order to provide an absolute frame of reference for the sociometric responses.

The interest of these experimenters was in the use of sociometric choice for the prediction of morale and productivity. Consequently it was not feasible for them to carry their work into the area of group structure. However, on the basis of their data, need structures could be constructed. Individuals could be identified as performing patterns of need-functions, and interpersonal relationships could also be characterized according to the need patterning involved.

Task-Behavior Criteria

Most specific of the role criteria is the one stating a component of a job or other activity. This question is directed specifically toward the analysis of task process. Thus the chooser in the case of leadership functions expresses preference for a person to give him orders, advise him on work matters, or represent his interests with higher echelons.

Because of the necessity of covering various aspects of task process in order to determine how it is perceived or formally prescribed as well as accepted by members, the task-behavior criterion is likely to be used in combination with other types of questions. Illustrative experimental material will therefore be discussed after perceptual criteria are presented.

Role-Perception Criteria

These questions which ask for perception of rather than preference for certain interpersonal relationships are not, strictly speaking, sociometric. However, the subject's naming of specific individuals interacting in some way is so closely related to personal preference that role-perception criteria may be considered essentially of a sociometric type.

Perceptual criteria recognize the fact that the structure of the group serves as a backdrop against which selections are made. Perceived structure might be called the individual's "interaction perspective" of his group. It includes his observation of role prescriptions, individuals' manner of carrying out their obligations, and task or social relations between persons. Choice of associates thus cannot occur in a perfectly free manner but must take account of the framework within which it can successfully operate. Jennings points out that the restrictiveness of this framework becomes greater as the criterion is more task related, and calls the interaction perspective the "group-role-view" (1950, p. 259).

The perceptual aspect of reciprocation is the concern of Tagiuri's "relational analysis," in which the subject not only chooses others but estimates who will choose him and what persons other subjects will choose (1952). Thus, for each subject there is produced a Leibnitzean monad, or view of the group and of its structure as desired by the members. The interaction perspective is reflected in the finding that mutual pairs are more *visible* than nonreciprocal relationships, and that the leader's choices are more visible than those of other persons even when we allow for the leader's greater number of reciprocal relationships. People vary in their transparency or openness to accurate perception, and leaders may be especially transparent (Tagiuri, Kogan and Bruner, 1956; Tagiuri, 1958). Thus relational analysis contributes to problems of the social visibility of individuals and of roles, although the criterion used is not cast in role-differentiated form.

Perceptual criteria of a more role-oriented type ask the individual to designate persons he observes to be performing certain functions in relation to himself. Or he may report on his perception of prescribed relations, in other words, who *is supposed* to do *what* to him. Such questions can be combined effectively with others based on preference.

Combinations of Criteria

Illustrative of task-structure research based on a variety of sociometric criteria is the *multi-relational sociometric survey* developed by Massarik, Tannenbaum, Kahane, and Weschler (1953). This method was aimed at the study of interpersonal relations as formally prescribed, as perceived by group members, and as preferred by them. The experimenter derived the official structure from organizational charts and manuals and from interviews with top administrators and personnel specialists. He then obtained the perceived prescribed structure through such questions as "Who is *supposed* to give you directions in your work?" The actual structure as perceived was reflected through, "Who *actually* gives you directions?" For the desired structure the type of corresponding question was, "If it were up to you to decide, *whom would you* choose to give you directions?" Since the experimenters were interested in organizational effectiveness, they used the resulting data as a means of developing scores expressing the extent to which prescribed relations are correctly perceived and the extent to which actual behavior conforms to prescribed behavior.

The authors point out further that a different type of analysis would note "the combinations of activities in which a specific relation appears for any pair of individuals. For example, it might be that persons who are actual order-givers, frequently also are individuals with whom personal problems are discussed and from whom advice is solicited. Thus, order-giving, advice-seeking, and discussing personal problems may form a cluster, as defined by the appearance of the actual relation" (1953, p. 23). The application of such cluster-study to leadership positions is obvious.

One of the most structurally oriented of sociometric investigations, using both role acceptance and perceptual criteria, was carried out by Roby (1956). He asked each air-crew member to designate, for example, those associates with whom he found close cooperation, those easy to get along with, and those he might want as companions on a lonely outpost. Various indexes were derived from clusters of such behavior. For predicting group effectiveness, two of these seemed better than the usual sociometric measures. These were, first, *role-behavior centralization* (or differentiation of role in the group) and, second, *pattern conformity* (or approximation of actual social linkages to those required by the job).

Returning to the definitions of Hemphill and others quoted earlier, we can indicate possible contributions of multiple-role criteria to the understanding of various aspects of leadership. A measure of leadership success in Hemphill's sense would be provided by the degree of choice acceptance in any specified leadership role or function. Social-process or task-process functions could be measured through perceptions or preferences of role occupants or associates. Such results could also be presented in terms of Levinson's role definitions which were concerned with behavior clusters as organizationally prescribed, as seen by the occupant of the position, and as actually adopted by the incumbent. Hemphill's leadership effectiveness is a more difficult problem for sociometry. Expressions of preference have been used as criteria of effectiveness; for example, "Which of your junior officers would you prefer to retain in your command?" But they do not cover the task aspects of efficiency which are measured more objectively by such methods as those of Bass (1955). In the area of task effectiveness, suitable role-playing tests, although difficult to develop, offer some promise. Aside from these possibilities, sociometry must, for a complete picture of effective leadership, rely on methods of combining its results with other data.

The unique contribution of the sociometrist to leadership study seems to stem from the use of multiple criteria to delineate patterns of interpersonal orientation and discover the individual frames of reference which mold such orientation patterns. Occupants of different roles derive their strength and satisfaction from each other. Different criteria can therefore be used to measure the interlocking attractions of leader for follower and of follower for leader, information necessary to an understanding of leadership in its dynamic setting. The result would be a picture of the social-process functions of the different group roles. If there is a general factor of leadership ability, it seems likely that it would appear as facilitation of the social process rather than the task process, since the former seems less affected by situational factors. Therefore sociometry may yield fundamental leadership insights of wide applicability.

Although research on choice has provided an approach to the interrelationships of all group roles, it has leaned rather heavily in the direction of the perceptions and attractions expressed by followers rather than by leaders. From the standpoint of the follower's role, the leader appears as a person well, but not intimately, assimilated into his group's system of pair interactions in which individuals most fully share with each other attitudes central to their self-concepts. To a greater extent, the leader is a part of the more generally shared group experience to which all members are expected to contribute. This ability to perform a public transparent role, to be social in a relatively impersonal way, provides the leader with the group support which he requires in order to influence task performance. But in operating from such a base he must be dependent on followers in ways yet to be determined through study of how he perceives his reliance on others and how his subordinates view their support of him.

The need of a more rounded view of leader-follower relations brings out aspects of interpersonal perception which could be ignored by the traditional one-dimensional sociogram based on nonrole criteria. The meaning of role relationships to those involved comes into focus and proves to be an intricate pattern. Some discussion is therefore required of the types of problems raised by the deceptively simple request for expression of preference.

THE MEANING OF LEADERSHIP CHOICE

The choice stimulus is brief and clearly phrased. Yet it can be analyzed into several elements, each leading to complications of interpretation. It specifies an interaction between chooser and chosen, and it implies that this interaction can actually be put into effect. The specified interaction often consists of complementary responses of chooser and chosen. The interaction occurs within a setting of similar responses made by the rest of the group members. This system of interactions is important to participants. The expression of a preference can possibly change the interaction toward greater satisfaction for the chooser.

The resulting complexity of the choice stimulus raises problems that can only be solved by a variety of experiments approaching different aspects of sociometric criteria. Action-related questions are necessary for precise definitions of the stimulus, but they do not guarantee how the actions they specify will be perceived or how these perceptions will lead to further action. Problems therefore center around the extent to which a stated interaction may be taken symbolically so that choice expresses an attitude or response readiness broader than expectation of performance in a given activity. Research already completed on leadership choice has indicated how some experimental interpretations will need to be revised.

A case in point is the tendency to infer that implementation of a preferred interaction must be anticipated by the chooser. The emphasis on reciprocation in Moreno's discussions rests on this assumption. Actions associated with choice are of course commonly expected, but this is not necessarily so. Fiedler, Hutchins, and Dodge (1959) found, for example, that individuals choosing others as confidants often did not report actually discussing personal problems with them, and the designated confidants frequently were not aware of receiving such requests for advice. Roby (1953) reported some evidence that choices of leaders under specific criteria such as attending a party or loading cargo were essentially a common expression of general interpersonal loyalty.

Choice also may be used to express acceptance of or desire for a person in a certain potential role rather than as an attempt to establish a pair relationship. Thus choices may not always be made with expectation of reciprocation, and nonreciprocal relationships may be natural to some positions, such as leader, in which the role function involves relating to a number of people at once on a less than intimate basis. Jennings' (1950, p. 265) results on sociogroups and psychegroups indicate that choosers under sociocriteria expect less reciprocation and more differentiation of status.

On the other hand, the chooser might sometimes expect reciprocation when this is seemingly not warranted by the criterion. The writer has pointed out that role criteria (such as leader, follower) represent one-way choices in that the chooser cannot logically expect reciprocation under the same criterion (Criswell, 1949). Research is necessary to determine to what extent this one-way restriction is actually operative on the chooser. Do persons sometimes expect to reciprocate each other as leader? Here Tagiuri's relational analysis can be of assistance to determine the relative amount of anticipation of pairing in one-way and two-way choice.

Another restriction seemingly imposed by one-way choice is that different persons should be chosen for complementary roles such as leader and follower. Logically, one role implies another interlocking with it and a person chosen for one of these activities should not be chosen to perform the other. Yet Hollander and Webb's (1955) results in this area have shown a nearly perfect correlation between a person's status as leader and his status as follower, each status measured in terms of choices received.

Related to the preceding idea is the expectation that choices made by a person under a given need criterion should be positively correlated with choices received by him under a complementary one. If he rates his group very high as satisfying his need for dominance or nurturance, for example, advice giving, he should be rated high by them as satisfying their need to submit or receive advice. Gardner and Thompson (1957, pp. 77–81) expected this result but found that no correlation appeared. Again, at least in the eyes of the experimenter, relationships required by roles did not occur.

In the case of Hollander and Webb's results, choosers seem to be ordering persons chosen under complementary criteria along a single continuum, probably one of leadership ability, in spite of the partitioning of duties occasioned by the interlocking roles. The same ability ordering may occur in the case of complementary roles in general. The Gardner-Thompson findings point to a different problem: the internal and external meaning of need. If a person reports high satisfaction for his dominance need, does he actually behave in what he considers a dominant manner and, if so, does he appear dominant to other members? This field of investigation can prove a rewarding one, especially if a variety of measures of meaning are employed.

The preceding research relating to meaning has been summarized in order to raise just a few of the questions that must be dealt with as the sociometric approach to leadership continues in its development of different role criteria. The final problem produced by the use of multiple criteria is the representation of preference structures in ways not provided for by the old sociogram. A consideration of developments in this area will therefore close our discussion.

THE REPRESENTATION OF LEADERSHIP CHOICE STRUCTURES

Results based on role criteria present relatively few difficulties if treated one-dimensionally. In this area choices of leader, for example, are easily set up in matrix form. The resulting pattern is one of group members' acceptance of each other as occupants of a hypothetical role. Such a pattern can be operated upon in well-known ways in order to determine such things as degree of hierarchy in the group (Hohn, 1953; Katz, 1954), and degree of conformity between this structure and others (Hohn, 1953; Katz and Powell, 1953; Roby, 1956). Additional measures applicable to role acceptance matrices have been discussed in reviews by Glanzer and Glaser (1957) and Proctor and Loomis (1951).

The role-acceptance chart based on one criterion is thus amenable to straightforward treatments already developed. However, a second and more difficult type of diagram is required by multiple-role criteria. Methods must be developed for setting up multidimensional charts of structure and for identifying and relating roles played by individuals. Role diagrams have been used by Moreno (1953, pp. 149, 325) but only for connecting roles within an individual's life space, such as, his roles as father, husband, supervisor, or friend, not for systematically representing an entire group structure.

An effort to chart group-role structure was presented by Massarik and associates (1953) for their *multirelational sociometric survey*. This method provided a three-dimensional block cut into slices, each of which represented a criterion activity such as giving orders, making merit ratings, or handling grievances. Each slice was a choice matrix in which a given individual cell indicated the presence or absence of each of five possible relationships between a pair of individuals. For persons A and B the corresponding cell indicated whether their relation under a criterion such as order-giving was prescribed, perceived by A as prescribed, perceived by A as actual, and accepted or rejected by A. Thus each cell recorded a many-faceted relationship. The block of matrices was useful as a basis for computing indexes, such as those already mentioned, and for deriving such measures as percent of prescribed relations perceived as actual. However, the matrices as arranged do not seem suited to the use of operations of matrix algebra.

Both Massarik and associates (1953) and Roby (1956) developed mathematical methods for identifying the role most characteristic of each person. Individuals so characterized can be charted in relation to each other and connected by relevant choices. A further problem arises here in regard to the measurement of connecting choice patterns themselves. For example, if two persons are connected through one choosing the other as leader and being chosen as adviser, how should such a relation be characterized?

For the role diagram, then, two types of measures must be developed, the first identifying role, preferably in the form of a pattern of elements, the other characterizing choice relationships. The most convenient solution is to identify each individual as to role and set up a matrix relating each pair through a single score representing their complex of interrole choices. Because of the dependence of the role diagram on different types of mathematical treatment, it is unlikely to yield a unique configuration, as does the sociogram. Thus it is important to develop systematic methods for giving this diagram a precise operational definition. Only in this way can reliable measures of the place of the leader in the structure be provided.

A third type of chart that can be derived from role criteria is the most complex and least developed. This is the diagram of the optimal make-up of the group as it should be reorganized to maximize member satisfaction and productivity. Construction of such diagram is at present an art; few rules have been established for translating choice findings into recommended organization. A major difficulty arises from the fact that choice findings cannot be used alone but must be combined with other knowledge.

It cannot, for example, be assumed that positive choice should be maximized. Excessive cohesiveness produced by such a method has been discussed by Maucorps (1949) along with other problems of reorganization. Fiedler's conclusions (1958, p. 31) also indicate that in some cases nonreciprocation of choice may be desirable. He found that a leader establishing too small a social distance between himself and his men can nevertheless be successful if he works through an assistant or key man for whom he had low sociometric preference. Schutz's results (1955) on fundamental motivations in group interaction indicate that use of sociometric attraction in the composition of groups must be supplemented by measures of compatibility of leader–follower needs. Even if the problem can in certain cases be restricted to maximization of attractions, Roby's work (1954) indicates that complex mathematical problems become involved and vary with the different definitions of attraction maximization which can be given.

It may be concluded that of all types of sociometric charts, the reorganization diagram is the most variable, the most affected by other group measures, and the most resistant to scientific systematization. Yet it has traditionally been the stated consummation of the sociometric experiment and can in fact be regarded as one of the important applications of psychology. Although sociometry's persistent linkage of applied payoff with basic research has sometimes caused undue emphasis on the former, group-reorganization concepts have contributed to an important theoretical problem: the optimal composition of groups. The work of Fiedler, Schutz, and Roby indicates the direction that might be taken by research on group reorganization. When further work along these lines has been done, it will be possible to enrich the role diagram and establish between it and the optimal group composition that bridge from theory to practice which has been envisaged but never attained by sociometry.

SUMMARY

Although first formulated as a therapeutic approach to group inter-action, the sociometric philosophy and method are relevant to the less intimate and more structured relationships involved in leadership functions. This is made possible by the preference technique in which the choice criterion specifies activities of importance to the group. Through systematic manipulation of different criteria, the meaning of the choice stimulus can be understood better, and thus the bases of preference structures involving leadership can be revealed.

Since the original formulation by Moreno, the sociometric method has progressed from the use of a single undifferentiated question to the employment of a variety of role criteria dependent on prescribed and perceived as well as desired relationships. Use of this multicriterial approach to choice promises contributions to theory but raises new problems of the meaning of preference and of the representation of structure.

Sociometric research indicates that the position of the leader in the preference structure of a group must be a part of the analysis of leadership acts or roles. The roots of effective leadership lie remotely in the intimate personal relations of group members and more immediately in relatively impersonal group-oriented social relations shared by all members. The support thus afforded the leader is a source of power for him and of need satisfaction for himself and followers. Of particular future interest will be sociometric analysis of the interdependence of superior and subordinate, thus illuminating from both viewpoints involved the meaning of leadership choice and of optimal group organization.

REFERENCES

Bass, B. M. Increased attraction to the group as a function of individual and group goal attainment. Technical report No. 2, ONR Contract N7onr 35609, NR 171–029, with Louisiana State University, Baton Rouge, La., 1955.

Criswell, Joan H. Sociometric concepts in personnel administration. *Sociometry*, 1949, *12*, 287–300.

Criswell, Joan H. The psychologist as perceiver. In R. Tagiuri and L. Petrullo (Eds.), *Person perception and interpersonal behavior.* Stanford, California: Stanford, 1958, pp. 95–109.

Fiedler, F. E. Interpersonal perception and group effectiveness. In R. Tagiuri and L. Petrullo (Eds.), *Person perception and interpersonal behavior.* Stanford, California: Stanford, 1958, pp. 243–257.

Fiedler, F. E., Hutchins, E. B., and Dodge, Joan S. Quasitherapeutic relations in small college and military groups. *Psychol. Monogr.* No. 473, 1959, *73*, 28 pp.

FORSYTH, ELAINE AND KATZ, L. A matrix approach to the analysis of sociometric data: preliminary report. *Sociometry*, 1946, *9*, 340–347.

GARDNER, E. F. AND THOMPSON, G. G. Group administered forms of the Syracuse scales of social relations. Annual report, February 1957, ONR Contract Nonr 669(01), NR 170–125, with Syracuse University, Syracuse, N. Y.

GARDNER, E. F. AND THOMPSON, G. G. *Social relations and morale in small groups.* New York: Appleton, 1956.

GIBB, C. A. The sociometry of leadership in temporary groups. *Sociometry*, 1950, *13*, 226–243.

GLANZER, M. AND GLASER, R. Techniques for the study of group structure and behavior: I: Analysis of structure. *Psychol. Bull.*, 1959, *56*, 317–332.

GLASER, R. Descriptive variables for the study of task-oriented groups. Technical report, June 1956, ONR Contract N7onr 37008, NR 154–079, with American Institute for Research, Pittsburgh, Pa.

HARARY, F. AND NORMAN, R. Z. *Graph theory as a mathematical model in social science.* Ann Arbor, Mich.: Institute for Social Research, 1953.

HEMPHILL, J. K. Administration as problem solving. In A. W. HALPIN (Ed.), *Administrative theory in education.* Chicago: Midwest Administration Center, Univ. of Chicago, 1958.

HOHN, F. E. Some methods of comparing sociometric matrices. Technical report, 1953, ONR Contract N6ori 07135, NR 171–106 with University of Illinois, Urbana, Ill.

HOLLANDER, E. P. AND WEBB, W. B. Leadership, followership, and friendship: an analysis of peer nominations. *J. abnorm. soc. Psychol.*, 1955, *50*, 163–167.

JENNINGS, HELEN H. Sociometry of leadership. *Sociometry Monograph 14*, New York: Beacon, 1947. Also *Sociometry*, 1947, *10*, 32–49.

JENNINGS, HELEN H. *Leadership and isolation* 2nd ed. New York: Longmans, 1950.

JENNINGS, HELEN H. Sociometric structure in personality and group formation. In M. SHERIF AND M. O. WILSON (Eds.), *Group relations at the crossroads.* New York: Harper, 1953. Pp. 332–365.

KATZ, L. A new status index derived from sociometric analysis. *Psychometrika*, 1953, *18*, 39–43.

KATZ, L. A probability model for one-dimensional group organization. Univ. of Michigan seminar in applications of mathematics, Memo. 23, 1954.

KATZ, L. AND POWELL, J. H. A proposed index of the conformity of one sociometric measurement to another. *Psychometrika*, 1953, *18*, 249–256.

LEVINSON, D. J. Role, personality, and social structure in the organizational setting. *J. abnorm. soc. Psychol.*, 1959, *58*, 170–180.

MASSARIK, F., TANNENBAUM, R., KAHANE, M., AND WESCHLER, I. R. Sociometric choice and organizational effectiveness: a multi-relational approach. *Sociometry*, 1953, *16*, 211–238.

MAUCORPS, PAUL H. A sociometric inquiry into the French army. *Sociometry*, 1949, *12*, 46–80.

MORENO, J. L. *Who shall survive?* Washington, D. C.: Nervous and Mental Disease Publishing Co., 1934.

MORENO, J. L. The advantages of the sociometric approach to problems of national defense. *Sociometry*, 1941, *4*, 384–391.

MORENO, J. L. *Who shall survive?* Beacon, N. Y.: Beacon, 1953.

MORENO, J. L. AND JENNINGS, HELEN H. Sociometric methods of regrouping with reference to authoritative and democratic methods. *Sociometry*, 1944, *7*, 397–414.

NEWCOMB, T. M. Social psychological theory. In J. H. ROHRER AND M. SHERIF (Eds.), *Social psychology at the crossroads.* New York: Harper, 1951. Pp. 31–49.

PROCTOR, C. H. AND LOOMIS, C. P. Analysis of sociometric data. In MARIE JAHODA, M. DEUTSCH, AND S. W. COOK (Eds.), *Research methods in social relations.* New York: Dryden, 1951, 561–585.

ROBY, T. B. Relationships between sociometric measures and performance in medium-bomber crews. Research Bulletin 53–41, November 1953, Project No. 511–023–0002, Human Resources Research Center, Air Research and Development Command, Randolph Air Force Base, Texas.

ROBY, T. B. Prerequisites of pair-scores to be used for assembling small work groups. Research Bulletin AFPTRC–TR–54–13, April 1954, Air Research and Development Command, Randolph Air Force Base, Texas.

ROBY, T. B. Sociometric index measures as predictors of medium-bomber crew performance. Research report AFPTRC–TN–56–46, April 1956, Air Force Personnel and Training Research Center, Lackland Air Force Base, San Antonio, Texas.

SCHUTZ, W. C. What makes groups productive? *Human Relations*, 1955, *8*, 429–465.

TAGIURI, R. Relational analysis: an extension of sociometric methods with emphasis upon social perceptions. *Sociometry*, 1952, *15*, 91–104.

TAGIURI, R. Social preference and its perception. In R. TAGIURI AND L. PETRULLO (Eds.), *Person perception and interpersonal behavior.* Stanford, California: Stanford, 1958. Pp. 316–336.

TAGIURI, R., KOGAN, N., AND BRUNER, J. S. The transparency of interpersonal choice. In J. L. MORENO (Ed.), *Sociometry and the science of man,* Beacon, N. Y.: Beacon, 1956. Pp. 368–379.

WHERRY, R. J. AND FRYER, D. H. Buddy ratings: popularity contest or leadership criteria? *Sociometry*, 1949, *12*, 179–190.

3

Emergent Leadership and Social Influence[1]

E. P. Hollander

School of International Service,
American University

The term *leader* is used so broadly that it is best to define our use of it at the outset. In general, leader denotes an individual with a status that permits him to exercise influence over certain other individuals. Specifically, our concern is directed toward leaders deriving status from followers who may accord or withdraw it, in an essentially free interchange within a group context. Group consent is therefore a central feature in the leader-follower relationships touched on here, although this limitation does not mean that we will totally neglect the possible implications for all kinds of groups, from the simple dyad to the institutionally based formal group or society.

Primarily, our intention is to offer some observations and empirical findings which strike at the persisting notion of a dichotomy between leadership and followership; we will first present some results of sociometric research, followed by a theoretical model that treats the emergence of status and assertion of influence as outputs from interaction centered in interpersonal perception. Finally, we will introduce some findings from a laboratory experiment with groups to underscore particularly conceptions

---
[1] This paper summarizes work carried on under ONR Contracts 1849(00) and 760(06) with the Carnegie Institute of Technology. The author is grateful to Kurt W. Back and John G. Darley whose constructive comments have proved useful in preparing the final version.

from this model which concern the different effects of perceived competence and conformity on the emergence of status and the assertion of influence.

STATUS IN GENERAL

There are different bases for status and different expectations regarding its operational features. These defy ready cataloguing, but in our usage here, status refers to the placement of an individual along a dimension, or in a hierarchy, by virtue of some criterion of value. To say that an individual has "status" does not describe an intrinsic attribute nor a stable pattern of his behavior; rather it describes the relationship of that individual to certain others and their attendant behavior toward him. Interpersonal perception is a necessary part of this process.

Who perceives what about whom is of central importance not just in terms of the literal case, but also in terms of expectancies. The behavior of the object person is not seen just by itself; it is also effectively *matched* against a standard of expectation held by the perceiver. Before a status distinction can arise, therefore, two things must hold: an arousal of a socially conditioned expectancy, and a flow of information regarding the object person. The perceiver will have had some exposure to the perceived through direct experience or through secondary sources; this leads to a perceptual differentiation which underlies a shift in "behavior toward."

Granting, as an example, that a millionaire possesses a fairly uniform degree of higher status in our society, he operates without it if unshaven, unkempt, and unknown, he moves about among strangers. Even though an economic criterion and an expectancy already exist for a status distinction, the relevant information is absent. In this instance, the emergence of status is linked to one kind of standard, though a wide variety of others could apply (Hyman, 1942). What the relative impact of these will be resides in complex issues of value. In any case, status is not a sole and stable function of some given feature of social interaction between two particular individuals. Cross-pressures of time and place affect the balance.

If leaders occupy a given status relative to followers, this is one function of the way the former are at some moment perceived and reacted to by the latter. Gibb (1954, p. 915) has made the point this way: "Followers subordinate themselves, not to an individual whom they perceive as utterly different, but to a member of their group who has superiority at this time and whom they perceive to be fundamentally the same as they are, and who may, at other times, be prepared to follow." Being a follower is not inconsistent with being a leader, in time. This begs the question of the persisting dichotomy, which makes a bit of history useful here.

THE CHANGING APPROACH TO LEADERSHIP

The tradition of concern and controversy about leadership extends far back into the history of social philosophy. This was to stamp related empirical work with a decided bent toward enumerating qualities of the leader. While recent research has seen the leader displaced from this traditional position at center-stage, not very long ago it was typical to indulge in a quest for broad traits of leadership.

Though essentially a matter of emphasis, as in the work of Cowley (1931), traits were selected without regard for situational variants. Gradually a useful distinction between appointed leaders and those who emerged through the willing response of followers was recognized. This was partly a reaction to the burgeoning interest in informal groups with their self-generating status hierarchies, and partly a result of the accessibility of sociometric devices which provided means for studying the consensual choice patterns of various groups.

During this phase, popularity as a feature of group-emergent leadership was given disproportionate importance. Much of the earlier sociometric work equated choice as a roommate or study companion with choice as a leader, and several well-known and substantial studies gave credence to this presumed parity, though only within a limited context (for example, Jennings, 1943).

Eventually, both the trait and popularity emphases were subordinated to an approach which focused on the varying demands for leadership imposed by an immediate situation (Hemphill, 1949; Carter, Haythorn, Shriver, and Lanzetta, 1951). The literature survey by Stogdill (1948) on personal factors associated with leadership was quite decisive in pointing up the disordered state of the earlier viewpoint, which disregarded situations. It was not as though the situational view prevailed entirely, however; influential as it was, the literature reflected some dissent (Gibb, 1950; Bell and French, 1950). We have this appropriate comment by Gouldner (1950, p. 13): "The group contexts of leadership must be specified if a formalism sterile of action utility is to be avoided. Leadership must be examined in specific kinds of situations, facing distinctive problems. The opposite shortcoming must also be detoured; in other words, the similarities among *some* leadership situations or problems must be emphasized. Failure to do so would enmesh our investigation in an infinite analysis of unique situations as devoid of practical potentiality as the formalist approach."

Still another refinement within the situational framework was an awareness that followers define a situation in responding to leadership; they are not passive creatures of a frozen social matrix. Of his research on the follower as an alert participant, F. H. Sanford (1950, p. 4) has said: "There is some justification for regarding the follower as the most crucial factor in any leadership event and for arguing that research directed at the follower will eventually yield a handsome payoff. Not only is it the follower who accepts or rejects leadership, but it is the follower who *perceives* both the leader and the situation and who reacts in terms of what he perceives. And what he perceives may be, to an important degree, a function of his own motivations, frames of reference, and 'readinesses.'"

Thus it is seen, several viewpoints have been held concerning leadership and followership: first, a search for characteristics of the leader on the supposition that there is some universality among these; second, a concern with group-emergent leadership where popularity among followers may be of significance; third, a focus upon situational factors that determine, or program, the demands made upon leadership and for leadership; and finally, an interest in the more subtle interplay of motives and perceptions between followers and their leaders.

If any current leaning is discernible, it seems to be toward a focus upon the interaction between individuals and its relation to influence assertion and acceptance. In this way, we are becoming more acute in noting how interpersonal perception affects and is affected by status differentiation, as shown, for example, in the recent work of Jones and deCharms (1957) and Dittes and Kelley (1957).

While it is true that two individuals may bear a stable relationship to one another in a given situation, the demands made upon them in a changing situation could reasonably alter their interpersonal behavior, assuming the necessary volitional conditions; being a leader or follower through the course of time or within a given group setting is not then a fixed state. The context for study consequently becomes more than the immediate situation in which interactions occur, since it includes the past interactions of the parties involved and their impressions of each other as well. The development of newer sociometric approaches has abetted this focus.

SOCIOMETRIC TECHNIQUES IN THE STUDY OF LEADERSHIP

Leadership and interpersonal attraction have been studied more by sociometric techniques than in any other way. It is useful, therefore, to note in perspective the changing complexion of the service these techniques have provided. In early work with the sociogram the essential thing was the interpersonal choice pattern, especially in indicating group members to be isolates or stars. In time, scores were generated through the adaptation of peer nomination as one kind of peer-rating procedure for evaluation (Hollander, 1954a and 1954b). This approach makes it possible to derive useful indexes of a person's qualities as seen by his fellow group members. A significant parallel development centers about the attempt to determine the basis for group members' perceptions of one another. This extension answers questions regarding the locus of evaluation—whether in the perceiver, the perceived, the situation in which they are immersed, or various possible combinations and weightings of these. Use of sociometric techniques in this more analytic fashion exposes bases for interpersonal attraction and reciprocal choice (Tagiuri, 1952).

For the simple case of two persons interacting, attraction is often attributed to a similarity of perception (cf. Homans, 1950; Newcomb, 1956). The literature on complementary roles bears out the contention that a common frame of reference, some commerce of understanding, disposes toward interpersonal attraction (Mead, 1934). Thus, in the simplest case of friendship formation, mutually reinforcing patterns of behavior derive from a shared perception or attitude.

For several reasons, though, it is mistaken to take this as a direct paradigm of leadership choice. Jennings (1947) has made a useful distinction in this vein, that between "psyche-tele" attraction directed by personal feelings, and "socio-tele" attraction governed at least in part by a group standard. The chooser is of course the interpreter of this standard. Nevertheless, a greater degree of restraint is introduced into the process of choice by imposing this group set. The situational demands of the group or encompassing institution have a discernible impact on the chooser, as is evident from sociometric analysis. Thus, depending upon the context, members of a group do indeed distinguish between those they like as friends and those they would wish to have as a leader, and this has been amply demonstrated in a number of studies. In one such study (Hollander, 1956), the friendship choices of officer candidates at the Newport OCS were found to be related variously to choices for other positively loaded continua, that is "leadership qualities," "probability of success in OCS," and "interest in and enthusiasm for training." Simply liking an individual did not mean a positive evaluation of him so far as these other characteristics were concerned. A counterpart of this finding occurs in the laboratory work of Bales and Slater (1955), among others.

The traditions of sociometry set limits, however, on our understanding of leadership and followership. We continue to find, for instance, the supposition of an identity between leadership and such criteria as "want to study with" or "want to play with." Their utility for pinpointing leadership in the influence sense is questionable. In this regard, Criswell (1949) has noted that these "sets" involve choice in the face of some expectation of reciprocation, thus making mutuality important; leadership choice makes it less important. Generally speaking, whether the leader chooses those who choose him is quite irrelevant to the more central consideration of the *frequency* with which he is chosen by others.   1168834

A collateral issue has to do with the criteria set for leadership and the extent to which these are rigorously specified within an operational setting. If we conceive of the leader's influence in terms of a continuum of power, then we may have a *low* power loading, as in the case of "lead this group in a discussion," or a *high* power loading, as in "command this squad in combat." Though an obvious distinction, it has too often been plainly absent from research; one suspects that a push is made for "some measure of leadership" or a "sociometric," and anything at hand or easily concocted gets used. No wonder then that the potential follower, asked to make an evaluation, seeks in vain for a meaningful frame of reference, and then either haphazardly makes a choice or bases his decision on some abstract orientation toward the class called "leaders."

These particulars are directed only incidentally at clarifying the use of sociometric techniques. More to the point, are the related and troublesome rubrics that still pervade the study of leadership. One of the more basic of these holds that some members of the group are perceived to have qualities appropriate to leadership and thus are frequent choices for that status. This may be referred to as the "pyramid model," with its peak comprised of leaders and its base of followers; it also may be reduced to a simple continuum from those of high choice, presumed to be leaders, to those of less choice, presumed to be followers. In either case, the assumption is implicit that there exists a universe of peers among which individuals, placed in the vantage point of followers, differentiate others perceived to be leaders. Followership thus becomes defined by sheer exclusion.

But supposing followership to be more active than passive, this would hardly prove an adequate basis for its appraisal. Is the follower, after all, just someone who is *not* a leader? To really pursue this one should invert the usual question of "whom to follow?" so as to render it "whom to have follow?" Group members thus placed in the position of leader would be called upon accordingly to differentiate individuals regarding characteristics appropriate to followers.

If the pyramid or continuum models are sound, one would expect that such an inversion of procedure would yield a diffusion of choice reflecting the operation of a friendship variable, or at least it should be so if followers are mainly friends. This might mean that some of the individuals otherwise selected as leaders would also be selected as followers, though on the whole one would expect that leaders should have a relatively lower standing on followership than the average standing for group members.

RESEARCH FINDINGS ON THE PYRAMID MODEL

A study taking account of the aforementioned points was completed by the author with Webb, and reported in 1955. Prominent among the considerations prompting that research was the view that the traditional sociometric model of leadership and followership might be open to challenge. Since our procedure followed the approach discussed rather directly, our data serve to address the issue squarely.

Eight sections of aviation cadets (total $N = 187$) were asked to complete three peer-nomination forms upon graduation from a sixteen-week preflight course at Pensacola. The first two of these were on leadership and followership, the third on friendship. On both the leadership and followership form each cadet was asked to assume that he was assigned to "a special military unit with an undisclosed mission." Then, for leadership, he was directed to nominate in order three cadets from his section whom he considered best qualified to lead this special unit and three cadets from his section whom he considered least qualified. A similar set was presented for followership with the instruction that the cadet assume that *he himself had been assigned to the leadership* of this special unit; from among the members of his section, he was instructed to nominate three cadets whom he would want as part of his unit and three whom he would not want.

Both forms stressed that selections were to be made with regard to abilities that the *nominator* considered to be important for these positions. The third form solicited the names of three cadets in his section whom the nominator considered to be his best friends.

Scores from the former two nominations were derived by a weighting procedure of the three-two-one variety used elsewhere in similar projects (Hollander, 1954a). The corrected split-half reliabilities for these variables were high: leadership, .94; followership, .91. Friendship, at .41, reflects the operation of mutuality in such choice.

Correlational analysis revealed leadership and followership nominations to be related to a high degree, r = .92. Friendship had a significantly higher relationship with followership, r = .55, than with leadership, r = .47. But apart from this, friendship nominations were not found to bear appreciably on the basic leadership-followership relationship. Of the three friendship nominees designated by each subject, an average of more than two were not mentioned at all in the leadership nominations made by these same subjects.

One further finding deserves attention in light of the previous remarks. If, as has been contended here, followership may be studied in terms of the desires of potential leaders, then one may question whether actual status on the leadership continuum renders a difference in followership choice. An analysis then correlated the followership scores derived from nominations made by individuals in the top half and by those in the bottom half of the leadership score distribution. Its value for followership scores independently summed from these two nominator segments was .82. It would seem therefore that chooser status did not make an appreciable difference in the choice of followers within these groups.

On this the results were clear: the more desired followers tended to be chosen from the upper extremes of the leadership distribution; indeed, the correspondence was marked. Furthermore, the influence of friendship, so often taken for leadership under the heading of "popularity," had little effect on this relationship.

In a later study by Kubany (1957) quite comparable results were found with medical school *graduating seniors* (N = 87). A high correlation obtained between peer-nomination scores for choices on "family physician" and "turn over practice to" (r = .85). Neither of these were as highly correlated with "friend and social associate," and each was differentially correlated with peer-nomination scores for professional knowledge, skill, and favorable interpersonal behaviors, with professional knowledge and skill typifying more closely the "family physician" choice. We may consider that where one physician is prepared to give himself over to another for his own personal care and that of his family, the latter may be viewed as a leader. Though operating within a professional relationship, his influence in interpersonal relations may be quite real; therefore, choices for "family physician" betray a view of the individual more in keeping with leadership. On the other hand, when one physician sees another as someone to whom he would "turn over his practice," this signifies a disposition more in line with followership since the chooser says in effect that this is someone whom he believes would take his directions and conscientiously fulfill them as a self-surrogate (Hollander, 1958b).

These data bolster the previous findings, but mainly in highlighting competence as a valued feature in a multiplicity of joint work situations. That individuals should choose potential leaders as those whom they would also wish to have as followers is not in itself surprising. For one thing, institutional hierarchies plainly create such demands, so that responding well as a follower is apt to be demanded at all levels. Common areas of competence are to be expected, but more important is the way in which competence may contribute to the development of leadership status, particularly when combined with still other interpersonal characteristics. Beyond one's ability at the task, followership holds an incipient state of leadership. Consequently, any model of leadership is deficient if it fails to account for transitions in status, especially as these are occasioned through the time-linked features of interaction.

SOME THEORETICAL IMPLICATIONS [2]

For emergent status, the findings amassed suggest that two things in particular are important in an individual's attainment of leadership. First, that he be seen as competent in the group's central task; and second, that broadly speaking he be perceived as a member of the group—what Brown (1936) has called "membership character." To put it another way, an individual must be in a group long enough for others to note his part in fulfilling group goals and to develop a degree of trust in or esteem for him.

The first of these elements relates essentially to a task concern, flavored with the demands of the situation, the latter to a social concern. An individual manifesting both should eventually reach a point where it becomes more propitious in the eyes of the group for him to assert influence; to the degree that his assertion is accepted, he is a leader.

The particulars of this process follow obvious lines. Any group member is bound by certain expectancies—whether norms or roles—which prevail at a given time. To directly challenge these would very likely limit his upward mobility, unless a person were extremely competent and, what is more important, widely perceived as such. It is unlikely that just anyone in a group could achieve leadership by a suggestion for change at an early stage of membership. The social context is not yet favorable; this is the dilemma of the neophyte who is discontented with the current state of affairs. It is a common observation in virtually all freely interacting groups that the neophyte is frequently the most restricted of all. This leaves aside, of course, cases of status in one group readily redeemed in

---

[2] A definitive presentation of the theory of idiosyncrasy credit is to be found in Hollander (1958a).

another, or of the "expert" not introduced by the traditional rites of admission.

In most instances, however, adherence to the prevailing expectancies of the group is essential for the group member's acceptance. We are in effect speaking then of conformity, but not in the usual sense of fixed behavioral norms to which all group members are expected to display manifest allegiance. Following Sears' (1951) view of dyadic relationships and their characteristics, we conceive of conformity in terms of *group expectancies* which may be person-specific and fluid or more generally applicable and static. Thus, what may be perceived to be nonconforming behavior for one group member may not be so perceived for another. Moreover, this is a function of status accumulated from past interactions. Here we introduce the construct *idiosyncrasy credit* to refer to status as a summative consequence of being perceived by others as contributing to the group's task and living up to expectancies applicable at any given time (Hollander, 1958a). These credits are in essence positively disposed impressions of a person held by others; operationally, they provide the basis for influence assertion and its acceptance. The apparent paradox that leaders are said to be at once innovators and also to be conformers to group norms may be seen therefore as a matter of sequence.

So long as the person does not lose credits by sharp breaks with a past record of competence and conformity to expectancies, he rises to a level of credit which permits deviation from, and even open challenge of, prevailing social patterns of the group. In attaining this level, however, the particular expectancies applicable to him will have undergone change, so that it may be less appropriate to behave in the same way. For the attainment of leadership, then, it would seem that two personal conditions must be fulfilled: accuracy of social perception and modifiability of behavior.

The relationship of these points to research on emergent leadership is evident in several ways: the finding, for example, that leaders appear to be more socially perceptive (Chowdhry and Newcomb, 1952) is accounted for in these terms. In maintaining leadership, however, the leader could lose status and find his latitude diminished if he should violate those particularized expectancies associated with his commanding position; this would represent a loss of credit. Thus, if the leader's motivation to belong —assumed thus far—were to appear weak or insincere to followers, such an outcome could be predicted. Even more, if the group expects innovation in the face of a perceived change in the situational requirements, inaction by the leader would be far from a safe course. Which person achieves and retains leadership will therefore depend upon the perceptions held by others, residing in credits accrued from past interactions. The incipient leader must be attuned to these, and this stochastic interchange involves a continual checking against the situation perceived to confront the group.

EXPERIMENTAL WORK ON IDIOSYNCRASY CREDIT

Guided by this model, a controlled study with problem-solving groups was conceived so as to test the effects upon influence acceptance produced by the nonconformity to procedural norms of a task-competent member (Hollander, 1960).

In general, it is predictable that with a relatively high level of task competence a group member should, in time, have increased influence to some maximum. However, if he does not conform to the procedural norms of the group, this should curtail his influence. More precisely, it follows from the model that given the display of a constant level of competence by this person on a task, his early nonconformity should diminish his effectiveness in gaining influence acceptance; and, to the contrary, late evidences of nonconformity—following the accumulation of credits—should yield the reverse effect: once having attained higher status, he should be subject to a shift in expectancies which make this kind of nonconformity a confirming feature of status, thus enhancing his influence.

Twelve groups, each composed of male juniors from the College of Engineering and Science at Carnegie, were engaged in a task involving a sequence of fifteen trials requiring group choices from among row alternatives in a seven-by-seven payoff matrix (see Table 1). The alleged object was to anticipate a system and maximize winnings. A confederate, always the same individual, irrespective of treatment, was present in all groups

Table I

	GREEN	RED	BLUE	YELLOW	BROWN	ORANGE	BLACK
Able	−1	−12	+5	−1	−2	+15	−4
Baker	+10	−1	−2	−7	+4	−3	−1
Charlie	−5	+5	−3	+3	−11	−1	+12
Dog	+5	−7	+10	−2	−5	+1	−2
Easy	−4	−1	−1	+1	+13	−10	+2
Fox	−6	+15	−5	−1	−3	−1	+1
George	−1	−1	−2	+10	+4	−2	−8

Group members were instructed: "In any one trial, the task involved is for the group to agree on just *one* row—identified by Able, Baker, Charlie, etc.—which seems to have strategic value. Once the group has determined a row, the experimenter will announce the column color which comes up on that trial. The intersecting cell indicates the pay-off."

as a fifth member among four subjects. All communication was carried on through a sound-system of microphones and headsets. The participants had only aural contact with one another from individual, partitioned booths.

The key manipulation was nonconformity by the confederate, through various zones of five trials each, to procedures previously agreed upon by the group in a pretrial discussion. The fifteen trials were considered as three zones—early, middle, and late—with the discussion taken to be part of the first zone. A group choice, whether by majority rule or otherwise (this determined by the group) was required for each trial, following the three minutes permitted for considering alternatives. At the conclusion of each trial, the experimenter announced the outcome, that is, a negative or positive sum of varying magnitudes representing funds won or lost.

Six treatments were used: nonconformity throughout; nonconformity for the first two zones; for just the first zone alone; for the last two zones; for just the last zone alone; and not at all, as a control condition. Each subject was heard to report his recommended choice at least once during every one of the trials. Had it been *accepted* by the group as its own, the choice recommended by the confederate would have yielded the higher payoffs on all but four trials (the second, third, sixth, and twelfth), where a loss would have been sustained from accepting his recommendation.

Subjects were designated by number in communicating with one another; the confederate in the first set of treatments was number 5 and, in the replication set, number 4, to test possible position effects. A ready measure of the group's acceptance of the confederate's influence on the task was provided in the number of trials by zone where his recommended response was accepted as the group's, in addition to interaction measures and postinteraction assessments secured from the subjects.

The matrix was specially constructed for this study to present an ambiguous but plausible task where alternatives were only marginally discrete from one another. It derives, at least in spirit, from a small matrix used with success by Moore and Berkowitz (1956) in a group study of their own. The considerably greater number of rows and columns was selected to enlarge the range of possibilities beyond the number of group members, while still retaining comprehensibility. Though the rows are unequal in algebraic sum, this appears to be less important as a choice element than the number and magnitude of positive and negative values in each; there is moreover the complicating feature of processing the outcome of the last trials in evaluating the choice for the next. All considered, the matrix was admirably suited to the requirements for ambiguity, challenge, conflict, immediate reinforcement, and ready manipulation by the experimenter.

The confederate, operating either as 4 or 5 in the group, suggested a solution which differed trial by trial from those offered by other members of the group. This was prearranged but subject to modification depending upon unforeseen eventualities. Though contrived, this was in no sense unique behavior since subjects rather typically perceived alternatives differently.

The device of a pretrial discussion, during which the communication system was tried out, had special utility for establishing common group expectancies (procedures) from which the confederate could deviate when deviation was called for in the design. The subjects had been brought to their booths individually and without knowledge of the other participants. Each had then been given a set of written instructions and the matrix to look over briefly, in advance of the experiment. The first indicated order of business was to make use of the communication arrangement to have the group members, always identified by an assigned number, determine certain procedures. They were to decide on an order of reporting; on whether a majority rule should apply and, if so, how large a majority should determine group choice; and on the division of funds later. In the pretrial discussion, predictable decisions on these matters were reached: members would report their views in order at the beginning of each trial; simple majority rule would prevail; and funds would be shared equally. These were routine decisions, and all were subject to revision during the trials; their importance, however, lay in having a *public statement* of intent in which members had shared.

In the zones calling for nonconformity, the confederate violated these procedures by speaking out of prescribed turn, by questioning the utility of majority rule, and by unsupported—but not harsh—challenges to the recommendations made by others. He manifested such behaviors on an approximate frequency of at least one per trial with a mean of two per trial considered optimum. Thus, he would break in with his choice immediately after an earlier respondent had spoken and before the next in sequence could do so; when there were periods of silence during a trial, he would observe aloud that maybe majority rule didn't work so well; and he would show a lack of enthusiasm for the choice offered by various others on the matter of basis. Lest he lose credibility and become a caricature, in all instances he chose his moments with care and retained an evident spontaneity of expression.

The task gave quite satisfactory signs of engrossing the subjects. There was much talk about the "system" and a good deal of delving into its basis;

one corroboration of this was found in the returned matrices, littered with diagrams, notations, and calculations. Withal, the confederate's tentative accounts of his reasoning, though quite meaningless in fact, were treated with apparent seriousness. But this was probably as much a function of the contrived time constraint, which prevented probing, as it was of his jargon regarding "rotations" and "block shifts." In any case, the confederate at no time claimed to have the system completely in hand. He delayed his response from the sixth trial onward to suggest calculation of an optimum choice in the face of conflicting alternatives; and the four trials where he was wrong were so placed as to suggest progressive improvement, but not total perfection.

Most pertinent, however, is the fact that there were no manifestations of suspicion concerning the confederate's authenticity; the others seemed to believe that he was one of them and that he was "cracking" the system; the post interaction data fully substantiated this point.[3]

Table 2 provides the basis for determining the effects of three major variables on the acceptance of the confederate's influence. The analysis is

Table 2

MEAN NUMBER OF TRIALS OF FIVE EACH FOR THREE ZONES OF TIME WHERE A GROUP ACCEPTS CONFEDERATE'S RECOMMENDED SOLUTION WITH AND WITHOUT PROCEDURAL NONCONFORMITY BY HIM FOR THE CURRENT ZONE AND IMMEDIATE PAST ZONE OF TIME

| | ZONE I (Trials 1 to 5) | | ZONE II (Trials 6 to 10) | | ZONE III (Trials 11 to 15) | |
	With	*Without*	*With*	*Without*	*With*	*Without*
With Procedural nonconformity in immediate *past* zone	1.67 6*	—	3.25 4	3.00 2	4.00 4	5.00 2
Without Procedural nonconformity in immediate *past* zone	—	2.00 6	5.00 2	3.75 4	5.00 2	4.75 4

* Indicates number of groups upon which cell is based.

---

[3] This presents an opportunity to note my great indebtedness to H. E. Titus, who not only took the confederate's role here but served as my close associate in every phase of this study.

arranged by zones (Z) of trials, and in terms of the confederate's non-conformity (NC) in the *current* zone and immediate *past* zone.[4] The means given in each cell indicate the number of trials, of five per zone, on which the confederate's choice was the group's choice. In a chi-square test, the effect of position upon this measure was found to be nonsignificant and is therefore omitted as a distinction in the analysis of variance for the table's data.

The significant F secured from Zones may be interpreted to accord with prediction. It reveals the ongoing effect of task competence in increasing influence acceptance over time, seen in the rising means across zones. While current nonconformity does not yield a significant effect, past non-conformity does. Horizontally, one finds that the means for *without past NC* exceed the means for *with past NC* in all instances but one. Regarding a significant interaction of *current* and *past NC,* the combination *without-without* yields values (2.00, 3.75, 4.75) characteristically greater than does *with-with* (1.67, 3.25, 4.00), again matching prediction. Finally, the maximum value of 5.00 in Zone II for the combination *without past NC* but *with current NC* confirms the model's key prediction, at least within the context of the relative magnitudes available here. The same value is also to be seen in Zone III for the identical combination; still another reading of 5.00 holds there, however, for the inverse combination, but in a tight range of values quite beyond separation of effects for interpretation.[5]

Considerable consistency was found too in the post interaction data. On the item "over-all contribution to the group activity," 44 of the 48 subjects ranked the confederate first; on the item "influence over the group's decisions," 45 of the 48 ranked him first. Two things bear emphasis in this regard: subjects had to individually write in the numbers of group members next to rank, hence demanding recall, and their polarity of response cut across all six treatments, despite significant differences among these in the literal *acceptance of influence.* That the confederate made an impact is clear; but that the impact had selective consequences depending upon the timing of his nonconformity is equally clear.

It remains to be said that, although the operational variables for studying influence were confined to the task itself, the matter of transfer of effect

---

[4] For Zone I, the past zone refers to the discussion period. If he were to non-conform there, the confederate would question majority rule and suggest that the division of funds be left until the end of the experiment rather than agree then on equal shares.

[5] For a fuller consideration of this analysis see Hollander (1960).

to nontask elements remains an important one insofar as it betrays alteration of common expectancies, apart from deviation from them. On this point some unquantified but clearly suggestive data are worth noting. In those groups, for example, where the confederate began nonconforming after the first zone, such behavior was accepted with minimal challenge; by the third zone, his suggestion that majority rule was faulty typically netted a rubber-stamping of his choice. Again, if he had already accrued credit, the pattern of interrupting people out of turn was simply imitated by others. Not so, however, when he exhibited nonconformity from the outset; in that event, quite opposite effects were elicited from the others, notably such comments of censure as "that's not the way we agreed to do it, five." Essentially, these findings support the model in corroborating differential impressions conveyed by the confederate's behavior in time.

SUMMARY

Two concerns have especially guided the emphasis in this paper: first, the variables yielding status differentiation in terms of potential influence; and second, the basis for an acceptance of influence. It has been shown that social interaction gives rise to what may be thought of as an implicit interpersonal assessment, and that this is compounded of task-related elements and behaviors matched by the perceiver against some social standard, referred to here as an "expectancy."

Where an individual fulfills these conditions in some combination over time, he is said to have accumulated "idiosyncrasy credits" and, at some threshold, these credits permit innovation in the group as one evidence of social influence. Thus the task-competent follower who conforms to the common expectancies of the group at one stage may become the leader at the next stage. And, correspondingly, the leader who fails to fulfill the expectancies associated with his position of influence may lose credits among his followers and be replaced by one of them. The research findings offered above demonstrate features of this interchange.

REFERENCES

BALES, R. F. AND SLATER, P. Role differentiation. In T. PARSONS, R. F. BALES ET AL., *Family, socialization, and interaction process.* Glencoe, Ill.: Free Press, 1955.

BELL, G. B. AND FRENCH, R. L. Consistency of individual leadership position in small groups of varying membership. *J. abnorm. soc. Psychol.* 1950, *45,* 764–767.

BROWN, J. F. *Psychology in the social order.* New York: McGraw-Hill, 1936.

CARTER, L. F., HAYTHORN, W., SHRIVER, BEATRICE, AND LANZETTA, J. The behavior of leaders and other group members. *J. abnorm. soc. Psychol.,* 1951, *46,* 589–595.

CHOWDHRY, KAMLA AND NEWCOMB, T. M. The relative abilities of leaders and non-leaders to estimate opinions of their own groups. *J. abnorm. soc. Psychol.,* 1952, *47,* 51–57.

COWLEY, W. H. The traits of face-to-face leaders. *J. abnorm. soc. Psychol.,* 1931, *26,* 304–313.

CRISWELL, JOAN H. Sociometric concepts in personnel administration. *Sociometry,* 1949, *12,* 287–300.

DITTES, J. E. AND KELLEY, H. H. Effects of different conditions of acceptance upon conformity to group norms. *J. abnorm. soc. Psychol.,* 1956, *53,* 100–107.

FIEDLER, F. E. Assumed similarity measures as predictors of team effectiveness. *J. abnorm. soc. Psychol.,* 1954, *49,* 381–388.

GIBB, C. A. Leadership. In G. LINDZEY (Ed.), *Handbook of social psychology,* Vol. II, Cambridge, Mass.: Addison-Wesley, 1954.

GIBB, C. A. The principles and traits of leadership. *J. abnorm. soc. Psychol.,* 1947, *42,* 267–284.

GIBB, C. A. The sociometry of leadership in temporary groups. *Sociometry,* 1950, *13,* 226–243.

GOULDNER, A. W. (Ed.), *Studies in leadership.* New York: Harper, 1950.

HEMPHILL, J. K. *Situational factors in leadership.* Columbus: The Ohio State Univ., 1949.

HOLLANDER, E. P. Buddy ratings: military research and industrial implications. *Personnel Psychol.,* 1954, *7,* 385–393. (a)

HOLLANDER, E. P. Studies of leadership among naval aviation cadets. *Journal of Aviation Medicine,* 1954, *25,* 164–170, 200. (b)

HOLLANDER, E. P. The friendship factor in peer nominations. *Personnel Psych.,* 1956, *9,* 435–447.

HOLLANDER, E. P. Conformity, status, and idiosyncrasy credit. *Psychol. rev.,* 1958, *65,* 117–127. (a)

HOLLANDER, E. P. Some further findings on leadership, followership, and friendship. ONR Technical Report. Pittsburgh: Carnegie Institute of Technology, Nov. 1958. (b)

HOLLANDER, E. P. Competence and conformity in the acceptance of influence. *J. abnorm. soc. Psychol.,* 1960. In press.

HOLLANDER, E. P. AND WEBB, W. B. Leadership, followership, and friendship: an analysis of peer nominations. *J. abnorm. soc. Psychol.,* 1955, *50,* 163–167.

HOMANS, G. C. *The human group.* New York: Harcourt, 1950.

HYMAN, H. H. The psychology of status. *Arch. Psychol., 269,* 1942.

JENNINGS, HELEN HALL. *Leadership and isolation.* New York: Longmans, 1943.

JENNINGS, HELEN HALL. Sociometry of leadership. *Sociometry Monographs,* 1947, *14,* 12–24.

JONES, E. E. AND DECHARMS, R. Changes in social perception as a function of the personal relevance of behavior. *Sociometry,* 1957, *20,* 75–85.

KUBANY, A. J. Evaluation of medical student clinical performance: a criterion study. Unpublished doctoral dissertation, Univ. of Pittsburgh, 1957.

MEAD, G. H. *Mind, self, and society.* Chicago: Univ. of Chicago, 1934.

MOORE, O. K. AND BERKOWITZ, M. I. Problem solving and social interaction. *Tech. Rep. No. 1, Contract Nonr–609(16).* New Haven: Yale University Department of Sociology, November, 1956.

NEWCOMB, T. M. *Social psychology.* New York: Holt, Rinehart and Winston, Inc., 1950.

NEWCOMB, T. M. The prediction of interpersonal attraction. *Amer. Psychologist,* 1956, *11,* 575–586.

SANFORD, F. H. *Authoritarianism and leadership.* Philadelphia: Institute for Research in Human Relations, 1950.

SEARS, R. R. A theoretical framework for personality and social behavior. *Amer. Psychologist,* 1951, *6,* 476–482.

STOGDILL, R. M. Personal factors associated with leadership: a survey of the literature. *J. Psychol.* 1948, *25,* 35–71.

TAGIURI, R. Relational analysis: an extension of sociometric method with emphasis upon social perception. *Sociometry,* 1952, *15,* 91–104.

4

The Ego, FIRO Theory
and the Leader as Completer

William C. Schutz

Institute of Personality Assessment and Research[1]
University of California, Berkeley

> *The leadership functions in the small group are the same as the ego functions within an individual personality.*

The purpose of this paper is to make this statement plausible and to explore some of its implications.[2] To do this it will be necessary to discuss some of the latest developments in psychoanalytic theory—specifically, ego psychology—and to elaborate these developments by using the theory of interpersonal behavior presented in FIRO (Schutz, 1958c). Further, this paper will discuss the fruitfulness of making the connection between ego and leader functions by presenting some implications of ego psychology for the understanding of leadership, and some implications of leadership and small group research for personality psychology.

The parallel existing between ego and leader is expressed by the general proposition: *a person is a group and a group is a person.* (The word "is"

[1] Now at the Department of Education, University of California, Berkeley.

[2] Many of the ideas in this paper were originated and developed in the research seminar at the Massachusetts Mental Health Center, Boston, in 1957–58 under Public Health Training Grant 2M6378. In particular, the notion of a group as a person and of the leader as completer was introduced to me and elaborated, along somewhat different lines, by Elvin Semrad.

is used in the sense of "follows the same laws as.") This thesis has been elaborated earlier (Schutz, 1958a) with respect to the psychological phenomena of levels of consciousness, development and maturity, defense mechanisms, and cognitive processes. Before dealing directly with the problem of ego and leader, let us present the general conceptual model of the person as a group.

A PERSON IS A GROUP

For centuries the notion has been advanced that there is considerable similarity between the functioning of an individual person and of larger human systems such as small groups, organizations, institutions, and nations. (See, for example, Herbert Spencer, 1862). This similarity has been commented on by literary men probably as much as by scientists. However, there has been relatively little done to work out in detail the specific connections between systems on various levels, both with regard to points of correspondence between levels and to general laws that might hold equally for the individual and for larger groups.

If such a detailed correspondence could be carried out successfully, many advantages would result. For instance, (a) any finding on the level of individual, small group, organization, or society would have implications for all other levels. Thus, hypotheses with considerable antecedent probability could be generated extensively across levels. (b) One special case of these connections is worth noting in particular. Understanding of the dynamics of personality may be increased by observation of group phenomena. The possibility of using the group as a model for the individual has great theoretical and experimental potentialities and will be discussed below. (c) There are practical implications for training and therapy groups in that the conceptual framework can aid both the trainer and the group members in understanding the group process more easily.

The assertion that a person is a group is not merely an attempt to establish an analogy. It is a contention that the same laws hold for both levels, so that the substitution of corresponding variables from different levels will result in correspondingly true hypotheses. In other words, the reason a parallel can be made between a person and a group is that an individual is assumed to have a group within him. Initially, there are many ambiguous figures in the infant's environment who are unconsciously and gradually brought into focus and differentiated. These individuals are then introjected to various degrees and allocated differential influence on the behavior of the individual. Within the individual there exists a struggle to determine which of these introjected figures will emerge pre-eminent.

As the individual matures, he must deal with the positive and negative feelings these people have toward each other and toward the individual's own impulses. These feelings must be brought in concert, if the individual is to emerge as productive and well-integrated.

The individual may therefore be conceptualized as a small group of which he is the leader. This group is composed of all his introjects, especially of his early years—all those people whom he has incorporated into his own ego. His leadership of this group varies from moment to moment and also with developmental phases. Very likely he is going to lean heavily on the group opinions when he is younger, but as he acquires experience and confidence, he will take over the leadership more strongly.

Just as some leaders seem to be dominated by one group member, so may an individual be influenced by a particular introject. Just as external forces influence group behavior, so do an individual's external personal relations affect the interaction of his introjects. Just as a group acts although torn by dissension, so does an individual act in spite of internal conflict. Just as groups vary in becoming welded into a cohesive unit, so do individuals vary in their integration. Groups become immobilized and unproductive just as do people. Just as in groups certain people are more influential in some areas and others in different areas, so do different introjects take over in different areas within an individual person.

To be a mature, well-integrated person, one must have a well-integrated group of introjects. This means, also, that the group, including the leader, must form a complete, well-functioning unit.

An individual personality may be regarded as composed of both inherent basic needs and parts of many persons introjected to varying degrees. An individual arriving at a decision may be regarded as symbolically working out the interaction of the group within himself to reach a decision. Thus the group equivalent of individual behavior is a group decision, or a topic that a group discusses, as opposed to idiosyncratic topics. This decision behavior is equivalent to ego functioning.

PSYCHOANALYTIC EGO PSYCHOLOGY

One of the important recent developments in psychoanalytic theory is the shift in emphasis from id psychology to ego psychology (see, for example, Gill, 1959). The following report on psychoanalytic ego psychology is drawn mainly from the writings of Heinz Hartmann (1939, 1950), David Rapaport (1954), and Anna Freud (1936). These analysts have been associated with the study of ego psychology for approximately twenty-five years. The main topic in ego psychology relevant to small group leadership is the development of the ego. Hartmann (1950, p. 79) speaks about ego development in the following way:

> We come to see ego development as the result of three sets of factors: inherited ego characteristics (and their interaction), influences of the instinctual drives, and influences of outer reality.

The influence of outer reality on the development of the ego is fairly straightforward. It is one of the functions of the ego to deal with outer reality, that is, all those things outside of the skin of the individual, including situational, inanimate factors and the existence of other people. The ego develops in part through its contact with these objects and through its efforts to deal with them in such a way that their threat is minimized, and the interaction of the person with these factors is enhanced. For conceptual consistency the interaction of outer-reality factors as well as the factors themselves will be added to Hartmann's list of the influences on ego development.

The term *instinctual urges* is used in its usual psychoanalytic sense, referring primarily to the sexual, aggressive, and sometimes the self-preservative drives, which are posited to exist inside the organism. Much of the intended meaning is preserved and much more may be gained by translating "instinctual drives" into "interpersonal needs." Traditionally, a stumbling block to the use of psychoanalytic theory in empirical investigations has been the concept of instincts with its connotation of inbornness, and its physiological basis. These implications need not be dealt with before the terms are useful. Instead, the behavior patterns characterizing the drives, especially his interpersonal dealings, may be identified for each individual as they manifest themselves in his daily life.

Hence, the term *interpersonal need* seems to be a rendering of *instinctual urge* that is reasonable in the sense of maintaining the intended meaning and also allowing for empirical investigation. Parenthetically, the three needs posited to be fundamental (Schutz, 1958c) are very close interpersonal counterparts of the three primary instinctual urges: inclusion parallels self-preservation, control parallels aggression, and affection parallels sexual urge. Again to maintain conceptual consistency, to the interpersonal needs shall be added their interaction as factors in the development of the ego. Therefore in part, the ego develops through dealing with the interpersonal needs and their interaction within the individual.

The inherited or autonomous factors are the newest set of variables— the ones that demarcate the ego-psychology movement. Here ego psychologists contended that, contrary to some interpreters of Freud's early writings, the ego does not develop *only* as the result of repressed, desexualized, neutralized energy from the instinctual drives taken over by the ego, usually in the form of sublimation. On the contrary, a *part* of the ego function exists at birth and develops autonomously. This part of the ego Hartmann calls the "conflict-free ego sphere." Although ego psychologists have not made a definitive list of the contents of this sphere, they usually speak of perception and motility as being within this sphere. In addition, Hartmann (1950, p. 75) mentions:

> Freud has always emphasized those which center around the relation to reality: "The relation to the external world is decisive for the ego." The ego organizes and controls motility and perception—perception of the outer world, but probably also the self . . . , it also serves as a protective barrier against excessive external and . . . internal stimuli. The ego tests reality. Action . . . and thinking . . . are functions of the ego. . . . Many aspects of the ego can be described as detour activities; they promote a more specific and safer form of adjustment by introducing a factor of growing independence from the immediate impact of present stimuli.

Also included in ego functions are defense mechanisms (Anna Freud, 1936), a person's character, and the coordinating or integrating tendencies known as the integrating function.

Thus, the conflict-free ego sphere may be thought of as comprising at least perception, motility, action, thinking, defensive behavior, and integrating or organizing activities.

The existence of this sphere does not imply that there is no part of the ego which is in fact a result of repressed instinctual drives, but it does assert that there is a definite independent development of part of the ego. Further, the conflict-free ego sphere does not necessarily remain conflict-free. It is theoretically possible and empirically frequent that part of the content in this sphere does become subordinated to some of the instinctual drives. For example (Hartmann, 1950, p. 81), ". . . in analysis we observe how the function of perception, which is certainly an autonomous aspect, may be influenced and frequently handicapped by becoming the expression of oral libidinous or oral aggressive strivings." In other words, there may come a time, as was recently demonstrated in the "new look" experiments, when perception, a fraction of the autonomous part of ego, becomes subordinated to an instinctual drive (interpersonal need) and becomes distorted; as for example, when Father is seen as much larger physically than he actually is due to the desire for his omnipotence.

Hartmann and the ego psychologists make clear the distinction between that aspect of behavior determined by the so-called irrational forces, that is, influenced by the instinctual urges, and that aspect determined by the rational forces, which are autonomously developed in the conflict-free sphere of the ego. Hartmann (1939) says, "To what extent is realistic regulation of action determined by intention and rational motivation, and . . . to what extent does action motivationally or genetically involve rational forces, that is, instinctual drives, and so on?" (p. 87). Thus, the third set of factors which influence the development of the ego are those autonomous aspects comprising the conflict-free ego sphere and their inter-action.

To translate freely Hartmann's discussion of ego development: The ego develops through coping with three sets of factors. It must organize and integrate the needs and demands of autonomous ego factors, interpersonal needs, and outer reality. This task is complicated by the interaction among the factors in each of these spheres separately. In other words, the ego must resolve such conflicts as those between control and affectional needs, physical limitations and climactic conditions, the results of thinking and acting, as well as conflicts arising between spheres.

The introduction of a rational sphere of the ego brings up the question of the meaning of "rational." Hartmann says (1939):

> The term "rational" has many meanings, but we will discuss only those aspects of rational action which are directly relevant to our problem. Rational action has goals and means. Here we are particularly interested in those two types of action which Max Weber (1921) has distinguished as "goal-rational" and "value-rational." According to Weber, "a man's action is goal-rational if he considers the goals, the means and the side effects, and weighs rationally means against goals, goals against side effects, and also various possible goals against each other." If a man acts upon ethical, esthetic, religious convictions disregarding foreseeable consequences, then his action is purely value-rational: "Value-rational action (in our terms) is always action in accord with 'commandments' or demands, 'which the actor believes he must follow.' " Weber's distinction is obviously analogous to the familiar one between action in the service of the ego and action in the service of the superego. But, let us add, this is not an absolute contrast: the ego may take up and sanction the superego's demands (p. 67).

Attempts at clarifying or dimensionalizing the conflict-free ego sphere are scarce. However, the following factors may indicate some areas for investigation, helpful for rendering the concept empirically usable. (1) The determination of one's hierarchy of values or goals. (2) Some of the psychological functions discussed by Jung (1923), especially thinking-feeling, sensing-intuition, and judgment-perception. (3) The variables known as cognitive style, including such characteristics as tempo of work, speed of learning, height of threshold for stimulation, and general capacity for activity. (4) Individual abilities such as intelligence and physical dexterity.

These by no means exhaust the conflict-free ego sphere, but may serve to characterize the area more specifically.

This completes the discussion of those concepts from ego psychology that seem relevant to leadership phenomena in small groups: the autonomous factors, outer reality, and instinctual urges; the conflict-free ego sphere; the phenomena of this sphere coming under the influence of instinctual urges; and the conception of goal-rationality and value-rationality. The parallels and coordinations that may be made between these concepts and the phenomena of small group behavior, in particular, leadership behavior, will now be discussed.

COORDINATING CONCEPTS BETWEEN EGO PSYCHOLOGY AND GROUP PSYCHOLOGY

In drawing a parallel of leadership between individual and group, individual ego is comparable to the leader of the group, or more accurately, ego functions of the individual are coordinate with leader functions of the group. Using this coordination, what conceptions of group leadership arise from the above discussion of ego psychology?

Just as the ego develops by dealing with its three areas of influence, leadership functions of the group can be said to develop through the interplay of the three factors of outer reality, interpersonal needs, and an autonomous or conflict-free area. Before examining these factors in more detail, it is interesting to note the congeniality of this notion of ego development with the excellent description of group development given by Bennis and Shepard (1956)—in particular, their mention of the group's contention with interpersonal problems finally resolved by the "unconflicted" members of the group in a given area. The unconflicted element might be called the "conflict-free group sphere."

Outer Reality

Consider first the outer reality necessary for group or leader. The ego must take on adaptive functions. It uses intelligence, perceptual ability, motility, and action in the service of adapting itself to the external world. It does this in two major ways. Hartmann, following Freud, discusses "autoplastic" and "alloplastic" adaptation. Alloplastic adaptation is becoming harmonious with one's environment by changing the environment, while autoplastic adaptation is becoming adjusted to the environment by changing oneself. These two techniques are open to the leader of a group who is attempting to adapt himself and his group to outer reality. A group member thus can perform a leader function either by changing the part of the environment that is not satisfactory, or by altering his group. In small-group literature there are several parallels to the notion of outer reality. Homans' "external system" (1950) is one example.

Interpersonal Needs

With instinctual urges or interpersonal needs, the problem for the group leader is to gratify those that exist within the group. These include group needs (existing commonly for several group members) and individual needs. In addition, the group leader must deal effectively with the inter-action among these various needs. Leadership function develops in the small group in part through dealing with interpersonal desires within the group. This interpersonal sphere has been discussed by several students of small groups, for example, the "socio-emotional problems" of Bales (1950).

Conflict-free Sphere

With autonomous factors, the leadership function is to mobilize and utilize all of the conflict-free spheres that he has available in the group—the general reservoir of talent, intelligence, perceptual ability. Leadership functions develop also through the attempt to utilize the conflict-free sphere within the group. This area is probably the most frequently mentioned in discussions of small-group researchers, Benne and Sheats' (1948) area of "task roles" being one example.

Rationality

Another set of ego psychology concepts for which coordinate group concepts are to be found are *goal-rational* and *value-rational*. Suppose all demands of outer reality and interpersonal needs have been met in a group and it is acting rationally. What does rational mean?

It can mean that the group is acting according to its own goals or according to its own values and beliefs. Before the ego in an individual can guide him rationally he must possess a fairly clear notion of what his goals and values are. Correspondingly, the group leader has the function of making clear, or helping the group to make clear, what its goals and values are. A more useful way of stating this is to talk about not the values, but the "hierarchy of values" of goals of the group. If the group is clear about its values or goals and their allocation in the hierarchy, then it can make a rational decision about what course of action it wants to take toward achieving them. (This point has relevance to the problem of whether or not a group will pursue a goal that is imposed upon it.) Depending upon its place in the group's hierarchy, the group will or will not go along with a leader's attempt to get them to achieve an external goal.

The parallel in group psychology to Hartmann's discussion of the relative role of the rational and irrational parts can be found most directly in Bion (1949) and Stock and Thelen (1958), who follow his concepts. They distinguish the "work" and "emotionality" parts of group behavior. All behavior in the group may be conceptualized as being made up of two parts: one is motivated basically by the attempt to solve interpersonal problems, the other is based more on the here and now and is rational or appropriate. These two form almost a constant sum. Rational, conflict-free factors operate to the degree interpersonal problems (either within the group or between the group and reality) are solved. The more interpersonal problems are solved, the larger the proportion of behavior determined by rational factors. This idea is logically the direct coordinate of the ego psychologists' primary distinction between rational and irrational forces.

In thus concluding the coordination between the concepts of psychoanalytic ego psychology and group psychology especially relevant to the problem of leadership, one naturally asks, of what assistance is this in understanding either leadership or individual psychology? Therefore, each of these coordinate concepts will now be dealt with in more detail to demonstrate primarily some of the contributions of ego psychology to leadership theory. Later, some contributions in the reverse direction will also be mentioned. In discussing these areas, it is necessary to use theoretical tools that are more detailed than those developed so far in ego psychology. For that purpose certain concepts from interpersonal behavior are used, in particular those presented in *FIRO* (Schutz, 1958c).

CONTRIBUTIONS: EGO PSYCHOLOGY TO LEADERSHIP PSYCHOLOGY

Analysis suggests an approach to describing necessary group functions or roles. Ego psychology presents a set of influences that contribute to development of the ego. Similarly then, it could be said that these influences are the ones that contribute to the development of leadership functions in a group. Hence, if a leader can enable the group to perform all the functions needed to integrate these three spheres, he will have done all that is required of him.

THE EGO, FIRO THEORY AND THE LEADER AS COMPLETER   •   57

Of the many approaches to the problem of basic group functions or functional roles, none has provided a satisfactory over-all framework from which roles are derivable. Most attempts are based on observation of existing patterns of behavior. Those that appear to recur are simply listed as "functional roles." They are rarely related to an underlying theory. Actually, it is difficult to know the degree of necessity of each role. What happens if there is no "task leader," for example, or no "joker"? Does the group disintegrate, or is it just a different type of group?

The suggested framework for integrating group roles consists of listing all those things needed for a group to cope successfully with outer reality, interpersonal needs, and conflict-free factors. It is at this point that the FIRO theory of interpersonal behavior seems to offer a method of enumerating the necessary behaviors for coping with at least two of the three spheres. This theory states that there are three fundamental interpersonal needs—inclusion, control, and affection—and in order for an individual (or group) to function optimally he must establish and maintain a satisfactory relation in all three areas, with other people or with symbols of people. The application of these notions to each area of influence of ego and leader development will now be pursued. The totality of requirements in these three areas may be considered necessary group functions for optimal group performance within the ego psychology—FIRO theoretical framework.

Outer Reality

The kinds of things that may go wrong in outer reality, the things that make it necessary for the leader to take some kind of action, are those in which the interpersonal needs of the group are not compatible with the requirements of external reality, or where somehow outer reality does not enhance (or even inhibits) the expression of the conflict-free area of the group. This suggests a way of categorizing outer reality for groups. *FIRO* describes various types of compatibility holding between people and suggests that this type of analysis can be expanded to include situations. Types of incompatibilities that can exist between the group and external reality may be described, parallel to person-person incompatibilities. Since, according to FIRO theory, individuals have three basic interpersonal needs—inclusion, control, and affection—there may be an incompatibility between a group and its environment in any of these three areas.

In the area of inclusion, a group can be incompatible with outer reality in that it wants either more or less contact and interaction with outer reality than it has. Too little contact is exemplified by military groups that live at isolated outposts. If such a group, as a whole, wants more interaction with people than the setting provides, this dissatisfaction may be the source of incompatibility between the group and its environment. On the other hand, a family group for example, including a famous person, may be constantly besieged by invitations, visitors, and by other experiences that do not permit them to maintain sufficient privacy. In this case, outer reality becomes incompatible with the group by not allowing them sufficient withdrawal from interaction with their environment.

In the area of control, outer-reality incompatibility means that the group either has too little or too much control over its environment. Too little control is exemplified by a group living at the foot of an irregularly erupting volcano. Here, there is a fundamental incompatibility between the group and outer reality because the group has too little control. On the other hand, a group that is forced to control its outer reality too much is likely to feel it has more responsibility than it can handle. For example, in wartime, aboard key ships, young, inexperienced tactical radar teams have the enormous responsibility of controlling the actions of planes in combat with the enemy. In this case control is sometimes too great, and these groups would often be quite happy to be relieved of much of their control.

In the area of affection, a group may be incompatible with outer reality because it has too few or too many affectional ties with the environment. It often happens that a particular kind of group such as the Central Intelligence Agency is required to act in a very dignified and secret manner. This group is not allowed to become intimate with any other group because of the nature of its work. This aspect of too few ties may be unsatisfactory for most group members. On the other hand, intimacy and closeness for other groups may be excessive and may be forced upon them by the external situation. This is true of certain families living in suburbia, where the great closeness of their living forces them to become close and intimate with many people in their surroundings in ways they do not desire.

The above, then, are examples of a way in which, if one accepts the FIRO framework, all possible incompatibilities between a group and outer reality might be categorized. An area of influence on ego development as elaborated by FIRO theory indicates the following.

Leadership functions re outer reality

(1) Establish and maintain sufficient contact and interaction with outside groups and individuals to avoid isolation of the group, but not so much contact that the group loses its privacy.

(2) Establish and maintain sufficient control over outer reality that the group can function satisfactorily without outside interference, and yet not so much control that the group is forced to undertake more responsibility than it desires.

(3) Establish and maintain sufficient closeness and intimacy with outside reality that the group can feel the pleasures of friendship and affection, and yet not so much intimacy with outside reality that the actions of the group become distorted and detrimental to group objectives.

Interpersonal Needs

The leader functions for establishing and maintaining satisfactory relations among members follow the same lines as those given for outer reality, except that the compatibility must be among members within the group rather than between the group and outer reality. An extensive discussion of the problems of compatibility of this type is given in *FIRO* (Schutz, 1958c). For the present purposes, the primary leadership functions for each area are discussed.

Satisfaction of interpersonal needs is obtained through the establishment and maintenance of an optimal relation among group members in their need areas. Hence, in order to function effectively, the group must find comfortable balance in the amount and type of contact and interaction, control and influence, and personal closeness and affection.

Leadership functions re interpersonal needs

Enough inclusion. It is necessary to maintain the group's existence. It therefore is desirable that everyone feels part of the group and to some degree knows he belongs. A desire for inclusion is motivation for efficiency in activities such as notifying members of meetings. Activities that foster these feelings include introductions and biographical stories to identify members.

Not too much inclusion. It is necessary to allow group members to maintain some degree of distance from other group members and some individuality. To accomplish this end groups are divided frequently into subgroups, labor is divided, and perhaps in a more subtle way differences are established between subgroups (male-female, Negro-White, Catholic-Jew, etc.).

Enough control. It is necessary for members to influence other members to some extent in order to make decisions. Without this influence or control of others no decision-making system could be effective. Techniques used to accomplish this end are election of officers, establishment of power hierarchies, employment of brute force, and so on.

Not too much control. In most groups it is necessary to establish behavior patterns leading to a restriction of the amount of control some members have over others. If this is not done, the value of the independent operation of some persons is lost, and some members acquire too much responsibility. The institutional procedures of majority rule and consensus are often used to limit control.

Enough affection. The necessity for this need is more controversial. For the present purposes it is assumed that affection is necessary for the effective functioning of a group. Hence, it is required that people relate to each other with sufficient warmth and closeness for group processes to proceed. If there is not enough freedom to express feelings among members, then the productivity suffers because of the tie-up of energy in the suppression of hostile impulses. Widely used behaviors attempting to gratify this need include side-whispers, subgrouping, after-meeting coffee, parties, bringing food to meetings and coffee breaks.

Not too much affection. Excessive intimacy and closeness may have the effect of detracting from the main purposes of the group, and also of personalizing task issues to an undesirable extent. Hence, it is necessary to limit the degree of closeness in groups. Techniques used for accomplishing this end are nepotism rules, fraternization rules, agenda and other procedural techniques, discipline and punishment for too much affectional play.

These functions constitute those of leadership in the area of interpersonal needs. The leadership function must see to their satisfaction by means acceptable to the group for the group to perform optimally.

Conflict-free Behavior

Leadership functions re conflict-free group sphere

1. The establishment and clarification of the hierarchy of group goals and values.
2. The recognition and integration of the various cognitive styles (modes of approaching problem solving) existing within the group.
3. The maximal utilization of the abilities and capacities of the group members.

The essential difference between this area of leadership and the others is that the supposed physiological or somehow "purely" cognitive, thinking, characteristics of the group members must be mobilized. This requires assessing what they are and enabling them to be expressed fully. The area of cognitive style may also be included in this area. Measures of variables of this sort are now being developed and appear very promising. They may aid in explicating the conflict-free area and eventually lead to usable dimensions.

Rational and Irrational

The ego psychologists say that although the conflict-free ego sphere develops autonomously, it may still come under the influence of instinctual urges. This is a phenomenon widely noted in group behavior as well. Past studies (Schutz, 1955) indicate that for groups the task situation is commonly used to gratify interpersonal needs that have not been satisfied in the group. For example, a task is used to achieve prominence or withdrawal, power or dependency, emotional closeness or distance, until satisfactory resolution of these needs is made. If a member's strongest need is high inclusion, he works to the degree necessary to be an integral part of the group; if control, he attempts to gain the respect of the group by performing competently; if affection, he tries to be liked by all, perhaps by working, or by joking, or by whatever technique he has found most effective. Similarly, people respond appropriately to the task situation if their interpersonal needs are gratified in the present group. *Appropriate* means "in such a way as to gratify themselves maximally in terms of their values and goals and within the limits of their cognitive capacities."

The Leader as Completer

In summary, by using the model of ego development presented by the psychoanalytic ego psychologists and elaborated by FIRO theory, a description may be made of the leadership functions in a small group. This description indicates the sameness of the problem for both the individual ego and the group leaders. In both cases, in order for the leader—or egofunctions—to develop optimally, the problems of the group, or individual, must be resolved: to outer reality with respect to contact, control and closeness; to interpersonal needs (or instinctual urges) with respect to contact, control and closeness; and to the autonomous conflict-free abilities and properties of the group or individual. In addition, the leader- or egofunctions must lead to a resolution of the interaction of these areas, partly through clarification and operation of value and goal hierarchies.

This approach leads to a somewhat more complicated picture of the leader function than those usually given—a picture which may be called the *leader as completer*. If all of the above-mentioned functions must be performed for optimal group operation, the best a leader can do is to observe which functions are not being performed by a segment of the group and enable this part to accomplish them. In this way he minimizes the areas of group inadequacy.

Specifically, whatever is required to enable the group to be compatible with outer reality and whatever is not being done by the group itself, the leader has to do or get done. If this means making contact with outer reality, or enabling others to do it, or becoming a spokesman to outer reality for the group, or absorbing the hostility of the external world heaped upon the group—an effective leader must perform these tasks. Occasionally it becomes necessary for the leader to become the scapegoat for interpersonal problems within the group because the incompatibility, leading to hostility, in the group is so great that no work can be accomplished. If the leader drains off some of this hostility by being the scapegoat, the group is able to continue to function. This conception also implies that when the group is fulfilling all its functions adequately, the most appropriate behavior for the leader is inaction.

This may be a somewhat different notion of a leader, since typically he is not looked upon as someone who puts himself in this position. From this analysis of the parallel with the psychoanalytic concept of the individual, the general properties of a leader become simply those functions required to maintain a certain kind of equilibrium between outer reality and interpersonal needs and the conflict-free functions of the group. These sometimes are very unpleasant, even "unleaderlike" activities.

One implication of this conception is that for some people, fulfilling these particular leadership functions would not be gratifying to their own interpersonal needs. For some, being the scapegoat voluntarily is not a pleasant way to interact in a group. Hence, the prime requisites for a leader are: (1) to know what functions a group needs; (2) to have the sensitivity and flexibility to sense what functions the group is not fulfilling; (3) to have the ability to get the things needed by his group accomplished; and (4) to have the willingness to do what is necessary to satisfy these needs, even though it may be personally displeasing. This whole conception of leadership is reminiscent of an old saying that "the good king is one whose subjects prosper."

Some Contributions: Group Psychology to Individual Psychology

In order to demonstrate further the usefulness of this model of ego and leader, a few examples of generalization from group theory to individual theory will be given. If the concept of an individual as a small group is a useful one, personality theorists should be able to profit from the studies of small groups.

One implication for the psychology of personality integration comes from Redl's (1942) analysis of group leadership, in which he distinguishes ten types of "central persons," that is, persons around whom groups form. If these types are related to the individual, they suggest ten ways in which individual personalities are integrated, that is, ten kinds of ego-integration. One may declare that people can be differentiated by ego-integration type. For example, one of the ways groups are formed, according to Redl, is through the use of the central person as an object of love. Another mode of group formation uses the central person as the object of aggressions. Perhaps these two processes occurring within one individual may be distinguishable by strong feelings of, on one hand, self-love, and on the other, self-hate. Two people having these two self-concepts, at an unconscious level, would parallel two groups organized around these two types of central person.

Another type of group formation centers around a common conflict solver, a person who acts in such a way as to resolve enervating conflicts in other group members. Where there is a great deal of conflict within an individual, he may select an unconflicted introject to orient his own ego, thereby allowing him to solve this problem. One might wonder, however, about the stability of such an individual, since for groups this formation is a very volatile one, the leadership pattern being dependent on the immediate conflict only. It may be that a useful classification of pathological conditions may be made on the basis of inadequate types of ego-integration. These types are derived not only from small group studies, but also from studying the etiology, weaknesses, and effect of various therapies on actual small groups organized around the different types of central person.

A second application of a group principle to individual psychology concerns the concept of compatibility. The kinds of group incompatibility that were delineated in *FIRO* (Schutz, 1958c) could now be looked upon as types of psychological difficulty. Among an individual's internalized introjects there are many kinds of compatibility that may exist, and these types can exist in different areas, namely inclusion, control and affection. What happens to individuals who have different kinds of incompatibility in their thinking? How do they look, how are they differentiated? One initial suggestion (Schutz, 1958c) is that difficulties in compatibilities in the area of inclusion are related to psychoses (aberrations in establishing contacts with people); in the control area, incompatibilities within the individual are related to psychopathy (the inability to control one's internal life or to build a superego often leads to psychopathic behavior); and difficulties with internal incompatibility in the area of affection are related to neurotic difficulties (usually associated with sexual and affectional inadequacies). There is, then, the possibility of a classification of pathology based on types of incompatibility derived from observations on small groups and applied to the internal groups conceptualized as existing within the thought processes of every individual.

This parallel leads to lines of research in which the group, conceptualized as one individual, becomes the basic tool. Attempts can be made to reproduce, in the group, various kinds of individuals. Since it is ordinarily easier to see more phenomena in a group than within an individual, experimental personality research can be expedited with the use of the small group.

SUMMARY

The purpose of this paper is to elaborate the general theoretical notion that a group and an individual may be understood using the same theoretical framework with the specific focus on the coordination between leader function in a group and ego function in an individual. A short exposition of some relevant aspects of psychoanalytic ego psychology was presented and then translated into terms appropriate to group leadership, equating the group with the individual and the leader with the ego.

Then using the FIRO theory of interpersonal behavior as a tool for elaborating the concepts of ego psychology and putting them in terms usable for investigating leadership, the implications of ego psychology for leadership were explored. It was found that optimal group functions could be described and necessary leadership behavior could then be illuminated. This led to the notion of the *leader as completer,* the one who enables the group to fulfill any function the group is not doing for itself, either by having it done or by doing it himself. This is a somewhat different notion of leadership in that, for example, it encourages the leader in scapegoat behavior at certain times.

Finally, the fruitfulness of the original model was shown by presenting a few implications of group research for personality theory. Redl's (1942) notions of central persons were related to different types of personality organization, and the idea of group compatibility was related to types of psychological disturbance.

REFERENCES

BALES, R. F. *Interaction process analysis: A method for the study of small groups.* Cambridge, Mass.: Addison-Wesley, 1950.

BENNE, K. AND SHEATS, P. Functional roles of group members. *J. soc. Issues,* 1948, 4, 41–49.

BENNIS, W. AND SHEPARD, H. A theory of group development. *Human Relations,* 1956, 9, 415–437.

Bion, W. Experiences in groups: III, IV. *Human Relations,* 1949, 2, 13–22; 295–304.

Freud, Anna. *The ego and mechanisms of defense.* New York: International Universities Press, 1946 (originally published 1936).

Gill, M. The present state of psychoanalytic theory. *J. abnorm. soc. Psychol.,* 1959, 58, 1–8.

Hartmann, H. Comments on the psychoanalytic theory of the ego. In *The psychoanalytic study of the child.* Vol. V, New York: International Universities Press, 1950.

Hartmann, H. *Ego psychology and the problem of adaptation.* New York: International Universities Press, 1958 (originally published 1939).

Homans, G. C. *The human group.* New York: Harcourt, 1950.

Jung, C. G. *Psychological types.* New York: Harcourt, 1923.

Rapaport, D. The autonomy of the ego. In Knight, R. P. and Friedman, C. R. (Eds.), *Psychoanalytic psychiatry and psychology.* New York: International Universities Press, 1954.

Redl, F. Group emotion and leadership. *Psychiatry,* 1942, 5, 573–596.

Schutz, W. C. What makes groups productive? *Human Relations,* 1955, 8, 429–465.

Schutz, W. C. The group mind revisited. Paper presented at Eastern Psychol. Ass., Philadelphia, 1958a.

Schutz, W. C. The interpersonal underworld. *Harvard Business Review,* July-August, 1958b.

Schutz, W. C. *FIRO: A three-dimensional theory of interpersonal behavior.* New York: Holt, Rinehart and Winston, 1958c.

Spencer, H. *First principles.* New York and London: Appleton, 1900 (originally published 1862).

Stock, Dorothy and Thelen, H. *Emotional dynamics and group culture.* Washington, D. C.: National Training Laboratories, 1958.

5

Defense Level and Influence Potential in Small Groups

Jack R. Gibb

National Training Laboratories

During the course of a series of studies of defensive behavior[1] within small groups it became increasingly apparent that the level of defense in a small group is related significantly to the influence potential of a given group-member act. Investigations led to the determination of certain functional relationships between the success of member influence attempts and each of three empirical variables: (1) the *role boundaries* prescribed by the group, (2) the *role repertoire* of the influencing member, and (3) the *consonance* of the member act with the group goal system. Further studies indicated that the defense level in the small group is systematically related to each of these three variables.

The influence potential of a given member act may be viewed as being a function of the interaction between a group-member act and the group state at the time of performance. Influence is a relationship. One can investigate the relationship by looking at properties of the member act, of the group context, or of the relationship itself. The three variables mentioned above represent three selected aspects of the influence relationship.

[1] These studies were financed in large part by funds from Contract Nonr–1147 (03) between the Group Psychology Branch of the Office of Naval Research and the University of Colorado, and Contract Nonr–2285(01) with the University of Delaware.

The role repertoire of the individual, the range and adequacy of his role behaviors, is a central aspect of the member-act side of the relationship. The effectiveness of these member acts is determined in part by the context in which the act is performed. Field observations have indicated that one significant contextual aspect in determining influence potential is the role boundary set up by the group for acts of each group member. The role boundary for an individual functions as a kind of perceptual selectivity screen that determines the responsiveness of the group to particular member acts. Field observations have indicated that a significant relationship variable in determining influence potential is the consonance of a member act with the group goal system existing at the time of action.

The three variables listed are illustrative of each of the three classes of variables: individual, contextual, and relationship variables. It is not known whether these three variables are the primary determiners of influence potential. How much each contributes to total variance in specific situations is a matter for further research. Of primary significance to our total research program is the intermediary role played by defense states in these relationships.

The primary data upon which the generalizations in this paper are based are taken from two major sources: (1) a series of laboratory experiments upon college students performing assigned laboratory group tasks, and (2) a series of field experiments and field observations upon adult groups engaged in human-relations training of various kinds. The focus was upon the intermediary role of defensive behavior in determining influence potential. *Defensive* behavior was viewed as any group-member act which was motivated, in substantial part, by an individual's need to preserve a stable perception of the self or to defend the self from perceived attack or potential attack. Measurements were made by interview, coded behavior observations, Likert-type scales, or projective tests. Defensive behavior included overt and covert representations of a wide variety of generalized states such as aggression, withdrawal or dependency. Defensive behavior was viewed for our purposes as a unitary construct. That is, it is demonstrably possible to differentiate consistent clusters of genotypical as well as phenotypical patterns of defensive behavior, but for the purposes of our studies we were interested in the determiners and effects of a generalized defense level in the individual, dyad, or the small group. It was our original assumption, corroborated in large part by a series of experiments, that the raising and lowering of defense levels would have predictable antecedents and consequences.

Because the term *leadership* has often led to ambiguity, due in part to its diverse historical associations, we have tended not to use it in conceptualizing our studies. One central aspect of the historical problem of leadership is the degree to which group members, from whatever formal or informal position in the group structure, can exert influence upon other members. Influence potential, like leadership, can be viewed for methodological purposes as a characteristic of the individual, of the group field, or of a certain relationship that exists at any given moment. We have used the term *tractability level* to refer to the degree to which an individual or a group can be changed by a given group-member act. The group is said to have high tractability when goal direction or role distribution is easily changed by a given member act. The individual is said to have high tractability when his behavior is easily changed by action of another group member. We have used the term *inductivity index* to refer to the change induction potential of the individual, that he carries as a constant variable in small-group situations. Inductivity and tractability are interactive variables. We could for various purposes independently vary the inductivity of an individual, the influence potential of an isolated and describable member act, or the tractability of a given group. Any of these could be studied in a particular moment of time or in an extended period of time. The inductivity of a particular individual, if generalized to situations, corresponds to one definition of what has been historically described as a leadership trait. Although such a view is not popular at the moment, the amount of stability in degree of variance contributed by individuals across influence situations is an empirical question. The significant research question is concerned with the degree of generality, not with its presence or absence. The manipulability of tractability levels in small groups is a matter that is of accelerating interest to a variety of social technologists as well as to students of the influence processes.

ROLE BOUNDARY

One series of field observations and laboratory studies indicated that a major determiner of influence potential of a given group-member act is the role boundary prescribed by the group. The role boundary for an individual refers to the boundary that encompasses the member acts the group will accept from the individual. The role area is both inclusive and exclusive. The actor may or may not be conscious of the boundary. The group may consciously or unconsciously impose the boundary. There seems to exist for each individual in a particular group at a particular time a certain range of behaviors to which the group will be optimally responsive.

Interviews and observations indicate that members respond to role actions outside of the role boundary by not seeing or hearing the behavior, by ignoring the behavior, by subtle fighting if this trespass is but dimly seen, by open rebellion if the circumvention of the boundary is seen as deliberate, by encapsulating the individual or forcing his withdrawal, by various perceptual distortions, or, in general, by using whatever means of behavior control the group has evolved as a norm.

Often the role boundary is a relatively formal one and exists as a manifestation of a formal set of agreements among members, such as the agreed-upon specification that the discussion chairman will be neutral on all issues confronting the group, or that the chairman will inform members when they are off the agenda, or that the host will tell the group when it is time for refreshments. Violations of formal role boundaries are visible and dealt with in a relatively easy manner by group members. Much more powerful and less controllable are covert boundaries that seem to prescribe that the group will accept certain members' remarks as humorous, will tolerate aggression from other members, will accept digression from some, and will respond immediately to an action initiation from others.

Members are differentially aware of boundaries imposed upon their behavior or of their contributions to the imposition of boundaries upon the behavior of others (Gibb, 1951; Smith, 1957). Interviews to test the strength of certain observer-perceived role prescriptions may get a firm denial of awareness of the consistencies in behavior which lead to the observer inference (Gibb, in press).

That the boundary is determined by fairly stable role expectations of role members has been shown by Schopler, Lott, and Gibb (1954). In a laboratory experiment, four conditions were studied in which systematic variations were made in sequence of style pattern used by pairs of leaders, one member of each pair following the other member of the pair in a group problem-solving situation. In one condition leaders with a specific prescribed range of behaviors, A, a restrictive kind of controlling leadership, were followed by leaders with a specific prescribed range of behaviors, B, a freedom-giving kind of leadership. In three other conditions the following orders obtained: B was followed by A; A by A; and B by B. Thus in two conditions leader behavior was followed by a congruent style of leader behavior, and in two other conditions leader behavior was followed by an incongruent style. Group members accepted and responded more readily to leaders who followed other leaders with the same prescribed range of behaviors. Furthermore, members were less defensive and more productive in problem solving in the congruent conditions than in the incongruent conditions. These and similar results indicate one of the conditions under which boundaries may be established. The results indicate that boundaries produce selective and differential responses of group members to member acts, depending upon the individual who is performing the act. Collective expectations seem to stabilize and impose restrictions upon the role interactions of group members.

Assumptions about role boundaries in relationships between leaders and group members often act as restraining forces to adaptive role distribution. There is some evidence that role distribution is associated with task efficiency over a long period of time (Gibb, 1959). Thus, as groups learn to work together stereotypic assumptions develop, both at a conscious and at a vaguely intuitive level, about the roles that members take or will take in problem solving. Interviews reveal these assumptions: "I was hoping someone would break the tension, perhaps Bill or Olin"; "I thought it was time that the leader stepped in and brought us back on the topic"; "We desperately needed someone to summarize"; "He had suggested that three times and I just didn't want to do anything he suggested." These role restraints may develop because of personal feelings directed toward individuals, assumptions about role prerogatives of discussion leaders or blackboard recorders, assumptions about ability or power hierarchies in the group, or because of habitual differential responsiveness to other group members. There is some evidence that these boundaries become more stabilized with time in long-term groups (Gibb, 1959) and that they become more permeable with greater development or maturity of the group. Group training, using process-oriented and defense-reductive methods, causes greater flexibility of role distribution, and reduces the rigidity of such assumptions (Gibb, 1952).

In our field observations and interviews in classroom groups there is evidence that group members often fail to perform roles they perceive as critical because they assume these roles to be the prerogative and responsibility of the teachers. This constraint upon adaptive role distribution serves as one source of decrement in problem solving. These states of role deprivation can occur over long periods in formal classrooms (Gibb, 1956) or can occur during brief periods in discussion groups. Expectations are built quickly, with minimal cues, and survive over long periods. Expectations can become so stabilized that periods of relatively severe role deprivation can occur in training groups, periods in which groups become immobilized from lack of certain roles necessary for proper locomotion or goal accomplishment.

In another study (Gibb, 1956) in which prolonged lecturing produced decrements in learning, the decrement was interpreted as partly a function of norms about boundaries of the teacher and student roles. In the experimental groups, interviews indicated that for some students in the frequent-lecture situation the role prescriptions for the teacher evolved into the conception of the teacher doing the organizing, goal-setting, initiating, preparing, and reality-testing, and the student doing the listening, memorizing, and following. In the experimental groups where lectures did not occur and in which students had a vigorous role in the organization of classroom activities, other assumptions developed about role distribution; role prescriptions for teachers and students were more similiar on the part of both students and teachers; less stabilization of boundaries occurred; and greater overlap existed between the actions of teacher and student. The lecture groups did less well on several different measures of learning, possibly due in part to stereotyping of role boundaries and to contingent group effects.

Interviews indicate a profitable area of investigation in the false assumptions made by group members about the role boundaries ascribed to them by the group. Remarks occur in interviews such as these: "People never pay any attention when I start things"; "I could never get the group to do anything." In some instances these feelings of role inadequacy are based upon valid perceptions of the group and are corroborated by behavior observations and interviews with other group members. In other instances they represent autistic representations of the group perceptions. In one study, feedback about interpersonal perceptions and assumptions—centered upon role boundaries—reduced the ambiguity of the role boundaries and greatly increased the boundary for certain individuals (Lott, Schopler, and Gibb, 1955). One significant finding was that people frequently chosen in sociometric tests tended to stay within the realistic boundaries prescribed by the group. Individuals less frequently chosen were more likely to violate boundary specifications. This may have been partly due to the fact that individuals more often chosen had wider boundaries and more role space in which to move.

We have evidence that role boundaries can be successfully imposed by verbal instructions (Gibb, 1959); that such manipulation affects the performance and inductivity levels of the small group; and that role boundaries can be affected by participative training methods (Lott, Schopler, and Gibb, 1955).

Relevant to an adequate theory of group action and to a sound technology of group change is the degree to which these role boundaries are related to the defense level in the small group. In a series of studies we were able successfully to raise and to lower the defense level. Defensiveness was increased by induced polarization (Gibb and Gorman, 1954); instructional sets; increasing the size of the group (Gibb, 1951); violating role expectations; and by giving distorted interpersonal feedback

(Gibb, 1956; Lott, Schopler, and Gibb, 1955). Defensiveness was decreased by feeling-oriented feedback (Lott, Schopler, and Gibb, 1955); sharing of negative self-perceptions in a training group (Gibb, 1956); informality of group atmosphere (Gibb, 1951); discussion of role expectations (Smith, 1957); and sustained permissive leadership. When high defense levels were induced role boundaries became more rigid; boundaries were less accurately perceived (Gibb and Gorman, 1954); and boundaries were more difficult to change with training (Gibb, 1959). Specific role actions were less influential when defense levels were raised.

This relationship between defense level and influence potential was seen in both the laboratory groups and in the adult training groups. When a dichotomous coding of initiating acts was made into (1) those acts which led to productive integration with subsequent acts, and (2) those acts which did not lead into productive integration with subsequent acts, the percentage of acts which led to productive integration was higher in groups where the defense level was lower. That is, influence potential seemed to be negatively correlated with defense level in a wide range of situations. We do not have a rigorous check on the contamination of this relationship by the fact that under high defense and resultant high rigidity of role boundaries less likely-to-be-rejected initiations may be made. There is some evidence that group members "play it closer to the vest" when defense is high.

It was possible to identify in training groups, in classrooms, and in laboratory groups, periods of relatively sustained high defensiveness which were labeled *defensive atmospheres* (Gibb, 1960). Analysis of tapes of 164 two-hour training-group sessions indicate that these identifiable periods were characterized by one or more of the following manifestations of defense: persuasive speech; expressions of powerlessness of individuals and unpredictability of events; polarized and relatively unproductive conflict; interpersonal attack and punishment; and low-integration sequences of role behavior. Thus it was possible to identify defensive atmospheres in field situations and to reproduce similar states in experimental laboratory groups. Greater rigidity of role boundaries occurred in defensive atmospheres than in what are described in the following paragraph as supportive atmospheres.

It was possible to identify in field training groups, in classrooms, and in training groups composed in the laboratory certain states in which relatively sustained periods of low defensiveness occurred. These periods, labeled *supportive atmospheres,* were characterized by one or more of the following manifestations of low defense: expressions by individuals that members were in control of the group and could exert legitimate influence; feelings of relative comfort in the group and with the decisions of the group; conflict directed toward problem solution and integrated into group locomotion rather than into periods of unproductive trauma; high interpersonal support; high integration of sequences of role behaviors; and high acceptance of deviant opinions and willingness to listen to deviant suggestions. Analysis of the tapes indicated less rigidity of role boundary in states of support.

ROLE REPERTOIRE

One series of field observations and laboratory studies indicated that another major determiner of influence potential of a given group-member act is the role repertoire of the member. *Role repertoire* refers to the range and adequacy of the role behaviors of an individual or of a small group. Thus it is possible to speak of the role repertoire of a person and also to distinguish small groups on a dimension related to role repertoire. There are large individual differences in the number of roles that a person characteristically performs in small group situations, and large differences in the adequacy with which such roles are performed. A study of the observation records of a wide range of individuals in training-group situations indicates that examples can be found of a number of different types of response to group problem-solving situations. Some individuals focus upon a few roles and perform them well, seldom widening their range. Others show little consistency in their individual roles, seemingly more influenced by the situation in which they find themselves. A number of individuals attempt almost all roles, performing some with particular skill and others poorly. Individuals vary in degree of skill at a particular role, number of roles attempted, and ratio between roles attempted and roles taken well. Some individuals are seemingly well aware of role limitations, and act in deliberately restrictive ways in group situations. Interviews indicate that individuals differ in ability to assess their own role adequacy, role spread, and role repertoire. Some individuals are well aware of their role limitations, others are not aware of the band of restrictions in their behavior. Role repertoire is related to consistent perceptions by other group members of level of adjustment and leadership ability (Gibb and Platts, 1950).

Influence of role taking was measured by coding response to the role. A profile chart was then drawn for each individual. This profile indicated the range and adequacy of his roles taken within the given time sample. Considerable difficulty in getting sufficient coding reliability was experienced, particularly with quality of role taking. Reliability sufficient for discrimination between experimental conditions was obtained with training of observers.

There is a partial redundancy in saying that influence potential is a function of role repertoire, but one definition of role adequacy used in the experiments was conceived in terms of the influence value of the role taking. In one sense, what is being said is that it is possible empirically to demonstrate that individuals differ in terms of influence potential of their acts. It is also true that individuals with the greatest role repertoire, that is, with the greatest range and general potency, tend to show a greater influence potential in a specific describable act. This is evidence for a trait theory of leadership. It is possible that certain negative findings in this area are due to inability of experimenters to center upon traits *relevant* to influence potential. We are currently attempting to determine generality of selective role-taking propensities.

Repertoires can be significantly influenced by training. Gibb (1952) found evidence that the role repertoire of individuals is a function of at least three factors: (1) the adequacy of the *diagnosis* of the situation, (2) the adequacy of *hypotheses* formulated about the requisite role for a high-influence entry into a given group situation, and (3) the adequacy of role-taking *skill* once an appropriate hypothesis had been formulated about entry. That is, a particular member act may have low influence because it represents an inadequate diagnosis of the situation, an inadequate hypothesis about the behavior required to change the diagnostic situation, or an inadequate performance *qua* performance of the role. Basing a training design upon this analysis, Gibb and his associates (Gibb, 1955) significantly changed the role repertoires of college students and determined whether this change was due to changes in diagnostic, hypothesis-taking, or role-taking skills. They did so by intensive, threat-reductive, "participative" training over a period of 16 weeks. These changes persisted for at least a six-month period, with decrements apparently associated with the supportivity or defensiveness of the climate in the immediate post-training reference groups.

As indicated in the preceding section, it was found possible to increase or to diminish the defense level in problem-solving and training groups by specific acts of an experimenter or group trainer. From observations of experimental groups in the laboratory and of field training groups it is clear that the role repertoire of individuals is negatively correlated with the defense level in the group. When the defense level was significantly reduced a statistically significant increase in role-taking adequacy was seen in the groups. Many individuals were particularly susceptible to the effects of atmosphere change, as has been indicated in prior experimentation. For those individuals who were particularly sensitive to climate change, role repertoire changes were most dramatic. That this change may be at least partially a conscious or deliberate one is indicated by the fact that degree of awareness of climate is positively correlated with degree of change in role repertoire. Interviews indicated that there were large individual differences in the degree of awareness of such changes. Examples were found in which people deliberately tried more initiative when threatening members were absent or when they "felt accepted" in the group. Other similar changes in tractability level were correlated with defense level. Cases were found in which members expressed great surprise when informed of consistencies in their behavior under high defense levels. Whether or not members showed awareness of their sensitivity to defense level, observers reported tractability changes correlated with defense level.

Analyzed in terms of the role categories, it is particularly clear that appreciable decrease in defensiveness of the climate of the group is accompanied by a greater number of ideas produced, more reality testing, greater expression of negative feeling when present, and stronger initiatory attempts. It is apparently true that some categories of role are less susceptible to the influence of group climate and are more dependent upon specific training or upon more enduring idiosyncratic responses. Thus, summarizing and consensus testing do not appear to change appreciably with change in defensiveness of atmosphere, but do increase in incidence with long term training. The incidence of such role taking seems more related to level of insight or skill than to threat level.

ROLE CONSONANCE

Observations of training groups and classrooom groups indicate that the influence potential of a given member act is a function of its *consonance* with the group goal system. There is some indication that group actions, once started, tend to persist and even to build up strength and ongoingness as the collective goal tends to subsume and to merge with the goals of individuals who "come aboard" or identify with the course of action. This process is analogous to the functional autonomy of individual behaviors. Group activities, once initiated, tend to become functionally autonomous. This property of goal directedness, and the persistence and intractability of this directionality gives rise to member anxieties about lack of influence potential of their acts.

Field observations indicate that goal integration occurs at many levels (Gibb, 1955; Gibb, in press). A given, persistent, group activity tends to meet at least three levels of need. The members have motivations to accomplish the task as verbalized or as present in the perception of a majority of the members—task needs. Members seem to have certain group needs to maintain the "groupness," to succeed as a unit, or to relate to each other as a team. Members seem to have various individual needs that may or may not be directly related to the ongoing goal as seen by the group. Group activities which are most durable, least tractable, seem to provide a basis for integration of these needs at some level.

Observations indicate that member acts which are concurrent with this multi-level goal system tend to be influential. That is, initiations or regulations that are consonant with the goal system tend to be accepted and integrated into group work. Initiations which are dissonant with the group goal system tend to be ignored, misperceived, rejected, or accepted only under power or status pressure.

Dissonance may occur over long periods of time, during which members may be seen by observers to be continually fighting the ongoingness of the group—continually out-of-phase with group activities. This kind of dissonance appears as a style difference, with possible personality or depth implications. Interviews of individuals indicate differential awareness of this dissonance. Interviews contain such statements as the following: "Nothing I say seems to have much effect upon the group"; "The group was getting into all this trouble, but no one paid any attention to me or asked my opinion about the matter." Dissonance may be a matter of person-rejection growing out of continual affective miscommunication. Some individuals seem to be so goal-dissonant as to be opposed on almost all suggestions.

Some forms of dissonance come apparently from poor timing on the part of the intervener. The group goal state may change subtly over very brief periods of time—at a particular moment the group resists certain actions, and at a point a few moments later responds to the same type of intervention with appropriate and integrated initiatory action. Individuals differ in timing skills, and in ability to diagnose these differences in readiness. Interviews contain remarks like the following: "I had made the same suggestion ten minutes earlier, but when Bob made it the group accepted it immediately"; and "I resented the group taking Oliver's point so well when they had ignored the same suggestion from me earlier" (Gibb, 1958).

A study of training-group leaders at the summer laboratory of the National Training Laboratories at Bethel, Maine, illustrates the kind of difference that may be found in an individual's ability to respond with consonance, and hence influence the activities of the group (Gibb, 1959). Our studies of trainer behavior indicate that these leaders differ greatly in diagnostic sensitivity and in timing skills. One of the aims of most trainers was stated as that of having groups accept a process-oriented intervention by continuing to talk about the process. In an analytic task, observers tabulated the times that trainer interventions led to meaningful process discussion and the times that trainer interventions were ignored in the immediate post-intervention discussion. Note that this categorization ignores possible, even probable, latent accumulation of effects of interventions. In any event, some trainers were able to intervene in such a way that 80 percent of their interventions met with meaningful interaction commensurate with stated influence goals. Other trainers were able to do this in less than 25 percent of the intervention attempts during the periods measured. We have not as yet been able to isolate the contribution to this success of diagnostic skill from the contribution of other factors such as trainer role-repertoire. Indirect indication that the skill was at least partly a matter of diagnostic ability was obtained by asking the training-group leaders to make a series of estimates of group-member ratings of satisfaction, cohesiveness, and other training-related variables at various stages of training. Similar large individual differences occurred in these skills. There is a statistically significant positive relationship between ability to predict correctly these group-state ratings and the ability to make successful interventions, in the situations studied.

In several studies (Gibb, 1956; Gibb 1959) there is clear evidence that the ability to diagnose group goal states has been improved by training. Further evidence indicates that this diagnostic ability is accompanied by greater feelings of ability to influence the group, and by greater integration of individual actions into group action, which state of affairs is at least indirect evidence that influence behavior is accepted more favorably by the group. We have no direct evidence that greater ability to diagnose group states leads to greater influence over group actions. The problem is being investigated. The fact that training leads to both increased diagnostic sensitivity and to improved group behavior in so many kinds of situations suggests that such a relationship may exist.

The evidence that consonance is greater with higher supportivity of climate and with lowered defense levels is found in several studies. For instance, in field studies we found that during supportive atmosphere periods high goal integration is associated with maximum tractability levels, during which members find it relatively easy to exert influence upon the direction of group activities. With supportive climates members listen and modify activities in response to what are seen as legitimate influence attempts. During periods of maximum supportivity and defense reduction, the asynchronous ideas of the least-chosen of low-sociometric members will be listened to and reacted to. Conversely, during maximum defense climates, the same low-sociometric persons will be more often ignored or their ideas rejected. Interviews of group members indicate that members are aware differentially of rejecting influence bids of such members during periods of stress or defensiveness.

One familiar phenomenon in defensive climates is a kind of cyclic recurrence of brief readiness periods between relatively long periods of low tractability. After long periods of polarization, fight, or neurotic persistence of group goal-states the group will come to brief readiness periods during which any influence attempt, however fortuitous or meaningless to the total group, will be seized upon by the group and accepted as at least a momentary goal.

Another familiar group phenomenon is seen as a kind of closure gradient during which as the group nears the end of the scheduled session, an otherwise highly intractable group will respond seemingly to any reasonably work-oriented effort to move the agenda forward to completion.

A distinct impression from our field observations is that much feeling of power or influence in a group situation is produced by the ability of certain individuals to assess the group goal-state before it is verbalized by other members, to verbalize this goal-state as an initiation, and thus to appear to self and to others as having performed a particularly successful influence intervention. While occasionally group members recognize this behavior in themselves and deliberately use this mechanism as an influence technique, our impression is that more often this is done intuitively. Much leadership is thus an illusion both to the leader and to the group. This kind of influence sequence is particularly prevalent in defensive atmospheres. The activity of the group gets inextricably tied in with the defense needs of the members and the defense work persists in a way that is only controllable by the kind of leader who is able, or willing, to move in front of the inexorable process. Leaders move to keep ahead of a group in order that they may appear to be leading it. The political leader is able usually to perform this kind of service to the community. The scientific leader, who fancies that his studies of intelligence, authoritarianism, or frustration influence the direction of scientific research, may well be following a prepotent social trend that is reflecting a defense-work dynamic of the culture.

It is clear that, in training groups, to be influential members must be to a high degree consonant with developing goals of the group. The ongoing norm-structure of the group is a powerful and prepotent determiner of group behavior. This is shown by the studies of training groups (Gibb, 1955) on the Colorado campus in which the discussion content, group goals, and process work in leaderless training groups was essentially similar to the content, goals, and process work of training groups who had skilled trainers. There is some evidence that this similarity was mediated by gradually evolving norms within the college community from which the trainees were drawn and by similar norms evolving within the training community itself (Gibb, in press). Given powerful norms within the training community, groups will select goals and perform activities commensurate with these norms. Trainers and therapists to be effective either make their interventions consonant with the evolving goal and defense-work system, or they make interventions during readiness periods to influence the evolving norms. The susceptibility to this "illusion of influence" is seen in trainers in the results of interviews with seven trainers whose groups were studied in detail and whose groups followed patterns highly similar to those of the trainerless groups. Each of the seven interviewees took satisfaction in having influenced the direction of the training activities in the group during the period, and each was positive in feeling that trainers were highly necessary in groups if such phenomena were to take place.

The higher the defense level the more rigid in appearance is the positive relationship between consonance and influence potential. One gets the impression of inexorability of the goal system under high threat or high defensiveness. Interviews with persons immediately following such states indicate a kind of fatalistic and cynical feeling about acts influencing the process. Members feel impotence, experience some resentment at the group, express discouragement—"anything I would do wouldn't make any difference in this group." There is a curious paradox that arises during such states. This very cynicism gives rise to a counter-feeling of "let's do something—anything—just so we can get moving." The ready acceptance of initiations that occur during this momentary period of extreme readiness gives the impression of high tractability. This tractability is of short duration and is in part illusory. It is usually followed by long periods of extreme nontractability where members are likely to refuse even the most reasonable initiatory attempts on grounds that "we already made that decision, let's stay with it." It is possible that the only way to lead or influence high defense groups is to assess, intuitively or consciously, the group goal-state before it is verbalized by other members, to verbalize this goal-state as an initiation, and thus to appear to have performed a successful influence intervention.

Another effect of high defensive climates is that the influence of status of the initiator is heavily weighted. Under supportive climates status and power inductions are weighted less heavily. Thus it is probably true that different kinds of influence are exertable under supportive rather than under defensive climates. This relationship has been observed in field situations but not tested under laboratory conditions.

The above discussion has presented illustrations from a program of studies which have indicated a possible approach to the study of influence. The studies illustrate the value of using a mediating unitary construct such as defensiveness in attempting to predict the influence potential of group-member acts. The defense level in a small group has been shown to be correlated with three empirical influence-related variables: (1) the role repertoire of the individual, (2) the role boundary prescribed by the group, and (3) the consonance of the influence attempt with the group goal system. Evidence is presented that leaders or group members can engage in activities that have a direct influence upon the defense level of the group. The practical applicability of such findings is obvious. Specific alternatives are open to administrators, teachers, therapists, trainers, and parents who wish to increase the induction strength of influence attempts.

REFERENCES

GIBB, J. R. A climate for learning. *Adult Educ.*, 1958, 9, 19–21.

GIBB, J. R. The effects of group size and of threat reduction upon creativity in a problem-solving situation. *Amer. Psychologist*, 1951, 6, 324. (Abstract)

GIBB, J. R. Effects of role playing upon (a) role flexibility and upon (b) ability to conceptualize a new role. *Amer. Psychologist*, 1952, 7, 310. (Abstract)

GIBB, J. R. *Factors producing defensive behavior within groups, II.* Annual Technical Report, Office of Naval Research, Contract Nonr–1147(03), NR 170–226, February 15, 1955, 24 pp.

GIBB, J. R. *Factors producing defensive behavior within groups, IV.* Final Technical Report, Office of Naval Research, Contract Nonr–1147(03), NR 170–226, 1956, 16 pp.

GIBB, J. R. *Factors producing defensive behavior within groups, VI.* Final Technical Report, Office of Naval Research, Contract Nonr–2285(01), 1959, 26 pp.

GIBB, J. R. Socio-psychological process of the instructional group. Chapter in G. E. JENSEN, ET AL. (Eds.), *The dynamics of instructional groups. Yearb. nat. Soc. Stud. Educ.*, 1960, 59, Part II. Pp. 115-135.

GIBB, J. R. A norm-centered view of T-group training. Chapter in L. P. BRADFORD AND J. R. GIBB (Eds.), *Theory of T-group training*, in press.

GIBB, J. R. AND GORMAN, A. W. Effects of induced polarization in small groups upon accuracy of perception. *Amer. Psychologist*, 1954, 9, 367–377. (Abstract)

GIBB, J. R. AND PLATTS, GRACE N. Role flexibility in group interaction. *Amer. Psychologist,* 1950, *5,* 491. (Abstract)

LOTT, A. J., SCHOPLER, J. H., AND GIBB, J. R. Effects of feeling-oriented and task-oriented feedback upon defensive behavior in small problem-solving groups. *Amer. Psychologist,* 1955, *10,* 335–336. (Abstract)

SCHOPLER, J. H., LOTT, A. J., AND GIBB, J. R. The effects of congruity of expectations upon group processes. *Amer. Psychologist,* 1954, 9, 582. (Abstract)

SMITH, E. E. The effects of clear and unclear role expectations on group productivity and defensiveness. *J. abnorm. soc. Psychol.,* 1957, *55,* 213–217.

6

Homeostasis Theory of Groups Implications for Leadership

F. Kenneth Berrien[1]

Rutgers, the State University
New Brunswick, New Jersey

More than thirty-five years ago Walter B. Cannon proposed the concept of homeostasis as a unifying principle to describe physiological functions and their interrelations. Toward the end of his brilliant and productive career he began to see certain similarities between biological organisms and the body politic. He raised questions of this sort: "May not the devices developed in the animal organism for preserving steady states illustrate methods which are used, or which could be used elsewhere? . . . Might it not be useful to examine other forms of organization— industrial, domestic, or social—in the light of the organization of the body? . . . May not the new insight into the devices for stabilizing the human organism which we have examined, offer new insight into defects of social organization and into possible modes of dealing with them?" (1932; 1945.)

Cannon followed his own suggestions by developing some sociological analogies, and he has been followed by a number of persuasive commentators and theorists who have professed to see in social organizations a process akin to homeostasis (Roethlisberger and Dickson, 1939; Homans,

---

[1] The author is much indebted for statistical advice and other aid to Dr. W. H. Angoff, Educational Testing Service, Princeton, New Jersey.

1950; Stagner, 1951; Hendrick, 1947; Bales, 1953; and Parsons and Shils, (1954).

One comes away from this literature impressed with the near absence of serious efforts to *test* the homeostasis propositions with hard data. Homeostasis has been used primarily as an interpreter of facts already held, or as an over-the-shoulder view of a problem.

GROUP HOMEOSTASIS THEORY

It is clear, from Cannon's statement (1945), that one of the criteria evincing homeostasis is the *perpetuation of the system*. Stated in another way homeostasis is assumed to exist if the system continues to function in a steady manner. To translate such a statement into one that applies to groups requires a definition of system.

System, Boundary, Defined

The universe is assumed to be made up of systems and subsystems, the largest being the universe itself and the smallest being the most minute subdivision of the universe (Miller, 1955).

System refers to a collection of interrelated processes or events encompassed by a recognizable boundary. The processes or events produce effects both on the system's subsystems (except in the case of the smallest) and the suprasystem (except in the largest) of which it is a part. Moreover, the system's effects are a resultant not just of its internal operations but are also influenced by the conditions surrounding it. The definition applies, for example, to the respiratory system of an organism, as well as to non-living but self-correcting servomechanisms. The common feature running through these systems is their characteristic homeostasis.

A human group considered as a system is a collection of individuals related to one another producing effects on the larger context in which it exists, and whose influence is also detectable on the individuals composing it. Furthermore, the group's interactions are themselves partly determined in frequency or quality by the larger context (suprasystem).

The *boundary* of a human group is defined by the nature of the communications and interactions. Communications and interactions within the boundary are different in quality and frequency than across the boundary. Clearly the communications within a family, for example, are different from the communications between families in a neighborhood. The same may be said of a naval task force as contrasted with the task force plus its enemy; a work group and the company; a church membership committee and the church; a United States Senate committee and the Senate. Communications within the group are different from the communications between groups.

Criteria of Group Homeostasis

It must be emphasized that the moment a system (in this case a human group) ceases to exist three things occur. First, it ceases to perform its function(s). Second, the compensatory interrelations among the system's components cease and, third, the unique nature of interactions within the boundary (as contrasted with those across the boundary) also disappear. The mere existence of a human group over a time span is the most fundamental criterion of homeostasis. It is also the least sensitive as a measuring criterion. For research purposes such a criterion has limited usefulness. We need a criterion for the group comparable to the concept of health in biological organisms.

We propose two such criteria that must be satisfied if the group is to perpetuate itself. First, the group must discharge the function for which it has been organized. An aircraft factory cannot long exist if it fails to turn out airplanes. A bank must make loans. A political party must win elections. There exists for each organization one or more *formal achievements,* whose accomplishment or lack of it influences the group's continued existence. The specific formal achievements have to be defined for each.

This does not argue that each system is sufficient unto itself. Obviously a system can be destroyed by disruptions in the larger context in which it exists. Contrariwise, the larger system's existence is influenced by the extent to which the subsystems discharge their functions. Moreover, a suprasystem may demand that the formal accomplishment of the system steadily rise in level rather than maintain a dead level. This seems to be true, for instance, of our economic system. Homeostasis therefore in some instances may refer to the maintenance of a *level* of accomplishment or to the maintenance of a given *rate* of increase or decrease in accomplishment.

So far as groups are concerned, a second type of function can be identified. It is axiomatic that people will not *willingly* continue to associate with and act in a group unless by so doing they satisfy some need of their own. Compliance with, or participation in, group activities can be coerced, but this is necessary only when group activities by themselves do not satisfy personal needs. Forcible compliance is assumed to be a condition of artificial, external pressure imposed on the group designed to perpetuate the group, but any such pressure is obviously a substitute for internally generated cohesive forces. Western culture tends to support the conception that an organization is better if coercion imposed from without is minimal. In any event, since internal cohesion stands in an inverse relationship to externally imposed coercion, knowledge of one may provide a basis for inferring the other. More specifically, do the members have a sense of belonging and acceptance by other members? The group's continued survival is influenced by these factors as surely as by the achievement of its formal functions. These we shall call *group-need satisfactions.*

Both formal achievement (F.A.) and group-need satisfactions (G.N.S.) are susceptible to measurement in degrees.[2] Both can be operationally defined. It is at least conceivable that a range of measured formal achievement and group-need satisfactions can be established which will represent something comparable to the normal variation in biological health. That is to say, we recognize that such phenomena as blood pressure, or body temperature, or respiratory rate may all vary within certain specified ranges and yet the organism remains normal or healthy. Likewise, formal achievement and group-need satisfactions also may vary within a statistically defined normal range of scores and still indicate that the system is stable homeostatically. Just how these two criteria are interrelated and how much variance can be tolerated within each are research problems capable of solution.

Homeostasis Predictors

What group variables compensate among themselves to create a relatively constant level of G.N.S. and F.A.? What are the group analogues of processes like the secretion of adrenaline liberating sugar from the liver, permitting prolonged muscular action useful in emergencies? If a group is disturbed, in what dimension or dimensions will it be affected other than in F.A. and G.N.S.? Statistically speaking, we must seek predictors of F.A. and G.N.S.

Without taking the time to justify each of the variables chosen, the following list is included with this preamble: Evidence is available in the literature suggesting that each one is related to one or the other of the homeostatic criteria.

1. Satisfaction with the leader's interpersonal relationships. To what extent do group members find their superior or supervisor to be agreeable, decent, considerate, as a person? (An effect of the external system on the group.)
2. Homogeneity of group attitudes. To what extent do group members see eye-to-eye on a variety of questions both work-related and otherwise? (Sometimes called cohesiveness—a property of the group itself.)
3. Satisfaction of group members with tangible rewards such as wages,

---

[2] Many persons have made essentially the same distinction in the "outputs" of groups but not with these labels. See Barnard (1938), Bass (1952), and others.

promotions, fringe benefits. (Source of satisfaction is external to the group.)

4. Pressures felt by members to remain in the group originating in the family, community, or trade union. (Again the source is external.)

5. Pressures from immediate supervision felt or perceived in the form of disciplinary threats. To what extent are these pressures sensed by group members? (Source is external to the group.)

6. To what degree do group members have confidence in the technical skill and knowledge of their immediate supervisors? (An external condition as perceived by the group members.)

7. To what extent do group members perceive their superior's behavior and his expectations of them in the way the superior intends his behavior and expectations to be perceived? (Consequence of group with larger system.)

8. To what degree is there freedom of communication within the group? (A group property.)

9. What is the degree of free communication between group and superior? (Is the group in contact with its external environment?)

10. To what extent are the group members personally task-oriented, task-involved? Is the task significant to them in its own right? (A group property.)

11. To what extent are group members satisfied with the organization as a whole? (An effect on the group of the external system but more remote than variables *1, 3, 4, 5* or *9*.)

12. To what extent does the group feel it can adjust to work changes? (A group property.)

It may be objected that some of these variables, particularly *1, 2, 6, 8* and *11* are merely aspects of G.N.S. and therefore confound this criterion. The same might be said about variables *2, 8, 10, 12* (the properties of the group). Critics might further say that if these predictors are highly correlated with the criterion this would be evidence of the confounding. On the other hand unless a predictor is correlated with the criterion it cannot be a predictor. Therefore, whether the predictors are or are not confounded with the criterion cannot be determined by an appeal to the correlation coefficient. Moreover the same considerations lead us to reject a factor analysis of all measures as a means of determining the degree of confounding if any exists.

It is therefore necessary to examine the variables in terms of the way they behave in other respects. That is, if the predictor variables show changes over a period of time among themselves but the criterion remains constant, this would suggest but not *prove* minimal confounding. Or, if the predictors remained constant but G.N.S. fluctuated over time this would also suggest little confounding even if there were a moderately high correlation at any one time.

Furthermore, in presenting this list of predictors it is not suggested that these are necessarily the most important nor necessarily sufficient to predict either criterion. The chief justification for the list is that investigators have reported that these conditions are related to either G.N.S. or F.A.

Within this framework the following specific propositions can be drawn:

1. If groups maintain a stability between time *1* and time *2* in one of the criteria of homeostasis in the face of disturbances, any difference between the time *1* and time *2* predictor variables represents a homeostatic set of responses.

2. If groups when disturbed fail to maintain a stability over time in one of the homeostasis criteria, alterations in the predictor variables will not represent a homeostatic set of responses.

3. Patterns of change in predictors which occur in *1* above, should be in some way different from the pattern of changes occurring in *2*.

4. The pattern of predictor changes in a homeostatic system will depend on the kind or severity of the disturbances.

To test these propositions under ideal circumstances would require about 60 or more bona fide groups consisting of 10 or more persons each, working together on a common task and having a long enough history to assure that each group member has a fund of reliable experiences with and about other group members. Reliable measures of F.A., G.N.S. and all predictors listed above would be necessary. Furthermore the groups should remain intact over a time period sufficiently long to permit some disturbance to occur and show its effects on the groups. Finally, all group measurements would be taken at least twice and preferably several times— before, during, and after the disturbance. These conditions are not impossible to achieve but to date we have not been able to meet all of them. Instead, we have made some preliminary analyses with data collected for other purposes. These data are clearly inadequate for a definite test of the above propositions but have been used as a preliminary test of methodology.

We want to make explicit an assumption underlying the analyses to be presented below. It is evident from the above hypotheses that homeostasis is a time-linked phenomena. The data so far analyzed were collected at a single time on groups, some of whom we had reason to believe were disturbed and some were not. Nevertheless, for the purposes of this preliminary test, we assume the data approximated measures taken on the same groups at two different times—once when they were undisturbed and once when disturbed. The following is a cross-section study, and consequently our interpretations as they relate to time changes must necessarily be tentative. On the other hand, test development measures are often taken on say eight-year olds, nine-year olds and ten-year old children at a single time and assume that the difference between the eight, nine and ten-year olds represent longitudinal changes, when in fact, they are not. We are making the same kind of assumption in this study.

A PRELIMINARY TEST OF GROUP HOMEOSTASIS

The first study involved an analysis of an attitude questionnaire prepared and administered by The Survey Research Center, University of Michigan,[3] to 32 employee groups of a sponsoring company engaged in the delivering of packages and cartons to private homes. The questionnaire contained 121 items, of which 58 were appropriate for our purposes. The items were categorized into seven of the variables mentioned above.

Within the questionnaire were three items which pertained to adjustability, satisfaction with work standards, and to sharp changes in work loads. We therefore divided the 32 groups into two subsets on the basis of their scores on these defining questions. It was our hypothesis that if the groups were homeostatic, their failure to adjust satisfactorily to sharp changes in work load would be compensated by increases in some other group variable. If well-adjusting and poorly-adjusting groups are equivalent in group-need satisfactions and formal achievement, the predictor variables should be different in each case but the net effect of these differences will keep both criteria stable. Essentially, the poorly adjusting groups represent disturbed systems.

The statistical design required two pairs of multiple regression equations: (a) one pair predicting G.N.S. in poorly and well-adjusting groups; (b) the other pair predicting F.A. in poorly and well-adjusting groups.

Group-Need Satisfactions

The means, standard deviations and b-weights for seven predictor variables for the G.N.S. equations are presented in Table 1. It is to be noted

[3] The Survey Research Center has been extraordinarily cooperative in supplying data from their files for this project. It is a pleasure to express appreciation for their considerable help.

that the means of all predictor variables are higher for the well-adjusting set of groups. This finding was contrary to expectations since we had anticipated some compensatory differences at this level. Examination of Table 1 furthermore reveals that the mean differences are significant in five of the seven predictor variables but interestingly enough, the *group-need satisfactions were not significantly different between high and low groups*. This latter fact satisfied one of the requirements for a homeostatic group.

We are therefore required to explain how group-need satisfactions are maintained in the face of a disturbance which adversely affected the predictor means. The b-weights provide a possible answer. They not only change in magnitude but also in sign. A covariance analysis of these data showed that the total system of b-weights represented in the high group was not significantly different from the total system of b-weights as given in the low group.

In spite of this finding it is still possible that the b's for particular predictors are different. At this point a statistical impasse is reached for we know of no method to test such differences, when the predictor values themselves are different. Therefore from this point on pairs of b-weights can only be examined for suggestive hints about homeostasis.

Let us assume as a standard the system of b-weights for groups *high* in their ability to adjust to schedule changes. We have assumed that such groups are undisturbed. Hence the b-weights for the high group may serve to represent the pattern from which other groups having less adaptability to schedule changes may be expected to deviate. Subtracting comparable b-weights of the high and low groups provides a set of values presented in the last column, Table 1.

We assume that declines in b-weights represent *adverse* effects of poor adjustability, while increases in b-weight values are the *compensatory adjustments* necessary to overcome the adverse effects if, as in the case here, group-need satisfactions are to remain about constant. That is to say, a decline in the b-weight if unchecked would ultimately lower the predicted criterion and hence have a depressing effect on G.N.S. Under this assumption the present data show that poor adaptability to work-load changes adversely affects:

> Felt discipline
> Satisfaction with supervisor's competence
> Satisfaction with company

Table I

SUMMARY STATISTICS FOR GROUPS DEFINED AS HIGH AND LOW WITH RESPECT TO ADJUSTMENT TO CHANGES IN SCHEDULE

Criterion: Group-Need Satisfactions

	High Group			Low Group			σ d.m.	t	Diff. in b's
	Mean	σ	b-weight	Mean	σ	b-weight			
1. Satisfaction with leadership	32.30	5.73	−.07	26.73	4.97	−.09	1.96	2.84*	−.02
5. Felt discipline	10.42	1.04	.21	8.95	1.22	−.20	0.41	3.56*	−.41
6. Satisfaction with leader's competence	8.72	1.18	.60	7.41	0.91	.01	0.38	3.41*	−.59
7. Discrepancy	26.81	1.75	−.17	25.86	2.45	−.18	0.78	1.22	−.01
9. Freedom of communication with supervisor	17.72	2.09	−.20	15.08	1.56	.14	0.67	3.92*	.34
10. Task involvement	7.51	.40	−.28	7.12	.83	.36	0.24	1.64	.64
11. Satisfaction with company	14.71	1.70	.12	11.71	1.47	−.23	0.58	5.17*	−.35
Criterion: group-need satisfactions	8.62	0.69		8.38	0.87		0.50	0.25	

* Significant at 1% level.

Compensating for these adverse effects are larger weights on

> Freedom of communication
> Task involvement

Some predictor variables do not appear to change in b-weights, namely—
satisfaction with the leader's interpersonal relations and *the discrepancy
between the supervisor's view of the job requirements and the view of the
employees.* Because of this counterbalancing among the separate b-weights
it is perhaps understandable that the total system of b-weights for high
groups is not statistically different from that for low groups.

In interpreting these statistics we have assumed that b-weights represent
the relative importance subjectively assigned by group members to the
predictor variables. No direct evidence of subjective importance exists in
the data at hand. However, the implication appears sound. The b-weights
are a function of the correlation between a given variable and the criterion.
If the correlation between a criterion and variable is high and the b-weight
is consequently large, this implies that the variable does in fact affect a
member's group-need satisfactions, and therefore has an importance in
proportion to the closeness of that relationship. We therefore infer that
differences in b-weights represent differences in subjective importance.

One may now ask the question: Importance for what? The importance
of a variable is always a relationship to something else. It may be highly
important, for example, for an employee to have a supervisor whose technical competence is high, because it helps the employee do his job. Such a
supervisor may not be at all important to the group-need satisfactions the
individual experiences. On the other hand, having attitudes which are in
harmony with those of fellow workers may not be important for getting
the job done but may be important so far as group-need satisfactions are
concerned. The subjective importance, therefore, of a condition or a
variable is always an estimate of that condition's relevance to something
else, and it furthermore may be different for several criteria. In addition
it is not unrealistic to assume that the importance assigned to a variable
will change over time in response to some stress or disturbance.

If these propositions are accepted, we may hypothesize that in this
instance *the seat of the homeostatic process lies in the compensatory
adjustments in importance assigned by group members to the predictor
variables in relation to one or the other criteria of homeostasis.* In order
to maintain an acceptable level of group-need satisfactions in the face of
disturbances, the group members must adjust the subjective importance
of the modified variable or some other variable. If such adjustment in

value does not take place, or takes places imperfectly, then group-need satisfactions or formal achievement, or both, can be expected to change and the criteria of homeostasis are not fulfilled.

We have therefore presented in Table 1, last column, a picture of homeostatic adjustments within a system of seven variables, such that stability in G.N.S. was maintained in spite of difficulties in adjusting to changes in work load. The major adjustments occur in Variables *5, 6, 10* and *11.*

Formal Achievement

It will be recalled that the predictor means in Table 1 can be employed with a separate set of b-weights to predict formal achievement (F.A.) in high and low groups. Table 2 presents this list of weights together with the observed formal-achievement levels for both high and low groups. It will be noted that the Mean Driver Productivity (F.A.) for the high groups is lower than for the low groups. This is an inversion in the statistic caused by the fact that productivity was measured in time units.

Table 2

b-Weights Predicting F.A. in Groups High and Low
on Adaptability to Work Changes

VARIABLES:	High	Low	Low - High*
1. Satisfaction with leadership	.02	−.10	.12
5. Felt discipline	−.01	−.24	.23
6. Satisfaction with leader's competence	−.17	.37	−.54
7. Discrepancy	−.06	.00	−.06
9. Freedom of communication with supervisor	.02	−.02	.04
10. Task involvement	.42	.03	.39
11. Satisfaction with company	−.15	.13	−.28
Criterion: mean driver productivity	1.73	2.18	−.45**

* Signs in this column are reversed because of an inversion in the criterion statistic. Negative b-weights in the first two columns have a net effect of raising the production (lowers the speed of work). Hence the difference column correctly indicates by negative sign the adverse effect of the difference.
** Significant beyond .01 level.

Stability in a criterion of homeostasis has not, in this case, been maintained in the face of disturbances. Hence the differences in b-weights between the high and low groups do *not* represent homeostatic changes. The covariance test shows that the system of b-weights in the high group is not significantly different from the system of b-weights in the lower group. However the major differences between the two sets of b-weights occur in Variables *5, 6, 10* and *11*. Three of these (*5, 6* and *11*) were the major contributors to differences between high and low groups in the G.N.S. systems.

Figure 1 presents a graphic display of the two sets of b-weight differences: one from the presumably homeostatic G.N.S. system, the other from the nonhomeostatic F.A. system. It is seen from this figure that among the three variables (*5, 6* and *11*) which accounted for the major part of the differences in both the G.N.S. and F.A. systems only one (*5*) has a positive difference for F.A. and a negative difference for G.N.S. Translating this statistic into psychological language suggests that groups not adjusting well to schedule and work changes attribute *less* importance to felt discipline so far as G.N.S. is concerned but *more* importance to felt discipline in getting the job done. The latter shift in emphasis seems to have contributed most to the failure to maintain a "homeostatic" F.A.

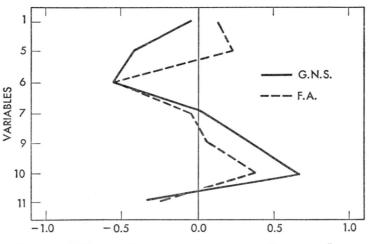

Fig. I. *b*-WEIGHT DIFFERENCES BETWEEN HIGH AND LOW GROUPS ON ADAPTABILITY TO WORK CHANGES

Let us spell out this interpretation a little more: groups that report difficulties in making adjustment to fluctuation in work also, in fact, are less productive but maintain a feeling of belonging as strong as those that handle work changes easily. The poorly adjusting groups assigned *less* importance to discipline, supervisor's competence, and the company as a whole so far as feelings of belonging were concerned. But in getting the job done, these groups believe discipline to be of *greater* importance. At the same time they experienced less discipline and pressure from supervisors (*see* Table 1, columns 1 and 4). This suggests that supervision may have been somewhat lax in the poorly adjusting groups—at least it was less than adequate in the light of the groups' self-assessment of adjustability to schedule changes.

In summarizing, statistics appear to prove that there may be identifiable distinctions between a homeostatic and a nonhomeostatic system, although we have no means to evaluate the differences point by point as displayed in Figure 1. On the other hand, it has been shown, first, that stability in G.N.S. can be observed. Second, a pattern of interdependent conditions has been observed which was *not* associated with stability in a criterion of homeostasis. This second pattern, exhibiting many similarities to the first, appears in some respects to be different from the first although the significance of the differences cannot be tested.

Other Kinds of Disturbances

The data were reanalyzed twice more with exactly the method just described developing two pairs of regression equations, one pair for high groups, another for low groups. But the high groups defined, first, in terms of their satisfaction with the supervisor's interpersonal relations (Variable *1*) and secondly, in terms of the freedom of communication with supervisor (Variable *9*). Essentially, we have repeated on two occasions the study just described using the same data and the same groups, analyzing them in the same way, but asking essentially that the groups be disturbed by two other sources of irritation.

Basically, we found the same events transpiring in the two repetitions as we did in the original study. Constancy was maintained on G.N.S. but not on F.A. The means of predictor variables are generally higher for the high groups and lower for the low groups.

Since we are interested primarily in *b*-weights predicting G.N.S. and F.A. for high and low groups respectively, the data are presented in Table 3. Moreover, *b*-weight differences between high and low groups are given in Table 4 for the two additional divisions of the data. The difference in profiles is given in Figures 2 and 3. A study of these figures should supply a clue as to the validity of hypothesis No. 4 (page 87). Once again, the statistical impossibility of evaluating the differences or similarity presented in this family of profiles must be pointed out. The chief contributors to the differences between high and low b-weight systems predicting G.N.S. are Variables *6, 10* and *12* for Figure 2; and Variables *5, 6, 11* and *12* for Figure 3. It is noteworthy also that the b's for Variables *1* and *7* are altered very slightly in all comparisons.

Table 3

b-Weights

| | SATISFACTION WITH SUPERVISOR'S RELATIONS | | | | FREEDOM OF COMMUNICATIONS | | | |
| | G.N.S. | | F.A. | | G.N.S. | | F.A. | |
	High	Low	High	Low	High	Low	High	Low
1. Satisfaction with supervisor's relations	—	—	—	—	−.05	−.07	−.30	−.03
5. Felt discipline	.04	.12	.21	−.34	.15	−.09	.03	−.17
6. Satisfaction with supervisor's competence	.34	−.50	−.14	−.16	.16	−.12	.23	.12
7. Discrepancies	−.16	−.25	.03	−.06	−.14	−.17	.04	−.09
9. Freedom of communication	−.18	.10	.10	.02	—	—	—	—
10. Task involvement	.54	−.25	.32	.14	.18	.14	.42	.04
11. Satisfaction with company	−.04	−.34	−.16	.06	.01	−.43	−.15	.06
12. Adaptability to schedule changes	.55	1.18	−.13	−.10	.40	.96	−.12	.00

Table 4

b-WEIGHT DIFFERENCES LOW MINUS HIGH GROUPS

	SATISFACTION WITH SUPERVISOR'S RELATIONS		FREEDOM OF COMMUNICATIONS	
VARIABLES	G.N.S.	F.A.	G.N.S.	F.A.
1. Satisfaction with leadership	—	—	−.01	.00
5. Felt discipline	.08	.55	−.24	.20
6. Satisfaction with leader's competence	−.84	.02	−.28	.11
7. Discrepancy	−.09	.09	−.03	.13
9. Freedom of communication with supervisor	.28	.08	—	—
10. Task involvement	−.79	.18	−.04	.38
11. Satisfaction with company	−.30	−.22	−.42	−.21
12. Adaptability to schedule changes	.63	−.03	.56	−.12

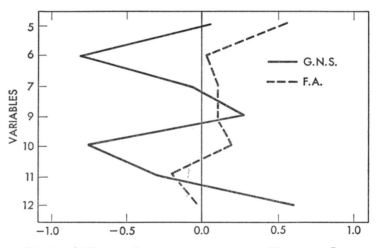

Fig. 2. b-WEIGHT DIFFERENCES BETWEEN HIGH AND LOW GROUPS IN SATISFACTION WITH SUPERVISOR RELATIONSHIPS

These observations on G.N.S. profiles suggest that the statistical model behaves as our psychological hypothesis predicted. Different kinds of disturbances produce different patterns of changes in the b-weights. Furthermore those sets of b-weights associated with the G.N.S. and satisfy-

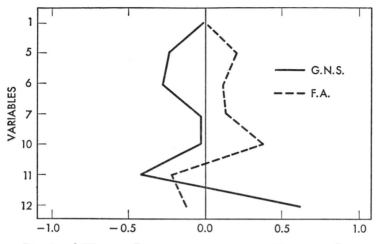

Fig. 3. *b*-WEIGHT DIFFERENCES BETWEEN HIGH AND LOW
GROUPS IN FREEDOM OF COMMUNICATIONS WITH SUPERVISOR

ing the criterion of homeostasis have a pattern of b-weight changes unlike those associated with F.A. which does not satisfy the homeostasis criterion.

It was hypothesized that the pattern of changes in b-weights for a system that did not maintain stability in its criterion would be different from one which did maintain stability. The examination just made of the profiles tends to support this hypothesis since the major contributors to the differences between high and low groups are not the same in the G.N.S. (stable system) as they are in the F.A. system (nonstable system).

Some Advantages of the Group Homeostasis Concept

It is possible that this view of groups, if it is eventually verified by additional tests, may provide somewhat better understanding of phenomena heretofore unrelated. Group resistance to change has been noted widely and studied in some detail (Lewin, 1947; French, 1948; Roethlisberger and Dickson, 1939; Peak, 1956). Presumably these phenomena can be partially understood at least in terms of the homeostatic process that tends to operate against external change agents to retain the established relationships within a group.

The effort in the industrial studies to relate wages, for example, to productivity, or morale to productivity, or cohesiveness to productivity, have, sometimes, been successful within certain ranges of the respective variables. However, when relationships break down at the extremes no adequate explanation has been possible as long as the investigator concentrates only on one-to-one relationships. Under the assumptions of the homeostatic model one might hypothesize that some other variable has compensated for, say low wages, to account for the failure of production to fall off as anticipated by the slope of the curve in the middle range of wages *versus* production.

Implications for Leadership

If one assumes that leaders have some responsibility for so arranging conditions to maximize both G.N.S. and F.A., it then becomes clear that the leader has before him an exceedingly complex task. It does in fact appear that it is not possible to maximize one without regard for the other. Instead the task of the leader appears to maintain a balance between G.N.S. and F.A.

The data just reviewed suggest, for example, that dissatisfaction with the supervisor's human relations skills will first show itself in disturbances in productivity rather than in group-need satisfactions. Is it possible that the group-need satisfactions are themselves more resistant to disturbances than productivity? Within the groups we have analyzed this appears to be the case. Whether it is true elsewhere or not cannot be determined with these data, although there is some indication from other studies that this may be true.

These researches re-emphasize that the leader of a group, like the pilot of an aircraft, must be constantly alert to many instruments, some of which have greater importance at one point in time and lesser importance at another. That is to say, if the leader changes a condition of work, a condition of communication, or senses some dissatisfaction with wages, with his own competence, or something else, efforts to rectify these disturbances may have repercussions in several other dimensions of the group. The leader not only has to read the instruments but he must constantly integrate this information by some sort of equation similar to those presented herein. Finally, he must solve that equation for the criterion—either group-need satisfactions or formal achievement.

This view of the leader's task emphasizes that he is dealing with a system of interdependent variables, linked in a complex way. We have already made reference to the similarity between the leader and the aircraft pilot. Each is operating within a dynamic system. If the pilot pulls back on the stick he gains altitude but at the cost of air speed. If air speed is to be maintained while climbing, he does this at the cost of increased fuel consumption. Here are three interdependent variables. Curves have been developed for each type of aircraft that show the optimum rate of climb for least increase in fuel consumption at given air speeds. The curves for one type of aircraft are not appropriate for another.

We are suggesting that ultimately curves will be needed of this sort which leaders may use, for example, to display the group rewards needed for increasing production, and to show what that increased production will cost in terms of G.N.S. Furthermore, the particular curves must be established empirically for different types of groups.

This is no new and brilliant insight into the complexities of leadership which have already become too well known to practitioners and researchers alike. It is, however, a systemized picture of this confusing complexity.

REFERENCES

BALES, R. F. The equilibrium problem in small groups. In PARSONS, T., BALES, R. F., AND SHILS, E. A. *Working papers in the theory of action.* Glencoe, Ill.: Free Press, 1953. Pp. 111–161.

BARNARD, C. I. *Functions of the executive.* Cambridge, Mass.: Harvard, 1938.

BASS, B. M. Ultimate criteria of organizational worth. *Personnel Psychology,* 1952, *5.*

CANNON, W. B. *Wisdom of the body.* New York: Norton, 1932. P. 305.

CANNON, W. B. *The way of an investigator.* New York: Norton, 1945. Pp. 113–114.

COCH, L. AND FRENCH, J. R. P., JR. Overcoming resistance to change. *Human Relations,* 1948, *1,* 512–532.

HENDRICK, I. *Facts and theories of psychoanalysis.* New York: Knopf, 1947. P. 93.

HOMANS, G. C. *The human group.* New York: Harcourt, 1950.

LEWIN, K. Group decision and social change. In NEWCOMB, T. M. AND HARTLEY, E. L. (Eds.), *Readings in social psychology.* New York: Holt, Rinehart and Winston, 1947. P. 335f.

MILLER, J. Toward a general theory for the behavioral sciences. *Amer. Psychologist,* 1955, *10,* 513–531.

PARSONS, T. AND SHILS, E. A. *Toward a general theory of action.* Cambridge, Mass.: Harvard, 1954. P. 223ff.

PEAK, HELEN. Factors in resistance to change. Technical Report 1, Contract NR 171–039. Ann Arbor, Mich.: Univ. of Michigan, 1956.

ROETHLISBERGER, F. J. AND DICKSON, W. J. *Management and the worker.* Cambridge, Mass.: Harvard, 1939.

STAGNER, R. Homeostasis as a unifying concept in personality theory. *Psychol. Rev.,* 1951, *58,* 5–16.

7

A Theory of Leadership and Interpersonal Behavior Under Stress

E. Paul Torrance

*Bureau of Educational Research,
University of Minnesota*[1]

The recent mushrooming of research concerned with behavior under stress with its scattered and sometimes apparently contradictory results makes a theory of leadership and interpersonal behavior under stress highly desirable. Some theory is needed to organize, interpret, and clarify the rapidly accumulating results; in this paper, an attempt will be made to sketch in bold outline such a theory.

What will be presented is a combination of known and unknown elements. It should be regarded much as Mendeleev's (Schwartz and Bishop, 1958, p. 821) "Periodic Table of the Elements" was regarded in 1869. In trying to piece together a comprehensive theory, it has been necessary to make predictions about the characteristics of the unknown elements.

First, the crucial character of stress which makes it different from "non-

---

[1] Most of the studies referred to in this paper were conducted by this author and his colleagues between 1951 and 1957 during which time he was director of the Survival Field Research Unit of the Air Force Personnel and Training Research Center in a program of research in support of Air Force Survival Training.

stressful" conditions will be discussed. Next, an attempt will be made to sketch a model of the processes of adaptation, with special emphasis on the mediation of stress through dimensions of time and intensity. One of the conceptual schemes which has seemed most useful in studying leadership and interpersonal behavior will then be sketched. Finally, some ideas about how leadership and interpersonal behavior under stress can be improved will be outlined.

CRUCIAL CHARACTER OF STRESS

It is this author's contention that the distinctive element in stress is to be found in the lack of structure or loss of anchor in reality experienced by the individual or group as a result of the condition labeled "stressful." In the group situation, this lack of structure or loss of anchor in reality makes it difficult or impossible for the group to cope with the requirements of the situation, and the problem of leadership and interpersonal behavior becomes one of evolving or supplying a structure or anchor and of supplying the expertness for coping with the demands of the situation.

Any of several sets of circumstances may make it difficult for the perceiver to structure the situation, or to cope with the situation after structuring has occurred. The situation may be unfamiliar to the group or require rapid shifts in customary activities. The group may not know what to do and, even if they know what must be done, they may not know who should do what with whom. The situation may also constitute a dangerous threat to central values of the group as a group, or of group members. This may blind the group to some important realities of the situation. Loss of structure may be occasioned by the instability of the situation or of group members or by confusion concerning the demands of the situation. There may be a lack of cues or too many cues. The changes may be too rapid to process adequately, or the requirements may overwhelm the group because it has inadequate skills for coping with them.

Groups spontaneously, sometimes perhaps unconsciously, do many things to safeguard the means for maintaining structure under stress. It is fairly well documented (Torrance, 1958) that groups prefer continuity in leadership from nonstressful to stressful situations. Even established leaders, however, must continue to validate their leadership or power roles by providing the structure and expertness necessary for group survival. Thus, leaders of long and distinguished experience must go to great lengths to demonstrate again and again their expertness.

When there is no designated leader, whoever is able and willing to provide the essential structure emerges as leader. Thus, in a department store fire, the lowly stock boy (Tyhurst, 1958) leads the second-floor employees to safety through the roof over the path he had frequently taken to escape the watchful eye of his employer. A formerly despised minority group member (Duguid, 1956) spontaneously leads a group to survival in a South Pacific jungle because of his 14 years' experience in jungle terrain.

There may be conflicts or even failure to survive, when the designated leader fails to provide the essential structure and expertness (Torrance, 1954a). Some leaders delegate leadership functions to someone who is able to supply the structure and expertness or to utilize the resources of the group in making decisions. In other cases, an able and popular individual spontaneously may assume command either by mutual consent or at a somewhat unconscious level. The incompetent leader may be abandoned or otherwise disposed of by the group and in rare instances may be removed by mutinous action. The sanctions against mutiny are so strong, however, that there are strong barriers to the emergence of a leader other than the designated one (Torrance, LaForge, and Mason, 1956).

PROCESSES OF ADAPTATION TO STRESS

Adaptation, it seems to the author, can most profitably be conceived of as a process through which specific stressors lead to an array of consequences which are mediated by such variables as duration, intensity, and leadership and interpersonal behavior. This conceptualization is presented schematically in Figure 1. In the "stressors" box can be listed the specific conditions which produce a loss of structure and place difficult demands upon groups. In the "consequences" box may be listed the common negative and positive outcomes. Theoretically, *any* of the specific stresses may lead to *any* of the consequences or symptoms. For example, continued or severe and unexpected failure in the group's mission may result in apathy and collapse or in hostility and defiance. The same consequence or symptom may also arise from quite dissimilar sources. The ability and structure of the group, the quality of its leadership and interpersonal behavior, however, might be such that there would be an overcompensation and all-out effort which would result in distinguished performance and heroic success. In other words, there is an interaction of the mediating variables.

Next, let us examine the course of adaptation when viewed along the dimensions of duration, intensity, and group characteristics.

Stressors	Mediating Variables	Consequences
Failure of group mission or objectives; unrealistic goals	DURATION	Panic, disorganization, lack of group-task efficiency
Attack by hostile individuals or groups		Apathy, lack of effort, loss of will-to-live
Difficult tasks; frequent repetition of events		Excessive hostility, defiance, destructiveness, lawlessness
Sudden emergencies		Exhaustion, collapse, dissolution of group
Deprivation of physical, social, emotional, cognitive, and/or esthetic needs		Overcompensation, all-out effort, victory over superior forces
Discomfort from cold, heat, fatigue, lack of sleep	INTENSITY	Increased speed and group-task efficiency
Lack of group-task structure		Control of panic, maintenance of will-to-live (continue adaptation)
Rigid group-task structure		Excessive disharmony, interpersonal strife, "survival of fittest"
Presence of an incompetent, competitive, hostile, erratic, unpredictable, disloyal, or other deviate member		Lack of trust, mutiny
History of internal strife	LEADERSHIP AND INTERPERSONAL BEHAVIOR	Planning, good group decisions, cooperation
Inadequate training for individual and group tasks		Mutual support and self-sacrifice of members
Loss of a group member		Inventiveness and creativity

Fig. 1. TYPICAL GROUP STRESSORS AND THE MEDIATION OF THEIR CONSEQUENCE

Duration of Stress

To the extent that we have been able to assess group performance under stress along a time continuum (Torrance, LaForge, and Mason, 1956), the data appear to conform quite closely to the process described by Selye (1950) for physiological adaptation and by J. G. Miller (1957) for psychological adaptation. When there is mastery of stress, this process may be represented schematically by the theoretical curve shown in Figure 2. In other words, when the stress is suddenly encountered, there is an initial shock or resistance to accepting the seriousness of the situation. This lag is followed by rapid overcompensation and recovery with a leveling off of performance as control is gained.

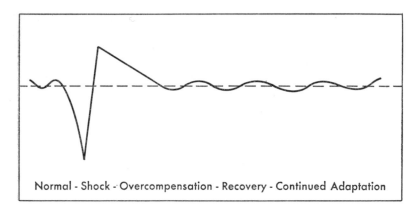

Normal - Shock - Overcompensation - Recovery - Continued Adaptation

Fig. 2. THEORETICAL CURVE OF GROUP PERFORMANCE UNDER STRESS OVER TIME IN CASE OF MASTERY OF STRESS

If the stress is continued long enough, regardless of the intensity of the stress and strength of the group, fatigue occurs and ultimately there will be collapse or breakdown, as represented in Figure 3. There may be vast differences, however, in the length of time required for different groups under different intensities of stress to reach a "breaking-point." Before the breaking-point is reached a variety of both positive and negative effects may be manifested. There may be confusion, inefficiency, recklessness, apathy, fatigue, hostility, changes in leadership, and the like. In fact, such actions may occur almost until the break appears. In such cases, the break may seem sudden. Prior to the break, the signs of approaching breakdown may have been denied or ignored. Usually after the break has occurred, the warning signs can be recalled.

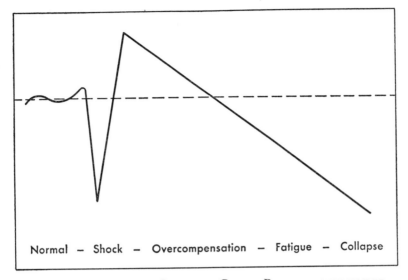

Normal — Shock — Overcompensation — Fatigue — Collapse

Fig. 3. THEORETICAL CURVE OF GROUP PERFORMANCE UNDER CONTINUED STRESS (ULTIMATE COLLAPSE OR BREAKDOWN)

Since there are interaction effects among the three classes of mediating variables, it should be recognized that there will be a number of important special cases.

Intensity of Stress

A number of laboratory studies of individual behavior (Harris, Mackie, and Wilson, 1956) indicate that mild stress tends to result in improved response, increased activity, and the like, and that extreme stress results in deterioration of performance. Our accounts of group survival in emergencies and extreme conditions and our observations of aircrews in survival training support a similar conclusion for groups. This relationship is represented graphically by the curve shown in Figure 4. The curve rises with increasing stress up to a point and then descends.

Character of Leadership and Interpersonal Behavior

It is within the framework which has just been sketched that the character of the leadership and interpersonal behavior of a group mediate the effects of stress. There are many ways of conceptualizing or labeling leadership and interpersonal behavior. One useful way of studying the process of adaptation of groups through effective leadership and interpersonal behavior is to think in terms of the linkages or forces which

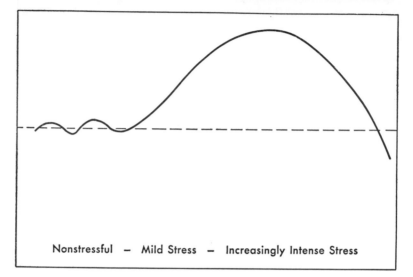

Nonstressful — Mild Stress — Increasingly Intense Stress

Fig. 4. THEORETICAL CURVE OF TYPICAL GROUP PERFORMANCE
UNDER CONDITIONS OF INCREASING INTENSITY OF STRESS

hold groups together, for example, affect, power, communication, and goals (Torrance, 1954b).

To use affect (liking-disliking) linkages as an example, theoretical functioning over time may be represented by the curve in Figure 5. According to this model, after a brief period of dislocation and momentary estrangement, there are manifestations and expressions of increased affect and feelings of closeness. In many groups strong interpersonal hostilities and repulsions change to strong positive affect, at least for a time. In time this increased affection returns to normalcy. If the stress continues unabated, however, there may be a deterioration of these affectional relationships. People become irritated with one another's faults and have no other objects available upon which to project feelings of aggression resulting from frustration.

Effective leadership and healthy interpersonal relations may be expected to decrease the lag at the onset of stress and prolong the period of continued adaptation in the face of unabated stress. Two special models of ineffective leadership and unhealthy interpersonal relations might, therefore, be added to the one represented by Figure 5. During the overcompensatory phase, affect linkages may be strengthened only to collapse after the first feeling of safety has been experienced. This relationship is the same as that depicted in Figure 3. At first, common danger draws

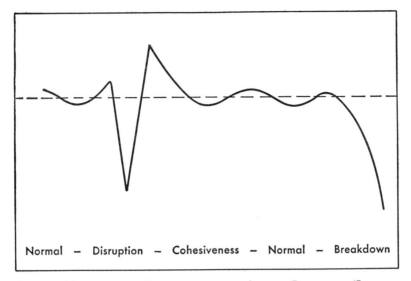

Normal — Disruption — Cohesiveness — Normal — Breakdown

Fig. 5. Theoretical Functioning of Affect Linkages (Liking-Disliking) in Groups under Stress Over Time

individuals together. Once the first danger has been passed, however, some members feel that they no longer need the others. They may even feel angry that they have "weakened" in feeling kindly toward their fellow group members. Under such conditions, some groups because of the quality of their leadership and interpersonal behavior collapse while others rebound, as shown in Figure 6. In this case, the group has retained its capacity to diagnose its ills, interpret the feedback.

If affect linkages are viewed in terms of sociometric structure, our evidence (Torrance, 1957b) indicates that instability occurs under stress. Effective groups show greater stability in sociometric structure than ineffective ones. Measures of leader and crew behavior increase in variability under stress. Group members become better acquainted with one another, less aware of prestige differences, and less harmonious. Official social structures tend to give way to informal structures under stress; and, in extreme stress, social structure tends to break down and not to be replaced.

Power, communication, and goal linkages appear to operate in much the same way as affect. When stress is first experienced, there is a tendency for power linkages to be exercised more firmly. As time goes on, the leader may (because of his inexpertness, lack of interest, or personal maladjustment) fail to validate or maintain his power and as a result lose the support of the group. Collapse is then imminent. Similarly, com-

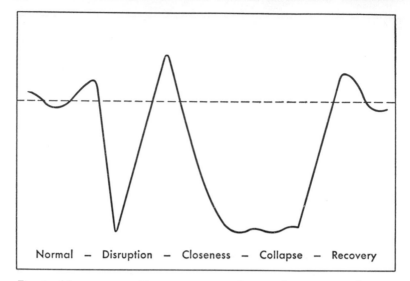

Normal — Disruption — Closeness — Collapse — Recovery

Fig. 6. THEORETICAL FUNCTIONING OF AFFECT LINKAGES IN GROUPS UNDER STRESS OVER TIME (COMEBACK FOLLOWING COLLAPSE)

munication and goal linkages tend at first to become stronger and then weaken and finally collapse if the stress is too prolonged. Furthermore, there is an interaction effect among the four types of linkages discussed. For example, the effects of weak affect linkages may be counteracted by strong power, communication, and goal linkages.

The theoretical functioning of affect linkages under increasing intensity is the same as shown in Figure 4. As intensity increases, affect linkages increase in strength until some theoretical limit or apex is reached. After this, there tends to be decline in strength. Power, communication, and goal linkages appear to function in essentially the same manner. With increasing stress it has been commonly observed that the leader tends to tighten up, delegate responsibility and power to subordinates, and check their performance more closely. After a certain intensity, however, the leader feels so threatened that he either takes away all power from others or abdicates his own power role. In some cases, he does both concurrently and this is when the group really falls apart. Under moderate stress, communication tends to become more frequent, but under intensity, communication breaks down. Under moderate stress, goals tend to become more important, more worthwhile. Under intense stress, group goals tend to become less salient, less worthwhile.

IMPROVING LEADERSHIP AND INTERPERSONAL BEHAVIOR

From the foregoing models concerning leadership and interpersonal behavior as mediated by duration and intensity of stress, it seems important to know what group mechanisms impede or facilitate the overcompensatory response and maintain or interfere with continued adaptation as stresses accumulate. Ultimately, experiments involving techniques of covariance and multivariate analysis may make possible the discovery of the dynamics involved in accomplishing this important objective. Until this is accomplished, it will not be possible accurately to place many of our scattered findings in their proper place in the model which has been outlined. If the fundamental problems are examined, however, this can be done in a crude manner.

A fundamental characteristic of a stressful situation is its demand for a level and type of activity sharply departing from the customary behavior pattern of the group. This often demands the use of skills which have previously been of minor importance or completely unused in the group's usual task performance. Thus the process of adjustment to the stressful situation is aided by factors which reduce the abrupt nature of the change, factors such as readiness of the group to perceive and accept an emergency, good communication networks, willingness to experiment with new types of organization and new types of behavior, and the presence of relevant skills in group members. Reducing the lag and prolonging adaptation depends then partly on the degree of behavioral change required and partly on the resources which the group possesses. Since the concern here is for the improvement of leadership and interpersonal behavior, an effort will be made to place some of the facts we have discovered in relation to the four qualities already discussed: power, affect, communication, and goal-orientation.

Power Linkages

Thus far, our findings (Torrance, LaForge, and Mason, 1956; Torrance, 1958) suggest that the following behaviors or conditions affect adversely the power linkages of groups under stress:

1. A history of conflict among the various echelons of power.
2. Failure of official leaders to accept the informal leadership structure.
3. The breakdown of official units or subgroupings with the onset of stress with the tendency for those most capable of coping with the stress to form a unit, leaving those least able to cope with the stress in units lacking resources for meeting the demands of the situation.

4. Isolation of the leader or leadership group from the remainder of the group.

5. Reduction of the power of the group by the leader with an accompanying increase in hostility.

6. Abdication of power roles or functions customarily assumed.

7. Unwillingness of designated leader to "act outside of authority."

8. Attempts to function without a designated leader.

9. Changes in leadership or failure of leader to fulfill group's expectations.

10. The failure of the leader to resolve his increased feelings of loneliness and isolation.

A few of these findings need to be discussed in somewhat greater detail.

The desirability of having a designated leader in a small group under stress has been questioned frequently. Some survivors argue for the strategic advantages of having no official leader. A careful examination of group survival accounts of self-styled "leaderless groups" usually indicates the presence of an informal, yet rather powerful, leader. In spite of the evidence and indoctrination concerning the necessity of a leader under stress, about 17 percent of our aircrewmen subjects favored having leaderless groups. It is the author's impression that an even larger percentage of groups, much to their disadvantage, tend to operate on the assumption that it is undesirable to have a leader in a small group under stress.

Further, it follows that the leader of a small group under stress should be a regular member of the group and should be the same as the official leader under normal conditions. Such leaders prove to be far more influential than others in determining the behavior of members (Torrance and Mason, 1956). The intelligent leader is able to overcome technical deficiencies by using available outsiders and group members as resource persons in making decisions, while retaining the decision-making function. This does not always occur, however. From a practical standpoint, emergent leaders may have to be used when the formally designated leader does not function or is not present. Typically, such leaders emerge on the basis of uniquely qualifying experiences, previous experience in stressful situations, expert skills important to the group, superior training, and the like. In other words, the basis for their power is expertness.

In emergencies and extreme conditions, men generally expect their leaders to behave in much the same way as they usually behave, with the additional assistance of checking on things more closely (Torrance, 1958). They believe that stress does not warrant a change in the relationship of the leader to his men and that his decisions should not be questioned. Further, they believe that the leader should share the same hardships and dangers as his men, but that he should avoid being "just one of the boys." Although men appear to want their leaders to behave about as they usually do, leadership behavior actually becomes more variable under stress.

The loneliness and isolation of the leader is a common phenomenon and appears only to be intensified by stress, except when a leader abdicates his power role. If the stress is prolonged and intense, the leader may be overwhelmed by the tensions thus aroused and either establish an intimate, confidential relationship with a trusted subordinate or in some way commit suicide or lose his will to survive. In business, industrial, educational, and athletic groups this probably takes the form of resignation, retirement, or similar "leaving-the-field" behavior. Highly expert leaders, however, appear to be able to associate quite intimately with their men without apparent harm to their exercise of power. Some leaders consciously employ the strategy of taking into their confidence some member of the group both to reinforce their control and to provide psychological support for themselves.

Perhaps dynamically related to the phenomenon of the loneliness of the leader and the feelings of some that small groups under stress should function without leaders is abdication of power. This usually occurs only under relatively severe stress and apparently operates at an unconscious level.

Unwillingness to "act outside of authority" may paralyze a group and cause it to delay dangerously its adaptation to stress, and to incapacitate it in maintaining adaptive behavior. Many examples of this type of behavior occurred as a result of the German's unwillingness to do anything which was *verboten* (Guerlain, 1943).

Affect Linkages

On the basis of our data, the following conditions appear to disturb the affect linkages in groups under stress and interfere with the ability of groups to cope with stress:

1. Interpersonal stresses resulting from differences in values and from personality incompatibilities of members (Torrance, LaForge, and Mason, 1956).

2. Unwillingness of a member to respond to group pressures to conform and to perform role expectations.

3. Discrepancy between the values of the leader and the predominant values of group members.

4. Failure to give mutual support and to sacrifice personal goals for group goals (Smith, 1957).

From observations and accounts of group survival, we have reasonably good models for the adaptation processes involved in the first two conditions listed above. First, the group exerts pressure to influence the offending member to adapt. Official sanctions are then exercised by the leader along with possible isolation by group members. Finally they absorb his roles so that they do not depend upon him for the performance of the functions necessary for their survival.

If the leader deviates in some way from the rest of the group, the resulting disruption of affect appears to become aggravated under stress. For example, difficulties in making group decisions may be encountered if the leader differs too sharply in some crucial personality characteristic (such as authoritarianism) from the other members of the group. Leaders with moderate needs for conformity to the opinions and judgments of the group members appear to be more flexible than those with either high or low needs and to show more confidence in their group's ability to make good decisions. Groups which are highly attractive to members are also more flexible in decision-making and more confident than low-attraction groups (Ziller, 1953).

Of special importance in coping with stress is the problem of increasing mutual support and willingness to sacrifice individual goals for group goals. When man scents danger, he appears to have a peculiarly strong desire to be with others. At the same time, evidences of unwillingness to sacrifice for the welfare of the group and of "survival-of-the-fittest" behavior are frequent and strong. In giving and receiving aid in groups under stress there is a great deal of ambivalence, and this ambivalence appears to fluctuate with the duration and intensity of the stress. Under severe stress, everyone must have support but capacity to give support is extremely limited. Those who sacrifice most for the welfare of fellow group members appear to survive longest under severe stress. There is also a tendency for those who achieve apparent safety or some satisfaction of a deprived need to refuse to sacrifice for the welfare of the group.

In general, mutual support and willingness to sacrifice for the welfare of the group increase chances of survival and reduce the discomfort of the stresses, whatever they may be. Individuals who fail to give aid to other group members suffer losses in self-esteem. Withdrawal of group support through either calculated or unconscious rejection appears to be quite painful psychologically and detrimental to chances of survival.

Some of the factors which seem to increase willingness to sacrifice are: group integrity; agreement among group members; previous acquaintance or close friendships; similarity of cultural background, religion, and group mores and norms; national pride; internal self-government; group pressures; public notice of failures to sacrifice; influence of the leader; success of the central mission of the group; prevention of breaks in the cooperative pattern, and the like.

Actual accounts of group behavior under stress, observations of aircrews in realistically simulated emergencies and extreme conditions, and laboratory experiments support the notion that unwillingness to sacrifice for the group is increased by opportunities to keep secret one's failure in this regard (Smith, 1957). Under such conditions, threat also increases this unwillingness to sacrifice. However, when failures to sacrifice are not kept secret, threat has no significant effect on willingness to sacrifice.

Communication Linkages

The following conditions appear to be most prominent in destroying communication linkages necessary for survival:

1. Failure of a group member to inform others of what he is doing (Marshall, 1947).

2. Failure to pool information which would provide a basis for diagnosing the seriousness of the danger and reducing resistance to acceptance of its seriousness (Torrance, LaForge, and Mason, 1956).

3. Confining communication to dyads or cliques rather than to the entire group (Torrance, LaForge, and Mason, 1956).

4. Failure to use group judgments in making decisions, and the use of leadership techniques which interfere with this type of communication (Ziller, 1957).

5. Power differences which interfere with communication of information needed in decision-making (Torrance, 1954c).

6. Unwillingness to disagree in the decision-making process (Torrance, 1957a).

The first two conditions are too obvious and too widely known to require elaboration. S. L. A. Marshall (1947) during World War II established the importance of failure to tell others what one is about as a cause of panic during combat. Equally as well known is the danger of failure to recognize and accept the seriousness of impending or present dangers and the consequent failure of the group to take adaptive action. Perhaps less well established is the tendency of groups under severe stress to break down into dyads or other subgroup formations and to confine communication to these formations. Under moderate stress, however, there appears to be a tendency for the members of a group to polarize around a leader and to respond more precisely to his communications. In time, however, these subgroup formations tend to develop and to interfere with the communication linkages.

Many of our findings concerning group decision-making under stress relate rather directly to problems of maintaining communication linkages, but there is no way to relate them to the dimensions of duration and intensity. In general, leaders appear to feel a greater than usual need to seek the judgments of group members when conditions become stressful. At the same time, group members are increasingly willing to place their lives "in the hands of" a strong leader who promises to "get them out of the predicament." In spite of the haste with which many decisions must be made during emergencies and extreme conditions, experiences of survivors indicate that even in sudden emergencies leaders can profit from the judgment and information of group members in reaching decisions.

On the matter of leadership technique, it appears that group members react most favorably to a group-decision situation under conditions permitting self-determination and reinforcement from the leader (Ziller, 1957). Leaders using techniques of decision-making in which they have no knowledge of the group's opinion prior to stating their own are more reluctant than leaders using group-centered decision-making techniques to make a decision which may involve the risk of the lives of group members.

Concerning the consequences of power differences, it was found that influence on decisions is in line with the power structure of the group and that this may interfere markedly with the quality of the decision (Torrance, 1954c). In rearranged or temporary groups, as compared with intact or more-or-less-permanent groups, it was found that the effects of power differences are lessened. In three-man groups with well-defined power structures the occupant of each power position tended to be assigned or assumed interaction behaviors characteristic of his position. The person with highest status appealed to solidarity, obtained suggestions and opinions, and evaluated them. The persons of intermediate status tended to be freer to disagree, while the lowest-status member seemed to be afraid to disagree and tended to withdraw from the decision-making process. Permanent groups more frequently made decisions which indicated a willingness to make a personal sacrifice for a group member, while temporary groups more frequently made decisions of a more flexible, sequential type.

Disagreement during the decision-making process appears to contribute to the making of good decisions if the disagreement is task-centered rather than person-centered (Torrance, 1957a). Disagreement also has possible negative effects if there develops any "negative identification" among members of the group. The expression of disagreement tends to be inhibited by status or power differences, the permanency of the relationships of group members, leadership techniques, and negative criticism.

Goal Linkages

Some of the most salient factors which seem to weaken goal linkages are:

1. The making of concessions to immediate comfort.
2. Weakening of goals and loss of will to survive.
3. The absence of a plan or strategy for coping with the stress.

In accounts of both individual and group survival, the making of concessions to immediate comfort looms important in maintaining goal linkages. This phenomenon was particularly clear in our Blizzard Study (Torrance, LaForge, and Mason, 1956). Entire subgroups failed to build fires, dry footgear, and exercise other precautions against frostbite. Men lost important items of equipment, such as gloves, on their rough downhill trek and simply failed to exert themselves to pick them up. If subgroup norms had placed a value on recovering equipment instead of making such concessions to immediate comfort, this extra energy would have been expended by most individuals.

The loss-of-will-to-survive phenomenon has been an object of special study. Factors involved in the maintenance of will mentioned most frequently by survivors are: instincts of self-preservation, determination based on some kind of unwavering decision, something to live for (family, home, democratic way of life, mission, immediate purpose, and the like), dignity and self-esteem, concern for someone or something outside self, group influences, some reason for hope, all-out efforts, religious faith, and various combinations of these. Whatever leaders can do to reinforce the above factors should strengthen goal linkages. A field experiment and a laboratory experiment concerning group factors relevant to will-to-survive indicated that the following factors are significant: degree of pressure from others, legitimacy of pressures from others, internalization of pressures from others, attraction of the crew, personal goals, and ego strength (Zander, Thomas, and Natsoulas, 1957).

Many groups in our sample seemed to be on the verge of collapse until someone developed a plan or strategy for coping with the stress. The development of such a plan or strategy seemed to give the group new and unexpected resources for adapting to the requirements of the situation.

SUMMARY

To summarize the status of our understanding of leadership and interpersonal behavior in groups under stress, it might be said that we are just

116 • THEORIES OF LEADERSHIP AND INTERPERSONAL BEHAVIOR

reaching a point where it is possible to begin formulating an organized, relatively comprehensive theory. Many elements of the theory sketched herein can be accepted with a high level of confidence. For example, it has been shown repeatedly that stress produces increased variability of performance, that moderate stress tends to produce performance increments, while severe stress results in disorganized performance. There are, however, many gaps to be supplied. Since what we know fits into a fairly comprehensive conceptualization, we can have some confidence in those parts where systematic knowledge is missing. This includes the principles concerning intensity, duration and quality of leadership and interpersonal behavior as mediating variables. Much previous research needs to be re-evaluated according to these concepts and future observations, and experiments should permit tests and elaborations of these generalizations.

As tentative as the theory presented herein is and as incomplete as is the firm information available today, nevertheless it is believed that they provide some useful guidance for improving leadership and interpersonal behavior under stress. They should provide useful guidance in making decisions about what standards of achievement to expect of groups, what degree of efficiency or perfection to require, how frequent changes should be made, when and how to use competition, what degree of independence to permit, what speed of performance to require, what degree of relaxation to strive for, and how to schedule periods of relaxation and periods of maximum performance.

REFERENCES

DUGUID, J. *Green hell.* London: Pan Books, 1956.
GUERLAIN, R. *They who wait.* New York: Crowell, 1943.
HARRIS, W., MACKIE, R. R., AND WILSON, C. L. *Performance under stress: A review and critique of recent studies.* Los Angeles: Human Factors Research, Inc., July 1956. (Technical Report VI. Contract Nonr–1241(00).)
MARSHALL, S. L. A. *Men under fire.* New York: Morrow, 1947.
MILLER, J. G. Mental health implications of a general behavior theory. *Amer. J. Psychiat.,* 1957, *113,* 776–782.
SCHWARTZ, G. AND BISHOP, P. W. (Ed.). *Moments of discovery. Vol. 2.* New York: Basic Books, 1958.
SELYE, H. *The physiology and pathology of stress.* Montreal: Acta, 1950.
SMITH, E. E. Choice of own versus group attainment under threat and reduced threat and in overt and covert conditions. *Amer. Psychologist,* 1957, *12,* 366. (Abstract)
TORRANCE, E. P. *Psychological aspects of survival: A study of survival behavior.* Washington, D. C.: Human Factors Operations Research Labora-

tories, Bolling Air Force Base, 1954. (HFORL *Memorandum* TN–54–4.) (a)

TORRANCE, E. P. The behavior of small groups under the stress conditions of survival. *Amer. sociol. Rev.,* 1954, *19,* 751–755. (b)

TORRANCE, E. P. Some consequences of power differences in decision making in permanent and temporary three-man groups. *Research Studies of the State College of Washington,* 1954, *22,* 130–140. Also in A. P. HARE, E. F. BORGATTA, AND R. F. BALES (Eds.), *Small groups.* New York: Knopf, 1955. Pp. 482–492. (c)

TORRANCE, E. P. Group decision-making and disagreement. *Soc. Forces,* 1957, *35,* 314–318. (a)

TORRANCE, E. P. What happens to the sociometric structure of small groups in emergencies and extreme conditions. *Group psychotherapy,* 1957, *10,* 212–220. (b)

TORRANCE, E. P. Leadership in the survival of small isolated groups. In *Preventive and social psychiatry.* Washington, D. C.: NRC-Walter Reed Medical Research Center, 1958. Pp. 309–327.

TORRANCE, E. P. The influence of experienced members of small groups on the behavior of the inexperienced. *J. soc. Psychol.,* 1959, *49,* 249–257.

TORRANCE, E. P., LaFORGE, R., AND MASON, R. *Group adaptation in emergencies and extreme conditions.* Randolph Air Force Base, Tex.: Office for Social Science Programs, Air Force Personnel and Training Research Center, 1956. (*Technical Memorandum* OSSP–56–2.)

TORRANCE, E. P. AND MASON, R. The indigenous leader in changing attitudes and behavior. *Internatl. J. Sociometry,* 1956, *1,* 23–38.

TYHURST, J. Emergent leadership. In *Preventive and social psychiatry.* Washington, D. C.: NRC-Walter Reed Medical Research Center, 1958. Pp. 329–335.

ZANDER, A., THOMAS, E., AND NATSOULAS, T. *Determinants of motivation and performance under pressure.* Ann Arbor, Mich.: Research Center for Group Dynamics, Univ. of Michigan, 1957.

ZILLER, R. C. Four techniques of group decision-making under uncertainty. *J. appl. Psychol.,* 1957, *41,* 384–388.

ZILLER, R. C. Leader acceptance of responsibility for group action under condtions of uncertainty and risk. *Amer. Psychologist,* 1955, *10,* 475–476. (Abstract)

ZILLER, R. C. Leader flexibility and group cohesiveness: Determinants of group problem-solving processes and concomitant affective group member behavior. *Amer. Psychologist,* 1953, *8,* 459. (Abstract)

8

The Executive Function in Small Groups

Thornton B. Roby

Tufts University

The purpose of this paper is to discuss the relations between leadership in the popular sense and the over-all executive function in small group situations. The present section attempts to show what is intended by this distinction, and why the distinction is important. Following this, the less familiar concept of an executive function will be developed in some detail. A final section considers ways in which these two phenomena may interact and some implications for research on leadership.

The term *leadership in the popular sense* here means simply personal leadership, the totality of influence relationships emanating from a particular individual who may be either a designated or an emergent leader. It is not intended to disparage the wide use of this concept or to minimize the importance of the phenomena it connotes. Earlier elementary descriptions of leadership as a general guiding force and a unitary personality trait have long since been adjusted to account for the context of leader behavior, for the effects of situations, and for co-actors. However, there are several reasons for exploring supplementary processes that may be conceptualized in quite different terms.

One reason is the trend toward increasing sophistication in the treatment of personal leadership phenomena. There is a danger that this trend will, if continued far enough, lead to some vitiation of the real meaning of personal leadership. It is obvious that there are dynamic and emotional factors in the exercise of personal leadership that are immensely important for understanding group behavior, even though they may not be universally applicable. Any conceptualization of leadership that attempts to embrace all group processes is apt to be much too tame for those rare but interesting cases in which leadership is indeed paternal or even charismatic.

A second reason is the discrepancy that exists between visible leadership functions and the actual behavior of group members. Certainly since Tolstoi's penetrating comments on the Napoleonic battles it has been recognized that an ostensible leader—even in a military situation—can exert only loose-jointed control over the behavior of his subordinates, and that this control may be far from unidirectional. Conversely, there are iceberg aspects to leadership—many of its most vital functions are not accessible to external observation. The general inference must be that any relationship between measurable-leadership behavior and other behaviors occurring in group situations is tenuous or gross. Rather than stretch the notion of leadership out to fill this causal vacuum, it seems advisable to impose a supplementary framework directly on the units of workaday group behavior.

The term *executive function* as it will be used here is intended to cover the entire process by means of which group actions are selected from a pool of potential actions. This process entails the detection or reception of information; storage of this information; transmission of information; calculations; refinements and extrapolations based on information; and the final processes that are usually classed as judgmental or decision-making. Emphasis in this paper will be on the final stage rather than on the results of the earlier stages. While the antecedent subfunctions are absolutely vital, they are also well recognized as essential to group performance and have been extensively investigated. Furthermore, the latter stages of response selection or decision-making are most closely related to the phenomena of leadership. Distinctly novel problems arise in the process of response selection in the group situation as compared with individual decision-making. These will be considered informally after a few remarks on terminology.

Group actions are made up of various combinations of the *action units* of the constituent group members. In general, these action units do not simply summate but may interact with each other in occlusive or facilitative fashion. For this reason, it is best initially to think of each distinct combination of action units as a separate entity, to be referred to as a *response aggregate* (RA). The number of RA's may be very great but will ordinarily be less than the total number of combinations of action units, since many combinations may be physically impossible. It is this pool of feasible RA's from which the selection is made on any occasion.

The relative merits or *utilities* of the RA's are of course not fixed but are determined as a function of existing environmental conditions. More precisely, every environmental state (E-state) induces a definite valuation on the entire set of RA's. In the present discussion we assume, (a) that these utilities are uniform for all group members; and (b) that the values of the extended payoff matrix (that is, the utilities of all RA's under all E-states) are known to those group members engaged in making selections. In other words we are considering a situation in which, if all group members shared full E-state information, agreement on the RA of choice would follow automatically. The complications that are discussed arise wholly from the nonuniform and incomplete distribution of E-state information, and from the necessity for isolated persons to make decisions, or component decisions, that are binding on the entire group.

It may be well to consider here just how this necessity may arise. Why don't group members get together, merge their information and agree on the best course of action? Broadly speaking, there are two kinds of pressure—physical and psychological—that may prevent them from doing this. In many instances of small group behavior such as infantry squad operations, individuals may be completely cut off from direct communication with each other. Any action taken under these conditions affects the success of the entire group but cannot possibly be cleared with other group members. On the psychological side it may be possible for each of several specialists to have more information about the possible consequences of a course of action than can possibly be communicated to their co-workers. This may be true of the President's cabinet, as an extreme example. Here a number of recommendations are made on a given issue, each presumably based on fiscal, military, diplomatic, or social considerations that no one person could digest in their entirety. It seems entirely plausible that such a nonhomogeneous distribution of information, in less dramatic form, is quite typical of all types of small group decision-making.

Even more generally, it is true that any information that is not directly accessible to a decision-maker, but must be obtained through internal communication processes, entails elements of delay and risk of error. Much of the experimental literature on small group performance is concerned with various aspects of these communication "costs." Thus, even where information might be fully shared the alternative procedure of permitting decisions to be made at separate centers may be superior.

In order to study the resulting composite process more closely, a formal apparatus is required that will permit:

1. Description of environmental states
2. Description of the response units and the response aggregates
3. Description of the payoff matrix of RA's and E-states
4. Characterization of the constraints that prohibit full and uniform information distribution and consolidated choice
5. Description of *de facto* executive structure
6. Determination of the behavior of individual decision-centers (that is, persons or groups of persons with uniform information and common authority)
7. Characterization of composite selections (selections resulting from the merger of several independently selected courses of action)
8. General evaluation of executive structures in terms of performance criteria.

To paraphrase this, we want to know what the over-all response selection task is and how it is governed by psychological or environmental constraints. We want then to see how particular groups may adapt to this task, and what the comparative payoffs are for these different modes of adaptation. The particular modes of adaptation are to be described in terms of the independent decision centers that are operative, the special action choices made at these decision centers, and the information on which these action choices are based. The next section offers a preliminary framework for dealing with such problems.

THE EXECUTIVE FUNCTION

We define a set $\{R\}$ of RA's with generic members R_i, each R_i composed of one or more action units. Any R_i may be selected on any occasion. A set of E-states, generically E_s, is defined such that, given any E_s, the value of every R_i is determined. For convenience it will be assumed that all E-states are equally probable, since this entails no real loss in generality.

Table 1 shows a set of eight E-states and eight RA's together with the value of each RA at each E-state. Both E-states and RA's are doubly characterized: first, by means of the subscripts s and i respectively; and more descriptively, by enumerating the action units (a, b, c) or environmental conditions *(r, s, t)* of which they are comprised. The hypothetical "payoff" values are picked from a table of random digits—that is, a rectangular distribution from 0–9. The fact that there are as many RA's as E-states is coincidental and is not assumed to hold generally. Of course both the number of E-states and RA's is much less than would be encountered in typical group situations, but this particular example permits convenient discussion of the essential phenomena.

Table I

AN ILLUSTRATIVE SET OF RESPONSE AGGREGATES, AND THEIR VALUES UNDER VARIOUS E-STATES

	E_1 (o)	E_2 (t)	E_3 (s)	E_4 (st)	E_5 (r)	E_6 (rt)	E_7 (rs)	E_8 (rst)
R_1(o)	8	6	3	2	5	3	2	9
R_2(c)	3	3	4	4	8	0	0	2
R_3(b)	9	3	8	6	2	2	5	0
R_4(bc)	1	2	6	5	6	6	1	3
R_5(a)	9	1	9	5	8	3	3	4
R_6(ac)	9	2	0	7	3	8	3	1
R_7(ab)	7	7	9	4	6	6	4	6
R_8(abc)	4	6	4	7	2	2	8	5

The notion of a *jurisdiction grid* is central to the rest of our discussion and is defined as follows: before any decision is made, there is a completely free choice among all possible RA's—eight distinct response patterns in the hypothetical example. A decision center, usually an individual, has the authority to cut down this range of choice on any specific occasion to some subset of {R}. He may, for example, specify that only R_1, R_3, or R_5 should be considered. These subsets of restricted choice will be referred to as *prescription sets*. It is then assumed that the prescription sets associated with any single decision center constitute a *partition* of {R} —that is, a division of the elements of {R} into mutually exclusive and exhaustive subsets. The jurisdiction grid, $(R_1 R_3 R_5) (R_2 R_4) (R_6 R_7 R_8)$, or more briefly (135) (24) (678), indicates that the decision center in question may, on any occasion, stipulate that any one of the RA's included between a single pair of parentheses may be employed. The decision center, however, has *no* authority over selection within each prescription set.

Because of the way in which RA's are defined—as patterns of action units—it is reasonable to assume that there is no overlap between prescription sets. That is, an explicit prescription will usually stipulate that certain action units will or will not be employed, and will be silent or indifferent concerning other action units. Then all the RA patterns that are differentiated by the explicitly suggested action units will fall in different prescription sets: those RA's which differ only in the action units over which the decision center has no choice will fall in the same prescription set. Thus, the general authority or influence of a decision center is directly related to the number of prescription sets or the fineness of the jurisdiction grid. Total authority would be represented by a jurisdiction grid containing only one RA in each prescription set, and zero authority would be represented by a grid containing the single prescription set {R}.

Suppose that a given decision center A has the jurisdiction grid described above—that is, (135) (24) (678). Then an independent decision center B might have a different grid, say (1256) (3478). If A chooses his prescription set (135) and B chooses his set (1256) then the choice of response aggregates is narrowed to the intersection of these two—(15). The choice between the two elements in this joint prescription may be a result of intersection with still another prescription set or it may be largely a chance process. Thus, a group decision is defined simply as the intersection of all prescription sets at a given E-state. This intersection may consist of 0, 1, or many RA's.

This method of conceptualizing jurisdiction, suggested actions, authority, and consensus, entails some inversion of the figures of speech customarily used to describe such matters. It is justified in part by the fact that it is equally adaptable to positive suggestions, "let's do x," and to negative injunctions, "don't do y." In the positive case, the prescription set consists of all RA's containing x and, in the negative case, the prescription set consists of just those RA's not containing y, where x and y are action units or subsets of action units. The term *jurisdiction grid* implies that the decision center has some recognized authority to offer these prescriptions. If no such authority exists for certain choices in particular groups, it may be appropriate to treat these choices as results of chance, as noted above. A further advantage of this formulation lies in the very simple rules for combining prescriptions, namely, the rules of set intersection. The problems of combining prescription sets will be examined further after some consideration of the basis on which individual prescriptions are made.

First, it is of course assumed that individual prescriptions, like the final selections, are based on an effort to maximize response aggregate values. Hence, some preliminary conventions are needed with respect to the evaluation of prescription sets and joint prescription sets. This evaluation should have two features. First, it should be independent of the general goodness of RA values since it may be desirable to evaluate decisions or response selections quite apart from the response repertoire on which they operate. Second, the evaluation should be suitable for sets of RA's as well as single elements.

A natural measure to use for this purpose is the standardized values of RA's within a particular E-state and of course the mean of these standard values for sets of RA's. In the case of null decisions it appears quite appropriate to assign the value zero (a null decision is equivalent to permitting random response behavior). If the distributions of values are seriously skewed or multimodal it may be preferable to use distribution-free measures such as the centile value of a response aggregate, or of the median aggregate in a prescription set. For very small {R} sets, as in the example, it would be convenient to use median rank orders of the RA's in the prescription sets, setting the rank order of the null set at $n/2$, where n is the number of RA's.

Assuming that some such evaluation of RA sets is possible, the other factor in selection is the environmental information that a decision center may have. We use a notion analogous to that of the jurisdiction grid to define an information grid. Thus an information grid is a partition of all E-states into subsets within which discrimination is impossible for the individual. For example, if A's information grid is (1234) (5678), he can tell any one of E_1, E_2, E_3, E_4 from any one of E_5, E_6, E_7, E_8 but can't distinguish E_1 from E_2, etc. We will call the subsets of the E-states *information sets*. This usage is in conformity with that of the Theory of Games (Von Neumann and Morgenstern, 1947).

In the present exposition it is assumed that selection of prescription sets will be based on the mean value of all elements in a prescription set over all elements of the information set. At a particular E-state, that is, the decision center will select that prescription set which has the highest mean value for all E-states in the same information set. Suppose that A's jurisdiction grid is (135) (24) (678) and his information grid is (1234) (5678), then the means for the two information states are as shown in Table 2. Person A clearly picks the starred values—(135) under E_1-E_4 and (678) under E_5-E_8. The expected value of all aggregates, if no other prescriptions are offered, is the mean of 5.75 and 4.50, or 5.12.

Suppose now that B's jurisdiction grid is (1256) (3478) and that his information grid is (158) (23467). The mean values are shown in the lower half of Table 2. His prescription sets will be (1256) for information state (158) and (3478) for (23467) and the expected values based on his prescription alone will be 5.31. However, we are assuming that B's prescriptions are actually made in conjunction with A's, a situation which is schematized in Table 3.

For convenient reference the prescription sets and information states have been labeled A_1, $\hat{A}_8$ respectively. The conjunction of two information states, say $\hat{A}_1$ and $\hat{B}_2$, is indicated by $\hat{A}_1\hat{B}_2$, and similarly for the prescription sets.

If the actual E-state is E_1, then A will be in information state $\hat{A}_1$ and

Table 2

PARTITIONING OF THE PAYOFF MATRIX INTO JURISDICTION GRIDS AND
INFORMATION GRIDS, WITH RESULTING CHOICES

A's selections

	E_1	E_2	E_3	E_4	E_5	E_6	E_7	E_8
R_1	8	6	3	2	5	3	2	9
R_3	9	3	8	6	2	2	5	0
R_5	9	1	9	5	8	3	3	4
V		5.75*				3.83		
R_2	3	2	4	4	8	0	0	2
R_4	1	2	6	5	6	6	1	3
V		3.38				3.25		
R_6	9	2	0	7	3	8	3	1
R_7	7	7	9	4	6	6	4	6
R_8	4	6	4	7	2	2	8	5
V		5.50				4.50*		

B's selections

	E_1	E_5	E_8	E_2	E_3	E_4	E_6	E_7
R_1	8	5	9	6	3	2	3	2
R_2	3	8	2	3	4	4	0	0
R_5	9	8	4	1	9	5	3	3
R_6	9	3	1	2	0	7	8	3
V		5.75*				3.40		
R_3	9	2	0	3	8	6	2	5
R_4	1	6	3	2	6	5	6	1
R_7	7	6	6	7	9	4	6	4
R_8	4	2	5	6	4	7	2	8
V		4.25				5.04*		

will accordingly choose the prescription set A_1 or (135). B will be in information state $\hat{B}_1$ and will choose his prescription set B_1 or (1256). The resulting prescription is a mixture of the two common RA's, namely R_1 and R_5. Similarly, for E_2, E_3, or E_4, A will again be in $\hat{A}_1$, but B will now be in the information state B_2: the intersection of their prescription sets is the single RA, R_3; and so forth. The mean values for selected response aggregates are singly starred in Table 3.

In the case of the joint prescriptions of Table 3, the expected over-all mean is 4.93. This is poorer than the prescription of either decision center considered individually (5.12 and 5.31 respectively). It is considerably

Table 3

JOINT PRESCRIPTIONS BASED ON INDEPENDENT PRESCRIPTIONS BY
TWO DECISION CENTERS

	$\hat{A}_1\hat{B}_1$ (E_1)	$\hat{A}_1\hat{B}_2$ ($E_2E_3E_4$)	$\hat{A}_2\hat{B}_1$ (E_5E_8)	$\hat{A}_2\hat{B}_2$ (E_6E_7)
A_1B_1 (R_1R_5)	8.50*	4.33	6.50**	3.25
A_1B_2 (R_3)	9.00**	5.67*	1.00	3.50
A_2B_1 (R_2)	3.00	3.67	5.00	.00
A_2B_2 (R_4)	1.00	4.33	4.50	3.50
A_3B_1 (R_6)	9.00	3.00	2.00*	5.50**
A_3B_2 (R_7R_8)	5.50	6.16**	4.75	5.00*

poorer than the prescriptions that would be obtained if A and B acted as a unit, sharing both information and jurisdiction. The expected value for the latter situation, computed by selecting the highest means in each column of Table 3 (doubly starred) and weighting for the number of E-states in each, is 6.44. It might be noted that the selections obtained from independent choice by A and B do not agree in any case with the optimal selection.

Although the present paper is primarily concerned with the implications of the executive structure for questions of leadership, some further examination of executive structure per se may be useful. This clearly is an immensely complex problem but some insights can be obtained by a slight modification, and specialization, of the paradigm discussed above.

While the response aggregates may be treated as distinct entities, it will be recalled that they may also be considered as sets of unit responses. Thus one RA would differ from another in presence or absence of one or more of these component units. Similarly, E-states will not, in general, be totally unrelated, but will reflect presence or absence of certain attributes or environmental conditions.

The simplest and most natural jurisdiction grid will be one in which each decision center controls the occurrence or nonoccurrence of one or more response units. As an example, the jurisdiction grid (1234) (5678) would correspond to control over a. The grid (15) (26) (37) (48) would correspond to joint control over bc. Similarly, the information grid (1357) (2468) would indicate that the decision center had full information on the state of the environmental attribute t.

This introduces a severe, but entirely natural, restriction on the number of possible jurisdiction and information grids that could be assigned to single decision centers. With this restriction it is not difficult to determine exhaustively the payoff values for each J-grid–I-grid combination. The mean RA values for all such information-jurisdiction combinations are presented in Table 4. As an example, the cell entry across from *ab* and down from *t* indicates that a decision center with information as to the presence or absence of *t* and with control over response units *a* and *b* could choose prescription sets with a value of 5.38. As would be expected, means increase as the lower right corner of the Table is approached—that is, as more of the interaction effects among information items or response units are brought into the prescriptions.

Table 4

EXPECTED RESPONSE AGGREGATE VALUES FOR INDIVIDUAL DECISION CENTERS
AT VARIOUS EXECUTIVE LOCI

	o	r	s	t	rs	rt	st	rst
a	5.00	5.00	5.00	5.00	5.00	5.00	5.00	5.06
b	4.69	4.69	4.94	4.69	4.94	4.69	5.16	5.25
c	5.06	5.06	5.06	5.06	5.06	5.18	5.06	5.31
ab	5.38	5.38	5.56	5.38	5.81	5.56	6.00	6.28
ac	5.63	5.63	5.63	5.75	5.75	5.94	5.75	6.37
bc	5.19	5.56	5.25	5.31	5.56	5.56	5.81	6.13
abc	6.06	6.06	6.19	6.31	6.56	6.69	6.81	8.09

In situations of practical interest there would usually be further constraint on the possible variety of J-grids and I-grids. For example, it may be necessary for the response units *a* and *b* to be controlled by different persons for physical reasons. Again, it may happen that specific individuals receive information on specific environmental attributes, such as *r* or *s,* as a matter of course. More broadly, there may be limits on the span of control or span of attention which require that jurisdiction and information be distributed among decision centers.

Starting with these constraints, it is clear that tentative recommendations as to optimal executive structures can be based on data such as that in Table 4. Suppose it was agreed that each of three decision centers should control one response unit, and should get information on two environmental attributes. Then a reasonable structure to consider would associate *a* with *rs; b* with *st;* and *c* with *rt.* Of course this could be checked by direct inspection of the means under this structure. As another example, if it were decided to assign response unit control to just two decision centers, it would appear advisable to combine jurisdiction over *a* and *b* or *a* and *c,* leaving the remaining unit to the independent center.

The reason for this is that the *interaction* gains for *a* are high as compared with its first order gains. To illustrate such "factorialized" structure, an executive structure based on joint assignment of *ac* to a decision center with information on *rt* and assignment of *b* to a decision center with information on *s* is shown in Table 5. The starred values again denote the RA actually selected for each information state, and it will be noted that exactly one RA is chosen for each occasion. The resulting mean is 6.00 so that very little is gained by the prescriptions made on *b*.

Table 5

A FACTORIALIZED EXECUTIVE STRUCTURE WITH RESULTING PRESCRIPTIONS

	o	s	r	rs	t	st	rt	rst
o	8	3	5	2	6	2	3	9
b	9	8	2	5	3	6	2	0
a	9*	9	8*	3	1	5	3*	4
ab	7	9*	6	4*	7	4	6	6*
c	3	4	8	0	3	4	0	2
bc	1	6	6	1	2	5	6	3
ac	9	0	3	3	2*	7	8	1
abc	4	4	2	8	6	7*	2	5

Perhaps the most reasonable conclusion to be drawn from the values in Table 4 is that every effort should be made to centralize information and jurisdiction. For example, the very large interactions among response effects, as shown in the last row of this table, would almost justify the assignment of all three response units to a single decision center even if that decision center had *no* information. On the other hand, the large interaction effects for environmental attributes would justify a determined effort to relay all information to a central decision point *even if message cost were very high.*

The foregoing observations are not offered as an adequate recipe for optimizing executive structures, but are intended to highlight considerations relevant for the leadership problem. For the sake of closure, we shall indicate merely further development in the present approach that might lead to a practical algorithm for group organization.

First, it must be recognized that the data on payoff scores and their relation to E-states will rarely be as precise or tidy as are those used in this hypothetical example. It would be necessary therefore to develop procedures that could be based on estimated relations and payoff values. One suggestion along this line comes from the obvious parallel between the layout of Table 4 and the conventional analysis of variance paradigm. The suggestion, namely, is that the cell entries in Table 4 might be replaced by variance estimates derived from empirical tests. These variance estimates can in turn be translated into estimates of the *best* response selections that could be made, using known characteristics of extreme score distributions (Cramèr, 1946; Gumbel, 1954).

A second obstacle in determining optimal executive structures is the tremendous combinatorial complexity that the typical realistic problem would present. Exhaustive inspection of possible structures would be out of the question for any task situation of practical interest. However, it seems likely that some modification of linear programming techniques could be developed to cope with this problem. In particular, it would appear that the procedures developed by Dwyer (1957) for handling the multidimensional assembly problem might be adapted to the present one.

It must be granted that the present formulation of the executive process leaves important substantive and formal questions unresolved. There do not seem to be any obstacles, however, that cannot be overcome by appropriate simplifying assumptions and more refined analytic techniques. We shall therefore summarize this section in terms of programmatic objectives rather than demonstrated results.

Essentially, it has been suggested that the entire process of response selection can be considered in terms of coincidence of certain kinds of information. This information concerns group goals; present environmental conditions; availability of action units; efficacy of various action units (for a given E-state); and, the interactive effects of other action units. Put in very broad terms, our hypothesis is that a good executive structure is one which maximizes the coincidence of these aspects of relevant information for each action unit in the group's active repertoire. To simplify the picture, we have confined the discussion to situations in which goal information, and information on the availability and effects of action units, are uniformly distributed. If these conditions are not satisfied the analysis would be much more intricate but not essentially different.

A rather pronounced departure of the present approach from existing formulations lies in its treatment of group consensus. It is assumed that a decision embraces every aspect of the group's behavior whether all these action units come up for active consideration or not. In a sense agreement, and indeed, commitment, as to certain courses of action may be tacit and is implied by acceptance of an executive structure. In the present view, no distinction would be made between action alternatives that came up for debate and those actions that are taken routinely. It is recognized, however, that for practical purposes of describing or analyzing executive structures, certain action units would be much more critical than others.

With regard to the leadership problem, perhaps the most pertinent feature of the present approach would be the extreme de-emphasis of individuals. Personalities and capabilities of individuals in a group are relevant only insofar as they are reflected in the types and amounts of information handled by the persons. The individual is a distinctive unit only if he is associated with a unique jurisdiction grid.

LEADERSHIP AND THE EXECUTIVE FUNCTION

The purpose of this section will be to trace the relation between the results of the foregoing section—or their programmatic extensions—and the more conventional aspects of leadership. To accomplish this it is necessary to strike a balance between the emphasis of the executive function approach on information and response categories and the more psychological concern with personal and social factors.

The introductory section warned against placing too much of the burden of explanation for group behavior on properties of the leader or of leader-follower relations, and it must now be recognized that this warning cuts both ways. It may be possible, but it is certainly neither natural nor fruitful, to squeeze all aspects of the decision-making problem into the executive-structure framework. In small groups, as in larger societies, government requires *both* laws and men.

We shall begin with a survey of the possible functions of a leader within the executive structure as described above. To avoid circumlocutions, reference throughout will be to an individual leader although the observations might apply without change to more widely distributed leadership acts. Also, it will be convenient to phrase all of the potential leadership influences in the positive, benign, sense. This simplification is explicitly dealt with at a later point.

A Catalogue of Leadership Functions

1. An assumption of the present model—and a necessity for integrated behavior—is that the goals and values of group members are similar or compatible enough so that the potential values of various response aggregates are similarly ordered. One function of leadership may be to bring about congruence of goals, and to emphasize existing congruences. Discrepancies will remain, but these discrepancies can be confined to issues which are comparatively tangential to the general group interest.

2. Effective group action requires not only an intelligent choice of

response aggregates but also a sufficiently large set of response aggregates from which to choose.

The leader can ensure that a reasonable balance obtains between the information processing efforts and facilities of the group, on one hand, and its response potential on the other. It is clear that, while these two aspects of group behavior cannot be treated as dichotomously separated there may be some conflict as to which aspect should be emphasized. A group may seem so preoccupied with finding out what is going on that they do not reserve enough time and energy for instrumental or remedial action. Contrarywise, the group may rush headlong into action without any clear notion of existing circumstances or desirable tactics. There are several stages at which an astute leader can correct tendencies toward either of these extremes. First, to avoid or counteract imbalances, he may recruit people who are especially fitted for one or the other function. Second, he can assign existing group members in such a way as to insure balance and take steps to guarantee that essential skills of observation or environmental manipulation are developed. Finally, he can make sure to some extent that the group becomes committed to tasks only if group members have the skills, experience, and motivations that are prerequisites for the task.

3. For a specified task, with a given set of external constraints, there exists an optimal executive structure—a decision-making structure that will focus the maximum relevant information on each composite decision. Without minimizing the difficulty of the problem of determining such an optimal structure, it remains true that an effective leader should provide a structure that incorporates all major relationships between information and action. Exceptional leaders can develop an intuitive grasp of these relationships that goes far beyond the obvious, and can organize executive structures accordingly. At the very least, a leader should prevent situations in which suggestions for action are based on utterly inadequate information. It is almost as important for morale, to avoid putting people with relevant information in positions without commensurate authority.

4. Once an executive structure is established, it is necessary to make sure that it functions as it is supposed to function. If information is required for a certain class of prescriptions, the leader must insure that this information is available at the decision center. Although we have stressed the final stage in the response selection process, there may be many preparatory activities which precede this and are absolutely vital for optimal response aggregate selection. It may be necessary not only for information to be made available, but for it to be available at a very precise time—neither too early nor too late. In essentially branched executive structures it is most

important for decisions at an earlier stage in the selection process to pre-cede decisions further down the line. Nothing is more frustrating for group members than to arrive at a choice among several alternatives only to discover that these alternatives are not open.

5. Within the general framework defined by the executive structure the leader may serve as an important, but undistinguished, element. The ten-dency is for leaders to act at the final, decision stage, of the executive function. Typically, they have jurisdiction over action components for which interaction is relatively important (as compared with outside infor-mation) and the necessity for a centralized selection is acute. At times, however, and particularly in groups that deal with other groups, the leader, as group representative, is the unique source of an important class of information. In action groups such as bomber groups, football teams, the leader may be the most important single contributor to the response pool.

6. Finally, in any real-life executive structure, constructed without the aid of our factorial schema, there will be conflicts between selections (null joint prescription sets) and equivocal selections. In these cases, the leader may function as an arbitrator in attempting to arrive at a unique selection. He may use additional information to tip the scales toward one selection or another, or he may just utter the last word in order to break a deadlock. In groups there may be well-defined rules of order that must be invoked whenever unacceptable joint-prescription sets occur; and the leader often acts as a chairman in observing the rules.

Functional Equipotential Leadership

Clearly, attention to all of these leadership responsibilities would con-stitute at least a full-time job. At the same time, one completes this enumeration of functions with the feeling that much of the real substance of leadership has slipped through the net. In part this apparent incom-pleteness of description is due to the kinds of things most readily asso-ciated with the terms *environmental state* and *response aggregate*. It is natural to fill in these conceptual blanks with very practical items such as *instrument readings* and *lever movements*. There is no reason in principle, however, why executive structures cannot be thought of as the diges-tion of information on personal attitudes and emotional states and the resultant selection of group therapeutic activity. With this more liberal interpretation of our basic terms (putting aside difficulties of measure-ment) the picture of the leader may take on a more lifelike hue.

Nevertheless, it remains true that none of the functions described appears to be an absolutely necessary and invariant part of a leader's role.

Leaders in some groups may perform some but not all of these functions, or may perform some of them at certain times but not continuously. At other times, or in other groups, these functions may be unnecessary or they may be subserved in other ways—for example, by procedural devices within the executive structure.

This leads to the contention that leadership may be characterized better by its equipotentiality than by any specific profile of activities. In other words, the ability of a leader to fill any breach in the executive process may be more significant than the particular functions he performs routinely. It would appear that the latter can almost certainly be delegated or institutionalized over a period of time so that no single individual's attention is indispensable. On the other hand, if the basic executive structure becomes inadequate because of unusual environmental demands or defection of group personnel, it may be most important to have a versatile and authoritative figure to keep things going.

It may be contended that it is just this aspect of leadership that invests it with its peculiarly personal quality. While the executive structure as such is based on access to task relevant information, the manifestation and acceptance of personal leadership may be based on personal or social characteristics that have little to do with the immediate task. Put somewhat differently, the leader has a fund of confidence or of externally derived power on which he can draw in special circumstances. This backlog of generalized authority permits him, if necessary, to violate the existing executive structure or even the evident logic of the group task.

Thus, personal leadership which does not derive from task-related information and experience, occupies a somewhat anomalous position with respect to the executive function. It may be highly essential on occasions to forestall catastrophic failure of the system. Its very necessity, however, is symptomatic of deficiencies in the normal executive structure, deficiencies that may be either chronic or the result of unforeseen environmental conditions. To the extent that it is a stopgap measure, it is apt to result in decisions that are inferior from the standpoint of immediate task effectiveness. Moreover, there is an element of risk in centralized personal leadership insofar as it makes group performance entirely dependent on the continued presence and good judgment of a single individual.

The present position should not, however, be construed as one rigid egalitarianism. Task environments are seldom so well defined or so stable as to rule out the occasional necessity for arbitrary or *ex cathedra* decisions. The authority to offer and impose such decisions must be conferred on an individual basis. Our analysis suggests that truly effective personal leadership depends upon its ability to recognize when its own operation is required; it depends equally on a readiness to surrender the reins when its purpose has been accomplished.

Some Implications for Research

It is clear that before any very precise study of the relationship between the executive process and personal leadership is possible, a considerable amount of spade work is required on the former topic. Of course as a formal theory it stands or falls on its conceptual manageability, which, at the present stage, looks promising. This by no means insures its usefulness as a paradigm for representing real-life decision processes; it must first be shown that the terms on which the paradigm is based lend themselves to empirical measurement and that they are stable enough to meaningfully characterize groups. To accomplish this, there appears to be no substitute for an extended natural history study of a variety of groups.

Following this, the present position suggests a series of longitudinal studies of groups in environments in which the payoff matrices are closely controlled. Such studies determine how various constraints on information access, or on jurisdiction, affect the development of group structures. In particular, they determine whether groups, left to themselves, gravitate toward executive structures that are optimal in the sense of the previous section. In addition an investigation could be made of those pressures, such as interpersonal attitudes or "empire-building" proclivities, that tend to distort or impede the development of optimal executive structures.

Such studies as these are not irrelevant to the understanding of leadership. Indeed this is exactly the course of investigation that is recommended for studying those aspects of leadership that fit directly into the context of the executive function as we have described it. There are however other problems bearing particularly on personal leadership that merit special investigation.

a) Under what conditions does a distinctly personal type of leadership emerge? The foregoing discussion suggests that it emerges only when there is occasion to make decisions that are inherently or apparently arbitrary. If the logic of the task, and the constraints on information and jurisdiction, permit each group member to share consistently in composite decisions—even in a minor way—there will be no clearly marked leader. Task manipulations which either encourage or preclude such distributed decision-making are readily suggested by the framework of the second section.

b) If conditions do favor the emergence of a personal leader, who will it be? To what extent is the identity of the leader determined by accidental or temporary circumstance; to what extent by a generally strategic position in the executive structure; and to what extent by purely personal factors? This is not a novel question in group research, of course, but it is given a sharpened form if considered within the context of the kind of framework presented here.

c) Once personal leadership is asserted, what factors tend to keep it in force? There are several aspects to this problem, one of which relates to the devices leaders may use to maintain their position, such as deliberate cornering of information access. A second aspect of the problem is the environmental circumstances and particularly reinforcement conditions that favor the continuation of personal leadership. In this, as in the preceding problems, it is supposed that the group is accepting such leadership in lieu of an executive structure that might lead to more effective use of available information.

In brief, then, a normative and nonpersonal framework along the lines here proposed may assist the study of leadership phenomena in two different ways. First, by providing a context within which the decision-making behavior of any single individual is understood in the same terms and as a part of a more general directive process. In addition, it supplies a sort of baseline for distinguishing authority relationships that are not, strictly speaking, "rational," and for defining the conditions under which this sort of authority is most likely to obtain.

SUMMARY

It is suggested that the study of personal leadership may be usefully supplemented by an analysis of the over-all process of response selection. Reasons are advanced for supposing that the investigation of leadership as an isolated phenomenon may be self-defeating.

A framework is presented for conceptualizing the selection of response aggregates. This framework hinges on the notion of a partition of possible response aggregates and of information states, different partitions being associated with each decision maker. The relation between the informational and jurisdictional partitions of individuals is critical in assuring that various prescriptions are based on adequate knowledge of conditions, and the relation between the separate jurisdictional partitions is critical in guaranteeing that composite decisions will not be inferior to the subordinate prescriptions.

In the last section, an attempt is made to describe the leadership role within the context of an executive structure. It is observed that the activities usually associated with leadership do not seem to have any necessary or consistent place in this pattern. Making a preliminary distinction between leadership as a direct function of superior task information—interpreted broadly—and leadership as a matter of sheer personal influence, it is suggested that the latter may invade the executive process only when the process is otherwise inadequate. Thus, even when personal leadership is essential to hold a group together, it may operate preemptively to inhibit the development of more enduring structures.

Finally an indication is given of the implications of this approach for empirical study. Since it is essentially a formal, and in some respects normative, approach, the principle empirical question concerns its aptness as a tool for analyzing and describing response selection. This question can best be answered by examining groups in a variety of task situations and trying to translate their response-selection procedures into present terms. In addition, there are problems suggested by the distinction between personal leadership and a distributed executive structure that require special research attention.

REFERENCES

CRAMÈR, H. *Mathematical methods of statistics.* Princeton, N. J.: Princeton, 1946.

DWYER, P. S. Mathematical procedures and multiple criteria for assembly of large work groups. AFPTRC Tech. Report. 57–9, Lackland AFB, Texas: October, 1957.

GUMBEL, E. J. Statistical theory of extreme values and some practical applications. National Bureau of Standards. *Applied Mathematics Series 33.* Feb., 1954.

MARSCHAK, J. Towards an economic theory of organization and information. In THRALL, R. M., COOMBS, C. H. AND DAVIS, R. L. (Eds.), *Decision processes.* New York: Wiley, 1954.

ROBY, T. B. The mechanics of environmental adjustment. *Behavioral Science,* 1959, 4, 107–119.

VON NEUMANN, J. AND MORGENSTERN, O. *Theory of games and economic behavior,* 2nd Ed. Princeton, N. J.: Princeton U., 1947.

9

Power, Influence and Pattern of Communication[1]

Kurt W. Back

Duke University

INTRODUCTION

The study of power and influence forms the meeting ground of several disciplines. Psychologists have considered the conditions of imitation and the influence of the primary group, sociologists the reasons for role differentiation. Political scientists have as their central problem the question of organized power; political philosophers search for justification of the existence of any kind of power. The basic question underlying this ramification of interest is quite simple: How does it happen that one person does what another person incites him to do? It is evident that it does happen, and it is also evident that this power is unevenly distributed. Some persons are more likely to be the instigators of actions and others are more likely to be instigated. This differentiation can be observed along the whole range of social relationships from small primary groups

[1] This paper was written as part of the program of the Organization Research Group of the Institute for Research in Social Science, University of North Carolina, which is supported by the Office of Naval Research [Nonr–855(04)]. The author thanks the members of the Organization Research Group, especially Drs. John W. Thibaut and Edward E. Jones for stimulating and critical discussions of early drafts of this paper. The helpful comments of the discussants at the symposium at Louisiana State University, Drs. E. Paul Torrance and Eugene L. Gaier are also gratefully acknowledged.

to large, organized, political units. However, the interest in specific questions has sometimes obscured the identity of the basic problem.

The unequal distribution of power is especially manifest in large political units, and it is here that we find early attempts to account for the fact that some people let others determine their actions. We shall not go back further than Hobbes to look for theories that account for this evolution. Theorists like Hobbes and his followers posited an early state in which there was no differentiation and that the differences were developed later either by force or by common agreement. A considerable amount of ingenuity was expended to describe the hypothetical original state of nature and of subsequent changes.

At the other extreme some psychologists noticed that differentiation of power occurs between individuals rather regularly and that some individuals are prone to exert power over others. They attempted therefore to study the traits of persons who were successful in having others do their bidding—the traits of leadership. It is easy to see that there was little common outlook between scientists who searched for the base of power differentiation in the distant past and those who tried to assess an individual according to his leadership ability. The other approaches which were mentioned above fall between these extremes but they too were likely to concern themselves with particular conditions.

It is now gradually becoming recognized that each approach may illuminate the problems of the other. For instance, instead of looking for the origin of power in the hypothetical past, it may be fruitful for political scientists to study the exertion of authority here and now, and instead of solely testing for leadership traits, it may be fruitful to study how power is exerted in society. In this way common problems may be recognized and common concepts be employed in their study as a preliminary to the investigation of particular refinements for varied conditions.

In this paper an approach is made to a common problem, namely the process through which power is exerted. We shall confine ourselves to studying the pattern of interaction and communication through which a person makes his intent to influence known to other people, and the different effects which these patterns may have. We thus shall omit all reference to conditions outside the interpersonal system, such as the source of power, possible sanctions, and the relation of the topics to other aspects of the life of the individuals. This restriction is similar to that made by French (1956). While his theory of social power concentrates on the pattern of channels through which power is exerted, the present paper is concerned with the pattern of messages within these channels.

Before attempting an abstract theoretical scheme on the function of communication in this context, let us first define a few terms which have been used up to now almost interchangeably: power, influence, and authority. We are considering only situations in which one person wishes to change another's behavior.[2] The degree to which he is able to do so will be called *power*. We can conceive of a person as a system with a describable input and output, and we can infer the internal state. The overt output we shall call *action;* the inferred state of the internal system which determines the likelihood that certain outputs will be used shall be stipulated as *attitude.* That kind of power which changes attitudes is defined as *influence,* and that which changes or produces action as *authority.* It is thus possible to have influence without authority and authority without, or with little, influence. However, authority combined with influence will be more enduring as the predisposition of the person to act spontaneously at a later date is changed, while direct authority is represented typically by compliance to one command.

In the following sections we shall propose several hypotheses about conditions under which influence and authority are exerted. Before doing so we shall develop a general mathematical model from which specific relations can be derived. In turn, these relations can be interpreted as the proposed hypotheses. The type of model developed is logical but not strictly arithmetical. It shows functional relationships, such as "more" or "less," or "more or less probable."

There are several reasons for tying specific hypotheses about communication and power to a general mathematical system. Higher abstractions make it possible to find applications of the same theory in widely different fields; and we shall see later how the concepts can be used to tie together a variety of phenomena. The mathematical definition has in general a clearer denotation than a purely verbal definition and thus the essentials of the theory become clear. Further, the mathematical treatment shows where more precise operations are needed and in what way this can be accomplished; a later section will treat new ways to measure communication. Finally, additional hypotheses can be derived from the larger system and these can be applied and tested. Confirmation of any part of the system increases the initial plausibility of each hypothesis and thus leads to a fruitful interplay of empirical data and theoretical interpretation.

MATHEMATICAL FORMULATION OF POWER AND INFLUENCE

General Specifications

Let there be a system P with a series of possible inputs and another of possible outputs. A certain input C at time t_1 can be connected with a

---

[2] These distinctions are similar to those made by Easton (1958).

certain probability with some outputs B at some later time, say t_2. It can also change P in such a way that the probability distribution for outputs with the same C at a later time is different.

Thus, a certain output B is a probability function f of some C at a previous time and of the state of P at that time. Assuming for simplicity's sake only one C:

$$B (t_2) = f[C(t_1), P(t_1)] \qquad (1)$$

In the same way, P at time t_2 is a probability function of its own previous state and any C's at a previous time:

$$P (t_2) = g[P(t_1), C(t_1)] \qquad (2)$$

Looking at the two equations we see that any input can have two kinds of effects on outputs: a direct effect and an indirect one by changing P in a way that the probability of P's responding at a later date with an output is changed. The formulas are general in the sense that a C may have one effect or another or both in varying degrees, that is, the functions g or f may or may not be identically zero.

The two equations may also be considered as specifications of P. The system must be designed in a way that these relations are possible. We shall now construct a model of such a system and from this deduce some properties of C relating to different f and g functions.

Automata Theory

Models of this kind have been constructed in automata theory. This theory will be used here only as mathematical method, not as a representation of actual processes within P (the person). Although the elements in this algebra are called nerve-fibers because of the physiological origin of the theory, they are used only as mathematical concepts, not as representation of physiological events. It may be a comfort, however, to the physiologically minded, that the mathematics presented here is at least not inconsistent with an application to nerve-nets.

One system of automata in particular designed by Von Neumann (1956) can be applied to fulfill the requirements which we have stated. We shall now sketch this system and then select appropriate parts to fulfill the conditions of P.

Fiber

The basic unit in automata theory is the analog of a nerve-fiber (Figure 1). This is a system with several inputs and one output; each input and output is represented by a line. The output reacts (the fiber fires) after a time delay when a certain number of inputs are stimulated. The number of inputs necessary for firing is a characteristic of the fiber. In addition, some inputs can be inhibitory cancelling out active stimulation. Thus a fiber which will fire when one input is stimulated needs two stimulations if one inhibitory input is stimulated.

Fiber

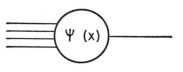

Fig. I. FIBER (*From* Von Neumann, 1956, p. 46)

Out of this simple fiber, various systems can be constructed to execute any logical operation, to count, to store information, and so on. One operation which will be important is the scaler. This system counts to a certain number and fires only when this number has been reached. That is, it will "remember" how often it has been stimulated.

By making a feedback circuit—by connecting an output back to an input—the unit can keep firing, or need less stimulation for the next firing.

Organs.

Specific types and combinations of fibers can be constructed and are called organs. One of these, the majority organ, is important for application of the theory: it is a fiber which will fire if a majority of its inputs are stimulated. For instance, if there are three inputs the organ will fire only if at least two of them are stimulated. Logically this corresponds to a disjunction of three conjunctions [if we call the three input lines a, b, c, then (a and b) or (a and c) or (b and c) or (a and b and c) must be active]. It can be shown that this organ is sufficient by itself to perform all logical operations. In other words, a message, analyzed into its logical components, can be put into the input and the output pattern will represent this message. This is, of course, true only if the unit is free of error and operates on a certainty, not a probability relationship.

Corrections of Error

If there is a probability of error, some complications have to be introduced for the output to achieve a high degree of reliability. The simplest way to check errors in messages is to repeat the messages. Similarly a simple way in this system is to carry the same message in a different form on several lines of a fiber or in different fibers, that is, to have bundles for input and output. The messages carried by the different lines in the bundle can then be compared and organs constructed which can reconstruct the original message with high probability of correctness. This process is called multiplexing. A multiplexed fiber is shown in figure 2.

Multiplexing

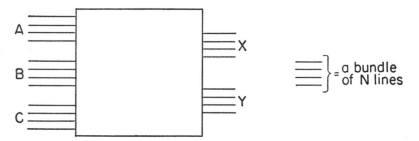

Fig. 2. MULTIPLEXING (*From* Von Neumann, 1956, p. 63)

The majority organ is a mechanism capable of selecting multiplexed messages which are more likely to be correct. The adaptation of the majority organ is shown in figure 3. In the example, there are three

Multiplexed Majority Organ

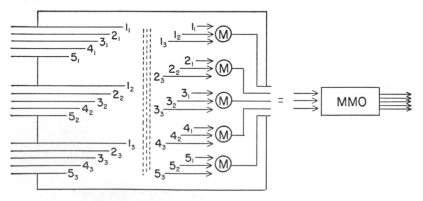

Fig. 3. MULTIPLEXED MAJORITY ORGAN
(*From* Von Neumann, 1956, p. 70)

input bundles of five lines each and five output bundles of three lines each. The output fibers are connected to the input fibers in such a way that each bundle has one fiber from each of the input bundles. In the figure the lines are not actually connected but coded by input and output. Thus 1_1 means that the line goes from the first input to the first output bundle, 1_2 from the second input to the first output bundle, 2_1 from the input to the second output bundle, etc. Here we have a system which can act according to a certain probability of input or, conversely, act with a certain probability to different types of input. Let us assume that the correct input consists in the stimulation of all ten lines in two bundles which would fire all the output lines. If there is a twenty percent error and only eight of the lines fire, it is still practically certain that the majority of the output lines fire. That is, even an error of this size is corrected in the system.

Complete System

We are now ready to proceed to construction of the system which will conform to our original requirement. The system consists of a combination of majority organs and scalers and is shown in figure 4.

The system must have two levels of functioning, both of which work like majority organs. That is, inputs of the same bundle are distributed over all the units and a certain critical proportion of live inputs in one unit is necessary for that unit to fire; a certain proportion of firing units is necessary for the whole system to fire.

(a) The first system is further distinguished by a scaler. A stimulation of any kind may leave an input live and thus less stimulation is needed the next time for the whole system to fire. The scaler may include a memory, thus it may be more easily stimulated after earlier stimulations. We shall call this first set the A-system.

(b) The second set is a simple majority organ without scalers. It fires when a specified majority of its input system has been stimulated. As its inputs are the outputs of the A-system, this means that it will be active if a stated majority of the A-organs is fired. We shall call this system the M-system.

We have now constructed a system P (consisting of the two sub-systems A and M) which fulfills the conditions laid down in equations (1) and (2). Inputs may change the A-system without leading to any output, but in doing so they change the probability of a later output. If the A-set is in a favorable condition then an additional stimulus may fire the M-set and hence produce an output for the whole system, without changing the A-set appreciably.

Complete Model
(only 3 of 5 parts shown)

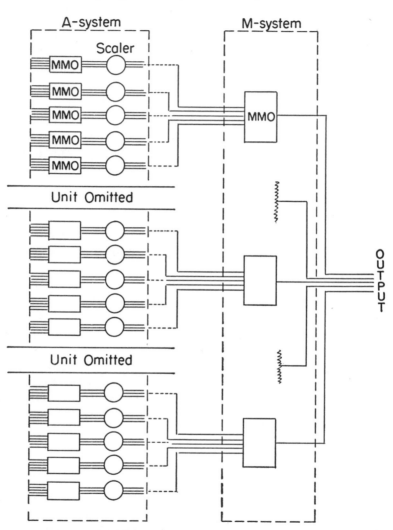

Fig. 4. COMPLETE MODEL (only 3 of 5 parts shown)

Interpretation of the System

The mathematical model just described is adaptable to an interpretation that illuminates the problem we are concerned with in this paper. The following coordinating definitions will be made:

The system P is defined as the person;

the inputs C are defined as communications;

the outputs B are defined as behavior;

the sub-system A (within P) is defined as attitude (of a person);

the sub-system M (within P) is defined as motoric or action system (of a person).

The two equations (1) and (2) are now interpreted as meaning:

(1) Behavior at any time is a function of communication and of the state of a person at a previous time; this describes the effect of authority communication.

(2) The state of the person at any time is a function of the state of the person at a previous time and a communication at a previous time; this describes the effect of influence communication.

We can further interpret multiplexing (the uses of bundles of inputs) as repetition of the content of messages in different form. One bundle corresponds to a certain kind of information, but each fiber corresponds to a different way of putting the message across.

Four Hypotheses

The system leads to some derivations about the effect of particular kinds of inputs or communications. Let us assume that some of the fibers in one bundle are stimulated. This will change some of the organs in the A-set toward a higher probability of firing. Increase in stimulation can proceed in two ways: an increasing number of fibers in the same bundle can be stimulated or some fibers in the other bundles can be stimulated.

In the first case, there will be an increase of readiness in all the parts of the A-set. The change in probability will thus be widespread, affecting an increasing number of elements in the A-system, but it amounts to only one unit in each part. This situation is therefore unlikely to fire the A-system itself, and to transmit an impulse to the M-system. Interpreted, this means that the same content transmitted in different forms will change attitudes, but is unlikely to lead to corresponding actions.

In the second case, fewer of the units or elements of the A-set are likely to be stimulated, but in some of the elements the increase will amount to several steps. Hence some of the units will have the sufficient proportion of live inputs and will be active and there is an appreciable likelihood of the whole A-system firing and stimulating the M-system. With a great distribution of input bundles being stimulated weakly, it is possible that just barely enough impulses will come out of the A-system to fire the M-system. In this case we have an output from P, but the situation is clearly unstable and depends on the input being kept up. This means that many messages of different content will lead to action, especially when favorable attitudes are present, but the action is unlikely to be kept up.

Thus, we have two hypotheses about the power of differing types of communication:

1. Repetition of the same or similar content in different form will lead to change in attitude, but not necessarily to corresponding actions; that is, these messages will have influence.

2. Single messages of differing content will lead to transition between attitude and action; this type of communication is appropriate to the exercise of authority, with only a fleeting change of attitude.

Going beyond the individual system, it is possible to make some inferences about the conditions under which different types of communication will be used and under which authority and influence will occur.

For this purpose we have to consider several systems P connected with each other, that is, a number of persons who interact and communicate with each other. Insofar as the output of each system is verbal, it can become a communication and hence an input for the other systems. What is the nature of the relationship between the systems necessary for two kinds of distribution of messages to result?

Let us consider the situation in which the A-systems of all participants are stable and also similar to each other. Stability will occur when in each unit more fibers than the critical proportion are stimulated. Then the units will keep firing even if some lines are changed to inactive conditions. Messages which run counter to the prevailing attitude—which neutralize part of the input—will be insufficient to change the attitude. The output of P, in this case, will reflect a fairly constant A-set and thus be constant itself. It will stimulate whole bundles or be repetitious in content. As the attitudes overlap, most of the communications will be conforming to the attitudes already existing and thus reinforce these attitudes. These are the conditions for producing influence.

The conditions describe the situation of individuals who agree strongly on many issues, whose interaction serves mainly to reinforce this common core in various ways until the attitudes (A-sets) are identical. This also implies that no individual has a different function from another, that the roles are interchangeable. This description tends to identify a team, in the sense of a group with "we-feeling" or "group spirit." As the theory does not include the motivation of members to enter a group but only the communication patterns, the usual definition of the group in terms of cohesiveness cannot be used. It has been shown, however, that groups defined in the two ways are closely related.

Because of the high redundancy, the relation of output to input in these systems will be low. However, the possible long-run effects may compensate for this low efficiency in the short run, and result in the creation of common attitudes which will lead to easier triggering and hence greater efficiency on later occasions. The relationship of amount of communication to efficiency depends therefore on the kind of redundancy, whether content or form, and on the time span considered.

The opposite condition is one in which all the systems are different and have unstable A-sets: They are likely to send out varied impulses resulting in behavior by other systems. This behavior will be varied as different parts of the A-sets are activated by different messages. As the messages will differ in content they will stimulate different bundles and perpetuate the differences in output of the different systems. These differences are not random variations as they are determined by the outputs of the other systems. In fact, we have here a model of functional interdependence.

The conditions of the systems describe a situation in which each member of an organization has a different role or function; hence his messages will be different, pertaining to a certain action which the recipient has to carry out. All recipients will be ready to carry out these actions, but their general attitudes are not likely to be affected. The processes described are thus characteristic of a formal organizational setup, the condition for authority relation.

We can summarize the results of our considerations of the interactions of the systems in two additional hypotheses:

3. Communication which is redundant in content but varied in form (corresponding to a few whole bundles) is

a. Likely to occur in cohesive groups

b. Likely to lead to a common framework of attitudes within a social system.

4. Communication which consists of messages on different topics with little redundancy in content is

a. Likely to occur in functionally interdependent formal organizations

b. Likely to lead to effective action within a social system.

Types of Conditions

This set of hypotheses can be summarized by constructing four types of communication situations out of the combination of redundancy of form and content:

1. If both form and content are low in redundancy, we have the vivid kind of discussion, varied in content which is characteristic of interpersonal, sociable situations.

2. If the content is high on information and the form is stereotyped or redundant, we have the organizational setup which performs work without changing opinions.

3. If content is redundant but the form is varied, the communication is of the kind which we associate with primary, face-to-face groups which have influence on attitudes but frequently do not lead to any corresponding actions.

4. Finally, if both form and content are redundant, communication becomes a ritual. This ritualistic communication is mainly characteristic of the sacred type of social structure, uniting a great number of people in common beliefs and common actions.

THREE APPLICATIONS OF THE MODEL

A. A Field Experiment: Communication in Planned Social Change

The preceding four hypotheses provide a set of relationships between group structure, communication, and the effects of attitudes and action. Although they have been stated as four different principles, the significance of the whole set will be illustrated to clarify the implications of the system and the operational meanings of the terms. The following is an experiment on educational methods of promoting family planning in Puerto Rico; (Back, Hill, and Stycos, 1957a; Hill, Stycos, and Back, 1959). The same experiment was replicated in its essential features in Jamaica and led to substantially the same results (Stycos and Back, 1957).

As subjects of this study a representative sample of rural lower-class families was selected. The wives in the families were matched on attitude toward family planning, adequacy of family organization (adequate communication between husband and wife), and information about methods of family planning. On the basis of previous research, these three sets of variables were assumed to represent the internal set necessary for action on family planning. The subjects could be classified into those who were favorable on all three factors and those who were deficient on one of them. The content of the educational program was designed to produce favorable changes in one or more of the factors.

The educational program was transmitted by two methods: group meetings and distribution of pamphlets. One set of respondents attended three meetings in which the topics of ideal-family size, communication with the spouse, or birth-control methods were discussed and demonstrated by various means such as movies, role playing, and analysis by a physician, while another set received the same information in a series of pamphlets. A third set was interviewed twice during the same time interval as a control group.

The two methods correspond roughly to the two modes of communication described in the previous section. Meetings employed a variety of techniques which put the main points into different forms and the effort to have all group members participate resulted in much repetition and weighing of the same content from different points of view. This method thus can be looked at as an application of the first type of communication. The use of pamphlets is an application of the second mode. Pamphlets are of necessity much more direct and less repetitious. In this case especially, the text was kept to a low-literacy level which prevented elaboration of the points to be made and kept the language structure to the repetitiousness of primer level.

The effect of the two methods shows a sharp division in change of readiness for action, start of action, and consistent continuation of it. Some of the respondents had been using contraception, although not consistently or efficiently, while others had never used any. We can divide the respondents according to previous use, in addition to the division by readiness for use (favorable preconditions of value, family organization, and information). After the experimental programs, the women were interviewed on two occasions: a reinterview after eight weeks and a follow-up after a year. Table 1 shows the effects of the educational methods on the different respondents who had and who had not practiced birth control previously. Only those subjects who were interviewed on all occasions are included. The data can be summarized and interpreted according to the influence model as follows:

Table I

INFLUENCE OF TYPE OF COMMUNICATION ON START, CONSISTENCY AND
REINFORCEMENT OF USE (FIELD EXPERIMENT IN CONTRACEPTION).

	NONUSER		USER		
	Meetings	Pamphlets	Meetings	Pamphlets	
Positive Effect* in					
Reinterview	31%	55%	50%	29%	
User in follow-up	67%	58%	79%	80%	
Nonuser in follow-up	33%	42%	21%	20%	
No Positive Effect in					
Reinterview	69%	45%	50%	71%	
User in follow-up	38%	19%	89%	56%	
Nonuser in follow-up	62%	81%	11%	44%	
N	42	60	38	35	

* Positive Effect means any use of contraception by nonusers and change to a better method or improvement in regularity by users. (From Table 127, Hill, Stycos & Back, 1959.)

a. Pamphlets were more likely than meetings to result in prompt action. More than half of the respondents who had received pamphlets and who had never used contraceptive methods previously did so in the weeks following the experiment while less than a third of nonusers in the meeting groups did so. The difference is even more striking in the ready group, who were initially favorable in all three factors. Of all the "ready" nonusers in the pamphlet treatment, who were contacted in the reinterview, seventy percent changed to users, while only forty-three percent in the meetings did so. Among the other respondent groups the difference is much smaller: thirty-two percent for the pamphlet condition against twenty-eight percent for the meeting condition. In fact, half the "ready" women in the control condition started using birth control in these weeks, the interview acting presumably as a message.

The individual messages distributed over a variety of content were just sufficient to fire enough of the A-system to activate the M-system; the effect of the pamphlets on the ready groups has been described as *saliency*.

b. Meetings tended to insure that action was consistently maintained and had a stronger effect on those women who had been using some birth-control method. In addition, the follow-up interview after one year showed that action which began as a consequence of the meetings had a greater chance to be maintained than that which followed receipt of pamphlets. The meeting had indeed a delayed effect which frequently manifested itself only after the reinterview.

The repetitious messages in meetings stabilize a few parts of the A-system. If sufficient parts are activated at all, and sometimes later events or perhaps even the stimulation of reinterview will do that, the resulting activation of the M-system will result in a consistently maintained action.

These results are in accordance with the first two hypotheses. The conditions under which these two communication systems were employed corresponded almost of necessity to the group and functional organization: the meetings were conducted in groups and techniques were adapted to the creation of influential group atmospheres. On the other hand, the pamphlets were delivered, without any discussion, by a messenger who had a clearly defined, somewhat distant, function from the respondents. In addition, further spread of the information in the communities followed corresponding lines: information about the meetings was more likely to be given to friends, that is, in group context, while information about the pamphlets was more likely to be given to those who were most in need of it, that is, along functional lines (Back, Hill, and Stycos, 1957b; Hill, Stycos, and Back, 1959). These data are explications of the third and fourth hypotheses. The meetings correspond to the primary face-to-face group situation in the typology mentioned above, while pamphlet distribution is more similar to the organizational setup.

The distinction of types of communication made here does not correspond to that of mass media and interpersonal communication. Both of these can have varied, redundant attitude-changing modes and direct, salient, high-information action-provoking modes. Under the particular conditions, among respondents who rarely receive pamphlets by mail or by personal messenger, printed media were the salient ones, while meetings gave the attitude-changing background. In the replication of the experiment in Jamaica, an additional method—individual casework—was used. The caseworkers were successful in inducing action, especially among rural (less ready) respondents. The pamphlets were still salient in effect, but the visits had the advantage of being tailored to the needs of the particular respondent. In this case, a personal contact method produced action, while another personal method, meetings, produced mainly change in attitude.

Other studies which have concentrated on an immediate effect on conforming action have found similar, sometimes surprising, effects. A case in point is an educational experiment by Torrance and Mason (1958) on persuading airmen to eat pemmican. This was a field study undertaken during actual survival maneuvers. Two methods showed themselves to be most effective in making the men eat the biscuits during the exercise and in inducing them to say that they would eat it again. They were instructed that part of the evaluation of their performance in the course would be their eating pemmican, and purely matter-of-fact information was supplied by the instructor. In contrast methods depending on example by the instructor and individual discussion showed a boomerang effect—they were less effective than the control group. As in the fertility studies, the control groups showed a considerable effect by themselves. The results can be summarized as: little communication with extremely intensive content (defining the problem as part of the general course or purely factual information) has considerable effect, and indirect communication (the gestural communication of example or personal discussion) has extremely little effect. As no follow-up on continued use was possible, we can interpret these data as an example of elicitation of initial action. In a functional organizational context and with formal, highly informational communication this type of effect can be attained. It is interesting to note that in an early experiment on a similar problem—eating a large number of salted crackers during an experimental session—the two most effective methods were: giving exact instructions for each part of the eating process and redefining the situation (Frank, 1944). Both these methods are similar to those found effective in Torrance's field experiment.

Brim (1954) makes a distinction between trial and adoption in a field experiment on changing mothers' feeding methods to greater permissiveness. Trials of the recommended system depended on the mothers' belief that the experimenter was a physician. This belief in authority did not lead, however, to consistent adoption of the method. Brim found three factors which did lead to adoption: acceptance of other sources giving the same advice, approval by the husband, and improved behavior of the child. All three of them implied reinforcement through other channels, that is, transmission of the same message in a new form. Here we can see the conditions which lead to consistent behavior in distinction to those which lead to only a few trials.

The two field experiments on different topics, with populations different from the Puerto Rican and Jamaican experiment, confirm the results and interpretations of the fertility studies.

B. Microscopic Analysis: Application to Content Analysis

Analysis of ordinary communication by amount of information, and of redundancy has not been attempted rigorously. Shannon and Weaver (1949) are explicit about omitting meaning and content and, even in the development of a semantic theory of information, only extremely simplified situations have been considered (Carnap and Bar-Hillel, 1952). If we want to analyze some actual communication within the framework presented here, we need at least an approximation to a method of content analysis which will provide an analogy to the different types of input.

We shall deal here with only two communication patterns, the pattern with high redundancy in content and low redundancy in form and the opposite one, low redundancy in content and high redundancy in form. These two patterns provide the best contrast to approach the analysis of communication. Here the type of redundant information which we associate with the stimulation of several lines in the same bundle is not simply a repetition of the same message, but the rephrasing in a different form. On the other hand messages, in which each clause carries new information frequently have a standardized form which makes it easy for the recipient to attend to the content. Thus one message can activate a line and lead to action.

Redundancy and variety in form of the message can be measured by comparing the length and structure of the different sentences in the message. An analysis of parts of speech can give a rough measure of the quantity of information in a passage or a message. If we want to send a message which contains a maximum of information in a minimum of words (as in a cable with high word rates) the main words to be used will be nouns or adjectives. It is reasonable to use the ratio of nouns and adjectives to total words as a measure of information.

In line with the first two hypotheses, communications which have as their main intent and effect change of attitude will show great variation in form and a relatively low percentage of the "content words" (nouns and adjectives), and the reverse will be true of communications which intend to initiate action. An analysis of this kind was made on two topics in which action or attitudes may be induced: politics and religion.

As an example of political power, two speeches by Franklin D. Roosevelt were analyzed (Zevin, 1946). Both were given in the same year, 1940, were carried over national radio networks, and hence had the same potential audience. The context of the two speeches was different, however. The first was given at the beginning of the year, at a Jackson Day dinner for party officials. It was directed mainly at people with a favorable attitude quite in advance of any concrete action (election campaign). This speech was intended principally to reinforce attitudes. The second speech was given at a party rally at Madison Square Garden, one week before the presidential election. This speech was directed immediately at obtaining votes, hence to initiate a specific action. The two speeches represent an attitude and an action appeal.

In the field of religion, sermons of two contemporary ministers with considerable popular appeal were compared: Billy Graham and Norman Vincent Peale. Both religious leaders exert their power in favor of a religious revival, both appeal to wide-range audiences which probably overlap considerably. Graham is a revivalist who urges an immediate "testimony" of revelation, while Peale exhorts his listeners to follow a general way of life ("positive thinking"). Graham represents an action-arousing and Peale an attitude-changing message. One of each minister's most effective sermons was used: Graham's "America's Decision" (given in 1953) and Peale's (Poling, 1944) "The Power Flows from the Cross."

In each of the four speeches the first fifty sentences were analyzed. As measures of variation of form, the variances of the sentence length, of the number of subordinate clauses, and of the proportions of nouns and of adjectives to total number of words in the sentences were used. Measures of information in the sentences were the mean proportion of nouns and adjectives. Table 2 shows the results of this analysis. With one exception the variances are larger in the attitude communications than in the corresponding action communications, most of them significantly so. On the other hand, although there is a consistent numerical difference in the predicted direction of the mean proportion of nouns and adjectives, only one of the four is statistically significant. As the differences in variances may be related to corresponding differences in means, especially between the two religious leaders, the relative dispersions (coefficients of variation) are also shown. In general, these coefficients preserve the differences shown in the variances; only one difference, that in the variability of number of subordinate clauses between Graham and Peale, seems to be due to the differences in means. On the other hand, the large reversal— in the variance of proportion of adjectives between the same two speeches —is also accounted for by the difference in the mean proportion, and the coefficients of variance differ in the predicted direction.

The type of content analysis of communications which has been proposed here shows itself as a first approximation to consistent measurement of information content and as a lead to data which confirm the theoretical model. The action communications have more nouns and adjectives, they have more uniform sentences which vary less in length and organization than the attitude communications. At the same time, the method is still quite crude and needs supplementation. In a different context, Yule (1944) has developed a method of vocabulary analysis, counting the occurrences of different words in an author's work. Yule defines a statistic K which measures the degree of occurrences of words. A large K designates certain words which are more likely to be used than others. Repetition of a word implies a degree of redundancy, that is, repetition of information. We can thus advance the hypothesis that the size of the K coefficient will be related to the attempts to influence attitudes through writing. The ranking of K coefficients in texts analyzed by Yule is as follows: the Gospel according to St. John has the largest coefficient; next comes Thomas à Kempis, a medieval monk and devotional writer; next John Bunyan, the author of *Pilgrim's Progress;* then Jean Charlier de Gerson, a medieval theologian; and finally Thomas B. Macaulay, the historian. This order seems to correspond to the rank order of the intent to influence attitudes.

The same type of analysis has been applied to an experiment relevant to hypotheses three and four which the author has been conducting with Lloyd H. Strickland. Only data which relate to these hypotheses will be considered here. Groups of three students each were given the task of constructing a pamphlet. Three jobs were defined: research for data, selection of design, and coordination. The students were led to believe

Table 2

Uniformity and Information in Attitude and Action Appeals

	A — POLITICAL (F. D. Roosevelt)			B — RELIGIOUS		
	Attitude (Jackson Day)	Action (Madison Square Garden)	Significance of difference or of F ratio	Attitude (Peale)	Action (Graham)	Significance of difference or of F ratio
VARIABILITY IN FORM						
Words per sentence						
Variance	558.08	182.81	<1%	206.00	69.70	<1%
Coefficient of variation	.8544	.5696		.6239	.5543	
SUBORDINATE CLAUSES PER SENTENCE						
Variance	1.91	1.05	<5%	2.97	.76	<1%
Coefficient of variation	1.50	1.13		1.32	1.5625	
PERCENT NOUNS IN SENTENCE						
Variance	118.00	36.78	<1%	88.52	76.19	n.s.
Coefficient of variation	.4862	.2527		.4613	.3856	
PERCENT ADJECTIVES IN SENTENCE						
Variance	63.00	57.55	n.s.	30.08	110.46	[<1%]*
Coefficient of variation	.8277	.6465		.8145	.0852	
MEASURES OF INFORMATION						
Mean percent of nouns	22.42	23.98	n.s.	20.40	22.64	n.s.
Mean percent of adjectives	9.58	11.74	n.s.	6.74	12.32	<1%
N	50	50		50	50	

* Contrary to hypothesis.

that they would be assigned to different jobs. The actual tasks were performed separately and, in fact, each student was a designer. It was clear that the work of the designer—evaluating the design of an excessively large number of Chamber of Commerce pamphlets—could not be completed in the time allotted, and it was also apparent that the coordinator had sufficient time left from his own task to help the designer. Communication was possible only by written messages. Two experimental conditions were introduced: In the *group* condition, team work was stressed, rewards were given to the group as a whole, and positions were considered to be interchangeable, presumably assigned by lot. In the *organization* condition, efficient organization for the work was stressed, rewards were given to individuals (though they were not competing with each other), and different functions were distributed by ability, presumably on the basis of tests.

The students were given four opportunities during the experimental session to write messages. For our two measures of information, percentage of nouns and adjectives, we have thus four possible comparisons each or a total of eight comparisons. Table 3 shows the eight pairs of mean percentages. In seven of the eight comparisons the organization condition produced a higher percentage of "content" words (significant at 5 percent level by sign test). In addition, a measure of variability of sentence length could be computed. As in this case, when we are comparing the communications of several individuals within each condition, we cannot assume that all the sentences produced in the organization condition will be more uniform than those in the group condition. We can infer, however, that each individual in the organization will produce sentences of uniform length in all his messages. Hence, the variances of the words in all the sentences of each student's messages were computed. The means of the variances in each condition (or rather the logarithm of the variances for a more normal distribution) are shown in the last column in Table 3. The organization condition shows a lower variability, that is, smaller variances (significant at 5 percent level, one-tailed t-test).

By taking actual examples of communication, and communication under special experimental conditions, the systems of analysis proposed here show promise of measuring the semantic content of communication and of being able to test mathematical models of social communication.

C. Social Change: The Two-Step Theory of Communication

The distinction between communication which changes or reinforces attitudes and that which leads to action underlies the two-step theory of

Table 3

UNIFORMITY AND INFORMATION UNDER GROUP AND
ORGANIZATION CONDITIONS (EXPERIMENTAL DATA)

	Group	Organization	Direction of Difference (+ according to hypotheses, − contrary to hypotheses)
Sentence Length			
Mean 100 (log of variance)	129.44	107.77	+
N	36	35	
Message I			
Mean Percent Nouns	15.73	17.1	+
Mean Percent Adjectives	8.20	18.5	+
N	15	9	
Message II			
Mean Percent Nouns	12.39	14.47	+
Mean Percent Adjectives	5.97	7.29	+
N	33	34	
Message III			
Mean Percent Nouns	19.7	15.67	−
Mean Percent Adjectives	8.63	10.33	+
N	16	9	
Message IV			
Mean Percent Nouns	10.60	15.18	+
Mean Percent Adjectives	6.97	9.18	+
N	34	33	

information flow stated by Lazarsfeld, Berelson, and Gaudet (1944). An excellent summary of its development is given by Katz (1957). He tries to explain the working of mass media by showing that they do not affect an atomized audience, but that they affect certain individuals (the opinion leaders) and that these in turn influence other members of their primary groups through interpersonal influence. A great amount of significant work has been done in identifying the opinion leaders, their characteristics, and those of the person whom they influence. The application of the communication model may further strengthen this theory.

Opinion leaders have been found to be more socially supported, more exposed to mass media, and also more subject themselves to personal influence than nonleaders. These characteristics describe people who adopt changes early and also those who then influence others to adopt them—

the two functions of the opinion leader. In large-scale surveys in which these opinion leaders are identified we cannot, of course, determine the exact nature of communications. We can, however, relate these differences to the type of communication which generally occurs. Both leaders and nonleaders are exposed to the same kind of mass media which lead to having a favorable predisposition, a somewhat prestimulated A-set in our model. The communications which they receive in this way are thus of the general attitude-arousal type. Why are certain persons more likely to start action? In accordance with the model, they are the persons who obtain more of the same type of communication which push their attitudes closer to action; further, they are more likely to receive pointed communications directed at them which make the A-system active enough to start the M-system. A unique action in the favorable direction (for example, a doctor using a new drug once, women trying some new food once) would not make them leaders within the group, and would not make them induce other people to follow the same action. But, exposing themselves to more media they become initially more favorable, and have more support for sustained action. Further, the central and socially secure position within their group means that their output—their known actions and communications—will be received by the other members of their acquaintance group. For the nonleaders this output will become action-directed communication only and will thus induce them to try this action. Thus among nonleaders action should depend primarily on their sociometric position while among leaders or isolates it would depend on the communications they receive. This has been verified in the studies on the two-step flow of communication.

A further corrollary can be stated, namely, that this type of opinion leadership is specific to the topic under consideration. This follows because opinion leadership is a combination of influence and authority. It is only possible in situations where a favorable predisposition exists originally, and additional exposure to the same type of communication—in addition to some direct action-communication—will lead one person to act and to continue to act in the same way. This additional interest which leads to the additional exposure will be distributed according to individual predilections. It becomes quite likely that on different topics other persons within the group will be in the equivalent position.

For this reason opinion leadership is different from political power and authority. This is generally concentrated in the same person notwithstanding the topic under consideration (Hunter, 1953). Hence, the communications are only action-directed, having, within limits, little regard to prevailing attitudes. On the other hand, they have to be repeated for each particular action or issue. Authority depends, therefore, on the social structure, on who is in a position to issue communications of this kind. The authority or community leader works within a functional organizational network, while opinion leaders work within primary, homogeneous groups.

RELATIONSHIP TO OTHER THEORIES

In general, psychological and sociological theories of power consider the relationships between more and less powerful persons, the bases for the existence of power, and the effect of power relations on group structure. The present theory, however, deals with the manner in which power is exerted, with the conditions and consequences of this manner. It is thus possible that this theory is compatible with several other theories; however, it will be instructive to indicate how the ideas used in this paper fit in with other concepts.

A person may be able to control another, that is have power in the sense indicated, for several reasons. Thus French and Raven (1959) distinguished five bases of interpersonal power: expertness, possibility of reward, coercion, attraction, and legitimacy. The first three clearly correspond to functionally interdependent relationships and can be expected to lead to authority relations with their appropriate communication patterns. Attraction, either personal or toward membership in a group, is likely to lead to a common framework of attitudes and hence is appropriate for influence. The last basis listed, legitimacy, represents a combination of the two types: if one person acquiesces to the power that can be exerted by another person having a specific relationship to him then communication from this source can change attitudes and behavior.

The bases of power appear in the present theory as additional organs, reinforcing the communication from a source and giving it an appropriate effect. Thus, legitimacy can be represented as an additional part of the A-set, being an attitude toward a person, which is already charged and which adds an additional impulse every time a communication from this person is received. A similar, partial, arrangement can be used to represent the working of the other bases of power, adding impulses only into the A-set or M-set respectively.

Kelman (1958) classifies power into three categories: compliance, identification, and internalization. Compliance is defined as acceptance of orders without a basic change of attitude; identification primarily as an effort to be like another person and consequent change in his direction; internalization as adoption of the content of an opinion. Compliance is analogous to activation of the M-system only; the difference between identification and internalization does not fit exactly into the present model. Kelman implies, moreover, that internalization leads to a more stable change than identification and also that internalization includes some rational acceptance and is more content oriented than identification. Identification would thus involve mainly a change in the A-set and be analogous to the attraction base of power in French's classification. This interpretation seems reasonable if one considers the connection between personal attraction and identification. Internalization, on the other hand, can be taken as the effect of legitimate power. Its effect can be represented in the model in a manner indicated above and, like legitimate power, includes authority and influence.

A different approach to the bases of power is taken by Thibaut and Kelley (1959). They view the power which one person has over another as a function of the gratification he can provide for him. The mutual possibilities for gratification and with it the power relationships can be formalized by payoff matrices. People will act in a way which maximizes their gratification insofar as they are able to do so. The adjustments of several members of a group in their attempts to secure the best possible outcome result in a certain pattern of behavior. This pattern then becomes accepted as a norm. This theory, then, views initiation of action as the basic power situation—the A-set is generated out of the M-set. The type of relationship with which they start is a bargaining condition, that is what we have called a functional, organizational relationship. In this situation initiation of action is the most likely effect of power. The formation of norms is accompanied by formation of cohesive groups, thus preserving the relationship which is hypothesized in the model of this paper.

Thibaut and Kelley's theory is different from the other theories of the bases of power as, instead of making qualitative distinctions, it describes only quantitative relationships, as shown in their interaction matrices. Their deductions as to the nature of the interrelationships between group relations and exercise of power at any one time are the same as our hypotheses three and four. However, they are led to the additional deduction that the activation of an M-system is always prior to the establishment of a settled A-system. This question is not covered in the present model.

The analysis of four types of social systems according to the kind of communication used has its parallel in other theories. One of them is the discussion of Kelman (1958) mentioned previously. Compliance corresponds to the organizational condition, the induction of behavior without corresponding change in attitude. Similarly identification corresponds to the primary, face-to-face group, and internalization to ritualistic communication. The missing type, the sociable situation, with low redundancy in content and form, leads by hypothesis to little attitude and behavior change and falls therefore outside of Kelman's discussion. By contrast Watson's (1958) analysis of styles of interaction concentrates on sociability. She defines three styles—work oriented, familial, and sociable—according to five criteria. One of the criteria, conversational style, deals with the manner in which topics are discussed and is similar to the classification proposed in this paper. The work style emphasizes progress, going to different topics, and thus corresponds to the organizational situation. The familial style is repetitive, or redundant, and is an example of ritualistic communication. The sociable style stresses both new content and a dramatic form, thus has low redundancy in form and content; it is named identically in both theories. The fourth category, the face-to-face group is not distinguished in Watson's theory from the work-directed style. This difference only becomes apparent if novelty and repetition are treated separately for form and content.

In the discussion of different theories of the bases of power, we have seen that the distinction between influence and authority helps in analyzing some implications of this theory. The principle of this distinction—and the corresponding distinction between the A-set and M-set within the model—is not new. Allport (1937) summarizes under the name of "determining tendency" a number of concepts which psychologists have been using. What the model does is to lead to an explicit statement of the relation between interpersonal relations and effect on attitude and action on one hand and with communication patterns on the other. This in turn can lead to a precise analysis of the communication itself and of its effects.

CONCLUSION

Starting with the common problem of several disciplines—how power is exerted—an attempt was made to approach this question through an analysis of the communication process. Using some recent developments in applied mathematics, automata theory, and communication theory a model was set up which could account for the effects of different kinds of communication. The main result of this analysis was the definition of two kinds of communication: repetition of a few main points by different means, and single transmission of many points in standard form. The former type was seen to be related to establishment of attitudes, that is to influence, and to occur in cohesive groups; the latter type was related to initiation of action, to authority, and occurs in functional organizations. The application of these hypotheses was then shown in several contexts; in field experiments, in content analysis, and in the theory of opinion leadership.

The task of a leader may be to exert authority or influence, or both. The present theory points up the need to relate the interpretation of a leader's style and communication patterns in the light of the social situation and the effect desired. The empirical data shown present several ways of measuring three variables—communication, type of interaction, and effect—in accordance with the concepts required by the model. Further development of the measures will make it possible to state the exact leadership style required under different, specified conditions. In the rough division which resulted in the four types of power situations, we can derive, even at the present stage, the appropriate leadership styles. The leader in the social situation actually has no power; he achieves a position of popularity through vivacious conversation which does not allow him to exert authority or attempt influence. The leader in the primary group situation will be most effective if he does not attempt to deal with many points but presents these by various methods. Further, he will achieve unanimity of opinion without being able to initiate efficient action. Conversely, if a leader is principally interested in establishing a common climate of opinion, without being concerned at present with actions, creation of primary groups and use of the corresponding kind of communication patterns will be appropriate. If, however, he is mainly interested in securing immediate action, he will be more successful in an authority situation, the organizational setup with prescribed forms of communication and the bare minimum of necessary content without redundancy. Finally, for the creation of an extremely stable social situation, the leader will content himself with highly ritualized, formal pronouncements which do less to communicate than to reaffirm the common values. This is the function of many official speeches, proclamations and rituals which keep continuity in societies and institutions while providing a basis for large-scale common actions.

At this point we reach again the question of the place of power in society. This theory deals with only one aspect of power, communication. It does not deal with the bases of power, the sanctions which are available, nor with the channels and interconnections of the society within which power is exerted. It can, however, be related to theories which deal with these problems and be helpful in their analysis. The theory starts with one of the basic ways in which interaction within any social system is possible. Assuming that a system is in existence, the interaction and communication between different parts of the system and between different persons can be measured; and from this measure the effect can be estimated. We can then see which relationships will lead to common attitudes and beliefs, which are conducive to command action, which to self-sustaining effort. We can analyze the communication process and derive from it the effect and the function which it can have and the kind of relationship where it is likely to occur.

REFERENCES

ALLPORT, G. W. *Personality.* New York: Holt, Rinehart and Winston, 1937.

BACK, K. W., HILL, R., AND STYCOS, J. M. The Puerto Rican field experiment in population control. *Hum. Relat.,* 1957, *10,* 315–334. (a)

BACK, K. W., HILL, R., AND STYCOS, J. M. Manner of original presentation and subsequent communication. *Psychol. Rep.,* 1957, *3,* 149–154. (b)

BRIM, O. G., JR. The acceptance of new behavior in child-rearing. *Hum. Relat.,* 1954, *7,* 473–493.

CARNAP, R. AND BAR-HILLEL, Y. An outline of a theory of semantic information. M.I.T., Res. Lab. Electronics Tech. Rep. 247, October, 1952.

EASTON, D. The perception of authority and political change. In C. J. FRIEDRICH (Ed.), *Authority.* Cambridge, Mass.: Harvard, 1958.

FRANK, J. D. Experimental studies in personal pressure and resistance, II. Methods of overcoming resistance. *J. gen. Psychol.,* 1944, *30,* 43–58.

FRENCH, J. R. P., JR. A formal theory of social power. *Psychol. Rev.,* 1956, *63,* 181–194.

FRENCH, J. R. P., JR. AND RAVEN, B. The bases of social power. In D. CARTWRIGHT (Ed.), *Studies in social power.* Ann Arbor, Mich.: Research Center for Group Dynamics, 1959. Pp. 150–167.

GRAHAM, B. *America's decision.* Minneapolis: The Billy Graham Evangelical Association, 1953.

HILL, R., STYCOS, J. M., AND BACK, K. W. *The family and population control.* Chapel Hill: Univ. of North Carolina, 1959.

HUNTER, F. *Community power structure.* Chapel Hill: Univ. of North Carolina, 1953.

KATZ, E. The two-step flow of communication: an up-to-date report on a hypothesis. *Publ. Opin. Quart.,* 1957, *21,* 61–78.

KELMAN, H. C. Compliance, identification and internalization: Three processes of attitude change. *J. Conflict Resolution,* 1958, *2,* 51–60.

LAZARSFELD, P., BERELSON, B., AND GAUDET, H. *The people's choice.* New York: Duell, 1944.

POLING, D. A. *A treasury of great sermons.* New York: Greenberg, 1944.

SHANNON, C. AND WEAVER, W. *The mathematical theory of communication.* Urbana: Univ. of Illinois, 1949.

STYCOS, J. M. AND BACK, K. W. *Prospects for fertility reduction.* New York: Conservation Foundation, 1957.

THIBAUT, J. W. AND KELLEY, H. H. *The social psychology of groups.* New York: Wiley, 1959.

TORRANCE, E. P. AND MASON, R. Instructor effort to influence: an experimental evaluation of six approaches. *J. educ. Psychol.,* 1958, *49,* 211–218.

VON NEUMANN, J. Probabilistic logics and the synthesis of reliable organisms from unreliable components. In C. E. SHANNON AND J. MCCARTHY (Eds.), *Automata Studies.* Princeton, N. J.: Princeton, 1956. Pp. 43–98.

WATSON, JEANNE. A formal analysis of sociable interaction. *Sociometry,* 1958, *21,* 269–280.

YULE, G. U. *The statistical study of literary vocabulary.* Cambridge, England: Cambridge, 1944.

ZEVIN, B. D. (Ed.). *Nothing to fear: The selected addresses of Franklin Delano Roosevelt.* Boston: Houghton, 1946.

PART II

*Leadership
and Interpersonal Behavior
in the Small Group*

10

The Contribution of the Leader to the Effectiveness of Small Military Groups

M. Dean Havron
Joseph E. McGrath

Human Sciences Research, Inc.

INTRODUCTION

This paper summarizes and discusses research findings on leadership from a series of studies of small military groups conducted by the authors and their associates.[1] The studies were supported by a series of sponsoring military research agencies, with the particular focus of each study varying according to the sponsor's area of concern.[2]

---

[1] A number of scientists contributed to the research program discussed in this paper. Major contributors include W. A. Lybrand, P. G. Nordlie, and J. A. Whittenburg, formerly of Psychological Research Associates, now of Human Sciences Research, Inc., and F. Loyal Greer, now with General Electric Company.

[2] Personnel Research Branch, TAGO: Studies of individual and group predictors of unit proficiency (*see* references numbered 1, 2, 4, 6, 7, 8, 9).

Survival Research Laboratory, AFPTRC: Studies of individual and group predictors of air crew proficiency in survival situations (*see* reference numbered 5).

Human Resources Research Office, George Washington University: Studies of the effectiveness of variations in infantry unit training (*see* reference numbered 13).

Operations Research Office, Johns Hopkins University and Combat Operations Research Group, CONARC: Studies of unit composition, organization and command as they affect proficiency of small infantry combat units (*see* references numbered 10, 11, 12, 14, 15).

None of these studies was oriented toward experimental study of leadership per se. However, since leadership is critical to selection, training, and organization of military groups, study results shed a great deal of light on problems of selection, training of leaders, and determination of optimal organizational size.

The studies were not designed as an integrated series. However, they used similar methodology and, in many cases, later work attempted to validate prior findings. A total of about 500 small military task groups were tested under simulated combat and survival conditions.

DESCRIPTION OF THE RESEARCH PROGRAM

Nature of the Criterion Tests

The field performance tests that provided criterion measures of unit effectiveness were small scale standardized field maneuvers of six to eight hours continuous duration. They were carefully built to incorporate most of the common and critical tactical duties of the rifle squads and the most common and critical evasion and survival duties of Air Force crews. Infantry squads were tested under daylight and night conditions. Air Force crews were tested in daylight only (5). Test-development procedures and test administration are described in various research reports (5, 6, 8, 9).

The criterion was developed from combat accounts and incidents and in close cooperation with personnel of the military schools responsible for establishing tactics and doctrine. Objective scores were obtained by trained umpires using detailed performance-rating forms.

Umpires were trained intensively to insure valid and reliable ratings. Reliability estimates were obtained on about 200 of the tested units. Average rater-rater reliability for studies of units selected from populations of Army and Air Force units was .87 (5, 8, 9). Average reliabilities of test scores of studies in which the research team trained or composed the units (and thus reduced individual differences between units) was .81 (13). These reliabilities, we feel, are remarkably high considering the fluid nature of the tactical performance situation in which they were obtained. Thus, the tests yielded criterion scores sufficiently reliable to permit assessment of the various predictive instruments.

Criterion scores were combined and analyzed in a number of ways. This paper is primarily concerned with those relationships in which characteristics of the unit *leader* are related to *unit* performance effectiveness.

The Predictive Instruments

A battery of paper-and-pencil tests was administered to units prior to administration of the criterion in an attempt to predict field performance. Beginning with our first Army unit study (6), our battery of predictive instruments continued to grow as we learned more and as additional researchers, with fresh points of view, joined our team. In later studies (3, 7, 8, 9) some 60 predictive instruments were used.

Leader predictors can be classified into three general areas: measures of personality characteristics of unit leaders; of intelligence, job knowledge, and the various abilities of leaders; and of leader motivation. Similar measures, including measures of interpersonal relationships, were obtained on group members. Each of these general areas was represented by several specific tests.

Some consisted of existing tests, or slightly modified versions of standard tests. For example, we used GCT scores from Army records as one indicator of intelligence. Other predictive devices were developed by the research team and were more specific to the tasks of the groups under study. For example, we developed an 80-item test of rifle-squad-leader job knowledge which turned out to be the best single predictor of *total squad* performance effectiveness.

Through the series of studies, many of these predictive instruments consistently showed significant relationships with unit effectiveness. A few measures which appeared to be significant in one study did not hold up in later validations. Only predictive instruments which showed consistently significant correlations between leader characteristics and over-all unit effectiveness are dealt with in this paper.

RESULTS AND DISCUSSION

Summary of Most Consistent Predictive Measures

Among Army squads (but not Air Force crews) the predictors which consistently showed the highest relationships with unit effectiveness were measures of leader job knowledge and measures of leader intelligence. On successive studies, both correlated between .35 and .50 with unit effectiveness scores (7, 8). However, we identified several cases of leaders who had low intelligence-test scores and high or fairly high job-knowledge scores, and whose squads scored high on the criterion.

The next highest set of consistent predictors were measures of leader knowledgeability (4). Although there were several variations of such measures, they were basically estimates of how accurately the leader could describe his men in terms of their (objectively tested) intelligence and abilities, their interpersonal attitudes, and their job-related motivations. These correlations were approximately .30, significant at the .01 level in the groups we tested. The good leader apparently "knows his men" and the poor one doesn't.

Two measures of leader characteristics which we developed showed next highest correlations among Army groups. These were measures of General Army Adjustment and measures of Peripheral Nervousness (an attempt to assess the emotional instability of the leader which is manifested as hypertension, nervousness and over excitability [9]). Scores on both of these measures correlated consistently and significantly (near .25) with the criterion for Army units. The measure of Peripheral Nervousness also correlated significantly with performance in those Air Force crews identifiable as highly motivated (5).

Another consistent predictor was a measure of the discrepancy between unit members' perceptions of an *ideal* leader and their perceptions of their *own* leader's actual role behavior. Men were asked how an ideal leader should act with regard to a particular situation, then how their present leader acted. Discrepancies between men's evaluations of actual and ideal leader for each group member were summed. Scores on this measure correlated significantly with unit performance differences *even though* the member-ideal varied from man to man in the *same squad,* as well as from one "good" squad to another. Thus, this finding indicates that the effectiveness of leader in role lies in his ability either to *appear* to behave in a manner consistent with the divergent expectations of each of the members, or by some means to make members form a leader ideal that is consonant with their perception of his actual behavior (7).

For Army squads, the predictive power of the entire battery approached a multiple R of .60. Of this total, a multiple correlation of approximately .50 can be obtained by use of leader-predictor measures alone. This seems to indicate that about two-thirds ($.50^2/.60^2$) of the predictable variance in small combat unit behavior is attributable to the leader, his characteristics and his performance. This inference is likely to be incorrect, however, and may in fact point up the limited methodology available for combining or weighting the contributions of characteristics of group members to total group performance.

Several groups of predictive measures which did *not* consistently relate to unit proficiency are also worth noting. These include sociometric measures (leader nominations given and received) and measures of authoritarian attitudes. The former showed a significant correlation in an initial pilot study of small Army units (1, 2), but the relationship did not hold up consistently for later studies (8, 13), neither did authoritarian attitudes of leaders or members predict unit proficiency. There were indications that similarity of authoritarian attitudes among members and between members and leaders may have a relatively weak correlation with unit proficiency. The same low but positive correlation is suggested with respect to homogeneity of other attitudes, though correlations between homogeneity of attitudes and the criterion are seldom statistically significant.

In summary, the leader's contribution to small military-combat groups appears to include his intelligence, his job skill, his knowledge of the skills and feelings of his men. His emotional stability and attitudes toward military life are important as is his ability to be perceived by his men as relatively near their leader-ideal. While these findings summarize leader characteristics that predict the proficiency of his infantry unit, the series of studies includes a number of not so well validated but highly provocative findings which shed light on the nature of the leader's role in small military groups. Some of these findings are discussed below.

Army *versus* Air Crew Studies

Many of the correlations between predictors and criterion found in the series of studies of Army units did not hold for the attempts to predict air-crew-survival performance. A number of factors in the test situation itself as well as the way in which tested units perceived their training and testing could have accounted for these differences in results (5). The field tests were usually perceived by the Army units tested, and especially by the squad leaders, as evaluations of them in their primary military job. On the other hand, Air Force crews undergoing the survival field test did not look upon either that test or the entire survival program as a part of their basic job. Many were members of interceptor or bomber crews; they took pride in their flying skills, but not necessarily in survival proficiency. Furthermore, in the Army situation good performance was rewarded in the form of favorable recommendations to platoon and company, and in the form of special passes for the best-performing units.

Unlike the Army situation, Air Force crews were tested during one day of a two-week training course. Our researchers had no control over this training course. Observations of Air Force crews and interviews with them indicated that most felt that survival training was a thankless task. There was no reward for the best crew. Crew members, by and large, had been assigned from desk jobs or from interceptor or bomber squadrons to strenuous physical training in the Sierra Mountains. There are strong, though not conclusive, indications from our data and observations that the prevailing student motivation was to reduce misery rather than to learn. It seems reasonable to conclude that in a situation where motivation is at a low ebb, or very possibly negative toward the task assigned by the formal structure, measures of job knowledge, individual personality characteristics, and so on, are not likely to show consistent correlations with a criterion. However, even in the cold and misery of the Sierra winter, students regarded the one-day tests developed and administered by our scientists as a highly valuable training experience.

Insights into "The Good Squad Leader"

Many insights about leadership were obtained from interviews with all members of the 13 best-scoring squads and the 13 that scored lowest on the criterion (7). Since these 26 were selected from a total of 67 squads tested, they represented fairly extreme values.

Rather marked differences between low- and high-scoring squads were noted. There were strong similarities among leaders and members in the low-scoring squads. They were not motivated; they were not responsive to their environment. Consequently, they appeared to be a rather colorless mass of men with few distinguishing characteristics of any sort. Within the high-scoring squads, however, there were often marked differences in personalities, direction of drive, and concepts of leadership. The leaders and often at least two or three of the members of these squads appeared more intelligent, more likely to initiate action, more interested in the field work and in the world about them.

These are largely clinical impressions. They are validated to some extent by the fact that leaders of high-scoring groups did score higher on intelligence tests and on measures of motivation. The important point, however, is that while leaders and certain members of high-scoring groups had apparently thought more about their problems, their individual means for solving them varied markedly. This fact, as well as other indications of marked differences among such high-scoring squads, has import for uses of statistical averages to compare effective and ineffective groups.

Perhaps in half of the high-scoring squads the leader approximated the usual stereotype of a "good leader." But there were notable exceptions. In the best squad of all, the leader had a low intelligence test score, and a mediocre job-knowledge test score. During the field test he did not seem to perform too well. However, his men gave him a tremendous amount of support and helped him through.

Another of the high-scoring squads was led by a man who was thoroughly disliked by most of his squad members, although they respected him for his thorough knowledge of his job as field leader. He was not interviewed because he went AWOL. Still another leader was highly respected by his men, although contrary to their belief, he felt little respect for them. He played the role of respecting his men, because, as he explained in the interview, this was the way to get things done.

We designated one of the statistically significant characteristics of leaders in the interview study as *willingness to act*. The measure of this characteristic was made on the basis of certain field observations. Many times when there was a plain call for exercise of leadership in a situation which was ambiguous and offered no clear-cut course of action, those leaders who took the initiative, who gave *some* order (even though not clearly the correct one), seemed to enjoy the confidence of their men and to receive more support than leaders who waited. This characteristic was tested in a situational test as follows: The experimenter seated the squad leaders of effective and ineffective squads one at a time in his interview room. During the interview he left the room on some pretext, walked to the next room and started ringing a field telephone, the other outlet of which was across the room from where the squad leader sat. Almost all of the effective squad leaders answered the phone, most of them after only a few rings. Most of the ineffective squad leaders did not answer it at all, even after ten rings.

This interview study produced several insights which we put to use in a later study of squad training. Discovery that one of the best squads was led by a man low in intelligence and average job knowledge was exploited, as we will indicate later. Another surprising finding was also exploited. We had assumed that the better the intrasquad leadership structure was understood, the better the squad would perform. From this assumption, we had hypothesized that squads in which *only* the leader gave orders would be the more effective. We tested this hypothesis in the interview study and found that not only was it false, but the contrary hypothesis was true beyond the .01 level of significance. That is, squads wherein members felt free to give orders to one another when the situation seemed to warrant such action performed better than those in which only the leader gave orders.

Leadership Training

In a study of squad training conducted under HumRRO sponsorship in 1955 (13), part of our effort was directed toward the development of a concept of leadership and a feeling of the need for good leadership in all members of the unit. Consequently, we set out early to impress trainees that the success and the very lives of combat-unit members are interdependent, that teamwork is required, that the careless mistake of one man can lead to disaster for the whole group. By both direct and indirect means we showed trainees that leadership was necessary, and that whatever the personality or capabilities of the leader, the leadership *function* must be properly performed.

As another guiding concept, we assumed that more than one type of leadership can be effective, and that the best leadership for a particular group depends in large part upon the make-up of that group and on the ability and personality characteristics of its formal leader. A common military concept has the leader originating all orders, announcing them, and supervising their execution. We encountered a number of leaders who wanted to run their groups in just this way and who were quite good at it. However, we found other personality characteristics often accompanied by lower level of ability and job knowledge among the trainee leaders, and successfully developed a training approach by which we could produce effective units, even with formal leaders of average ability or with leaders who did not wish to employ fully the authoritarian structure.

Observations from prior studies had indicated that leadership frequently breaks down because events occur too quickly for the leader to assimilate and act upon them intelligently. In this study, those conditions which overburden the leader were anticipated and squad members were designated as responsible for suggesting an order to the leader if he did not notice the occasion for it or remember to give it. Group members had to appreciate that the orders still had to be channelled *through* the leader, that is, the leader had to give them his sanction by repeating them. Further, he had to know what was going on. Thus, a man would suggest an order to the leader, who would generally act upon it by announcing it and supervising its execution. This system of leadership sharing greatly improved the leader's ability to handle fast-moving situations.

Perhaps the most remarkable aspect of this training program was that it generated in the groups in question a concept of leadership that was appreciated, irrespective of who held the particular leader position. We have excellent validation of this statement. At the conclusion of the training program one test was administered which involved a mission in which the leader and his assistant were both "killed." The problem of the unit was to complete its mission. We tested 24 squads we had trained and another 24 Army-trained squads in this "leaderless" mission. We encountered a finding that is rare in socio-psychological data. There was *no* overlap in performance scores between the two groups. All of the squads trained by methods we had developed scored higher than any of the

24 Army-trained squads (8, 13). It was obvious to those who umpired both groups that in the Army-trained squads the members depended entirely upon the leader to take initiative. As a result, once the formal leadership was withdrawn, the unit did a very poor job. On the other hand, in the squads trained by experimental methods, although both leader and assistant leader were removed and no one had been specifically designated as third leader, someone inevitably took over and the unit's performance on the mission was almost as good as the performance of those same squads when the leaders were present.

This is a dramatic illustration, we think, of one of the more important facets of leadership. A group can act effectively and in a co-ordinated way even with a leader of indifferent ability or can reorganize quickly without leaders, if the *concept of leadership and how it is to be exercised operationally* is learned and appreciated by all group members.

Leadership and Group Size

One key question investigated in the ORO sponsored studies of Army-unit organization (10, 11, 12, 15) was that of the optimal size of the basic unit. Since there are a variety of leadership structures, which confound the question of size as related to performance, we rephrased the research question: What is the optimal number of men that one leader, unassisted, can control and supervise?

The question, although apparently simple, is an extremely complex one in full tactical context. Obviously, the number of men a leader can effectively control is a function of the ability and training of both the leader and his men. Less obviously, the effectiveness of control of a given sized unit is a function of the type of mission, the nature of the terrain, the vegetation, changes in visibility from day to night, and a host of tactical conditions, not the least of which is the intensity and pattern of enemy action.

Nevertheless, some size has to be adopted for the basic unit, and we felt that we might be able to generate important information—at least with respect to upper and lower bounds to squad size—by an experimental approach. We organized, trained and tested a number of squads in each of several sizes (four-, five-, six-, seven-, eight-, and eleven-man units) with a single unassisted leader. We tested eight units of each of these types in a set of tactical missions extending over six hours and incorporating a variety of patterns of enemy action, terrain and vegetation.

When the number of men in the units was varied between four and eight (leader/men ratio of from one to three up to one to seven), there appeared at first to be a "zone of indifference," that is performance differences as a function of unit size did not vary markedly. However, when the more difficult tactical situations were analyzed (14), it became apparent that squad leaders of the larger units were maintaining unit effectiveness at a greater cost—a higher activity level, more leader exposure to enemy fire, and so on. As the difficulty of the situation increased, it became less feasible to compensate in this fashion with the larger-sized units, and effectiveness was degraded. The eleven-man squads wherein one leader tried to control ten men were definitely too large. Performances of eleven-man squads headed by a single, unassisted leader were quite poor.

Within the size range from four- to eight-man units, intensive analysis suggested that the six-man unit performed better than units of other sizes. We had, of course, experimentally controlled variables that could be so controlled practically. There were other variables that could not be controlled experimentally. Consequently, we carried out a number of covariance operations. Each of them tended to sharpen the bend in the curve at size 6. Thus, it appeared that somehow size 6 (one leader and five men) may be the optimum number of men for rifle squads that operate under the leadership structure used in this study.

SUMMARY

The findings of these studies contribute to a more effective understanding of leadership phenomena. Numerous measures of leader characteristics (ability, job-knowledge, knowledge of his men, emotional stability, role behavior, willingness to act) consistently predict total unit effectiveness. The differences between Army and Air Force crews indicate that motivation—of the leader and of all the men—is also an important contributor; in fact data obtained from Air Force crews suggest that adequate motivation is a necessary condition and must be fairly high before other measures designed to predict performance begin to operate.

It was found that there is more than one effective leadership pattern. Consequently, the scientist should talk of the *forms* of leadership rather than of a unitary concept of leadership. One important direction for future research is, of course, to try to trace out the various patterns of effective leadership, hopefully a few in number, and to tie down antecedent and consequent conditions associated with them.

While these studies were not designed to investigate leadership per se, the possibilities for training in effective leadership are evident from our results. We were able to develop highly effective units even with leaders of mediocre ability, primarily by inculcating in the men an appreciation of the need for leadership and by assigning them responsibilities for monitoring the leader and helping him to initiate action. The success of this training has general implications for training of leaders and groups.

REFERENCES

GOODACRE, D. M. Group characteristics of good and poor performing combat units. *Sociometry*, 1953, *16*, 168–178. [1]

GOODACRE, D. M. The use of a sociometric test as a predictor of combat unit effectiveness. *Sociometry*, 1951, *14*, 148–152. [2]

GREER, F. L. *Small group effectiveness.* Philadelphia: Institute for Research in Human Relations, 1955. (Contract No. NONR–229[00].) [3]

GREER, F. L., GALANTER, E. H., AND NORDLIE, P. G. Interpersonal knowledge and individual and group effectiveness. *J. abnorm. soc. Psychol.*, 1954, *49*, 411–414. [4]

GREER, F. L., PEARSON, W. O., AND HAVRON, M. D. *Evasion and survival problems and the prediction of crew performance.* Lackland Air Force Base, Texas: Air Force Personnel and Training Research Center, Dec., 1957. (Technical Report AFPTRC–TR–57–14, ASTIA Doc. No. AD 146 426.) [5]

HAVRON, M. D., FAY, R. J., AND GOODACRE, D. M. *Research on the effectiveness of small military units.* Washington, D. C.: Institute for Research in Human Relations, April, 1951. (Personnel Section Report No. 855–Department of the Army.) [6]

HAVRON, M. D., GREER, F. L., AND GALANTER, E. H. *An interview study of human relationships in effective infantry rifle squads.* Washington, D. C.: Institute for Research in Human Relations, December, 1952. (Personnel Section Report No. 983.) [7]

HAVRON, M. D., et al. *The assessment and prediction of rifle squad effectiveness.* Arlington, Virginia: Psychological Research Associates, Nov., 1954. (PRA Report No. 54–11.) [8]

HAVRON, M. D., et al. *The effectiveness of small military units.* Washington, D. C.: Institute for Research in Human Relations, Sept., 1952. (Personnel Section Report No. 980.) [9]

HAVRON, M. D., et al. *Experimental investigation of tables of organization and equipment of infantry rifle squads. Part I.* Washington, D. C.: Psychological Research Associates, March, 1954. (PRA Report No. 54–2.) *(CONFIDENTIAL)* [10]

HAVRON, M. D., et al. *Experimental investigation of tables of organization and equipment of infantry rifle squads. Part II.* Washington, D. C.: Psychological Research Associates, Jan., 1955. (PRA Report No. 55–1.) [11]

HAVRON, M. D., *et al.* *A research study of infantry rifle squad TOE.* Washington, D. C.: Psychological Research Associates, Dec., 1955, (PRA Report No. 55–11.) *(CONFIDENTIAL)* [12]

HAVRON, M. D., *et al.* *A research study of the tactical training of the infantry rifle squad.* Washington, D. C.: Psychological Research Associates, June, 1955. (PRA Report No. 64–10, HumRRO Subcontract 650–017.) [13]

KASSEBAUM, R. G., *et al.* *Effect of dense terrain on small unit controllability.* Washington, D. C.: Psychological Research Associates, March, 1956. (PRA Report 56–7.) *(CONFIDENTIAL)* [14]

WHITTENBURG, J. A., *et al.* *A study of the infantry rifle squad TOE.* Washington, D. C.: Psychological Research Associates, March, 1956. (PRA Report No. 56–3, Vol. 1–11.) [15]

11

Leadership and Leadership Effectiveness Traits: A Reconceptualization of the Leadership Trait Problem[1]

Fred E. Fiedler

University of Illinois

As far as most social psychologists are concerned, leadership-trait theory has gone the way of Theoretical and Applied Phrenology. Gibb (1954) summarized the prevailing thinking by his statement "reviews such as that by Stogdill reveal that numerous studies of the personalities of leaders have failed to find any consistent patterns of traits which characterize leaders." He acknowledged that leadership traits may well exist, although none have been recognized, and he advanced an alternative explanation that leadership is a complex job which probably does not call out a consistent pattern of functional roles.

And yet, we know of men who consistently managed to build up ineffective groups and sick organizations, while there are others "who could not

[1] This paper was written for the ONR–LSU symposium while the author was on sabbatical leave of absence on a Fulbright Research Grant at the Municipal University of Amsterdam. It is a pleasure to acknowledge the helpful comments by Prof. H. J. C. Duijker and Dr. N. Frijda of the University of Amsterdam, and Dr. C. Boekestein of the Free University of Amsterdam.

lead a troop of hungry girl scouts to a hamburger stand." Unless we close our eyes to these cases, we are forced to the conclusion—long held by laymen—that there must be some abilities or personality attributes which distinguish the good leaders from the poor ones.

One problem in this area has been the confusion inherent in the term, *leadership trait*. As the term is sometimes used the trait differentiates the leader from the follower or from the non-leader. In other cases, the leadership trait purports to differentiate *effective from ineffective* leaders. This paper will deal with leadership traits in the latter sense. It will re-examine the notion of leadership traits in light of some recent findings. Despite Gibb's and Stogdill's (1948) reviews, we shall explore the possibility that leadership effectiveness traits or attributes exist, and that they may not have been recognized because our conceptualization of the problem has been based on inadequate assumptions.

Previous studies of leadership traits were concerned with the problem of differentiating leaders from non-leaders on the basis of various personality attributes. These studies showed that leaders differed slightly from non-leaders within their own groups in a number of attributes such as intelligence, height, and specific task-related skills. Thus, a bowling team might choose its leader from among the best bowlers, and a gang of toughs might choose the toughest member as its leader, but differences across various types of groups were very slight and generally inconsistent. A posteriori we can easily see some of the reasons for this discouraging set of findings. A wide variety of causes may propel a man into a leadership position, and many of these causes are totally unrelated to personality attributes. One of the surest ways of becoming company president is to come from a family which owns the company. Another is to have unusual technical skills and to be available at the right time. Furthermore, men tend to rise to leadership positions as they gain in age and experience. This means that younger or less experienced men with leadership potential may remain non-leaders until they have gained the necessary technical qualifications or experience necessary to assume leadership positions. Leadership traits, if they exist, would, therefore, be masked by many effects, and hence difficult to identify.

A leader's work, typically, consists in directing, coordinating, and supervising the activities of group members for the purposes of attaining a common goal. Whether or not a man becomes an occupant of a leadership position is frequently a matter of chance. But a man's ability to motivate other men may well be related to one or more personality attributes. It seems, therefore, more fruitful to deal with *leadership-effectiveness* traits. These can be defined as personality attributes of the leader which promote a high level of group productivity. A leader is then effective to the extent to which his group is productive, or achieves its assigned goals.

Here, too, however, previous studies have proved to be disappointing. We may here disregard studies which assessed leadership effectiveness in terms of supervisors' or subordinates' ratings since such criteria are frequently unreliable. However, there still remain a sizable number of methodologically sound studies of leader attributes and group effectiveness which have not been able to identify leadership-effectiveness traits. Why have these studies failed to find leadership traits, and under what conditions can such personality traits be discovered?

A personality trait is generally defined as ". . . some consistent quality of behavior . . . which characterizes the individual in a wide range of his activities and is fairly consistent over a period of time" (Woodworth and Marquis, 1948, p. 89; Allport, 1937). A leadership effectiveness trait could thus be defined as a consistent, reliably measurable personality attribute which differentiates effective from ineffective leaders. As with other traits, we expect to find leadership-effectiveness traits to be distributed to a greater or lesser degree in all members of the population. *But the behavior relevant to these traits will manifest itself only under appropriate conditions.* We expect that a trait such as aggressiveness or dominance is present in all members of the population to a greater or lesser degree, but we would not expect to find many behavorial differences in dominance or aggressiveness during a Quaker meeting. Similarly, we would not expect to differentiate between effective and ineffective leaders *unless the individuals under study were actually in a position to influence their groups.*

This problem in the study of leadership traits has been frequently overlooked. The term *leader* is not precisely defined and has more than one meaning. We use the term to identify a person who occupies a leadership position, although he may actually have little real influence over his group members. We also call persons "leaders" if they are elected representatives of their groups (e.g., Congressmen), if they are most influential (as indicated by sociometric ratings), or if they are foremost in their field of endeavor. In studies of small groups, it is obvious that we cannot expect a relationship between the "leader's" personality traits and group behavior unless the individual in the leadership position is in fact able to influence his group. This is the case only when we are dealing with a person whom the group recognizes as its leader—a person who is not a figurehead. It is, therefore, not enough to search for leadership-effectiveness traits by comparing the men who occupy the leadership positions. We must assure that the formal leaders are leaders in fact.

In light of the foregoing theoretical considerations, can we point to at least one personality attribute of leaders which is related to leadership effectiveness?

A program of research is described here briefly which indicates that this is, indeed, the case. The personality attribute to which we shall refer is measured by Assumed Similarity between Opposites (ASo) scores. ASo can be obtained by asking a subject (S) to describe his most preferred co-worker on a scale sheet containing about 20 six-point graphic rating scales. Each of the scale items is bounded by a personality adjective and its antonym, for example:

S marks each of the scale items to describe the person whom he considers his best co-worker; he similarly completes a scale sheet describing the person whom he considers his poorest co-worker. The persons to be described may be people with whom S currently works, or someone he knew before. The descriptions of these two persons, who are opposites on the co-worker continuum, are then compared by means of the co-efficient D which is a measure of profile similarity (Cronbach and Gleser, 1953).

ASo is a highly reliable score with split-half co-efficients ranging from .85 to .95 for a 20-item test, and it is reasonably stable over time (Fiedler, 1958). The score is also consistent over persons: the correlations are of the magnitude of .6 and above when Ss are asked further to describe their second most- and second least-preferred co-workers, or the safest and least-safe individual they have ever known (Cleven and Fiedler, 1956). We are thus dealing with a personality trait measure in the commonly used sense of the term.

Assumed Similarity between Opposites scores have been interpreted as measures of psychological distance to co-workers. Low ASo scores, indicating that the subject perceives much discrepancy between his most and least preferred co-workers, are related to analytical, critical attitudes toward co-workers. High ASo scores indicate a tendency to accept co-workers in a relatively uncritical and unreserved manner (Golb and Fiedler, 1955). In effect, the low ASo person seems to express rejection of a potentially poor team member.

Within the past eight years, the score has been extensively utilized in a program of research on leadership effectiveness.[2] The major studies of

---

[2] These studies were conducted under Contract NR 170–106, N6–ori–07135 between the University of Illinois and the Office of Naval Research.

this program will be briefly summarized to illustrate the theoretical points presented earlier in this paper. (For a more detailed treatment see Fiedler, 1958, and Godfrey, Fiedler, and Hall, 1959.)

The first study dealt with 14 high-school basketball teams. The group effectiveness criterion was the proportion of games the team had won by midseason. ASo scores of the informal leaders correlated −.69 with the criterion.[3] A check sample of 12 basketball teams was tested toward the end of the season, and supported the earlier result ($r_{pb} = -.58$, $p < .05$). These findings were further confirmed in a study of 22 student-surveying teams where the accuracy of mapping land was the group-effectiveness criterion. Here, the informal leader's ASo score correlated −.51 with the criterion ($p < .025$). The basketball teams and surveying parties were informally organized task groups, that is, there was no appointed leader; hence, we could assume that the sociometrically most-chosen person had the greatest influence and was thus the informal leader of the group.

A second series of investigations dealt with highly structured groups, namely, small military combat units. These crews had formally appointed leaders as well as specialists in each crew position. One study utilized B-29 bomber crews with radar bomb scores constituting the criterion of crew performance. Although 53 fairly complete crews were available, in only 22 of these was the formal leader (the aircraft commander) also sociometrically chosen as the crew's informal leader. No significant relations were observed between the leader's ASo score and crew performance when all crews were included in the sample. However, significant, although statistically complex, relations were found in crews in which the aircraft commander was also the crew's informal leader. These relations were cross-validated on a sample of 25 army tank crews for which two independent criteria of effectiveness were available. A recent study of antiaircraft artillery units has further confirmed these findings.[4] Sociometrically accepted task-group leaders who are psychologically distant from their co-workers, especially their least preferred ones, have more effective crews than leaders who appear to be more permissive and accepting of their least-preferred co-workers (Hutchins and Fiedler, 1960).

Since military units are generally very short lived, we also studied 16 shifts of very stable open-hearth steel crews. Here the group's acceptance of the leader appeared to be less important. The group effectiveness

---

[3] A negative correlation indicates that the leaders of effective groups perceived little similarity between their most- and least-preferred co-workers, i.e., they were psychologically distant from least preferred co-workers.

[4] This study was conducted under Contract DA–49–007–MD–569 between the University of Illinois and the Office of the Surgeon General, Department of the Army.

criterion was the "tap-to-tap" time, which is a measure indicating the tonnage of steel produced per unit of time. The formal leaders of open-hearth shifts are the senior melter foremen. The correlation between the ASo scores of the senior melters and the effectiveness criterion was −.52 (N = 15, p < .05). It should be noted that men in these groups work together for unusually long periods; five to fifteen years are not uncommon. Under these conditions, it seems probable that the only people who remain in the same group are those who accept each other. However, we also considered the sociometric preference scores by limiting the sample to the shifts in which the senior melters were accepted by the other foremen in their groups, and who, in turn, endorsed their junior melters. Under these conditions the correlation rose to −.89—but on a sample of only six cases (Cleven and Fiedler, 1956). Nevertheless, this study again points to the importance of assuring that the formal leader of the group is also accepted by his subordinates.

A recent study of consumer cooperatives (Godfrey, Fiedler, and Hall, 1959) provides the clearest support for the contention of this paper that we cannot measure leadership-effectiveness traits in action, unless we confine ourselves to groups in which the formal leader has considerable influence over his group. This investigation dealt with 32 member companies of a large federation of consumer cooperatives. Each of the companies had its own board of directors and its own management. Personnel, products, operating and accounting procedures were nearly identical for all companies in the sample. Carefully collected data made it possible for the headquarters of the federation to provide valid indexes of the effectiveness of each member company. Two criterion measures were used in the study which is here described. The first of these was Net Income, an index based on the gross volume after deducting the cost of goods and services. The second index, Operating Efficiency, is based on the proportion of gross income which must be utilized for operating expenses of the organization. These indexes were not correlated with the size of the company nor with the economic prosperity of the area which the company served.

The formal leader of the management group is the general manager, who is also considered to be the most important official in the company. As in other corporations, he is responsible to a board of directors, and, in turn, supervises a number of assistant managers and various employees.

As expected, we found no correlation between the general manager's ASo scores and the criterion when all companies were included in the sample. These correlations successively increased as the sample was confined to groups in which the general manager enjoyed greater and greater influence (Table 1). It can be seen here that the manager's authority derives in large part from his superiors on the Board of Directors, as well as from his subordinate assistant managers. But this support, in itself, only gives the leader power to influence the group. It does not determine or affect the wisdom with which the formal leader will use his power. How well the company will succeed depends in large part on the accepted general manager's attitude toward his co-workers.

Table 1

CORRELATIONS BETWEEN THE GENERAL MANAGER'S ASSUMED
SIMILARITY BETWEEN OPPOSITES (ASo) SCORE
AND COMPANY EFFECTIVENESS

SAMPLE	N	NET INCOME	OPERATING EFFICIENCY
All General Managers	32	−.14	−.16
General Manager endorsed by staff	19	−.09	−.22
General Manager endorsed by Board	19	−.07	−.08
General Manager endorsed by most influential board member	23	−.39*	−.24
General Manager endorsed by staff and most influential board member	13	−.70**	−.59*
General Manager endorsed by staff and most influential board member, and Manager endorses key Assistant Manager	8	−.74*	−.73*

* p < .05 (one-tailed test)
** p < .025 (one-tailed test).

The studies in this series seem to show that a leadership-effectiveness trait has been identified. In three of the investigations—the first basketball sample, one half of the surveying parties, and the 25 tank crews—ASo scores were obtained *before* the groups had worked together intensively as a team. In the case of the surveying parties, the men were tested before they were assembled into groups. The tank crews had been assembled within a few days of testing and had just started to train as a crew. Many of the men did not yet know the names of their fellow crew members. Obviously, then, ASo was not primarily affected by the team's success, rather it seems to be a personality attribute, or a trait, related to leadership effectiveness.

Although the discussion of this paper has been confined to ASo scores, it seems reasonable to assume that other personality traits might yield equally good results. This requires, however, that we deal with men who are in leadership positions, and who are thus able to exert strong influence on group behavior as indicated either by sociometric or other suitable indexes.

This paper has dealt only with leadership-effectiveness traits. This should not be taken to mean that there is any conflict with the so-called interactional theories of leadership. Group effectiveness will necessarily depend on a number of factors unrelated to the leader's personality. Some of these are the group members' skills, the nature of the task, and the social context within which the group operates. Thus, there is some evidence to show that leadership effectiveness in task groups, such as those discussed here, requires different leader attitudes than those required in policy- and decision-making groups (Godfrey, Fiedler, and Hall, 1959). Moreover, the question remains why, or how, some men gain acceptance as leaders while others do not. It is to be hoped that increased attention to the conditions which are necessary for the manifestation of leadership-effectiveness traits will lead to a healthy revival of interest in this facet of leadership theory. We hope that it will lead to an overdue exhumation of a number of leadership traits which may have been prematurely buried.

REFERENCES

ALLPORT, G. W. *Personality, a psychological interpretation.* New York: Holt, Rinehart and Winston, 1937.

CLEVEN, W. A. AND FIEDLER, F. E. Interpersonal perceptions of open-hearth foremen and steel production. *J. appl. Psychol.,* 1956, *40,* 312–314.

CRONBACH, L. J. AND GLESER, GOLDINE C. Assessing similarity between profiles. *Psychol. Bull.,* 1953, *50,* 456–473.

FIEDLER, F. E. *Leader attitudes and group effectiveness.* Urbana: Univ. of Illinois Press, 1958.

GIBB, C. A. Leadership. In G. LINDZEY (Ed.), *Handbook of social psychology.* Cambridge, Mass.: Addison-Wesley, 1954.

GODFREY, ELEANOR P., FIEDLER, F. E., AND HALL, D. M. *Boards, management, and company success.* Danville, Ill.: Interstate Press, 1959.

GOLB, EILEEN F. AND FIEDLER, F. E. A note on psychological attributes related to the score, Assumed Similarity between Opposites (ASo). Technical Report *12* (mimeo.) Urbana: Group Effectiveness Research Laboratory, Univ. of Illinois, 1955.

HUTCHINS, E. B. AND FIEDLER, F. E. Task-oriented and quasi-therapeutic role functions of the leader in small military groups. *Sociometry,* 1960, *23,* in press.

STOGDILL, R. M. Personal factors associated with leadership: a survey of the literature. *J. Psychol.,* 1948, *25,* 35–71.

WOODWORTH, R. S. AND MARQUIS, D. G. *Psychology* (5th Ed.) New York: Holt, Rinehart and Winston, 1948.

12

Organizational Leadership in Task-Oriented Groups

Harold Guetzkow

Departments of Psychology and Sociology
Northwestern University
and
Executive Judgment Research Study
University of Chicago

Today there is considerable agreement that both personal traits and group situation compose the matrix within which leadership must be examined. No longer are we satisfied with a demonstration that traits do influence leadership activity, nor are we satisfied with an exhibition of the way in which the structure of a group influences leadership style. Are we now able to discover just how situation and trait interplay to produce leadership in organizations?

This essay attempts to display in detail an island of theory, quite incomplete, of how trait and situation yield organizational leadership in contrived task-oriented groups. It draws data from experimental work completed at Carnegie Institute of Technology, which have been reported partially elsewhere (Guetzkow–Simon, 1955; Guetzkow–Dill, 1957; Guetzkow, 1960).[1] An endeavor has been made to gain perspective about the nature

[1] The experimental work was supported by a grant from the research funds of Carnegie's Graduate School of Industrial Administration. Grateful thanks are due to Messrs. K. Hellfach, A. D. Martin, and F. Metzger and to Mrs. Martha Pryor, Miss Anne E. Bowes, Mrs. Marion Bement, and Mrs. Janet Stein for aid in conducting the investigation and help in analyzing its results. Professors Herbert A. Simon and William R. Dill stimulated the author in development of many of the ideas presented in this paper.

of organizational leadership by integrating our findings with those of others.

One may conceive of this experimental development of organizational leadership as an exemplification of the "initiation-of-structure in interaction" variable isolated in the Ohio State University Leadership Studies by Shartle and his colleagues. Many of the OSU researches have concerned themselves with the isolation of this variable, distinguishing it from such factors as "consideration" (Stogdill and Coons, 1957). The organization of roles into social structures in our experimental work would seem to be the consequence of such initiating by leaders within our contrived groups. We shall be concerned here with the micromechanisms through which "initiation-of-structure in interaction" develops, given ascendant impulse toward initiation.

A BEVY OF CONTRIVED ORGANIZATIONS

Distinguishing between task-performance and group development-and-maintenance functions within organizations continues to be an analytically fruitful way of separating activities in groups. Using the Bavelas-Leavitt situation for groups of five persons, an effort was made to modify their original experimental situation so as to separate the task-performance activities from those involved in the development of an organization for the performance of the task itself. A partial separation was accomplished by the expedient of allowing periods of communication about organizational matters between periods of task-performance. The use of precoded messages, which provided only for task activity during the performance periods, tended to restrict organizational activities to the intertrial periods when noncoded communications with any content were permitted.

This examination of the detailed processes by which organizational leadership developed in these contrived groups will be restricted to data obtained within a single communication net, for then net-related factors may be held constant. In these instances, less than half of the five-man groups managed to develop a hierarchical decision-making organization of some stability with role differentiations. This circumstance allows comparison of the leadership in groups which organized, contrasted with leadership efforts in groups which failed to use more than undifferentiated, personal decision-making procedures.

Forty-one five-man groups were placed for their task trials in a "circle" net, in which each position is connected separately by a two-way communication channel to each of two of the other positions.[2] Two hundred

---

[2] These forty-one groups consist of twenty-one "Circle" groups (Guetzkow and Simon, 1955, pp. 239–40) and twenty "Circle-AC" groups (Guetzkow and Dill, 1957, p. 190).

and five male freshmen engineering students at Carnegie Institute of Technology served as subjects. Each person in a group was given a different combination of five pieces of information from a standard set of six. The group's task was to determine which piece was held in common by all on a given trial. Each man immediately communicated his solution to the experimenter. The group's trial time, then, was determined by the last subject to report the correct solution. Intertrial periods of a maximum of two minutes in length were allowed each group between each of the 20-task trials. The time used for task completion varied from six minutes to less than a minute per trial.

By establishing a division of labor among themselves, the participants may structure a three-level organizational hierarchy for the sending of information to a central key point at which the solution is formed. These keymen then may or may not use this same hierarchy in reverse for distribution of the solution to members occupying each of the four other positions in the circle net. The two individuals adjacent to the keymen serve as relayers, receiving the answer for their own response and then forwarding it to the endmen, who are once removed from the central keymen. Although the two endmen are potentially linked to each other in the circle net, in the hierarchical organization this channel is seldom used for communication between them.

Fourteen of the forty-one groups established a hierarchical division of labor, averaging .48 minute per trial for completion of the task on their three fastest trials. Twenty-six of the groups remained essentially undifferentiated, exchanging information about who had what symbols with each other. Each individual gradually came to his own solution, thereby obviating need for any answer exchanges. These "each-to-all" and "undiscernible" groups averaged .73 minute per trial for completion of the task on their three fastest trials. In the following discussion, the former 14 groups will be designated as "organized" and the latter 26 groups as "unorganized." One of the groups was neither clearly organized nor unorganized; this group is not considered in this report.

SITUATIONAL CONTENTS OF LEADER INITIATIONS

It may appear that the organizational development described above is concomitant with the differentiation of such roles as keymen, relayer, and endmen. But such is *not* the case. We designate a person as occupying a role when he has performed the specified role behaviors for four or more consecutive task trials. The distribution of person in the three roles is presented in Table 1 for both organized and unorganized groups. Although 80 percent of the individuals in the unorganized groups developed roles for themselves, they were unable to interlock their roles into group structures. What is it that enables certain groups to articulate their roles into hierarchical organizations?

Table 1

DISTRIBUTION OF ROLES
(Number of Persons in Role)

ROLE	Organized Groups		Unorganized Groups	
Keymen	15	21%	30	23%
Relayers	28	40%	39	30%
Endmen	27	38%	35	27%
Persons without roles	0	0%	26	20%
Totals	70		130	

To interlock roles, perhaps it is helpful to be able to perceive the roles as they evolve. This hypothesis is confirmed in our experimental situation by checks on the extent to which persons in different roles were able to identify the roles of others, as presented in Table 2. Those in the organized groups perceived other members in their groups at least three times more accurately than did those in the unorganized groups. It is interesting to note that the individuals who were in keyman and relayer roles in both the organized and unorganized groups perceived others approximately two or more times as accurately as those in the endman role.

Table 2

ACCURACY OF ORGANIZATIONAL PERCEPTION BY ROLES*
(Correct minus incorrect role identifications over total roles present)

Role of Perceivers	ORGANIZED GROUPS		UNORGANIZED GROUPS	
	Mean	Standard deviation	Mean	Standard deviation
Keymen	.68	.46	.16	.42
Relayers	.58	.45	.18	.35
Endmen	.37	.47	.02	.29

Significance tests: t-tests of (Keymen plus Relayers) *vs.* Endmen were significant both in the organized groups (t = 2.1, p<.05), and in the unorganized groups (t = 2.0, p<.05).

* Number of persons occupying each role is given above, *supra* Table 1.

An analysis of the organizational-planning activities which occurred during the intertrial periods yields further insight into the way in which organizational leaders integrate the roles which they perceive into working hierarchical structures. During each of the 19 intertrial periods, approximately, 6.2 unit messages were sent by the five subjects within each group. About 15.4 percent of these units involved planning for the organization itself.

A more detailed breakdown of these organizational planning messages is given in Table 3. In coding the organizational messages that dealt with planning, we established three categories:

Table 3

INTERTRIAL MESSAGES CONCERNED WITH ORGANIZATIONAL
PLANNING BY ROLES*
(Number of units sent in 19 intertrials)

	ORGANIZED GROUPS		UNORGANIZED GROUPS	
3a *Messages Concerned with Specific Organizational Proposals*	*Mean*	*Standard deviation*	*Mean*	*Standard deviation*
Keymen	4.0	3.2	0.6	1.4
Relayers	1.7	2.4	0.5	0.9
Endmen	1.2	1.8	0.4	0.7

Significance tests: t-tests of Keymen *vs.* Relayers (t = 2.6, p<.02) and Keymen *vs.* (Relayers plus Endmen) (t = 3.6, p<.001) are significant in the organized groups.

3b *Promulgation of Specific Proposals*				
Keymen	1.1	2.0	0.4	0.7
Relayers	1.2	1.8	0.3	0.6
Endmen	1.4	2.1	0.5	1.3

Significance tests: none significant between roles in either organized or unorganized groups.

3c *General Organizational Matters*				
Keymen	1.7	2.2	1.0	2.2
Relayers	1.3	1.4	0.5	1.2
Endmen	1.1	2.2	1.1	2.2

Significance tests: none significant between roles in either organized or unorganized groups.

* Number of persons occupying each role is given above, *supra* Table 1.

a. Specific proposals for organization, suggesting the proposer himself or others for particular tasks. (For example, a proposer might suggest the plan: "I will solve the problem and then send out answers." Or one group member, say G, might propose to K: "Send your information to S.")

b. Messages that merely promulgated a suggestion initiated by someone else. (For example, suppose P suggested to G that G should "send to S first." Then a follow-up message by G to M, "Let's keep it going to S," is a promulgation of the plan.)

c. Plans that were more general in nature. (Examples: "Why don't we send all our messages to one person?"; "Send all messages clockwise.")

In Table 3 note how these activities are related to roles in the organized *versus* the unorganized groups.

There is not much difference between the organized and unorganized groups in the volume of planning messages of a general nature, as shown in Table 3c. But the organized groups developed specific messages and then passed them about (Tables 3a and 3b). Further, note how specific organization planning tends to be done in the main by the keyman, while the promulgating is done by persons in all the roles. Examination of the specific messages indicates that the keymen were designating themselves as being the solution-formers, and that they promulgated messages to that effect.

Thus, it seems that although differentiation of roles is imperative for integration, such differentiation is not sufficient in itself to induce an interlocking of roles. In unorganized groups planning was deficient, not in its failure to secure behavioral differentiation of the functional roles, but in its failure to provide organizational leadership through which there might be interlocking of the roles already being performed. Specific proposals by these organizational leaders were related intimately to achievement of an integrated structure. Participants do not articulate roles by exchanging notes about general organizational plans. Further, not only must roles be differentiated (Table 1), but the participants must have highly specific knowledge of each other's roles in planning. The unorganized groups (Table 2) only minimally understood the other roles which were being played, as contrasted with those in the organized groups. Individuals in the latter groups, who averaged some accuracy in their identification of roles, were able to interlock their activities much more adequately than those in the unorganized groups, whose knowledge of the roles averaged but 12 percent (approximately) in accuracy.

Although Selznick's somewhat mystical treatment of leadership in administration fails to explore the mechanisms of organizational leadership, his analysis emphasizes the role of leaders in making value-commitments in the decision-making process (Selznick, 1957, pp. 119–130). Does the ability of our leaders to absorb and dispel uncertainty regarding the structure of the evolving organization resemble the value-commitments that organizational leaders make in the seas of competing organizational goals described by Selznick? Our contrived situation, regrettably, allowed no exploration of the origination of end-values.

PERSONAL MECHANISMS IN ORGANIZATIONAL LEADERSHIP

Given this analysis of organizational leadership in our 40 task-oriented groups, how do personal traits of our participants interplay with the situational contents to yield particular role behaviors in specified persons? Our experimental explorations in this area were limited to two variables: intelligence and personal ascendance.

Intelligence and Planning

An ACE score of general intellectual ability was obtained on each subject; then in composing the groups, the experimenters matched subjects so that each group had one person coming from each of five ACE levels. These data allow us to check whether role occupancy is associated with intelligence, as well as to determine indirectly whether intelligence played a part, per se, in the interlocking of the roles into organizational structures.

The average raw scores for persons in the three roles are presented in Table 4a. In the organized groups, the keymen and relayers are superior in their average scores to the endmen. In the unorganized groups, the keymen alone are superior in their scores to both relayers and endmen. Although the difference in the organized groups fails to reach the significance level of the difference in the unorganized, the findings seem not to be calculational artifacts. An ACE raw score of 131 (approximating the average keyman in both types of groups and the average relayer in the organized groups) places at the 83rd percentile on national, four-year college norms[3]; a score of 124 (approximating the average endmen in both types of groups and the average relayer in the unorganized groups) places at the 74th percentile. Role occupancy is associated with differences in intelligence, as in both organized and unorganized groups the key men are clearly superior to the endmen in the intellectual abilities measured by the ACE.

But does intellectual ability play a part in the interlocking of the three

[3] Percentiles based on Table 5, data for 94 four-year colleges, *Norms Bulletin, American Council on Education, Psychological Examination for College Freshmen,* 1949 Edition, Educational Testing Service, Princeton, N. J.

Table 4

PERSONAL CHARACTERISTICS BY ROLES

	ORGANIZED GROUPS		UNORGANIZED GROUPS	
	Mean	Standard deviation	Mean	Standard deviation

4a *Intellectual ability*
(Total ACE raw scores)

	Mean	Standard deviation	Mean	Standard deviation
Keymen	129.9	22.9	131.9	21.2
Relayers	132.5	20.3	125.1	18.8
Endmen	123.2	18.8	125.1	23.3

Significance tests: t-test of (Keymen plus Relayers) *vs.* Endmen is not significant in the organized groups ($t = 1.7$, $p < .10$) but the t-test of Keymen *vs.* (Relayers plus Endmen) is significant in the unorganized groups ($t = 5.3$, $p < .001$).

Number of persons occupying each role in Table 4a is given above, *supra*, Table 1.

4b *Personal Ascendance*
(Raw sums on G-Z"A" scale)

	Mean	Standard deviation	Mean	Standard deviation
Keymen	5.9 (n = 11)	2.1	6.0 (n = 13)	2.0
Relayers	4.2 (n = 20)	2.0	4.8 (n = 24)	1.5
Endmen	4.6 (n = 19)	1.2	4.9 (n = 23)	1.4

Significance tests: t-tests of Keymen *vs.* (Relayers plus Endmen) are significant both in organized ($t = 2.4$, $p < .05$) and in the unorganized ($t = 2.2$, $p < .05$) groups.

Number of persons occupying each role is given in parentheses under each mean in Table 4b; see footnote 3 in Guetzkow and Dill (1957) for further details.

roles into organizational structures? The differing intelligence of the relayers in the organized *versus* the unorganized groups, as displayed in Table 4a, indicates that general ability is associated with the success groups have in organizing themselves for task performance.

Two activities were demonstrated earlier as integral in organizational leadership, namely, accuracy in perception of organizational structure and active planning for specific role establishment. Does intelligence predict the extent to which these activities are evoked within our participants? No. The product-moment correlations between ACE scores and the accuracy measure ($r = .03$) and the volume of specific planning ($r = .06$) are not different from zero. Because of the general intellectual superiority of our Carnegie Tech freshman (the average score of 127.5 coming approximately at the 79th percentile on the general national norms), intelligence may be functioning covertly as a necessary, but hardly a sufficient, condition for organizational leadership.

General intelligence, thus, is found to be associated with organizational leadership—in the differentiation of the more influential roles from the routine roles, in the interlocking of roles into organizational structures, and in the articulation of the relayers with their keymen. Yet the general intelligence scores, consisting largely of verbal and quantitative abilities, do not predict the extent to which participants perceive the organization's emerging structure, nor do they predict the extent to which the participants give organizational leadership. These results are not incommensurate with the factor-analytic findings of Berger, Guilford, and Christensen's (1957) studies of planning abilities. The components involved in planning activity there were found to be quite separate from the usual Verbal Comprehension, Numerical Facility, and General Reasoning factors which load intelligence measures. Our study did not gather scores on such factors as originality, conceptual foresight, and elaboration as possible predictors of planning activity.

Ascendance and Leadership

If general intellectual competence is but an underlying factor in organizational leadership in the development of our contrived organizations, might some personal characteristic more intimately related to the style with which an individual operates in interpersonal situations be associated with heightened activity in organizational development? The important part self-designation played in role establishment suggested that social ascendance should be explored. A number of the participants completed responses to the Guilford-Zimmerman Ascendance "A" scale before entering the group situation. When a table analogous to the one made for ACE scores is constructed for these self-rated questionnaires (Table 4b), the keymen are seen clearly to be more ascendant than the relayers and endmen. In the organized groups, it would seem that although superior intelligence is required for both keymen and relayers higher amounts of personal ascendance distinguish the keymen from the relayers. Personal ascendance is associated with the occurrence of self-nomination as keyman.

The fact that essentially identical findings were obtained for both organized and unorganized groups indicates that ascendance is *not* associated with the interlocking of roles into organizational structures. This contrasts with the impact of perceptual accuracy, planning activity, and general intellectual ability—all three of which were involved in the development of an interlocked structure as well as in the distribution of occupants in differentiated roles.

Our findings on the part played by ascendance in the self-selection of keymen are complemented neatly in the findings of Berkowitz (1956) on the effects of group position upon the expression of ascendant responses. In our work with groups in which the role structure is undifferentiated at first, ascendance is a significant factor in assorting individuals into roles. Berkowitz worked with roles which are structured initially by the imposed communication restrictions, and to which particular persons, with varying ascendance scores, are assigned by the experimenter. Berkowitz found that the group's structure importantly reduced the frequency with which persons having high-ascendant G-Z scores expressed ascendance behaviors—and, vice versa, augmented the frequency with which low ascendants increased their attempts at leadership because of position requirements.

When the group's structure is ambiguous and in process of formation, the participants' personal characteristics play an important part in allotting individuals to particular roles and even determine whether or not particular roles will become differentiated. Contrariwise, when persons with particular personal characteristics are assigned to occupancy of predetermined roles, their initial tendencies to respond in terms of underlying personal characteristics will be modified, acting to "minimize the personality-determined differences" (Berkowitz, 1956, p. 221) when the role contradicts the personal tendencies. When the role demands coincide with personal tendencies brought into the social situation, the personality-determined differences probably would be augumented.

LOCAL LEARNING versus PLANNING

Our analyses endeavor to display micromechanisms involved in the initiation-of-structure in social interaction. They explore the detailed way in which the contents of the situation interplay with personal traits of the group's members. By comparing our findings with those of Christie, Luce and Macy (1952), it is possible to gain further insight into the contingent nature of organizational leadership.

The differentiation of unstable, random-like message exchanges into stable, well-structured interactions undoubtedly is the result of some learning processes. But a local stimulus-reinforcement schema seems incapable of explaining the development of our hierarchical organizations. There was no random exchange of answers in our groups. There was a considerable drop over time in the information messages exchanged, but this drop seemed not to depend upon reinforcement by the reward of receiving answers. In the groups which eventually organized, the number of information messages received by those persons who had sent or had not sent answers during the previous trial was checked. Using *only* those trials before a final organization was reached, we found an average of 2.49 information messages were received by those who had supplied an answer in the previous trial, compared with 2.30 information messages by those who had not sent an answer, a difference without significance (Guetzkow and Dill, 1957, p. 184).

There is indirect evidence that local learning may even prevent eventual organization of hierarchical structures in these task-oriented groups. The interaction patterns of a hierarchically organized group necessarily are stable. But stability may also be achieved at a primitive undifferentiated level of organization (Guetzkow and Dill, 1957, Table 3 *vs.* Table 4). Does "premature" local learning "freeze" the groups into less well-adapted organizational arrangements? During the *first four* test trials the groups which eventually organized differed in their stability from those which eventually failed to organize. The former groups showed significantly more *instability* in the answer channels used during these initial trials (Guetzkow and Dill, 1957, p. 198). Thus, although local reinforcement did not aid significantly in the differentiation of hierarchical structures, an early stabilization of responses may have served to prevent the development of hierarchical structures. In our discussion of planning and innovation, my colleagues March and Simon hypothesized, "Whatever relations are established in the initial phase will be relatively stable" (March and Simon with Guetzkow, 1958, p. 187).

The strong impact of the environmental situation upon the mechanism by which the structures of interaction are organized is dramatically illustrated in the work of Christie, Luce, and Macy (1952) at MIT. They modified the original Bavelas-Leavitt experimental procedure by allowing no opportunity for communication about perceptions and plans. Each member of the group had only the coded task messages as the basis for the development of efficient message sendings. Yet the MIT circle groups did reduce their messages to but one of the minimum by the end of 25 trials. This re-structuring of the task situation allowed conditioning-type learning to bring success without organizational leadership. In the Carnegie experimental situation, where there was opportunity for planning, an organized leadership mechanism was evolved. Thus, we have the two extremes—one in which group structure is initiated without organizational leadership—and the other in which key persons plan the interlocking of group members into complicated hierarchies. It would seem that when one mechanism is prevented from being engaged, another may take its place. As we have put it elsewhere, "the less the complexity of the environment, the greater the use of local changes in programs" (March and Simon, with Guetzkow, 1958, p. 176). By permitting only communication about tasks, the MIT experimenters reduced the complexity of their subjects' environment so drastically as to allow change only through local learnings.

DISCUSSION

The Contingent Nature of Organizational Leadership

Likert and his colleagues in the Survey Research Center at Michigan work in ongoing, quasi-stable organizations, making rich multivariate analysis of their observations. In Seashore's exciting summarization of "Administrative Leadership and Organizational Effectiveness" (Likert and Hayes, 1957, Ch. 2), stress is placed upon the conditional nature of the interplay in leadership between situational and personal characteristics. For example, "it was found that the same leadership practice might have a positive result when carried out by a supervisor who is influential in the department, and have a negative result when carried out by a supervisor of little power" (Likert and Hayes, 1957, p. 65).

In a similar vein, the contingent nature of organizational leadership was demonstrated time and again in our contrived groups. The interlocking of roles into organizational structures depends upon leaders' perceptions of role differentiations. The allocation of roles themselves depends upon the situational placement of potential leaders vis-à-vis potential relayers. But perhaps even more dramatic is how the situation may determine whether or not any organizational leadership may be brought to bear. In certain communication structures, local role autonomy is so great that organizational leadership becomes irrelevant. As social psychologists explore the micromechanisms involved in leadership within organizations, we will be able to specify more accurately the contingent choices which need be made for more adequate leadership performance, as Seashore so persuasively argues (Likert and Hayes, 1957, pp. 55–60).

Face-to-Face Groups versus Organizations

Someday it may be possible to characterize human collectivities on a set of independent dimensions, so that "the definition of group and the discrimination of group from no-group [will] become arbitrary matters of convenience" (Borgatta, Cottrell, and Meyer, 1956, p. 223). In the meantime it seems fruitful to continue the distinction of small groups from organizations, so that the extension of theory from one to the other is done with circumspection. The term *groups* often refers to configurations of persons in interaction, with varying degrees of stability. *Interaction* designates the state of affairs in which the responses, or symbolizations thereof, of individuals serve as stimulus objects to other persons within the configuration.

Small groups then may be characterized as groups in which the interaction among the members is direct and face-to-face; the behaviors in the group are accessible simultaneously to all. Committees, work teams and families are examples of this kind of group. *Organizations* are distinguishable from face-to-face groups by virtue of the predominance of indirect, mediated interaction among members, so that the behaviors within the group are relatively inaccessible to any given individual. Examples are found in departments, bureaus, branches, companies, and government units (Guetzkow and Bowes, 1957, p. 380).

If this stress on the importance of mediation in interaction is useful, the contrived configurations developed in our experiments may be thought of as organizations rather than face-to-face groups. Researchers in the small-group area have created situations of indirect interaction among the experimental participants for reasons of experimental convenience. It is my contention that such a maneuver inadvertently has shifted significantly the position of their groups on this direct-indirect continuum of interaction. Perhaps the designation of groups as "small" then is fatuous, as aggregations of three, four, or five men may be organizations rather than face-to-face groups. In our experimental situation I believe we have so constrained the communication as to be working with contrived organizations rather than face-to-face groups. (1) The use of written messages, sent by one member to one other person only (rather than to all, as in face-to-face situations) and (2), the use of a circle net, in which every other person has his communications mediated by a third—these two characteristics would seem to have moved our five-man groups from the face-to-face to the organizational end of the continuum. If this analysis is correct, we then have less costly experimental research sites for the exploration of leadership in contrived organizations than when "largeness" is conceived as the key difference between committees and organizations.

SUMMARY

An endeavor has been made to display micromechanisms underlying the initiation-of-structure in groups through organizational leadership. The role of organizational planning in the development of contrived groups has been found to be a resultant of the interplay of situational contents and personal characteristics. The independence of intelligence vis-à-vis other planning processes has been demonstrated. The functioning of personal ascendance in the differentiation of roles rather than in the interlocking of roles into structures has been distinguished. The contingent nature of the processes involved in the exercise of organizational leadership is impressive.

REFERENCES

BERGER, R. M., GUILFORD, J. P., AND CHRISTENSEN, P. R. A factor-analytic study of planning abilities. *Psychol. Monogr.*, 1957, *71*, No. 6 (Whole No. 435).

BERKOWITZ, L. Personality and group position. *Sociometry*, 1956, *19*, 210–222.

BORGATTA, E. F., COTTRELL, L. S., AND MEYER, H. J. On the dimensions of group behavior. *Sociometry*, 1956, *19*, 223–240.

CHRISTIE, L. S., LUCE, R. D., AND MACY, J., JR. Communication and learning in task-oriented groups. *Technical Report* No. 231, Research Laboratory of Electronics, Massachusetts Institute of Technology, 1952.

GUETZKOW, H. Differentiation of roles in task-oriented groups. In Cartwright, D. and Zander, A. (Eds.), *Group dynamics: research and theory.* (2nd ed.) Evanston, Ill.: Row, Peterson, 1960.

GUETZKOW, H. AND BOWES, ANNE E. The development of organizations in a laboratory. *Management Science*, 1957, *3*, 380–402.

GUETZKOW, H. AND DILL, W. R. Factors in the organizational development of task-oriented groups. *Sociometry*, 1957, *20*, 175–204.

GUETZKOW, H. AND SIMON, H. A. The impact of certain communication nets upon organization and performance in task-oriented groups. *Management Science*, 1955, *1*, 233–250.

LIKERT, R. AND HAYES, S. P. (Eds.), *Some applications of behavioural research.* New York: UNESCO Publications Center, 1957.

MARCH, J. G., AND SIMON, H. A., WITH GUETZKOW, H. *Organizations.* New York: Wiley, 1958.

SELZNICK, P. *Leadership in administration.* Evanston, Ill.: Row, Peterson, 1957.

STOGDILL, R. M. AND COONS, A. E. Leader behavior. *Ohio State University Bureau of Business Research* Monogr., 1957, No. 88.

13

Why People Attempt to Lead

John K. Hemphill

Educational Testing Service

BACKGROUND AND INTRODUCTION

It is now generally recognized that leadership is in part situational. Reviews of earlier research on leadership have discouraged its study as simply a personal attribute or personality trait (Gibb, 1954; Jenkins, 1947; Stogdill, 1948). Personal characteristics do play a part in contemporary leadership theories, but primarily as they interact with situational variables.

Substantial progress has been made towards the understanding of leadership since we began to attend to its situational properties. There remain, however, serious difficulties which block the most rapid utilization of this approach. Obviously, leadership is a complex mixture of social behaviors. Therefore, it is doubtful that it can be profitably treated as one dimension of behavior or that it can be adequately understood without subdivision.

As part of a theory of leadership and group behavior and in an effort to divide leadership research into manageable areas, Hemphill (1958) has suggested the use of the concepts of "attempted leadership," "successful leadership" and "effective leadership." Each of these subdivisions of leadership research subsumes particular problems for investigation and understanding. It is likely that the variables or constructs most useful to the understanding of the problems in one of these three areas will not prove nearly as useful in the others.

An "attempted leadership" act is an act by which an individual intends to initiate structure into group interaction for the purpose of solving a mutual problem. That is, an individual who attempts to lead is trying to set the form by which the group may solve its problem. He is recommending a rule of organization, or a procedure, or a technique, or a consistent pattern of behavior for the group to follow. The major problem here is to account for the personal motives or the situational pressures which prompt group members to try to lead.

A *successful leadership* act is an attempted leadership act which has been followed, that is, an act which has initiated a structure into the group's interaction. As a result of a successful leadership act the group has taken a new course in its problem-solving activities. The major research problem particular to successful leadership is to account for the fact that the members of groups on many occasions behave in accord with a form suggested or directed by a single individual. Why do people follow the lead of another?

An *effective leadership* act has not only initiated structure into interaction but has also contributed to the group's solution of a mutual problem. The major research problems associated with effective leadership are criterion problems related to group effectiveness. Involved in these criterion problems are the standards used to judge when a mutual problem is solved. How do we decide that a course of action which has been suggested and which has been followed has also, in fact, contributed to the solution of a mutual problem?

The major part of this paper is devoted to a description of a series of four experiments, each of which was conducted to test hypotheses in the area of attempted leadership. Each of the experiments is concerned with why people try to lead. It is believed that their results illustrate the usefulness of dividing leadership into limited areas for specific study.

THE FOUR EXPERIMENTS

Each of the four experiments was conducted in a small-group laboratory at Ohio State University under contract N6ori T. O. III (NR 171–123) with the Office of Naval Research. Three of the four have been reported in detail elsewhere (Hemphill, Pepinsky, Kaufman, and Lipetz, 1957; Hemphill, Pepinsky, Shevitz, Jaynes, and Christner, 1956; Pepinsky, Hemphill, and Shevitz, 1958). The dependent variable in all four experiments was the frequency with which members of groups attempted to lead.

A. Experiment One

The first of the four experiments was undertaken to test the hypothesis that those group members who have more information relevant to the group's task would attempt to lead more often than those with less information. This hypothesis is closely related to a practical question which is still being debated: must a leader have superior proficiency in the task of his group?

The experiment was conducted according to a design which involved four different group tasks. Attempted leadership acts were recorded for each of four group members during the 15-minute periods he worked on each of the four tasks. The four tasks were an Assembly task, a Strategy task, a Construction task and a Discussion task.

The Assembly task required the subjects to assemble the components of a simple electronics circuit to conform with its schematic diagram. The Strategy problem was a modification of the game of Peggity, in which the group members competed with the experimenter by inserting pegs into a large pegboard, with the objective of getting eight pegs in an unbroken row. The Construction task was to build a model airplane from a set of commercially available materials called "The Toy." The Discussion task required the group to reach a consensus on an estimate of the total number of votes cast for the Republican presidential candidate in the state of Oregon in 1940.

The independent variable of primary interest was information supplied the members during a training period which preceded their work on the four tasks. During this training period each group member studied a booklet of information for forty minutes. Each booklet contained four short articles of approximately equal length but of varied relevance for the tasks. For each task, two articles were prepared; one was clearly relevant to successful performance of the task and the other, although related to the task, was not very relevant to its successful performance. The booklets were prearranged such that, in accord with the design of the experiment, a group-member's booklet might contain either relevant or irrelevant material for one or more of the tasks. Our hypothesis was that those individuals who had been given the more relevant information for a task would attempt to lead with greater frequency than those who had been supplied with less relevant information.

The number of times each individual group member attempted to lead during the 15 minutes he worked on each task constituted the dependent variable. An Observer Manual was prepared to train observers and contained detailed procedure for categorizing and tallying attempted leadership acts. Three observers were used in the experiment. Checks on observer agreement showed a reliability as indicated by an average interclass correlation coefficient of .83.

The subjects, 64 male students enrolled in elementary psychology at

Ohio State University, were volunteers who were found, on the basis of a short screening test, to be relatively naive with respect to all four of the tasks used in the experiment.

The number of each group member's attempted leadership acts was transformed into scores suitable for analysis of variance. Table 1 presents the basic results of the analysis.

Table I

ANALYSIS OF VARIANCE IN ATTEMPTED LEADERSHIP SCORES ASSOCIATED WITH GROUP DIFFERENCES (INITIAL INFORMATION AND TASK SEQUENCE) TASK DIFFERENCES AND RELEVANCE OF INFORMATION.

Source of Variation	df	Variance	F
Between tasks	3	87.36	45.98*
Between groups	15	7.63	4.02*
Between information	1	1.13	
Group information interaction	15	4.30	2.26*
Residual	221	1.90	
Total	255		

* Significant at .01 level.

The results of the experiment provide little or no support of the hypothesis. The subjects with the less relevant information attempted to lead as frequently as those with the more relevant information. However, the interactions of information with groups which involved the order in which the different tasks were encountered suggested that we might not be justified in rejecting the hypothesis entirely. Detailed examination of this interaction suggested that individuals who had relevant information on the first of the four group tasks, especially if that task was one in which there existed a close relation between information and successful task performance, rapidly accrued leadership status. Their status may have encouraged these individuals to continue to try to lead on subsequent tasks regardless of whether they had relevant information. It appeared that even on those tasks where other group members were better informed, earlier acquired leadership status was respected.

The results of this experiment demonstrated quite clearly a further point: wide differences among the four tasks in the over-all frequency of attempted leadership. Tasks which required decisions at frequency intervals, e.g., the Strategy tasks, produced far more attempted leadership acts than did the tasks which involved a single final group decision, e.g., the Discussion task.

B. Experiment Two

In the second of the four experiments, the hypothesis tested was that individuals with higher needs for achievement and lower needs for affiliation would attempt to lead more often, despite personal rejection which they associated with their attempts, than would individuals with lower needs for achievement and higher needs for affiliation. Acceptance or rejection by fellow group members was one variable and needs for achievement and affiliation was a second. The hypothesis involves a specific interaction of these two variables.

The task used in this second experiment was called the "manufacturing problem." This task required the four members of the group to organize themselves as a toy manufacturing concern and to operate their business for maximum profit. Tinkertoy parts were available at a "supplier's" table, and could be purchased and assembled to make either a toy "man," "top," "airplane," "wagon" or "step-ladder." Toys thus manufactured could be sold at a "buyer's" table. As beginning capital, each group was provided with three dollars. New buying and selling price lists were issued at the beginning of each five-minute period to simulate fluctuations in the markets. Two 20-minute sessions constituted the work period.

The first independent variable, "rejection-acceptance," was introduced into the experiment by two complementing procedures.

Each of the 24 groups were made up of two research assistants, who posed as subjects, and two bona fide subjects. To create the rejection condition, these assistants let a subject who attempted to lead know immediately and in no uncertain terms that they didn't like "bossy" people, resented people who told them what to do, and so on. In their "acceptance" role the assistants indicated, each time a subject attempted to lead, that they liked a person who could get things going and who could come up with a good plan. In neither role did the assistants themselves attempt to lead, nor did they refuse to carry out a suggestion made by a bona fide subject. They constantly displayed a keen interest in the task and frequently expressed a desire to do well at it. They were completely successful in not being recognized as other than fellow group members.

As a means of reinforcing the treatment given the subject by the assistants, an opportunity was provided by a "warm-up" period before the beginning of the experimental task and again by a break between the two sessions to obtain and "feed back" sociometric ratings. Ostensibly, these ratings were immediately tallied by the experimenter and presented as confidential "feedback" to the subjects. In actuality, the "feedback" was prearranged to reinforce the treatment the subject had been receiving.

The second independent variable, need patterns, was introduced by the selection of subjects. The subjects were 48 white male students, enrolled in the introductory psychology course at Ohio State University. A screening questionnaire followed by a 15-minute interview was used to locate two extreme classes of 24 subjects each. One class consisted of individuals who professed a long-standing and strong desire to achieve in many areas of endeavor and who also indicated relatively little dependence upon love and affection from others. The other class of subjects represented the opposite extremes with respect to their professed needs for achievement and affiliation. The reader should be cautioned to note that our procedure for determining these needs differs from that suggested by McClelland, Atkinson, Clark, and Lowell (1953) and Shipley and Veroff (1952).

As in the first experiment, the dependent variable was the number of attempted leadership acts as tallied by well trained observers. The analysis of the attempted leadership scores is presented in Table 2.

The second column of F-ratios in Table 2 presents the results of a more stringent test for the effects and is based upon a comparison with the interaction treatment X needs X blocks.

Table 2

ANALYSIS OF VARIANCE IN ATTEMPTED LEADERSHIP SCORES ASSOCIATED
WITH NEEDS, TREATMENTS, SESSIONS AND BLOCKS
(OF TWO GROUPS EACH)

Source of Variation	df	Variance	F_1	F_2
Between treatments	1	130.67	76.42**	21.92**
Between needs	1	0.38		
Between sessions	1	5.04	2.95	
Between blocks	11	4.86	2.84*	
Treatment X needs	1	1.49		
Treatment X sessions	1	0.67		
Treatment X blocks	11	5.35	3.13*	
Needs X sessions	1	0.37		
Needs X blocks	11	2.60	1.52	
Sessions X blocks	11	0.68		
Treatment X needs X sessions	1	4.17	2.44	
Treatment X needs X blocks	11	5.96	3.49*	
Treatment X sessions X blocks	11	1.17		
Needs X sessions X blocks	11	0.60		
Residual	11	1.71		
Total	95			

* Significant at .05 level.
** Significant at .01 level.

The results of this experiment demonstrated a definite effect of rejection or acceptance upon the frequency of attempts to lead. This statistical result is supported by a general observation that was made during the experiment: it was not uncommon to have 15 or 20 minutes of silence after the assistants had repeatedly rejected the subjects for attempting to lead. At such times, the two subjects quit trying to get things going and simply stood around the room showing great embarrassment. This refusal occurred in spite of the fact that the group members were thereby forfeiting an opportunity to earn money by doing well on a task which had been set for them by the experimenter. In marked contrast, when the assistants acted in their "accepting" roles, group activities moved at a rapid, if not hectic, pace. Individuals who apparently had rarely led before began to do so with great frequency. Moreover their style of leading often assumed a crude form of giving direct orders.

A point biserial correlation coefficient of .61 indicated that at least one-third of the observed variation in attempting to lead could be accounted for by the acceptance or rejection treatments.

Although the effects of rejection and acceptance were amply demonstrated, the experimental hypothesis had to be rejected (Treatment X Needs). There was no evidence that supported a difference between the two classes of subjects with respect to their reactions to acceptance or rejection. Individuals who had been selected as having high needs for achievement and low needs for affiliation were affected by rejection as much as were those who were classed as having lower achievement needs and higher affiliation needs. Our method of classifying subjects with respect to need categories may be open to question, but this experiment provided no support for these two personality variables as important in accounting for attempts to lead.

C. Experiment Three

The third of the four experiments was concerned with the effects upon attempts to lead of (1) motivation to accomplish the group's task, and (2) expectancy of being able to do it. One of our hypotheses was that group members who work on a task for which the rewards for its accomplishment are large and significant would attempt to lead with greater frequency than those who work on tasks involving lesser rewards. Our second hypothesis was that group members who could see clearly that work on a task would contribute to its accomplishment would try to lead more frequently than those who were less certain of the possibilities of accomplishment on the task.

The task used in this experiment was an adaptation of the manufacturing problem which has been used in the preceding experiment. The objective of the task varied with the two conditions of reward. Subjects exposed to "high" reward conditions worked to earn money. They worked on a task which was presented enthusiastically to them by the experimenter and which was represented as a very important research project that simulated manufacturing. Under the "low" reward conditions, on the other hand, the importance of the task and its inherently interesting features were de-emphasized. The task this time was presented by the experimenter without enthusiasm and as a pretest of a Tinkertoy test which might be more appropriate for children. Further the subjects exposed to "low" reward conditions worked merely to earn "points." Care was exercised not to alter the task in any way with changes in reward conditions which might affect the opportunities it afforded for group members to attempt to lead.

The second independent variable, expectancy, was introduced by the simple expedient of varying the "profit" margin between the "supplier's" and "buyer's" price lists. Under "high" expectancy, by comparing the two price lists, group members could easily find a "profitable" toy to build. Under "low" expectancy, however, their choice was either to break even or to lose—no opportunities existed for making a profit.

The experiment was run in two 20-minute sessions. The first 5 minutes of each session was reserved for planning, during which time the subjects were forbidden to do other work. The 5-minute planning period was provided to give the subjects an opportunity to become aware of the expectancy conditions under which they were to work. During the first of the two sessions, expectancy (i.e., the profit margin) was set at a moderate level and only the reward conditions were permitted to vary. During the second session, both independent variables were involved.

The subjects were 96 volunteer male students from the introductory psychology course at Ohio State University. They were assembled into 24 four-man groups without reference to other than scheduling convenience.

The results of this experiment are given in Table 3.

Unlike the previous two experiments, for which the results failed to support major hypotheses, both hypotheses involved in the third experiment were clearly supported. Members of the groups working under "high" reward conditions attempted more leadership acts than did those under "low" reward. When expectancy was varied in session two, those individuals who worked under "high" expectancy attempted to lead most. The interaction between expectancy and motivation conditions did not contribute a significant effect.

Table 3

ANALYSIS OF VARIATION IN ATTEMPTED LEADERSHIP SCORES
ASSOCIATED WITH REWARD AND EXPECTANCY

Source of Variation	df	Variation	F
Session I			
Between Reward Conditions	1	20.17	6.79*
Between Observers	1	10.67	3.59
Reward X Observers	1	2.03	.68
Group Uniqueness	20	4.78	1.61
Residual	72	2.97	
Total	95		
Session II			
Between Expectancy Conditions	1	33.84	11.87**
Between Reward Conditions	1	14.26	5.06*
Between Observers	1	33.84	11.87**
Expectancy X Reward	1	.10	.04
Expectancy X Observers	1	12.76	4.48*
Reward X Observers	1	1.76	.62
Expectancy X Reward X Observers	1	.02	.01
Group Uniqueness	16	3.42	1.20*
Residual	72	2.85	
Total	95		

* Significant at the .05 level.
** Significant at the .01 level.

The significant effect of observer differences in Table 3 needs some explanation. Observer differences were completely confounded with the time of day (A.M. or P.M.) at which the groups were run. One observer worked in the morning, another in the afternoon. A detailed analysis of subjective reports of the subjects after the experiment suggested that this effect could possibly be explained by a difference in the alertness between morning and afternoon subjects. Subjects run in the morning groups reported more accurate perceptions of the expectancy conditions, i.e., when no profit or gain could be made they realized it quickly. In the afternoon, there was a tendency for the subjects who worked under low expectancy to fail to perceive, until late in the session, that nothing could be gained by working on the task.

D. Experiment Four

The fourth experiment (Shevitz, 1955) was designed to repeat the first experiment, with special attention to controlling variables which had confused the result in the first case. In this experiment, the major hypothesis was again that those individuals with more relevant information would attempt to lead their group more often than would individuals with less relevant information. Rather than try to impart relevant information to the subjects at the beginning of the experiment by supplying it in the form of a booklet to be studied, we selected subjects who had already achieved expert knowledge in an area directly related to one of two tasks. Both tasks demanded a high degree of technical knowledge. One was a more difficult version of the electronics assembly task used in the first experiment. "Experts" for this task were recruited from the Columbus Amateur Radio Association. The second task was a statistical problem. "Experts" for this task had successfully completed a basic course in statistics.

Twenty-four three-man groups were used; each included one "expert" for the particular task on which the group was to work, an "expert" on the other of the two tasks, and a naive subject. The latter was selected because he had scored very low on a short achievement test in both electronics and statistics. Each group thus contained a member who was expert in an area relevant to the task and two who were not. Each expert worked on one task for which his special technical knowledge was relevant and also on a task for which he had no special qualification. Groups were reconstituted after each task so that the three members always started work as strangers. This avoided the possible effects of previously acquired leadership status noted in the first experiment.

Table 4 presents a summary of the results of this experiment.

Table 4

ANALYSIS OF DIFFERENCES BETWEEN ATTEMPTED LEADERSHIP SCORES, OF
TASK EXPERTS, NONTASK EXPERTS, AND NAIVE SUBJECTS
ON TWO DIFFERENT TASKS

| | Types of Subject | | |
	Electronic Expert (A)	Statistics Expert (B)	Naive Subject (C)
Electronic Assembly	6.58	4.00	1.47
Statistics Problem	3.76	6.09	2.71
t	8.06	3.59	2.18
p	.001	.01	.05

The results of this experiment clearly demonstrate that the "experts" in both electronics and statistics attempted leadership most often when working on tasks relevant to their special backgrounds.

DISCUSSION

In each of the four experiments, the effects of the experimental variables were observed in terms of the number of times members of groups attempted to lead their groups. It seems reasonable to infer that the effects of these variables upon how often individuals attempted to lead were mediated through changes in individual motivation. We may interpret the results of these experiments in terms of factors producing motivation to lead.

From this point of view, the experiments strongly suggest that individuals are encouraged to try to lead by (a) rewards that are associated with the accomplishment of the group task, (b) expectations that the group task can be accomplished, (c) specific task characteristics as yet not clearly understood but which create requirements for someone to lead, and (d) personal acceptance by their fellow group members which comes about as a result of attempts to lead. The experiments also suggest, although not as clearly, two additional sources of encouragement to lead: (1) possession of task relevant information not readily transmittable to others, and (2) previously acquired leadership status in the group.

An attempt to lead is an act through which the individual hopes to secure the satisfaction of a reward. With respect to the rewards associated with the accomplishment of the group's task, the more meaningful and important the reward is for the members of the group the more they are motivated to lead.

Although the amount or significance of task reward directly influences the individual's motivation to lead, he is also influenced by his estimate of his chances of obtaining the reward through work on the task. If he can see no connection between attempting to lead the group and achieving the reward, his motivation to lead is lowered. In situations where the objective conditions are such that it is unreasonable to expect that a reward can be obtained through attempting to lead, almost all such attempts can be traced either to a failure to comprehend the situation fully or to restructuring the task to involve a substitute reward. In the third experiment, almost all the attempts to lead made under the low-expectancy conditions occurred before the group members had fully realized that work on the manufacturing problem would produce no gain, or by an individual who refused to accept this objective reality. In order to be motivated to lead his group, the individual must not only want the reward that can be obtained by accomplishing the task, but he must also see some relationship between his attempt to lead and obtaining the reward.

Task rewards are not the only ones that are involved in determining motivation to lead. Perhaps of more importance is acceptance by other group members. Rarely did an individual continue to try to lead when he was aware that his attempt resulted in his rejection by other members of the group. Conversely, a strong reinforcement of attempted leadership acts was immediate approval of the individual by others in his group. To be liked and accepted by the group may be a more important consideration than task accomplishment.

The results of the first and fourth experiments, both of which were concerned with the function of relevant information as a source of motivation for leadership, give some insight into a complex relationship between technical competence and leadership. Possession of task relevant information is not in itself a mandate to lead. Such information can be communicated to other group members, who in turn can transform it into a recommendation for a course of group action. This latter alternative is a very probable choice if one of the other group members has status as the group's leader. If there already exists a recognized leader, the better informed group member may prefer to restrict his group participation to providing information and thus avoid challenging or interfering with the role of the established leader. However, if the group member clearly enjoys a vastly superior knowledge or competence, and especially if other group members are aware of his expert knowledge, he encounters great pressure to lead, for it may be difficult or impossible for him to transmit his information rapidly enough or fully enough to meet the requirements of the task. Under such circumstances, he is expected to make recommendations for courses of action for the group to follow rather than simply to volunteer his information.

Group tasks set widely different demands or requirements for leadership. The nature of the task thus becomes an important consideration in the complex of motivational factors related to the attempt to lead. A task that repeatedly presents occasions where a decision must be made produces many attempted leadership acts. Repeated decisions were necessary to carry out the strategy task, employed in the first experiment. It will be recalled that in work on the strategy task, the four group members played as a team against the experimenter. The game involved a series of alternating moves, first by the experimenter and then by the subjects. With each move, the group members faced the necessity of analyzing the consequences of the experimenter's play and deciding about their own strategy. Since the game was played within a time limit, decisions had to be made rapidly.

In contrast, the first experiment also included a discussion task, which required very little group decision making. This type of task is popular in the study of group interaction. Typically, group members are presented with a problem requiring a single decision. They bring whatever knowledge they have to bear upon the problem, and eventually render a single group decision. Since such tasks can be solved appropriately with but a single decision, fewer attempts to lead were made during the 15-minute period spent with the discussion task than were made in the case of the strategy task.

These observations about the nature of tasks and the frequency of attempted leadership make it necessary to digress to consideration of a major difference between attempted leadership as used here and attempted leadership as used by Bass (1953). Bass utilizes the gross frequency of participation (talking) as a measure of attempted leadership in group discussion tasks. He reasons that almost every opportunity a group member takes to participate in a leaderless group discussion can be considered as an attempt by that person to influence the perceptions or behavior of the other members toward his point of view, and thus as an attempt to lead. In the present study, however, merely presenting facts or information to the group or simply reasoning aloud were not considered attempted leadership. To be considered an attempt to lead, we required a clearly recognizable intention on the part of the group member to initiate or to make a change in the form of interaction which the group is to use in its mutual problem-solving activities. Giving information to the group or reflecting upon various possible courses of action without recommending one over the others were not considered attempts to lead. It is in the group discussion task that the differences between group participation and frequency of attempted leadership is most clearly seen. Verbal participation, although perhaps necessary, is entirely insufficient as an indication of an attempt to lead.

SUMMARY AND CONCLUSIONS

These four closely interrelated experiments provide some insight into a complex of personal and situational variables which explain what motivates a group member to try to lead. On the side of positive motivation, we find (1) large rewards promised by accomplishing the group's task, (2) reasonable expectancy that by working on the task it can be accomplished, (3) acceptance by other members of the group for attempting to lead, (4) a task which requires a high rate of group decisions, (5) possession of superior knowledge or competence relevant to the accomplishment of the task, and (6) previously acquired status as the group's leader. On the negative side, we find, (1) low task reward, (2) low expectancy of task accomplishment, (3) rejection by group members for attempting to lead, (4) a task which sets requirement for only a few decisions, (5) low competence on the task or little knowledge relevant to it, and (6) respect for the leadership status of another group member. Attempting to lead presents the possibility of receiving certain negative sanctions, probably the most severe being a rejection by fellow members of the group. Motivation to lead appears as a resultant of the probability of achieving rewards of task accomplishment and the probability of negative sanction.

A few experiments cannot be expected to answer all the questions of leadership motivation. The four reported here require replication and the leads which their results suggest need to be followed up. This is one recommended course for future leadership research. A second course is to direct attention to the research areas which have been identified as "successful" leadership and "effective" leadership. Investigation of these areas logically follows some understanding of why people try to lead.

It is hoped that the results of the experiments described and summarized in this paper demonstrate in a small way the fruitfulness of a more limited and directed approach to problems of leadership research. It is believed that progress can be made with systematic exploration of various parts or areas of leadership. We need better theories to suggest areas of problems and, further, to provide a system for adding together the results of different investigations. Perhaps the concepts of attempted, successful, and effective leadership can contribute in this direction.

REFERENCES

BASS, B. M., WURSTER, C. R., DOLL, PADDY ANN, AND CLAIR, D. J. Situational and personality factors in leadership among sorority women. *Psychol. Monogr.*, 1953, 67, No. 16 (Whole No. 366).

GIBB, C. A. Leadership. In G. LINDZEY (Ed.), *Handbook of social psychology.* Vol. II. Cambridge, Mass.: Addison-Wesley, 1954.

HEMPHILL, J. K. Administration as problem-solving. In A. W. HALPIN (Ed.), *Administrative theory in education.* Chicago: Midwest Administration Center, 1958.

HEMPHILL, J. K., PEPINSKY, PAULINE N., KAUFMAN, A. E., AND LIPETZ, M. E. Effects of task motivation and expectancy of accomplishment upon attempts to lead. *Psychol. Monogr.*, 1957, 71, No. 22 (Whole No. 451).

HEMPHILL, J. K., PEPINSKY, PAULINE N., SHEVITZ, R. N., JAYNES, W. E., AND CHRISTNER, CHARLOTTE A. The relation between possession of task relevant information and attempts to lead. *Psychol. Monogr.*, 1956, 70, No. 7 (Whole No. 414).

JENKINS, W. O. A review of leadership studies. *Psychol. Bull.,* 1947, *44,* 54–79.

MCCLELLAND, D., ATKINSON, J. W., CLARK, R. A., AND LOWELL, E. L. *The achievement motive.* New York: Appleton, 1953.

PEPINSKY, PAULINE N., HEMPHILL, J. K., AND SHEVITZ, R. N. Attempts to lead, group productivity, and morale under conditions of acceptance and rejection. *J. abnorm. soc. Psychol.,* 1958, *57,* 47–54.

SHEVITZ, R. N. *Leadership acts. IV. An investigation of the relation between exclusive possession of information and attempts to lead.* Columbus: Ohio State Univ. Res. Found., 1955.

SHIPLEY, T. E., JR. AND VEROFF, J. A projective measure of need for affiliation. *J. exp. Psychol.,* 1952, *43,* 349–356.

STOGDILL, R. M. Personal factors associated with leadership; a survey of the literature. *J. Psychol.,* 1948, *25,* 35–71.

14

Organization, Management Strategy, and Team Productivity[1]

Harold B. Pepinsky and Pauline N. Pepinsky

The Ohio State University

Increasing the productivity of work teams is, in everyday life, an important management problem. Managerial decisions are required not only to identify and assess past or present productivity, when it has occurred, but to make possible increased amounts of either known productivity or new forms of productivity in the future. In the present chapter a program of research, centered on this problem, is reviewed and discussed. Emphasis is given here to four laboratory experiments on motivation and productivity, performed in 1955–1957 under the sponsorship of ONR's Group Psychology Branch.[2]

[1] Work on this paper was partially supported under Contract AF 49(638)–373 between the Air Force Office of Scientific Research and the Ohio State University Research Foundation. An earlier version, Working Paper RF 857–12, was presented to a project seminar on "Organization and the productivity of research teams."

[2] The research was conducted under Contract N6ori–17, T.O. III (NR 171–123) between the Office of Naval Research and The Ohio State University Research Foundation. Detailed technical reports on all of the studies (H. Pepinsky, P. Pepinsky, and Pavlik, 1956; Florence, 1956b; P. Pepinsky, H. Pepinsky, and Pavlik, 1956; Pavlik, 1956; P. Pepinsky, H. Pepinsky, Robin, and Minor, 1957; H. Pepinsky, P. Pepinsky, Minor, and Robin, 1957) may be obtained on loan from the Gifts and Exchange Department of the Ohio State University.

THE FIELD STUDIES OF PRODUCTIVITY IN ORGANIZATIONS

A program of research on productivity in organizations has been under way since 1951 in the Ohio State University's Counseling and Testing Center.[3] This research has suggested to us a useful working definition of productivity as a measured amount of successful task accomplishment by an actor or a team of actors (H. Pepinsky, P. Pepinsky, and Pavlik, 1958, p. 305). In field and laboratory studies, this definition pointed to the selection, empirical definition, and measurement of the outcomes of activities engaged in by individuals or teams in organizational settings. Several useful generalizations emerged from the field studies (Clyde, 1956; Coon and H. Pepinsky, 1955; Fager, 1958; Florence, 1956a; Florence, 1956b; Hood, 1953; Hopwood, 1954; Love, 1957; Moss, 1955; Pavlik, 1955; Pendleton, 1955; H. Pepinsky, 1954b; H. Pepinsky, 1955; Siegel, Coon, H. Pepinsky, and Rubin, 1956; Stoltz, 1956; Stunden, 1955; Thrush, 1957; Thrush, 1958; Warman, 1958). The most important of these generalizations is concerned with the definition of productivity as a dependent variable—the problem of the criterion.

First, it became evident that each organization provided its own relevant, empirical definitions of productivity, in prescribing both the tasks to be performed and the criteria for their successful completion. In marked contrast, many students of organization make a priori assumptions about desirable activity outcomes to be obtained in natural settings and then attempt to structure empirical events according to their beliefs (for example, Churchman, Ackoff, and Arnoff, 1957), a procedure that has been challenged elsewhere (H. Pepinsky and Thrush, 1958; Howland, 1959). In designing our motivation and productivity experiments, we attempted to create task conditions and requirements similar to those observed in natural settings, so as to increase both the face validity of the tasks for the subjects who performed them and the generality of the experimental results. The generalized finding that definition and assessment of productivity were idiosyncratic to an organization supported a hunch that observable productivity would be linked to task conditions resulting from particular organizational norms of task accomplishment. In the laboratory, then, we were encouraged to make specific predictions concerning productivity differences as outcomes consequent to systematically varied task conditions.

Second, it became apparent that the concept of *task* varied considerably

---

[3] Then called the Occupational Opportunities Service. The senior author is grateful to the agency director, Frank M. Fletcher, Jr., for his continuing stimulation and encouragement of the productivity research.

within organizations in the explicitness with which it was defined by persons from whom productivity data were obtained in the field studies. Since productivity outputs might be expected to vary with the explicitness of antecedent task instructions, we attempted to specify clearly for our laboratory subjects the amount of time, space, and activity required for the performance of laboratory tasks. Third, the field studies revealed that definitions of productivity itself varied among persons within an organization. Further, these definitions seemed to vary with the positions held by persons within the organization. Therefore, in the laboratory we could expect subjects to define their productivity differently from members of the research groups who developed, assigned, and monitored laboratory tasks, and from nonparticipating observers who had still different views. We tried either to minimize or identify these differences through task instructions and checks on experimental procedure.

SOME BASIC DEFINITIONS AND ASSUMPTIONS

In this section, the above definition of productivity in organizations has been fused with a conception of effective management strategy to develop a rationale for the motivation and productivity experiments. The latter have as their prototype the "small group" experiment, in which the activity of an ad hoc group (Strodtbeck, 1954) of subjects is directed by and subjected to the contemporary assessment of a researcher or a group of researchers conducting the experiment (Guetzkow, 1950; Hare, Borgatta, & Bales, 1955; Riecken, 1958; Stogdill, 1959). As suggested in the preceding section, a deliberate attempt was made in the motivation and productivity experiments to use everyday events observed in natural settings as prototypes for laboratory situations. In turn, however, these experiments were planned to suggest possible manipulations of work conditions, by means of which task setters could manage more effectively teams of persons working with them.

A Conceptualization of Motivation and Productivity in Organizations

For a meaningful interpretation of our experiments, we may turn to the field studies of productivity in organizations and to relevant social (Gerth and Mills, 1946; Gerth and Mills, 1953; Parsons, 1951) and systems theory (Goode and Machol, 1957; Hitch, 1957). These suggest a definition of the social organization as a set of independent and dependent variables related to each other in a system of task related activities— together with their inputs and outputs—that establish and maintain the organization in an environment (after Howland, 1959). Among the independent variables we may assume that there are sets of persons who perform system tasks, for example, control, communication, selection, service, and supply (Howland, 1959), and who share responsibility for the accomplishment of system tasks. The control tasks of the system are assumed to include its task setting operations: (a) requiring specified tasks to be performed under stipulated rules of procedure, (b) specifying the criteria by which task performance is to be evaluated, (c) evaluating the performance of assigned tasks, and (d) selecting, rejecting, and developing system members on the basis of their success in performing assigned tasks. Members of the system are defined as "actors," persons who "act" or "behave as if"; each actor being required to perform assigned tasks in the system and being assessed by it for his performance. Task setting operations of the system are assumed to include the performance of actors whose task assignments consist of setting tasks for other actors. Hierarchies of actors setting tasks for other actors and having effects upon other actors' task performance also may be assumed. In this framework *productivity* is defined as the amount of success that an actor or team of actors has in the performance of an assigned system task, and *effect* is the modification of productivity resulting from another actor's strategies.[4]

In moving from the above conceptualization of the social system to the motivation and productivity experiments, we can anticipate the necessity of distinguishing between the task as defined (a) by the actor to whom it is assigned and (b) by the task setter who assigns it (see previous section). Therefore, we may define the task, in the latter view, as the confronting of an actor with a designated stimulus situation in which he is required to follow stipulated rules of procedure in responding to the situation, and in which he must attempt to satisfy specified criteria by which the amount of success of his acts is judged. (Note that "required," "stipulated," and "specified" are treated as variables in respect to explicitness and amount.) The task setter is assumed to be operating for the social system, both in stipulating the actor's rules of procedure and in judging the extent to which the actor satisfies the task setter's criteria of success. This is called the official task—to distinguish it from the actor's private task or problem, the actor's definition of a stimulus situation that

---

[4] In an earlier version of this conceptualization, it was assumed that the effect of one actor upon the actions of another depends upon the ability of the former to reward and punish the behavior of the latter, such "power" relationships helping to explain an organization's survival (H. Pepinsky, P. Pepinsky, and Pavlik, 1956, pp. 1–6). As Howland (1959) has indicated, however, it is conceptually helpful to differentiate, e.g., "service" (production) and "control" (power), tasks that contribute independently to the continuing existence of an organization. We are indebted to Daniel Howland for his concept of system, but he is not responsible for what we have done to it here.

he feels impelled to modify so as to realize some personally desired out-come. Thus, an actor may or may not respond to the assigned, official task as if it were a problem to him; the actor must be so motivated before he can be expected to act in accordance with the task setter's requirements of him (adapted from H. Pepinsky, P. Pepinsky, and Pavlik, 1958, pp. 305–306).

Productivity as Related to Effective Management Strategy

Stated baldly, the problem that we wrestled with in the laboratory was how to get three- and four-man teams of persons to do well what we told them to do. To accomplish this, we set up in the laboratory miniature social organizations in which particular members of a research group were designated as experimenters (*E*s) to act for us as task setters, and in which student subjects (*S*s) were treated as teams of actors performing tasks assigned to them by the *E*s—under working conditions prescribed for both *E*s and *S*s by the research group.

We propose in this paper, then, to shift our original perspective and to consider now the research group as a management team, with the *S*s cast in subordinate roles. It is argued that the decisions of a research group, as they were used to manipulate the working conditions of *E*s and *S*s, constituted management strategies. In another context Hemphill (1958) has provided a useful definition of these strategies—which he has called "attempted leadership acts"—as "acts governed by an intent to initiate structure-in-interaction . . . as part of the process of solving a mutual problem" (pp. 98–99). In the present context "mutual problem" has been defined as a shared responsibility for task accomplishment.[5] Through explicit instructions to the *E*s and the teams of *S*s who performed for our research groups in the laboratory, we tried to ensure that the *S*s knew what kind of task performance was expected of them. Through various independent checks we tried to find out whether the *S*s did accept such an allocation of responsibility—to what extent, if the *S*s saw the situation as a game, they were playing the game according to rules laid down for them by the *E*s, or were instead engrossed in counter strategies of their own (see Criswell, 1958).

It is argued, further, that when the explicit strategies of a research group, through the agency of designated *E*s, led to *S* behavior consistent

---

[5] The term *mutual problem* has alternative implications; e. g., Lewin's (1948, p. 165) belief in an "interdependence of fate" among Jews may be contrasted with Hemphill's (1958, p. 90) idea of a shared dissatisfaction among persons that requires satisfying behavior from each of the persons, the latter closely allied to Deutsch's (1949, p. 150) concept of the "promotively interdependent" pursuit of goals by a group.

with experimental prediction, then such strategies exemplified *effective management strategies* by the research group, regardless of whether the Ss' productivity increased or decreased. Again, we are consistent with Hemphill's (1958) definition of what he has labeled "effective leadership acts" as "acts that have initiated structure-in-interaction and that have contributed to the solution of a mutual problem" (p. 106). In this case the mutual problem of the research group is to increase its own ability to predict the behavior of the Ss.

Our research had the flavor of a betting situation, in which the research group itself was required for each experiment to forecast greater or lesser "payoff" (better or poorer performance by the Ss) for specified, alternative conditions imposed on the experimental teams of Ss (cf. Girshick, 1954; Marschak, 1954). Although the substantive content of the research varied from experiment to experiment, the dependent—or payoff—variable was made definitionally consistent for all experiments. In one of these, we took a benevolent attitude, and we set things up so that particular team members could be interested and satisfied while doing a relatively good job for us! Our principal dependent variable in every case, however, was *productivity,* defined as *a measured amount of successful task accomplishment by a team member or by an aggregate of team members. In every case, also, "successful task accomplishment" was given explicit, a priori definition by the research group.*

The selection of task performance as a measure of our major dependent variable was done arbitrarily. For the moment, other behavior was regarded as "out-of-system" (see Guetzkow, 1950). In so doing, we assumed that, in response to assigned tasks, the behavior of individual team members (1) could be observed and measured, and (2) could be classified as "correct" or "incorrect" in terms of specified criteria. We assumed, further, that (3) the two categories of behavior were mutually exclusive, and that (4) behaviors occurring in the two categories were inversely related (that is, more of one kind of behavior would be accompanied by less of the other).

Although we are still working toward the statement of a general rationale concerning the effects of management strategies upon worker productivity in organizational settings, we did employ a central notion in the motivation and productivity experiments. It was that "correct" and "incorrect" behavioral outcomes are mediated by *response competition,* itself engendered by variously manipulated experimental conditions assumed to make conflicting demands upon the actor.

We made use of this notion in formulating specific relational propositions for the experiments: in general, other things being equal, (1) an experimental condition that increases correct behavior will decrease incorrect behavior; (2) an experimental condition that increases incorrect behavior will decrease correct behavior; and, therefore, (3) since productivity is an outcome of correct behavior, individual or team productivity will be greater under condition 1 than under condition 2. For each experiment, of course, it was necessary to make explicit the experimental conditions that would be likely to increase correct or incorrect behavior. These statements helped us to predict, for the particular situation, greater and lesser amounts of productivity for individual team members and for the team as a whole. The predictions could be interpreted as "paying off" to the extent that (1) they followed logically from a particular experimental rationale; (2) the rationale was definitionally related to actual laboratory operations; and (3) the predictions were empirically supported by laboratory data.

In the experiments, the strategies of the research group were designed to control and manipulate experimental conditions antecedent to the Ss' task performance. Though the manipulated conditions were varied from experiment to experiment, their purpose throughout was to increase our ability to predict and account for individual and team productivity in the simulated organizations that we had created in the laboratory. We could infer that a team of Ss were more *motivated* toward task accomplishment if our experimental manipulations were followed by relative increases in productivity. Conversely, when such predictions were supported, we could infer that task relevant *motivational properties* could be attributed to the manipulated antecedent conditions.

In summary, each laboratory experiment could be conceived as a social system, in which teams of Ss shared with a research group responsibility for the performance of system tasks. In a simulated, miniature social organization, Es acted for the research group as task setters for Ss who performed assigned tasks. According to planned strategies, the research group managed the Ss through manipulations of experimental conditions, assumed to be motivating in that they were rationally calculated to increase the likelihood of either correct or incorrect behavior by the Ss. The research group's management strategies were inferred to be effective when accompanied by the repeated occurrence, in successive teams of Ss, of anticipated higher or lower productivity scores.

THE MOTIVATION AND PRODUCTIVITY EXPERIMENTS

Four different sets of manipulations were employed in the experiments, namely, (a) task relevant personal belief, (b) task complexity and time pressure, (c) group orientation and related type of task, and (d) confirmation *versus* contradiction of management policy commitments. An experiment was designed for each set of manipulations. The four experiments are summarized below.

Task relevant personal belief and task accomplishment (H. Pepinsky, P. Pepinsky, and Pavlik, 1956; 1958)

This experiment was based on the assumption that an important component of an actor's motivation to perform an organizational task is his belief in his ability to perform successfully a class of activities sampled by the task. Through repeated experience, the actor develops generalizations about classes of task events that he believes himself capable of performing more or less successfully. Hence, (Relational Proposition I) when organizational task and personal belief are compatible, motivation to perform the task is greater than out-of-system motivation; and (Relational Proposition II) when tasks and belief are not compatible, out-of-system motivation is greater than motivation to perform the task.

*S*s in the experiment were 56 white, male Ohio State University undergraduate students, selected on the basis of their responses to the Student Behavior Description, a forced-choice measure of undergraduate student belief about successful student behavior in the University (Florence, 1956a; Florence 1956b). Part I scores indicate which of five behavioral dimensions a student uses to characterize himself, and a Part II score shows where his self description places him on a General Level of Success dimension. Four classes of *S*s were selected for the experiment:

Class I: High score on an Organizational Leadership (OL) dimension, low score on a Scholastic Achievement (SA) dimension; high score on the General Level of Success (GLS) dimension.

Class II: High score on OL, low score on SA; low score on GLS.

Class III: Low score on OL, low score on SA; high score on GLS.

Class IV: Low score on OL, high score on SA; low score on GLS.

*S*s were divided into 14 four-man teams, each containing representatives of these four classes of students. Team members were equated for general scholastic ability. Every team performed two laboratory tasks, one devised to elicit behavior specified by highly loaded items on the Organizational Leadership factor (from which the OL scale of the Student Behavior Description was derived); and the other, to elicit behavior specified by the Scholastic Achievement factor (from which the SA scale of the SBD was derived). Performance criteria on both the *organizational leadership* and *scholastic achievement* tasks also were designed to correspond to behavior specified by OL and SA items, respectively, of the SBD. The two laboratory tasks were presented in a counterbalanced order, half of the teams first performing the *ol,* and the other half, the *sa* task. Three hypotheses, relating SBD score to task performance score, then could be tested. Procedural checks had established that the *S*s scores on the SBD were phenomenally relevant to their views of the two tasks and that general scholastic ability differences among the four classes of *S*s were unrelated to their task performances.

Hypothesis I was that on the *organizational leadership* task, *S*s with high Organizational Leadership scores on the Student Behavior Description would perform better than *S*s with low OL scores. The hypothesis was supported in that more of the high OL than low OL *S*s were viewed by their peers as organizational leaders, but only when the *ol* task was presented *after* the *sa* task. Observer rankings of the *S*s organizational leadership, however, though highly reliable, were not related to the *S*s' OL scores.

Hypothesis II predicted that *S*s who had obtained high scores on the Scholastic Achievement scale of the Student Behavior Description would perform better than low SA score *S*s on the *scholastic achievement* task. Because mean differences on the task measures were quite small relative to within group variation in task scores, the mean differences themselves were not significant, and this hypothesis was not supported.

Hypothesis III stated that on *both* laboratory tasks, *S*s with high scores on the General Level of Success scale of the Student Behavior Description would perform better than *S*s with low GLS scores. This hypothesis was clearly supported in the case of both peer nominations and observer rankings of *organizational leadership* task performance, but not for the *scholastic achievement* task. Again, peer nominations were more closely associated with OL scores when the *ol* task followed the *sa* task in order of presentation to the *S*s.

Always allowing for the possibility that either the scholastic achievement belief or its task measure was weak, we could, post hoc, make sense out of these results. One inference was that the *scholastic achievement* task may have been only too successful in duplicating for the *S*s the unfortunately often dull University routine of class attendance, study, and test taking. This experimental task may have been generally nonmotivating, and performance variability attributable simply to individual differences in task-related ability. A second inference was that the *organizational leadership* task may have been more successful in differentiating between *S*s with high and low General Level of Success as well as Organizational Leadership scores, because organizational leadership represented a more prestigeful accomplishment than scholastic achievement for our sample of

*S*s. This interpretation of the data was supported by Florence's (1956a; 1956b; Pepinsky, 1956) research in developing the Student Behavior Description. A third inference followed from the first two, namely, that task order itself was situationally motivating for the high OL score *S*s whose beliefs were relevant to the *ol* task. If we could assume that the high OL score *S*s who performed the *sa* task in the first experimental session were frustrated by it, we could also infer that during the second session their motivation to perform the *ol* task would be increased, and that under this condition they could be expected to receive higher OL scores (cf. Brown and Farber, 1951). These findings and the inferences we drew from them did lead to the conclusion that the cultural or subcultural value of an organizational task may be an important component of individual task motivation; to wit, organizational leadership was more highly valued than scholastic achievement in the student subculture, and this antecedent condition did affect our laboratory results.

The Effects of Task Complexity and Time Pressure Upon Team Productivity (P. Pepinsky, H. Pepinsky, and Pavlik, 1956; 1960)

This experiment was designed to test the effects upon team productivity of the complexity of the assigned tasks and the conditions of time pressure under which teams of *S*s worked in a simulated organizational setting. Our rationale (described in detail in P. Pepinsky *et al.,* 1956), in which increased time pressure was assumed to increase the drive level of the team members, led us to expect (a) for a simple task, a straight-line relationship between time pressure and team productivity such that productivity increases with time pressure, and (b) for a complex task, a curvilinear relationship between time pressure and team productivity in which productivity is greatest under an intermediate time pressure.[6]

Seventy-two volunteer male undergraduate students were assigned to 24 three-man teams in this experiment. Two task conditions were introduced, operationally defined as a relatively simple (task S) task, and a relatively complex (task C) task; each involved the repeated assembly and disassembly of as many replicas of a nonrepresentational tinkertoy model as possible during a 20-minute experimental session. The effect of organization structure was controlled by requiring the teams to follow a rehearsed procedure, performing interlocked operations in an order prescribed by the E. Time conditions included a high (H), medium (M), and low (L)

---

[6] Cf. Brown & Farber (1951), Taylor & Spence (1952), H. Pepinsky and P. Pepinsky (1954), Taylor (1956), and Fincher (1956) for the development of an analogous rationale about the effects of drive level and task complexity upon *individual* productivity.

time pressure, manipulated through systematic variation in the frequency of oral signals indicating the amount of time remaining in each session. The dependent variable, a team productivity score, was measured as an adjusted total of the number of operations performed by the team during a work session. Thus, comparable performance measures were available for both tasks. The experiment was conducted according to a factorial design, counterbalanced to permit separate examination of time condition, tasks, time conditions sequence, task sequence, and block effects. Post-experimental checks revealed that the Ss in general were clearly able to identify the more and the less complex task, and to perceive conditions of greater and lesser time pressure. Also, the Ss clearly preferred task C to task S, and the second to the first of two work sessions.

Three predictions were tested concerning team productivity: (1) that on task S output would be significantly greater under time condition H than time condition L, (2) that on task S productivity under time condition M would be intermediate between productivity under L and H, and (3) that on task C productivity would be significantly greater under time condition M than L or H. A complete analysis of variance failed to support these hypotheses, where time conditions and tasks were examined separately. Instead, greater task complexity was consistently related to team productivity, and the second session scores showed an equivalent practice effect for both tasks. Yet, changes in time pressure from one session to the next in interaction with direction of change in time pressure did have a significant effect upon difference scores. When time pressure was changed from low in the first work session to medium in the second, a significant increase occurred in team-productivity scores. A decrement occurred, however, when the time pressure was increased from low to high. These effects occurred regardless of changes in task and the effect of practice.

The results were interpreted as underscoring the importance of carefully specifying the stimulus characteristics of tasks employed in research on the effects of simulated organizations upon worker productivity. The study also provided precise tests of the effects of two situational variables previously used in conglomerate fashion, without empirical knowledge of their independent predictive value. Within the range of tasks examined, an increase in task complexity was inferred to have a positive motivational effect upon team productivity. Task motivation is higher when the task is sufficiently complex to have some variety and intrinsic interest than if it is so simple as to be highly monotonous and boring. Also, the fact— that differences between sessions in team productivity scores were meaningfully related to changes in time pressure—was interpreted as lending support to a revised curvilinearity hypothesis about the relation between low, medium, and high time pressures and team productivity. Thus, change in time pressure also could be inferred to have motivating properties. Contrary to expectation, however, the hypothesis was supported for the simple as well as the complex task. This suggests that, even if it is highly structured, the team as compared to the individual work situation, is so complicated that beyond a point, increases in pressure will produce a decrement in performance on even a quite simple task. A follow-up experiment by Pavlik (1956) failed to support the hunch that, given initial, individual differences in drive level, as inferred from scores on the Manifest Anxiety Scale (Taylor, 1956), time pressure alone would significantly affect individual performance on even a simple task.

The Effects of Induced Orientation and Type of Task upon Group Performance and Group Morale (P. Pepinsky, H. Pepinsky, Robin, and Minor, 1957)

A provocative experiment by Olmsted (1952; 1954) provided the impetus for this experiment. His observational notes had indicated that induced *Gemeinschaftlich* and *Gesellschaftlich* (Tönnies, 1940; Parsons and Shils, 1952) orientations produced typical differences in the process of groups working on the same tasks. In our study, we attempted to induce experimentally one or other of the two orientations in separate sets of 8 four-man teams, considered to be groups because of the induced attitude that the members of each team were assumed to share (see Hemphill's definition of a "group" as "a shared attitude," in Hemphill *et al.,* 1954, Appendix A) in the context of a simulated organization. A third set of eight teams served as controls and received no experimental orientation. All 24 teams of Ss performed the same two experimental tasks: (a) a "human relations" task, the *Treaty Problem,* designed to elicit responses compatible with a *Gemeinschaftlich* orientation, and (b) a "rational" task, the 30 *Questions Quiz,* intended to elicit responses compatible with a *Gesellschaftlich* orientation. Each experimental group performed first the task that was assumed to be compatible with its induced orientation; task order was systematically varied under the control condition. Productivity, one of the dependent variables, was measured by team performance scores on each task. Measures of the second dependent variable, group member "morale," were obtained from postsession responses to items concerned with "interest in the task" and "satisfaction with the group." Two general propositions were that (a) team productivity is higher when the group task and group value orientation arouse compatible responses than when task and group value orientation arouse competing responses; and (b) when group member morale is instrumental to success as defined by *both* the group's value-orientation and the task performance criterion, then morale and productivity are positively correlated; otherwise, no relationship exists between morale and productivity.

Postsession questionnaire checks on the experimental procedures indicated that the experimental orientations were successfully induced and that the Quiz task was compatible with the *Gesellschaftlich* orientation. In the *Ss'* views, however, the Treaty problem was not compatible with the *Gemeinschaftlich* orientation. Yet the *Ss* regarded the two tasks as equally interesting.

Five hypotheses were tested: (1) the highest productivity scores on the Treaty task would be obtained by the *Gemeinschaftlich* groups, and (2) the highest productivity scores on the Quiz task would be obtained by the *Gesellschaftlich* groups; (3) interest in the task would be positively associated with the productivity scores for the *Gemeinschaftlich* groups on the Treaty task only, but (4) positively related to productivity on both tasks for the *Gesellschaftlich* groups; (5) group satisfaction would be positively related to productivity scores only in the case of *Gemeinschaft-lich* groups working on the Treaty problem. Hypotheses 2 and 4, concerning the effects of the *Gesellschaftlich* orientation, were supported by the data. None of the predictions about the *Gemeinschaftlich* groups was supported.

The performance of the control groups provided an illuminating aspect of the study. Without any *experimentally* induced orientation, a post-experimental questionnaire showed that the control teams were oriented toward being "good subjects," i.e., toward getting along with others (a *Gemeinschaftlich* value) in the group and also toward doing well on the task assigned by the experimenter (a *Gesellschaftlich* value). For them, these objectives were mutually compatible. But the control teams received *lower* productivity scores on *both* tasks than either the *Gesellschaftlich* or *Gemeinschaftlich* groups, which indicates that some orientation by management (as represented by the E) has more motivational effect than none. The performance of the control teams on the *Quiz* task was significantly and positively related to *both* indices of morale; performance on the *Treaty* task was unrelated to either morale measure.

There was independent evidence from the procedural checks to suggest that where particular predictions were not borne out, the prior assumption of task and orientation compatibility had not been satisfied. What actually did occur was consistent with our underlying rationale.

A central empirical question remains unanswered by this study. Can it be shown that there *are* special circumstances where a process (for example, *Gemeinschaftlich*) orientation will maximize group task efficiency? Or, does such an orientation lead to superior group performance, or to group performance correlated with morale, only when process variables are employed as criteria of productivity?

A major general conclusion from this experiment was that group productivity in the simulated organization did depend in part upon the compatibility of the group's value orientation with the procedural requirements for task success. Also, there was evidence that the relatedness of group morale to group productivity depended on the correspondence of (a) behavior measured as an index of morale with (b) behavior demanded by the task *and* favorably sanctioned by the group's value orientation. Finally, the results suggested that regardless of the particular task, group members were motivated to perform better by knowledge of the rules of procedure and the criteria by which their work was to be assessed. Here, too, we see evidence, in the task views of the control teams, of an infusion into the laboratory situation of cultural values placed upon docile conformity to the expectations of those in authority.

Team Productivity and Contradiction of Management Policy Commitments (H. Pepinsky, P. Pepinsky, Minor, and Robin, 1957; 1959)

The likely consequence for worker productivity in an industrial plant of a management failure to honor its policy commitments suggested our final experiment. Here 80 white, male undergraduate students, comprising 20 four-man teams, performed an assigned toy manufacturing task (adapted from the task employed in Hemphill, P. Pepinsky, Kaufman, and Lipetz, 1957). An invariant task condition, simulating bureaucratic organization in the natural setting (cf. Gerth and Mills, 1946, pp. 196–224), was a three-level hierarchical group structure, including: (a) an E serving as *vice president,* who directed and limited the performance of (b) an S who was appointed as *department chairman,* and who in turn coordinated the task performance of (c) three other Ss who constituted *members of a subordinate work team.* Relationships with another E, serving alternately as *supplier* and *buyer,* were also required. All transactions between the work team and the vice president, supplier, and buyer had to be conducted for the team by their department head, and all transactions between department head and buyer-supplier required the vice president's prior approval. Two experimental conditions were provided in the form of prior commitments by the vice president to the department head. These were advance statements of the sanctions to be given any prospective transactions between department head and supplier: (1) a *confirmation* condition, in which the vice president, by his subsequent action, corroborated his prior commitment, and (2) a *contradiction* condition, in which the vice president failed to corroborate his commitment—his approval or disapproval of subsequent transactions was not based upon information available to the work team. Since a team under the confirmation condition could predict correctly the vice president's approval or disapproval of transactions and since, under the contradiction condition, a team could not predict such transactions correctly, we could propose that the likelihood of out-of-system behavior would be greater under the contradiction than under the confirmation condition. Hence, we could hypothesize that team productivity would be lower under the contradiction condition than under confirmation. Following an initial work session in which all teams performed under a control condition, 10 of the four-man teams performed under the contradiction and 10, under the confirmation condition.

Postsession questionnaires and interviews clearly established that the confirmation teams could predict, and that the contradiction teams could not ever learn to predict the vice president's pattern of approvals and disapprovals during the experimental sessions. It was interesting to note, however, that the department heads (in contrast to the other Ss) claimed that they could predict the actions of management, despite independent evidence that they could not. Though a majority of both sets of Ss stated that their motivation was increased by the experimental conditions, a significantly larger proportion of the contradiction teams reported that their teams become more disorganized and less efficient. Comparisons between the two sets of teams provided unequivocal support for the hypothesis: productivity as measured by either amount of profit or amount of profit per minute of actual work time was clearly superior under the confirmation condition.

These findings strongly supported our inference that response competition effects, in a team situation as in individual performance, could account parsimoniously for decreased productivity scores in the performance of a complex organizational task. The experiment corroborates directly the informal impression that uncertainty over supervisory or sponsor departures from policy commitments in an organizational setting may contribute to a decrease in relevant motivation among work teams and a resultant decrease in their productivity on assigned tasks.

SOME CURRENT RESEARCH ACTIVITIES

The motivation and productivity experiments summarized above suggest a number of motivating conditions that may be used as management strategies to increase individual or team productivity in natural settings, including the selection of already relevantly motivated persons for membership. But on the practical side, it is not always easy to determine what productivity means in a given situation, or when a person or an organization can be regarded as productive. We recognized these difficulties before we began our experiments, but we were able in them to make explicit the properties of the simulated organization, the task conditions, the criteria for their successful accomplishment, and the measured outputs of team members as productivity scores. Such clarity is not easily attainable in everyday life. One of the possible by-products of studying individual and team productivity in natural organizational settings, however, is that organizational goals and accomplishments become clearer to the membership. Nevertheless, one of us recently has been confronted with the magnitude of the criterion problem in a University general hospital setting, where an interdisciplinary research team is engaged in a study of "patient care." At least eight different reference groups, to which both the hospital and the research group must attend, are clearly visible. The task of defining patient care alone is very complicated.[7]

A second, related aspect of the criterion problem in the natural setting is the necessity of taking into account the social environment in which task-related activity takes place, including its cultural setting. We recognized the restricted character of our task conditions–task setter-actor(s) conceptualization, but chose to deal mainly with "situational factors" in our experiments, following a pattern set in previous small group studies. In a current research project, however, one of us has turned again to a study of productivity as related to the natural organizational settings in which it occurs. In collaboration with an anthropologist and an industrial engineer, the senior author is seeking to determine how "organization" can be represented so as to provide useful answers to questions that arise in natural settings. For example, it will be helpful to identify effects that organization has upon the definition and assessment of team productivity, or when a team is able to innovate productively, or how innovation develops historically in the context of culture and social organization. Research groups on this project have focused on the specific problem of "organization and the productivity of research teams." Here, it is already evident that a variable such as "effective management strategy" can be viewed as antecedent to "organization," as dependent upon it, as mediating between "organization" and "productivity," or as emerging with other variables from the institutionalization of an organization.[8]

---

[7] Daniel Howland is principal investigator, under Research Grant No. GN–4784, from the Division of Nursing Resources of the U.S. Public Health Service (see H. Pepinsky and Thrush, 1958).

[8] See H. Pepinsky, Howland, and Bennett (1958). This research is supported under contract No. AF 49(638)–373 between the Air Force Office of Scientific Research and the Ohio State University Research Foundation.

Finally, the other author of this paper is directing a project in which she is seeking to discover situational factors antecedent to what she has called "productive nonconformity." Her investigation has implications for the research-team study, cited above, but she has not confined herself to the research team as a metaphor for the kind of behavior in which she is explicitly interested. Beginning with three field studies, which were designed to yield testable hypotheses, she and her associates have begun a series of experiments to identify some conditions likely to increase the occurrence of individual behavior that is both socially productive and independent of the prevailing social norms.[9]

These current research projects have permitted us to be concerned with the problem of balancing individual needs and talents against the pressures of social organization (cf. Argyris, 1957). Others have warned that as our kind of research contributes to knowledge of how to control and manipulate individual and team behavior, we contribute also to social control in the form of greater organizational and societal efficiency and greater restriction upon individual freedom of action. It seems to us, however, that the potential richness of task activity outcomes is increased, along with increases in freedom of movement for the persons involved, when they are helped to obtain favorable contemporary assessment for innovative behavior. Thus, the search for effective management strategies to increase the productivity of others has become for us, as investigators, an ideological as well as a methodological problem.

A CRITIQUE

This paper has summarized a series of experiments on motivation and productivity, which followed earlier research on productivity in organizations at the Ohio State University. Both the background and a set of definitions and assumptions basic to the experiments were briefly described, and cursory reference was made to some of our current research on organization and productivity, as outgrowths of the laboratory studies. Fortuitous circumstances—in the form of initially unanticipated research grants, stimulating colleagues, and challenging publications—have contributed both opportunity and awareness, modifying our research ideas and practices over time. Yet we have been doggedly persistent in attempting to define and measure human productivity as manifested in natural and simulated organizations, and to determine how productivity is apt to be

---

[9] Under Contract Nonr–495(15) (NR 170–396) between the Office of Naval Research and the Ohio State University Research Foundation (see P. Pepinsky and H. Pepinsky, 1958).

assessed and why it occurs or does not occur in the context of different kinds of organization.

From the experiments themselves, especially where the results were "essentially negative," we have learned much that rarely sees the light of day in psychological journals, where space restrictions prohibit more than the barest abstracting of ideas. In viewing the actions of our research groups as management strategies, we have learned the hard way that fuzziness of conceptualization and procedure invariably reduce the accuracy of laboratory predictions. We learned early the value of taking careful account of empirical evidence available to us from the work of others and from our own studies. We are heartened by the appearance of such relevant articles as those by Criswell (1958), Riecken (1958), and Rosenthal and Fode (1959), which strongly support our own concern with the use of procedural checks to determine whether there was congruence between the Ss' and our own views of the organizational tasks that we assigned to them. Many an unsuccessful "dry run," however, stood between this objective and our accomplishment of it. We strove, nevertheless, to make our tasks the Ss' problems, and to find out how well we succeeded. Our hunch is that many a published experiment may have been erroneously interpreted, because the Ss actually responded out of different frames of reference from those imputed to them by the E.

We ally ourselves, in principle, with those who believe that human actions and their antecedents are potentially capable of being rationally synthesized and used to predict behavioral outcomes. March, Simon, and Guetzkow (1958) and Newell, Shaw, and Simon (1958) have illustrated how such information can be "programmed" into a digital computer, which is made to serve as an analogue for individual and group problem-solving activity. In the context of this paper, the ability to program successfully is an instance of effective management strategy on the part of the investigator. On the other side of this argument are those who imply that no rationally conceived experiment and no computer program can adequately represent a developing person or organization of persons in a natural setting (e.g., Machover, 1949; Selznick, 1957). In this view each organism has a unique natural history and its own, idiosyncratic present circumstances. Effective management strategy, in the latter view, must take into account the "institutionalizing" process, by which the object of study becomes infused with value as it acquires its own, distinctive character. Management strategies cannot be rationally prescribed for dealing with persons in teams or in more complicated organizations; leadership must emerge developmentally in response to the social needs and pressures exerted in a particular natural organization.

Certainly we do not claim to be on the side of the angels in tending to espouse the former view. For example, in our "task relevant belief" and "group orientation" studies, the post hoc discovery was made that our very laboratory situation had become for the Ss infused with the cultural values that they had brought into it. And we were forced to take these values into account in a revision of our rationales and predictions for the experiments. But we *could* program this kind of knowledge into the experiments. In this way, we could also increase the effectiveness of our research strategies. It is, indeed, as Criswell (1958) has emphasized, a major advantage of the laboratory that *because* of its very artificiality, the investigator can "determine the structure of the subject's perception of his problem, including his perception of the experiment, his own role, and the role of the experimenter as an experimenter" (p. 102).

It is unfortunate, perhaps, that one must choose up sides at all, for there is much to be learned from different strategies. As it is, distorted interpretations of fact undoubtedly occur in the partisan when data are viewed as having been gathered, on one hand, by "mush-headed, seat-of-the-pants, post-hoc explanatory, hot clinicians"; and, on the other, by "static-cross-sectionalizing, molecular-atomistic, and narrow-minded authoritarians"! If we are not yet able in the behavioral sciences to discard our partisanship, let us at least try to make more explicit use of "man's forgotten weapon" of self-awareness, of which Roe (1959) has reminded us, to recognize that though our vantage points differ, we share an opportunity to contribute toward the solution of problems, in which we have a common interest—and there is ignorance enough for all.

REFERENCES

ARGYRIS, C. *Personality and organization: The conflict between system and the individual.* New York: Harper, 1957.

BROWN, J. S. AND FARBER, I. E. Emotions conceptualized as intervening variables—with suggestions toward a theory of frustration. *Psychol. Bull.,* 1951, *48,* 465–495.

CHURCHMAN, C. W., ACKOFF, R. L., AND ARNOFF, E. L. *Introduction to operations research.* New York: Wiley, 1957.

CLYDE, R. J. An investigation of the construct validity of some Rorschach variables. Unpublished doctoral dissertation, Ohio State Univ., 1956.

COON, H. L. AND PEPINSKY, H. B. Contributing toward a language of emotional health. *Educ. Leadership,* 1955, *12,* 476–480.

CRISWELL, JOAN H. The psychologist as perceiver. In R. TAGIURI AND L. PETRULLO (Eds.) *Person perception and interpersonal behavior.* Stanford, Calif.: Stanford, 1958. Pp. 95–109.

DEUTSCH, M. A theory of cooperation and competition. *Hum. Relat.*, 1949, 2, 129–152.

FAGER, R. E. Student and faculty conceptions of the "successful student." *J. counsel. Psychol.*, 1958, 5, 98–103.

FINCHER, C. L. An investigation of associative and nonassociative factors in verbal performance. Unpublished doctoral dissertation, Ohio State Univ., 1956.

FLORENCE, EDWIGES DE C. The construction of a forced-choice technique for the evaluation of college students' goals. Unpublished doctoral dissertation, Ohio State Univ., 1956. (a).

FLORENCE, EDWIGES DE C. Motivational factors in individual and group productivity: II. Validation and standardization of the student behavior description. Columbus: Ohio State Univ. Res. Found., 1956. (offset) (b)

GERTH, H. AND MILLS, C. W. *Character and social structure.* New York: Harcourt, 1953.

GERTH, H. H. AND MILLS, C. W. *From Max Weber; Essays in sociology.* New York: Oxford, 1946.

GIRSCHICK, M. A. An elementary review of statistical decision theory. *Rev. educ. Res.*, 1954, 24, 448–466.

GOODE, H. H. AND MACHOL, R. E. *System engineering.* New York: McGraw-Hill, 1957.

GUETZKOW, H. (Ed.) *Groups, leadership and men: Research in human relations.* Pittsburgh: Carnegie Press, 1951.

GUETZKOW, H. Unitizing and categorizing problems in coding quantitative data. *J. clin. Psychol.*, 1950, 6, 47–58.

HARE, A. P., BORGATTA, E. F., AND BALES, R. F. *Small groups: Studies in social interaction.* New York: Knopf, 1955.

HEMPHILL, J. K. Administration as problem-solving. In A. W. HALPIN (Ed.), *Administrative theory in education.* Chicago: Midwest Administration Center, 1958. Pp. 89–118.

HEMPHILL, J. K., PEPINSKY, PAULINE N., KAUFMAN, A. E., AND LIPETZ, M. E. Effects of task motivation and expectancy of accomplishment upon attempts to lead. *Psychol. Monogr.*, 1957, 71, No. 22 (Whole No. 451).

HEMPHILL, J. K., PEPINSKY, PAULINE N., SHEVITZ, R. N., JAYNES, W. E., AND CHRISTNER, CHARLOTTE. Leadership acts: I. An investigation of the relation betwen task relevant information and attempts to lead. Columbus: Ohio State Univ. Res. Found., 1954. (offset)

HITCH, C. An appreciation of systems analysis. *J. Operations Res. Soc. Amer.*, 1957, 4, 466–481.

HOOD, P. D. Q-methodology: A technique for measuring frames of reference. Unpublished doctoral dissertation, Ohio State Univ., 1953.

HOPWOOD, KATHRYN L. Expectations of university freshman women. *Personnel Guid. J.*, 1954, 32, 464–469.

HOWLAND, D. Problems of research on the hospital system. Working Paper

RF 940–112, Operations Res. Group, Ohio State Univ., Rev. Aug. 28, 1959. (ditto)

LEWIN, K. *Resolving social conflicts.* New York: Harper, 1948.

LOVE, PATRICIA A. A follow-up study of the expectations of a group of university women. Unpublished master's thesis, Ohio State Univ., 1957.

MACHOVER, K. *Personality projection in the drawing of the human figure.* Springfield, Ill.: Thomas, 1949.

MARCH, J. G., SIMON, H. A., AND GUETZKOW, H. A. *Organizations.* New York: Wiley, 1958.

MARSCHAK, J. Probability in the social sciences. In P. F. LAZARSFELD (Ed.) *Mathematical thinking in the social sciences.* Glencoe, Ill.: Free Press, 1954. Pp. 166–215.

MOSS, H. Standards of conduct for students, teachers, and parents. *J. counsel. Psychol.,* 1955, *2,* 39–42.

NEWELL, A., SHAW, J. C., AND SIMON, H. A. Elements of a theory of human problem solving. *Psychol. Rev.,* 1958, *65,* 157–169.

OLMSTED, M. S. Small group interaction as a function of group norms. Unpublished doctoral dissertation, Harvard, 1952.

OLMSTED, M. S. Orientation and role in the small group. *Amer. sociol. Rev.,* 1954, *19,* 741–751.

PARSONS, T. *The social system.* Glencoe, Ill.: Free Press, 1951.

PARSONS, T. AND SHILS, E. A. Categories of the orientation and organization of action. In T. PARSONS AND E. A. SHILS (Eds.) *Toward a general theory of action.* Cambridge, Mass.: Harvard, 1952. Pp. 53–109.

PAVLIK, W. B. The relationship between expressed standards of behavior and group participation. Unpublished master's thesis, Ohio State Univ., 1955.

PAVLIK, W. B. Motivational factors in individual and group productivity: IV. The effects of personal and situational motivation upon individual performance in a small group setting. Columbus: Ohio State Univ. Res. Found., 1956. (offset)

PENDLETON, P. W. The academic role of the college student. Unpublished doctoral dissertation, Ohio State Univ., 1955.

PEPINSKY, H. B. Productive behavior. *J. counsel. Psychol.,* 1954, *1,* 57–59. (a)

PEPINSKY, H. B. Research on productive behavior. *Personnel Guid. J.,* 1954, *33,* 140–144. (b)

PEPINSKY, H. B. Cogito, ergo. . . . *J. counsel. Psychol.,* 1955, *2,* 285–289.

PEPINSKY, H. B. Productivity in the university. *Personnel Guid. J.,* 1956, *35,* 134–139.

PEPINSKY, H. B., HOWLAND, D., AND BENNETT, J. W. Research team productivity in the organizational setting. A proposal for research, Engineering Exper. Sta., Ohio State Univ., Jan., 1958. (offset)

PEPINSKY, H. B. AND PEPINSKY, PAULINE N. *Counseling: Theory and practice.* New York: Ronald, 1954.

PEPINSKY, H. B., PEPINSKY, PAULINE N., MINOR, F. J., AND ROBIN, S. S. Motivational factors in individual and group productivity: VI. Team productivity as related to the confirmation or contradiction by management of its commitments to an appointed leader. Columbus: Ohio State Univ. Res. Found., 1957. (offset)

PEPINSKY, H. B., PEPINSKY, PAULINE N., MINOR, F. J., AND ROBIN, S. S. Team productivity and contradiction of management policy commitments. *J. appl. Psychol.*, 1959, *43*, 264–268.

PEPINSKY, H. B., PEPINSKY, PAULINE N., AND PAVLIK, W. B. Motivational factors in individual and group productivity: I. Successful task accomplishment as related to task relevant personal beliefs. Columbus: Ohio State Univ. Res. Found., 1956. (offset)

PEPINSKY, H. B., PEPINSKY, PAULINE N., AND PAVLIK, W. B. Task relevant personal belief and task accomplishment. *J. counsel. Psychol.*, 1958, *5*, 305–311.

PEPINSKY, H. B. AND THRUSH, R. S. A note on research in the general hospital. *J. counsel. Psychol.*, 1958, 5, 224–228.

PEPINSKY, PAULINE N. AND PEPINSKY, H. B. Originality in group productivity. Annual Technical Report under Contract Nonr-495 (15) (NR 170–396) with the Office of Naval Research. Columbus: Ohio State Univ. Res. Found., Nov. 15, 1958. (offset)

PEPINSKY, PAULINE N., PEPINSKY, H. B., AND PAVLIK, W. B. Motivational factors in individual and group productivity: III. The effects of task complexity and time pressure upon team productivity. Columbus: Ohio State Univ. Res. Found., 1956. (offset)

PEPINSKY, PAULINE N., PEPINSKY, H. B., AND PAVLIK, W. B. The effects of task complexity and time pressure upon team productivity. *J. appl. Psychol.*, 1960, *44*, 34–38.

PEPINSKY, PAULINE N., PEPINSKY, H. B., ROBIN, S. S., AND MINOR, F. J. Motivational factors in individual and group productivity: V. The effects of induced orientation and type of task upon group member morale. Columbus: Ohio State Univ. Res. Found., 1957. (offset)

RIECKEN, H. W. A program for research on experiments in social psychology. From background paper prepared at the Behavioral Sciences Conference, Univ. of New Mexico, Summer, 1958. (ditto)

ROE, ANN. Man's forgotten weapon. *Amer. Psychologist,* 1959, *14,* 261–266.

ROSENTHAL, R. AND FODE, K. L. Three experiments in experimenter bias. Univ. of North Dakota, 1959. (mimeo.)

SELZNICK, P. *Leadership in administration.* Evanston, Ill.: Row, Peterson, 1957.

SIEGEL, L., COON, H. L., PEPINSKY, H. B., AND RUBIN, S. Expressed standards of behavior of high school students, teachers, and parents. *Personnel Guid. J.,* 1956, *34,* 261–267.

STOGDILL, R. M. *Individual behavior and group achievement.* New York: Oxford, 1959.

STOLTZ, R. E. A study of productivity in a research setting. Unpublished doctoral dissertation, Ohio State Univ., 1956.

STRODTBECK, F. L. The family as a three-person group. *Amer. sociol. Rev.,* 1954, *19,* 23–29.

STUNDEN, BARBARA. Some relationships among sex role, group participation, and expressed standards of conduct in adolescents. Unpublished master's thesis, Ohio State Univ., 1955.

TAYLOR, JANET. Drive theory and manifest anxiety. *Psychol. Bull.,* 1956, *56,* 303–320.

TAYLOR, JANET AND SPENCE, K. W. The relationship of anxiety level to performance in serial learning. *J. exper. Psychol.,* 1952, *44,* 61–64.

THRUSH, R. S. An agency in transition: The case study of a counseling center. *J. counsel. Psychol.,* 1957, *4,* 183–190.

THRUSH, R. S. Work measurement and perceptual studies within a university counseling center. Unpublished doctoral dissertation, Ohio State Univ., 1958.

TÖNNIES, F. (translated by C. P. Loomis) *Fundamental concepts of sociology.* New York: American Book, 1940.

WARMAN, R. E. Differential perceptions of the counseling role of a university counseling center. Unpublished doctoral dissertation, Ohio State Univ., 1958.

15

Some Familial Antecedents of Responsibility and Leadership in Adolescents[1]

Urie Bronfenbrenner

Cornell University

THE PROBLEM

It is a well-documented fact (e.g., Bandura and Walters, 1959) that adolescents who are problems in school and community come from families in which the parents tend toward extremes of rejection, punitiveness, or over-indulgence. Moreover, a number of investigators have recently demonstrated that this marked association between deviant behavior in parents and children persists even when adequate controls are introduced for the influence of socioeconomic factors (Bandura and Walters, 1959; Glueck and Glueck, 1956). The situation is somewhat different, however, with respect to the familial antecedents at the opposite end of the behavioral continuum—effective psychological functioning. Several studies (Harris, Rose, Clark, and Valasek, 1955; Martin, Gross, and Darley, 1952) do report a positive relation between warmth and permissiveness of the parent-child relationship and measures of such variables as responsibility and leadership. But the marked association, reported in these same

[1] The paper is based on research supported by grants from the National Science Foundation and the National Institutes of Health. The author acknowledges the invaluable aid of Ruth Amsden, E. C. Devereux, Joan Dodge, Christine Hume, R. Lesser, Carol Millsom, Rachel Simonhoff, and G. J. Suci in carrying through analysis of the data. Also, appreciation is expressed to Drs. Joan Dodge, M. L. Kohn, and L. Petrullo for perceptive and helpful criticisms of an earlier draft of the manuscript.

239

researches, of both sets of variables with socioeconomic status is yet to be controlled. The present paper is directed toward this objective. Specifically, it reports the results of an exploratory study of the relations between parental and adolescent behavior as these are mediated by sex of parent, sex of child, and the socioeconomic position of the family. The particular variables of adolescent behavior to be examined are responsibility and leadership as rated by high school teachers. Family relationships are measured by scores on 20 variables of parent behavior derived from the adolescent's descriptions of each parent on a 100-item check list.

Two interrelated conclusions have resulted from a review of current theory and research (Bronfenbrenner, 1958a, 1958b, 1960) bearing on problems of personality formation in middle childhood and adolesence:

1. Existing theories, mostly psychoanalytic in origin, regarding the effect of parent-child relationships on personality development, assume— and offer intricate explanations for—certain phenomena regarded as typical if not universal; yet there is little evidence in the research literature that these phenomena do in fact commonly occur. Specifically, existing theories assume that boys and girls are treated quite differently by the parent of each sex and that this differential treatment has markedly diverse effects on the child of each sex. For example, Freudian theory implies that punitiveness by the father is particularly traumatic for boys and withdrawal of love especially critical for girls (Freud, 1950; Bronfenbrenner, 1960). Yet, very little is known about the variation that actually exists in the treatment of boys and girls by the parent of each sex or about the possible effects of such differential treatment.

2. Existing research has, by and large, ignored the methodological and theoretical implications of the association, repeatedly demonstrated (Bronfenbrenner, 1958a), between the family's social position and the attitudes and actions of its members. Specifically, existing theories tacitly assume that sex differences in parental treatment are similar and have similar effects at all socioeconomic levels. This assumption is without doubt erroneous, but the precise facts are still to be established.

THE METHOD

Examination of these prior questions of fact calls for an exploratory study designed not to test hypotheses but to lay bare the empirical relations requiring hypothesis formulation. Curiously enough, the investigator who sets out *in advance* to do an exploratory study of this sort finds himself in uncharted terrain so far as method is concerned. True, exploratory studies abound in the literature, but most of these were, so to speak, born out of wedlock, since they represent unintended consequences of investigations that went astray—tests of specific hypotheses that yielded unexpected results and were rechristened as exploratory studies. The occasional researches that explicitly acknowledge an exploratory aim at the outset are no better suited for our needs since they tend toward one of two extremes —the intensive analysis of case studies at one pole—the extensive sociological survey at the other. Our problem was at once too modest in its dimensions and too structured in its form to be pursued through either of these somewhat diffuse procedures. Although we had no hypotheses, we did have the rudiments of a theoretical structure: a set of independent variables (parent practices), a set of dependent variables (adolescent responsibility and leadership), and a set of intervening or mediating factors (sex of parent, sex of child, and family's social position). In short, we were working at the level of what Merton (1957) has called "theories of the middle range" and, in order to pursue our investigations, needed corresponding "methods of the middle range"—experimental designs that could be employed not for the purpose of testing a priori hypotheses but for winnowing out from a large set of empirical relations those that are likely to be most salient and reliable.

In the absence of a tried technology available for this purpose, we decided, at the risk of charges of perversion from methodological purists, to corrupt to our own uses a procedure designed for different objectives but nevertheless adaptable to our needs. The technique is that of multivariate analysis of variance, and, in using it, we propose to resort to a procedure long condemned in statistical texts, as long "illegally" employed in practice, but recently legitimized by statistical theorists. The procedure is that of looking for statistically significant differences after the fact even though no predictions have been specified in advance. The arguments in justification of this practice are documented in a definitive paper by Ryan (1959).[2] The method is well-suited to our purpose since it permits

---

[2] Ryan also stresses the importance, in both a priori and a posteriori analysis, of computing probabilities not on the basis of each individual comparison (as is conventionally done) but for "the expected number of erroneous statements per *experiment*," or over a series of experiments, and he describes a number of methods for obtaining such "experiment-based" error rates. We have deliberately refrained from adopting these more exact and conservative procedures on strategic grounds. As Ryan acknowledges, "conservatism also means loss of power"; that is, in minimizing Type I errors, one increases the risk of errors of Type II or the likelihood of dismissing as chance phenomena relationships which are in fact both real and reliable. Yet, the aim of an exploratory study is to detect relationships precisely of this kind. Although Ryan argues that any increase in power should be obtained by computing exact probabilities and then accepting a liberal level of significance, we do not believe that such precision is sufficiently important in an exploratory study to justify the additional labor required.

examination of the relations between parental and adolescent behavior and of the independent contribution of sex of parent, sex of child, and family's social position in mediating these relationships.

The subjects for the exploratory study were the entire tenth grade of a medium-sized city in upstate New York. Data were obtained for all students (N = 400) attending school on a given day. Approximately 10 percent of the students were absent, the rate of absence being somewhat higher among boys and among children from the lower socioeconomic levels. To achieve a balanced design, an equal number of boys and girls (24 of each) were drawn at random from each of four socioeconomic levels for a total of 192 cases. On the basis of previous work (Bronfen-brenner, 1958a; Bronfenbrenner, Devereux, and Harding, 1960), the father's educational level was selected as the index of social class most practical and appropriate for the purpose at hand. Unfortunately, the only readily available source for this information was the student's own report, which was undoubtedly susceptible to errors arising from ignorance or distortion of the facts; nevertheless, the information was felt to be adequate for purposes of an exploratory study. The four educational levels employed (which reflect the sample bias of a university community) were as follows: (1) some graduate work; (2) completed college; (3) completed high school; and (4) did not finish high school.

Of the several techniques utilized to gather information from students and teachers, only two need concern us here:

1. *Parent-Activity Inventory.* This questionnaire consists of 100 items designed to measure 20 different dimensions of parent-child relationships. Following the conceptual distinction suggested by Parsons and Bales (1955) the variables are grouped into two broad classes: *expressive* functions, typically associated with the mother and including such variables as *nurturance, affection, indulgence,* etc.; and *instrumental* functions, traditionally connected with the father—for example, *physical punishment, power, principled discipline,* etc.[3] In the inventory as filled out by the students, the five items measuring each variable are scattered through the questionnaire. Subjects were asked to indicate, by rating on a five-point scale, the extent to which each item "applies to each parent's treatment of you as you were growing up." A list of the variables with examples of constituent items appears in Table 1.

2. *Teacher Rating Scales.* The scales include 22 variables sampling

---

[3] In point of fact, our results show that, probably because of the mother's more regular presence in the home, most of these instrumental functions (all except three) are performed more frequently by mothers than by fathers.

Table 1

THE TWENTY PARENT VARIABLES WITH EXAMPLES OF TWO REPRESENTATIVE ITEMS FOR EACH

Physical punishment and threat
spanked me
threatened physical punishment

Deprivation of privilege or property
punished me by taking away privileges
punished me by taking away my favorite possessions

Material reward
rewarded me for doing well by giving me money
rewarded me for doing well by letting me go to movies, shows, parties, or other special events

Power
decided how late I could stay out
decided on what music lessons, camp, or after school activities I could have

Achievement demands
pushed me to do well in school
pushed me to excel in everything I did

Social isolation
punished me by sending me out of the room
punished me by not allowing me to be with my friends

Instrumental companionship
took part in activities and projects with me
helped me with homework or lessons

Principled discipline
reasoned with me
apologized if they had treated me unfairly

Neglect
avoided my company
forgot my birthday

Parental absence
away from home and children for weeks and months at a time
missed supper with children at least two nights a week

Nurturance
took care of me when I was hurt or sick
consoled me and helped me when I was unhappy or in trouble

Affection
hugged and kissed me
said nice things about me

Protectiveness
wouldn't let me go places because something might happen to me
went along with me to make sure that everything would be okay

Affective punishment
punished me by withholding affection or friendship
punished me by trying to make me feel guilty or ashamed

Expressive rejection
ridiculed and made fun of me
compared me unfavorably to other children

Indulgence
let me off easy when I did something wrong
couldn't say no to me

Intercession
got my punishments reduced or eliminated
stuck up for me in family arguments

Affiliative companionship
spent a lot of time with me not doing anything special
had regular playtime with me

Affective reward
rewarded good behavior by hugging and kissing
rewarded good behavior by praising me

Parental presence
home for lunch
spent weekends with family and children

adolescent behavior in the intellectual, emotional, and social spheres. The two variables dealt with in the present report were defined as follows:

Responsible . . . . can be counted on to fulfill obligations
vs.
Irresponsible . . . cannot be counted on to fulfill obligations

Leader . . . . influences and directs group activities and is accepted in this role
vs.
Follower . . . looks to others for direction and decision, attaches himself to others, does not take initiative.

Each variable was rated independently by two teachers on a six-point scale. The lowest rating (1) was to be given to students "in the bottom 10 percent of tenth-graders I have known"; the highest rating (6) to the top 10 percent. The four intermediate ratings applied to the 25th and 50th percentiles respectively.

Scores on the 20 parent variables were analyzed by means of a variance design involving four main effects: sex of child, sex of parent, father's education (four levels), and adolescent's behavior (three levels). The three levels of adolescent behavior (responsibility or leadership) were established by classifying subjects of the same sex and father's education into thirds (high, medium, and low) on the basis of the mean rating secured from two teachers. Since our interest in levels of education and adolescent behavior was confined to linear trends only, linear sums of squares, with one degree of freedom each, were computed for the dependent variables. Because scores for the two parents are correlated, the design involved two different error terms, one for testing all main effects and interactions not involving sex of parent, the other for testing all components involving sex of parent.

The selection of *responsibility* and *leadership* as the variables to be examined was guided by the speculation that compliance with adult standards (as reflected in teacher's ratings of the adolescent's dependability in fulfilling obligations) might have somewhat different antecedents in parental treatment from acceptance as a leader by his classmates. The odds for realizing such an expectation were by no means high, however, since the two variables (responsibility and leadership) showed a substantial positive correlation ($r = .48$) which, unfortunately, was as high as the rater reliability of either (.44 and .41 respectively, uncorrected for attenuation).[4] The reliability of rating is sufficiently low to produce substantial errors of measurement thus decreasing the likelihood of obtaining statistically significant results even though a true relationship may exist.

Another factor which, on occasion, may operate to mask or attenuate differences that in fact exist is that of response set. For example, the juxtaposition of items for father and mother in the Parent Activity Inventory probably results in a higher similarity in behavior ratings for the two parents than is actually warranted. Since in an exploratory study it is perhaps an even more serious error to overlook true effects than to accept false ones, we shall consider differences worthy of examination even if they are significant only at the 10 percent level of confidence (two-tailed test).[5] So that the more reliable findings can be identified, levels of significance are cited where appropriate both in tables and text.

Nevertheless, along with open-mindedness, an exploratory study demands caution as well. In this connection, we would call attention to certain important limitations inherent in the data and study design.

1. All of the information on parents was secured from the adolescent himself. As a result, the information must be qualified on two counts. First, the adolescent may lack complete or accurate knowledge about his parents. Second, and more important, even though most of the items on which the adolescent is asked to report deal with overt behavior rather than subjective feelings and opinions, his perceptions and responses are probably subject to distortion, both willful and unwitting. Accordingly, any statement about parental behavior on the basis of the present findings must be qualified by the phrase "as perceived or reported by the adolescent."

2. Although a number of measures have been taken to minimize the influence of response sets in the rating scales and questionnaires, such influences cannot be completely eliminated. For example, even though the direction of scales has been frequently reversed from item to item, there are undoubtedly halo effects in the adolescents' and in the teachers' ratings. Moreover, as Tryon (1939) and others have shown, ratings of adolescent behavior by teachers tend to show a response bias related to the teacher's predominantly middle-class value orientation.

---

[4] Such low reliabilities are hardly surprising since the teachers saw students for only one period a day. Moreover, an inspection of ratings made by teachers from the two subject matter fields represented (English *vs.* health) suggests that the two groups have somewhat different conceptions of what constitutes responsibility and leadership in adolescents.

[5] This standard of acceptance is even more liberal than it seems since it follows the conventional procedure of computing error rate on the basis of each individual comparison rather than on the experiment as a unit (cf. Ryan, *op. cit.*).

3. All findings in this exploratory study are *post hoc,* and hence highly subject to errors of chance. This susceptibility is further enhanced by three considerations. First, a liberal standard of significance has been adopted. Second, the results of successive analyses are not independent since many of the parent variables show significant intercorrelations. Third, in a complex analysis of variance design involving multiple comparisons, a number of significant differences will occur simply by chance. The fact that the significant differences fall into a pattern, as they do with many of our findings, is reassuring but constitutes no guarantee against unwarranted conclusions. The issue can be settled satisfactorily only through replication.

4. Even if the findings relating parental and adolescent behavior are accepted as valid, they present difficulties for interpretation. Specifically, since both sets of data were obtained at the same time, one cannot make the comfortable assumption that significant correlations reflect the influence of parent treatment on the adolescent's actions. Not only may both be a function of some third uncontrolled common factor (for example, ordinal position, ethnic background), but the direction of causality may even be reversed; that is, the child's behavior may have served as a major determinant of the parent's treatment of him.

Although the limitations outlined above present serious difficulties for the interpretation of our data, these difficulties are not insurmountable. Once the possibility of their existence is recognized, there are a number of strategies that can be used to check for the operation of the various contaminating influences we have mentioned and to give them due weight in the interpretation of results. This task will be attempted in the next but last section of this report.

THE RESULTS

Findings are presented under four major headings: (1) sex differences; (2) differences associated with father's education; (3) relationships of parental behaviors to adolescent's responsibility; and (4) relationships of parental behaviors to adolescent's leadership.

1. Sex Differences

The basic data on sex differences in parental behavior are shown in Table 2.

As is evident from Column 5 of the table, that the mother exceeds the father in virtually every area. Her predominance is most marked in such

Table 2

Sex Differences in Parental Behavior

PARENTAL BEHAVIOR	MEANS				DIFFERENCES		
	Mothers		Fathers		5. Mothers Minus Fathers	6. Girls Minus Boys	7. Same Sex Minus Opposite Sex
	1. Girls	2. Boys	3. Girls	4. Boys			
Parental absence	1.62	1.32	3.28	2.88	−1.61‡	.35	−.05
Parental presence	14.71	15.40	9.69	9.44	5.49‡	−.22	−.47*
Affection	11.35	9.75	10.10	6.90	2.05‡	2.40‡	−.80‡
Nurturance	12.75	12.86	9.37	9.88	3.18‡	−.32	.20
Affiliative companionship	10.94	9.12	9.29	8.03	1.36‡	1.54*	.28
Affective reward	12.03	11.10	10.63	8.82	1.84‡	1.37*	−.44†
Material reward	7.70	7.38	7.18	6.72	.59‡	.39	−.07
Principled discipline	12.55	12.52	12.10	12.16	.40†	−.02	.04
Instrumental companionship	12.14	10.11	11.02	12.72	−.74‡	.16	1.86‡
Physical punishment	3.80	3.96	3.68	5.22	−.57*	−.85†	.69‡
Social isolation	3.55	3.98	3.21	3.31	.50‡	−.26	−.16
Deprivation of privilege	5.37	5.53	4.29	5.57	.52‡	−.72	.56‡
Affective punishment	4.56	4.59	3.33	3.64	1.09‡	−.17	.14
Achievement demands	6.04	7.94	5.34	7.46	.59‡	−2.01‡	.11
Power	8.58	8.06	6.87	7.12	1.32‡	.14	.38*
Indulgence	4.60	4.46	4.50	3.76	.40*	.44	−.30†
Intercession	6.37	6.47	5.31	4.82	1.36‡	.20	−.30
Protectiveness	6.56	6.48	5.50	4.67	1.44‡	.46	−.38*
Expressive rejection	4.03	4.19	3.17	3.85	.60‡	−.42	.26
Neglect	1.77	2.04	1.60	2.20	−.01	−.44	.16

In this and subsequent tables, levels of significance (two-tailed test) are designated as follows:

† = 10%   * = 5%   ‡ = 1%

traditional maternal spheres as nurturance, affection, protectiveness, and, above all, in just sheer presence. But, to a lesser extent, the mother also exceeds the father in negatively as well as positively toned relationships. Thus she is seen as the more important source of power, general discipline, demands for achievement, and even rejection. In fact, there are but two instances in which the father surpasses the mother, and even these hold only for boys. With sons, the father is more likely than the mother to be the agent of physical punishment and to spend time in activities involving skill or competition *(instrumental companionship)*. It would appear that, except for a slight tendency for the father to specialize (with boys only) in what Parsons calls the "instrumental functions," the mother is perceived by the adolescent as by far the more salient figure in most aspects of parental treatment—negative as well as positive.

The above generalizations must be qualified, however, in the light of differences associated with the sex of the child. Although neither as pervasive nor pronounced as those cited above, the main effects (Column 6) likewise show the expected pattern: girls receive more affection, praise, and companionship for its own sake; boys are subjected to more achievement demands and physical punishment (from fathers only). The signs of the nonsignificant differences in Column 6 reflect this same general trend on a broader scale, with girls experiencing more warmth and protectiveness, boys more discipline and negative affect.[6]

The sex of the child, however, is actually a more important determinant of variations in parental behavior than the above simple differences would suggest, for its relevance becomes fully apparent only when considered in conjunction with the sex of the parent. These significant interaction effects are shown in Column 7. The value tabulated is the difference between same-sex and opposite-sex parent-child combinations. Thus a positive value, such as that appearing for *physical punishment,* indicates that the child is likely to receive more discipline from the parent of the same sex. In other words, boys are more likely to be punished by fathers, girls by mothers. It will be observed that the significant positive values in Column 7 occur for those variables implying activity and authority, whereas negative signs appear for scales connoting a more passive, affectionate

---

[6] There are two groups of variables that repeatedly appear in our results to behave as relatively homogeneous and independent "clusters." To simplify communication, we have given these arbitrarily designated clusters arbitrary names. The first, to be designated henceforth as "warmth" or "affection," includes the following variables: *affection, nurturance, affiliative companionship,* and *affective reward.* The second cluster, to be referred to as "discipline" or "authority," involves *physical punishment, deprivation of privileges,* and *power.*

relationship. In other words, the results reveal a tendency for each parent to be somewhat more active, firm, and demanding with a child of the same sex, more lenient and indulgent with a child of the opposite sex. An examination of the actual means involved (Columns 1–4) indicates that the reversal is most complete with respect to physical punishment, with fathers being stricter with boys, mothers with girls. In the spheres of affection and protectiveness, there is no actual shift in preference, but the tendency to be especially warm and solicitous with girls is much more pronounced among fathers than among mothers. In fact, generally speaking, it is the father who is especially likely to treat children of the two sexes differently.

Taken together, the results on sex differences in parental behavior suggest that, within the family, boys and girls find themselves in somewhat contrasting situations. Girls receive more affection, attention, and praise than boys—especially from their fathers—whereas boys are subjected to greater pressure and discipline, again mainly from their fathers. In other words, particularly in their relationship with fathers, girls find themselves in a more supportive context than boys. From the point of view of minimizing pressure and maximizing affection, the boy is in a relatively better situation in his relationship with the mother than with the father. These differential contexts are emphasized here since they turn out to be of special relevance for interpreting the varying relations between parental and adolescent behavior to be reported below.

2. Differences Associated with Father's Education

Table 3 shows the significant linear relation between the parent behavior variables and the father's educational level.[7] Taken as a whole, Table 3 documents the pervasive influence of the father's educational background on the parental behavior of both father and mother. The general tenor of the findings shown in Table 3 is closely in line with the trend revealed in a large number of studies of class differences in socialization (cf. the review by Bronfenbrenner, 1958a): namely, as one descends the educational ladder, there is a marked increase in parental behaviors regarded as socially undesirable by middle-class standards. Thus, irrespective of the sex of the child, parents with less education spend less time with their

---

[7] A check was also made for curvilinear relationships associated with educational level. There were no reliable nonlinear main effects among the 20 parent variables; such relationships began to appear appreciably only in the interactions; there were three significant two-factor interactions out of a possible 40, and five three-factor out of 20. Even these curvilinear effects, however, were often monotonic in character.

children[8] and are rated as relatively more rejecting, punitive, indulgent, and over-protective.[9] Lower-class mothers are especially likely to be described as dominating, demanding, and materialistic. Lower-class fathers spend less time in purposeful activities with their youngsters, and are less "principled" in their discipline techniques.

With a rise in father's educational level, "disapproved" parental behaviors decrease in frequency. The parents, especially the mother, spend more time with the child, and are less severe in their punishments, while fathers, although more often away from home, are more likely to participate in projects and activities with their children.

But it would be a mistake to conclude that *all* "good" parental behavior occurs more often in better-educated families. There are four scales (*affection, nurturance, affective reward,* and *affective punishment*) that fail to show significant association one way or the other between the amount of schooling and behavior of either parent. They differ from the remaining sixteen in placing special emphasis on the parent's emotional involvement with the child—the giving and manipulation of affection. It would appear that parents from diverse educational backgrounds are more likely to differ in specific techniques of discipline than in the general nature and degree of emotional involvement with their children.

One may ask whether the sex differences in parental behavior reported earlier show any systematic variation with father's educational level. If one considers only the sex of the child, the answer is substantially "no." The tendency on the part of parents to be more affectionate with girls and more punitive with boys is apparent at every educational level with not even a suggestion of a consistent trend. Once the sex of the parent is considered, however, the data tell quite another story. First of all, as indicated in Column 2 of Table 3, even more than the father it is the *mother* whose behavior is especially influenced by the father's level of schooling. Indeed, further analysis (not shown here) reveals that the mother's behavior is linked more closely to the father's educational level than to her own. In other words, it would appear that it is the family's social position (as reflected by the father's educational status) rather than the mother's knowl-

---

[8] Although the presence score of both parents decreases at lower educational levels, the father's absence score shows a similar drop. An examination of responses to the specific items making up each variable suggests the following explanation for this paradoxical effect: poorly educated fathers are less often away from home but, when they are home, spend less of their time with their children.

[9] With increase in incidence of "mistreatment," it is not surprising that at the lower educational levels there is also more intercession by one parent with the other in behalf of the child.

Table 3

DIRECTION OF SIGNIFICANT LINEAR TRENDS IN PARENTAL BEHAVIOR ASSOCIATED WITH LEVELS OF FATHER'S EDUCATION

PARENTAL BEHAVIOR	DIRECTION OF RELATIONSHIP		
	1. Main Effects	*Interactions*	
		2. By Sex of Parent	*3. By Sex of Parent and Child*
Parental presence	+‡	+Stronger in mothers†	
Parental absence		+fathers only‡	
Affection			
Nurturance			
Affiliative companionship	+†		
Affective reward			
Material reward	—*	—Stronger in mothers†	
Principled discipline	+*	+Stronger in fathers‡	
Instrumental companionship		+in fathers only*	
Physical punishment	—‡	—Stronger in mothers†	—Strongest in mothers of girls, ‡fathers of boys
Social isolation	—*	—Mothers only*	
Deprivation of privileges	—*		
Affective punishment			
Achievement demands	—‡	—Mothers only‡	
Power	—*	—Mothers only*	
Indulgence	—‡		—Strongest in fathers of girls*
Intercession	—‡		—Strongest in fathers of girls, ‡mothers of boys
Protectiveness	—‡		
Expressive rejection	—*		
Neglect	—‡		

(Plus sign indicates that parental behavior increases with rise in father's education; minus sign that parental behavior decreases.)

edge (as indicated by her own schooling) which influences her treatment of the child.

In view of the marked changes in maternal behavior from one educational level to the next, one may ask whether the predominance of the mother as the major parental figure is equally pronounced at each of these levels. An examination of the actual means (not shown) associated with the interaction effects reported in Column 2 indicates clearly that the mother becomes increasingly influential as one descends the educational ladder. More specifically, the lower the father's education, the more the mother becomes the authority figure, especially for girls. Indeed it is only in the better-educated families that the father in any way approaches or surpasses the mother as a generally influential person in the child's life. Thus the relative predominance, noted earlier, of the father over the mother in "instrumental" companionship with boys occurs only in families where the father has had at least some college education. Similarly, it is only the better-educated father who serves as the principal agent of physical punishment for the daughter. Quite the opposite trend, however, appears for boys; here it is the *lower class* father who is most likely to administer corporal punishment to his son.

Finally, it is this last contrasting pattern that is reflected in the significant interactions tabulated in Column 3 of Table 3; namely, the tendency for each parent—and especially the father—to punish the child of the same sex but to indulge and intercede for the child of the opposite sex is most marked at the lowest educational levels and decreases as the family rises along the academic ladder. Indeed, examination of the actual means involved (not shown) indicates that the pattern appears only in the high-school group and even shows a slight tendency to reverse itself among families of college-educated fathers so that now it is the child of the opposite sex who is treated more firmly. Again we call attention to these differential trends because of their subsequent relevance in interpreting the varying relationships between parental and adolescent behavior to be reported below.

3. Relations between Parental Behavior and Adolescent's Responsibility

We come now to the major concern of the present inquiry: the relation between parental treatment and adolescent behavior. Turning first to the variable of responsibility, we should note by way of introduction that it shows the expected differences by sex and social class. Girls are rated as more responsible than boys, and better-educated fathers have more responsible children. But if sex and educational level are held constant, do children at different levels of responsibility vary consistently in their descriptions of the behavior of their parents? The answer to this question appears in Table 4, which shows differences in parental behavior between groups classified as High (upper third) and Low (lower third) in responsibility. Three variables show reliable main effects unqualified by interactions; *rejection, neglect,* and *affiliative companionship,* and mean scores

Table 4

MEAN DIFFERENCES IN PERCEIVED PARENT BEHAVIOR BY ADOLESCENTS RATED AS "HIGH" AND "LOW" IN RESPONSIBILITY

| | MEAN DIFFERENCES (High Minus Low) | | | | MAIN EFFECT | INTERACTIONS | | |
| | Boys | | Girls | | | | | |
PARENTAL BEHAVIOR	1. Fathers	2. Mothers	3. Fathers	4. Mothers	5.	6. Father Minus Mother	7. Boy Minus Girl	8. Same Sex Minus Opposite Sex
Parental absence	-1.13†	-.28	.59	-.16	-.24	-.05	-.92	-.80†
Parental presence	.31	1.50†	-1.44†	-.91	-.14	-.86	2.08†	-.33
Affection	1.28	.91	-1.13	-.75	.08	0	2.03	-.38
Nurturance	1.25	1.69†	-1.84*	-.28	.20	-1.00*	2.53*	.56
Affiliative companionship	1.59†	1.94*	0	.88	1.10†	-.61	1.33	.27
Affective reward	.69	1.25	-.84	-.63	.12	-.39	1.70	-.17
Material reward	.13	-.16	-1.19	-.72	-.48	-.09	.94	.38
Principled discipline	1.47	1.75	-.59	.16	.70	-.52	1.83	.23
Instrumental companionship	1.13	.34	-.41	-.63	.11	.50	1.25	-.25
Physical punishment	1.66*	.03	-.81	.34	.30	.23	1.08	1.39*
Social isolation	.06	-.13	-.72	.06	-.18	-.30	.30	.48
Deprivation of privilege	1.41†	.16	-1.22	-1.09	-.19	-.56	1.94*	.69†
Affective punishment	-.44	-.53	-.66	-.28	-.48	-.14	-.02	.23
Achievement demands	.69	.56	-1.31	-1.28	-.34	.05	1.92	.08
Power	1.69†	1.28	-1.97*	-.41	.15	-.58	2.67*	.98†
Indulgence	-.25	-.47	-.25	-.34	-.33	.13	-.06	.06
Intercession	.22	.41	-2.16‡	-1.94‡	-.86†	-.20	2.36*	.02
Protectiveness	.03	-.19	-1.66*	-1.09	-.72	-.17	1.30	-.39
Expressive rejection	-.81	-1.22	-1.44	-.78	-1.06*	-.13	.09	.53
Neglect	-.81	-1.16†	-.38	-.62	-.74†	.30	-.48	.05

for the Low, Medium, and High groups, shown in Table 5, indicate that the major gap occurs between the Middle and the Low categories. In other words, to speak in terms of the specific items making up these variables, the adolescent receiving lowest ratings in responsibility describes his parents as most likely to complain about and ridicule him, compare him unfavorably with other children, spend little time with him, and avoid his company.

Table 5

MEAN VALUES FOR PARENT BEHAVIOR VARIABLES SHOWING CONSISTENT
RELATIONSHIPS WITH RATINGS OF ADOLESCENT'S RESPONSIBILITY
(Possible Range 0-20)

VARIABLES	LEVELS OF RESPONSIBILITY		
	Low	*Medium*	*High*
Expressive rejection	4.50	3.48	3.44
Neglect	2.34	1.76	1.60
Affiliative companionship	8.72	9.50	9.82

At the same time, variables like *affection, affective reward,* and *nurturance* fail to show consistent positive association with levels of responsibility. Also, parental involvement in the more extreme form of *intercession, protectiveness,* or *indulgence* tends to correlate negatively with responsible behavior. It would appear that it is the presence of rejection rather than the lack of a high degree of warmth which is inimical to the development of responsibility in both sexes.

The above interpretation must be qualified, however, by the most salient feature of our findings—the contrasting pattern of relationships for boys and girls. As indicated by the recurring interaction effects in Column 7 of Table 4, the parental correlates of responsibility appear to be quite different for the two sexes. For sons, high levels of responsibility are associated with greater *presence, nurturance, affection,* and *companionship,* especially from the mother (Column 2), and—even more markedly—with increased discipline and authority from the father (Column 1). In contrast, for girls, virtually all these parental variables are negatively related to level of responsibility—this reverse effect being most marked for *intercession, protectiveness,* and *power.* Again, it is the father (Column 3) whose behavior seems to be especially critical.

Further light on the meaning of these results is shed by examination of the actual means (not shown) on each variable for the three levels of responsibility. To begin with father's discipline of the boy, the major gap in means again occurs between the Low group and the other two. In other words, it is the *lack* of discipline by the father which is associated with low responsibility in boys. Indeed, it was not the most responsible boys who received the highest discipline scores but those ranking in the middle, a fact which suggests that there is a critical point beyond which too much authority impedes rather than facilitates the development of responsibility in males.

The converse effect is apparent regarding girls. Here, it is the *presence* of strong paternal discipline, especially *power,* which is particularly debilitating. But the weakest levels of authority are apparently not the most beneficial, since once again it is not the most responsible girls but the middle group who receive the lowest discipline scores. Thus again we are led to the notion of an optimal level of authority, but evidently this level is considerably lower for girls than for boys.

Although no curvilinear effects were observed for either sex in variables connoting emotional support, the phenomenon of a differential optimal level for the two sexes is again apparent; that is, the nurturance and affection which seem deleterious for the development of responsibility in girls occur in an appreciably warmer context than the comfort and companionship which appear to foster dependability in the boy. These contrasting critical ranges in both support and control for the two sexes are but a reflection of the fact, reported earlier, that both parents, and especially fathers, tend to be more affectionate with daughters and more strict with their sons.

In concluding consideration of the data in Table 4, we should note the predominantly positive, and in four instances significant, interaction terms in Column 8. These reflect the fact shown directly by the mean differences in Columns 1–4, that it is primarily fathers whose absence, affection and, especially, authority have differential effects on both sexes.

To what extent are the above relationships mediated by the family's social position? Since the complete data are too extensive to present in tabular form, we shall confine ourselves to a summary of the most reliable findings. In general, the analysis shows that the differential effects of the father's behavior on the two sexes increases at lower educational levels. It is here especially that weak paternal power and participation reduce responsibility in sons whereas strong paternal authority and affection lower responsibility in daughters. As one moves up the educational ladder, these differential effects of paternal discipline decrease in magnitude until, at the graduate level, there is even a reversal in trend, with mother's authority becoming more influential for both sexes; that is, it is now mainly her discipline and activity which foster responsibility in boys and impede its emergence in girls. Possible explanations for these differential effects will be discussed shortly.

4. The Relationship of Parental Behavior to Adolescent's Leadership

To begin with the basic facts about this variable: like *responsibility,* it shows the usual positive correlation with social class, but, as might be expected, boys receive significantly higher ratings than girls. Given the fact that *leadership* and *responsibility* are substantially correlated (r = .48), it is hardly surprising that the two variables show a similar pattern of relationship with scales of perceived parental behavior. Nevertheless, there are important discrepancies.

To deal first with the common features: as indicated in Table 6, *expressive rejection* and *neglect* once again show reliable negative relationships across the board, but now parental *absence* and *protectiveness* also come into the picture. The means on all these variables reveal a steady decrease as one moves from the lowest to the highest levels of leadership. In the light of these facts, as well as the consistent pattern of main effects appearing in Table 6, it would appear that either extreme hostility or indifference on one hand, or over-protectiveness on the other, may undermine the adolescent's status in the classroom group.

As before, however, the most salient feature of the findings is the contrasting pattern of relationship for boys and girls, with parental interaction again facilitating the development of leadership in boys, but impeding it in girls. At the same time, there is a conspicuous difference between these and the earlier results for *responsibility*. Here it is primarily in the sphere not of authority but of positive interaction that parental behavior shows its differential effects. Specifically, *affiliative companionship, nurturance, principled discipline, affection,* and *affective reward* appear to foster the emergence of leadership in sons but discourage it in daughters.

As with the findings for responsibility, in considering the above results, it is important to keep in mind that the parental (and especially paternal) warmth and companionship which appear to impede the development of leadership in girls are appreciably more intense than the level of affection which seems to foster high status for the boy.

One additional feature of the data in Table 6 remains to be noted. As reflected by the three significant negative interactions in Column 8 (and the corresponding means in Columns 1–4), it is the parent of the *same sex* whose neglect, absence, or withdrawal of love are associated with low levels of leadership in the child.

As with the data on responsibility, many of the above relationships are mediated by the family's social position. The even more frequent inter-

Table 6

MEAN DIFFERENCES IN PERCEIVED PARENT BEHAVIOR BY ADOLESCENTS RATED AS "HIGH" AND "LOW" IN LEADERSHIP

PARENTAL BEHAVIOR	MEAN DIFFERENCES (High Minus Low)				MAIN EFFECT	INTERACTIONS		
	Boys		Girls					
	1. Fathers	2. Mothers	3. Fathers	4. Mothers	5.	6. Father Minus Mother	7. Boy Minus Girl	8. Same Sex Minus Opposite Sex
Parental absence	−1.84*	−.50	−.53	−1.60‡	−.99‡	−.26	−.36	−1.08*
Parental presence	.14	.56	−1.19	−.50	−.25	−.55	1.20	.14
Affection	.84	1.06	−1.90†	−1.08	−.27	−.52	2.45†	.30
Nurturance	−.10	1.10	−2.56*	−.88	−.61	−1.44‡	2.22†	.24
Affiliative companionship	1.10	.50	−1.81†	−1.63	−.46	.14	2.52*	.39
Affective reward	1.19	1.38	−1.22	−1.19	.08	−.11	2.58†	−.08
Material reward	.10	.16	−.88	−.38	−.25	−.28	.76	.22
Principled discipline	2.00*	1.53†	−1.50	−1.96*	−.02	.46	3.50‡	0.00
Instrumental companionship	.90	−.03	−1.28	−1.54	−.48	.60	1.84	.34
Physical punishment	−.09	−.34	−.09	.38	.04	−.10	−.36	−.36
Social isolation	−.13	.72	.47	.12	.30	−.25	0.00	−.60
Deprivation of privilege	−.12	.50	−.90	−.79	−.33	−.25	1.08	−.25
Affective punishment	−1.25†	.16	−.42	−.88	−.60	−.46	.10	−.70*
Achievement demands	.41	1.19	.34	−.03	.49	−.20	.64	−.58
Power	.10	.25	−1.12	−.66	−.36	−.31	1.06	.15
Indulgence	−.78	−.18	−1.44	−.78	−.80	−.62	.63	.03
Intercession	.34	.10	−1.28	−.50	−.34	−.26	1.11	−.51
Protectiveness	−1.38	−1.78†	−1.88*	−2.41‡	−1.86‡	.47	.56	−.06
Expressive rejection	−2.09*	−1.82†	−1.26	−1.53	−1.67‡	0	−.56	−.28
Neglect	−1.10	−.38	−1.06	−1.60*	−1.04‡	−.10	.59	−.63*

action effects point in the same direction: the salutary influence of affection, nurturance, companionship, and praise on boys, and their debilitating effect on girls increase markedly as one moves from the lower toward the upper educational levels, reaching a maximum among families where the father holds a graduate degree.

What to make of these patterns of continuity and contrast? Are they simply vagaries of chance? Or are they compatible with one another and with the results of other studies? Above all, do they make theoretical sense? We turn next to a consideration of these essential questions.

EVALUATION OF RESULTS

We begin the discussion with consideration of our initial and most pervasive finding: the consistent negative relation between scores on parental rejection and neglect on one side and, on the other, teachers' ratings of both *responsibility* and *leadership*. We have already observed that results of this kind are not uncommon in research literature. What makes them noteworthy in the present instance is their emergence in a balanced design including controls for father's educational level. Although investigators are now beginning to recognize the importance of control for social class variables, in research on parent-child relationships (e. g., Kohn and Clausen, 1956; Tiller, 1958; Miller and Swanson, 1958; Bandura and Walters, 1959), the writer was not able to find any study which bore directly on the present issue. Perhaps the most relevant work is that of Bandura and Walters, who investigated the parental antecedents of aggressiveness in a sample of twenty-six delinquent boys, each matched with a control of similar age, intelligence, and father's occupational status. To the extent that delinquency may be considered the opposite of responsible behavior, Bandura and Walters' results are at least partially consistent with those stated here. They found a "basic lack of affectional relationships" among families of aggressive boys, the relationship with the father being especially important. The father of the antisocial boy tended to be cold, harsh, and punitive. (It will be recalled that although in our results "weak" fathers had sons rating low in responsibility, the boys from families with the most extreme scores in paternal punishment obtained responsibility ratings which fell in the middle rather than in the highest groups.)

The Question of Reverse Causality

But even though the negative relationship between parental rejection and adolescent responsibility overrides social-class influences, one cannot conclude on this basis alone that the parental treatment has in fact influenced the behavior of the child. As we noted in our introductory discussion, consideration must be given to an alternative possibility which simply reverses the direction of causality; that is, children who are delinquent, aggressive, or irresponsible are perhaps more likely to be rejected and punished by their parents. Such an explanation would certainly be applicable to our data were it not for the striking reversal of relationships for the two sexes. If parental treatment is mainly a response to the behavior of the child, this hypothesis would explain the negative relation between parental discipline and adolescent responsibility for girls, but not the positive relationship for boys. Similarly, it is reasonable that a responsible boy be given more companionship and approval, but why then should a responsible girl receive fewer rewards of parental attention? In short, the hypothesis of reverse causality, while logical, does not seem to be easily reconcilable with the facts.

Sex Differences in Socialization: Some Facts and a Hypothesis

If one proceeds, however, on the equally tenable and more common assumption that adolescent behavior is a function of parental treatment, an explanation of the contrasting pattern of results for the two sexes does suggest itself. To begin with, it will be recalled that the girls in our sample reported considerably more affection, praise, and protectiveness than boys. Moreover, a correlational analysis of the twenty parent variables separately for each sex showed that, whereas among boys measures of parental affection and warmth were positively correlated with indexes of discipline and control, these two sets of variables were substantially unrelated among girls. Finally, analysis of these same data revealed a factor in the matrix for girls, not present in that for boys, showing heaviest loadings on *power, protectiveness,* and *deprivation of privileges.* In other words, our data suggest that affection and control are used in somewhat different ways, for somewhat different purposes, and with somewhat different effects when applied to the two sexes. Girls are given more warmth and less punishment but, at the same time when discipline is applied, it tends to be more restrictive and less leavened by affection. As Sears, Maccoby, and Levin (1957) have demonstrated, girls are more likely than boys to be subjected to "love-oriented" discipline techniques, and evidence is accumulating that such techniques are especially effective in bringing about socially-approved conduct and internalized controls for behavior (cf. Sears *et al.,* 1957; Bronfenbrenner, 1958a, 1960; Miller and Swanson, 1959). In contrast, a rather different pattern of child rearing is employed with boys. As indicated previously and in the data of Sears *et al.* (1957), in bringing up sons, parents are more likely to use physical punishment, to be permissive of and even encourage aggressiveness, to place less emphasis on conformity, and to foster independence and achievement.

Such findings, along with the recent data cited by Kohn (1959), indicate that the differential treatment of the two sexes reflects in part a difference in goals. With sons, socialization seems to focus primarily on directing and constraining the boy's impact on environment. With daughters, the aim is rather to protect the girl from the impact of environment. The boy is being prepared to mold his world, the girl to be molded by it.

These contrasting means and ends may explain in part the familiar findings (Terman and Tyler, 1954), reflected in our data, that girls are more obedient, cooperative and, in general, better socialized than boys at comparable age levels. At the same time, the research results indicate that girls tend to be more anxious, timid, dependent, and sensitive to rejection. If these differences are a function of differential treatment by parents, then it would seem that the more "efficient" methods of child rearing employed with girls involve some risk of what might be called "oversocialization." The qualities of independence, initiative, and self-sufficiency, which are especially valued for boys in our culture, apparently require for their development a somewhat different balance of authority and affection than is found in the "love-oriented" strategy characteristically applied with girls. While an affectional context is important for the socialization of boys, it must evidently be accompanied by and be compatible with a strong component of parental discipline. Otherwise, the boy finds himself in the same situation as the girl, who, having received greater affection, is more sensitive to its withdrawal, with the result that a little discipline goes a long way and strong authority is constricting rather than constructive.[10]

In short, our analysis leads to the hypothesis that typically the optimal balance of support and control is different for the two sexes and hence entails different risks in the process of socialization. For girls, with their greater sensitivity both to authority and affection, the principal danger lies in an overdose of either or both. For boys, who tolerate and require higher levels of discipline on an affectional base, problems derive most commonly from the failure on the part of parents to provide adequate emotional support and—especially—firm authority. Hence the contrasting pattern of

---

[10] A similar formulation is developed by Sears, Whiting, Nowlis, and Sears (1953). In an attempt to reconcile sex differences found in a study of child rearing antecedents of aggression and dependency in preschool children, these authors conclude: "Because of their greater tendency to identify with their mothers, girls actually suffer more severe punishment than boys do from a given rated amount of maternal punitiveness, and hence show more indication of generalized inhibition" (p. 220).

relationships found in our data, with parental warmth and discipline facilitating effective functioning in boys and impeding it in girls.

It should be recognized that the above formulation, while drawing on certain general hypotheses long familiar in the field of personality development (cf. Bronfenbrenner, 1960), is actually specific to a particular cultural context—the predominantly middle-class society from which our sample was drawn. Application of these same principles to a lower-class group or to a sample of delinquents such as that studied by Bandura and Walters would lead to a different prediction. In such settings, one might anticipate more frequent instances of boys exposed to punishment well beyond the theoretical optimum.. Under these conditions one would expect as an outcome not responsibility but rebellion.

However well the theoretical formulation we have developed may fit our own data or other hypothetical situations, it remains a *post hoc* explanation, for we have not been able, as in other instances, to look to other studies for confirmatory or contradictory evidence. Although a number of investigators (see below) deal with the effects of parental treatment on boys, studies on girls are few and far between and the writer could not find any directly relevant to the present issue.

Even if confirmatory evidence were found, one might argue that our theory overlooks the importance of genetic and maturational bases for sex differences in behavior. Such differences, in turn, would evoke differential response from parents thus setting in motion the very dynamic processes hypothesized here, but on a biological rather than psychological foundation. We are inclined to believe that genetic influences operate in exactly this fashion in the present instance. At the same time, we would call attention to a situation in which virtually the same psychological processes seem to appear and flourish without benefit of biological instigation or maintenance. Variations in child behavior and parental treatment strikingly similar to those we have described for the two sexes are reported in a comprehensive study by Schachter (1959) of differences between first- and later-born children. Like girls, first children tend to be better socialized but also more anxious and dependent, whereas second children, like boys, are more aggressive and self-confident. Moreover, a review of research on socialization practices for first and later children reveals differential treatment analogous to that we have described above and leads Schachter to develop a theoretical rationale very similar to our own.

Differing Antecedents of Responsibility and Leadership

An extension of one of our lines of argument also provides a possible explanation for the major difference found between the parental correlate of responsibility and leadership; namely the more salient role of parental discipline in the former and of parental affection in the latter. It seems reasonable to suppose that ratings of responsibility, particularly when made by teachers, involve more emphasis on conscience and internalized control than do ratings of the adolescent's acceptance as a leader by his classmates. In view of the demonstrated importance of discipline techniques in the formation of such superego controls (Sears *et al,* 1957; Miller and Swanson, 1959), one would expect parental authority to play a more prominent role in the development of responsibility than in the acquisition of leadership status with one's peers.

At the same time, the special relevance of parental affection for the leadership variable becomes more evident when we note the manner in which the negative pole of this trait was defined. The adolescent classified as "Low" was one whom teachers rated as "not taking initiative," "looking to others for direction," and "attaching himself to others." In short, the opposite of leadership was dependency. And, as Sears *et al.,* (1957) have shown, utilizing a theoretical orientation very similar to our own, dependency in children develops primarily as a function of the balance of parental love and its withdrawal.

Corroborative evidence for our findings regarding the parental antecedents of leadership comes from a recent research by Leiderman (1957). This investigator studied the effects of parent-child relationships (as rated from interviews) on the sociometric status of a sample of fourth-grade boys. She reports a positive correlation between popularity and parental warmth (particularly from fathers) but, as in our data, no relation with physical punishment. Although Leiderman's research included no controls for social class, confounding on this score should be minimal since she states that her families came predominantly from upper middle class. A more regrettable omission, from the point of view of our interest, is the restriction of the study to male subjects only.

Possibly contradictory evidence on the issue under discussion appears in a paper by Hoffman, Rosen, and Lippitt (1958). Also working with a sample of preadolescent boys, these investigators found support for their hypothesis that "successfully assertive peer-group leaders" tend to describe their parents as high both on coerciveness "punishes, threatens, hits") and autonomy (freedom from supervision). No information was obtained on such variables as warmth or affection. Moreover, with the possible exception of a measure of sociometric "liking," there is some question whether the indexes of child behavior employed in this research are comparable to the teachers' ratings of leadership in our own study, since the former give far greater emphasis to aggressive and achievement aspects of the leadership role (for example, directiveness, influence attempts, higher school performance). In one important respect, however, the Hoffman study reports findings similar to our own. The authors emphasize that their theory applies to boys only, since data on girls, though not yet completely analyzed, indicates quite different results. ". . . It seems likely that assertiveness in girls is less valued by others," and that girls are more likely to "respond to the emotional rejection that coercion implies" (p. 5).

A Statistical Hypothesis: the Influence of Variability in Score

To turn next to another major feature of our findings—the special importance of the father as a differential influence on the two sexes, particularly in the development of responsible behavior. Although one is tempted to jump immediately to social psychological explanations for this phenomenon, an inspection of the data suggests an initial approach on purely statistical grounds. It will be recalled that the parental behavior of mothers is much more closely associated with the father's educational level than the behavior of the father and that disciplinary techniques are particularly affected by the family's social position. It logically follows, and our data confirm the reasoning, that, within any social-class level, fathers exhibit considerably greater individual differences in disciplinary behavior than mothers. In other words, the substantially higher relations between father's control and adolescent responsibility may simply be a function of the greater range exhibited by the fathers' scores on measures of discipline.[11]

No such large difference in variance favoring the father occurs, however, in the affectional sphere. Indeed, with respect to boys, it is mothers who show the greater variability, a fact which may explain the somewhat stronger positive relation for mothers than for fathers between scores on warmth and nurturance and boys' ratings on both responsibility and leadership. Only with regard to girls do fathers show greater individual differences than mothers in demonstrativeness; accordingly, it is the father-daughter rather than the mother-daughter relationship which shows the stronger association with both dependent variables.

The same statistical rationale applies to the contrasting pattern of relationships with social class observed for parental correlates of responsibility and leadership. To consider responsibility first: here the association with

---

[11] Strictly speaking, the above generalization applies only to measures of the magnitude of association such as the correlation coefficient. It is highly likely, however, that the size of the correlation will itself be substantially correlated with the size of the mean difference between High and Low groups. Hence the influence of range cannot be ruled out of serious consideration as a factor affecting our research results.

paternal discipline is strongest at the lower-educational levels and decreases steadily with higher academic status of the husband until, among families of fathers with graduate degrees, there is even a reversal, with discipline from the mother now being the more important for both sexes. An examination of the variances involved indicates that this shift is quite consistent with our statistical hypothesis. It turns out that individual differences in severity of discipline are greatest among lower-class fathers, and decrease steadily as one moves up the academic ladder until, at the graduate level, it is the mothers who show greater variation.

Turning to correlates of leadership, we find something of an obverse trend. The relevant affectional variables show a steady rise in variance with social status; that is, individual differences for both parents are greatest at the college level. Hence it is not surprising that parental affection and companionship have their maximal salutary influence on boys and debilitating effect on girls among families where the father holds a graduate degree.

Some Substantive Interpretations

It would be a mistake, however, to regard these effects as mere statistical artifacts for they have social psychological significance as well. Thus the fact that parents of high-educational status show the greatest variation in affection and support suggests that there is less consensus in this group about how much warmth and attention should be given to the child. Moreover, the greater likelihood of extreme deviations in both directions at this level means that girls, who typically receive more affection than boys, are in greater risk of being "smothered," while boys, who get less support generally, may not receive enough to enable them to establish secure relationships outside the family. If so, we have a substantive explanation for the higher correlation at the upper-class levels between extent of parental warmth and its differential effects for the two sexes on acceptance by one's peers.

Similarly, if our findings on the parental antecedents of responsibility are valid, the fact that husbands exhibit greater variability in severity of discipline than wives means that fathers are the more important source of individual differences in the responsible behavior of their children. But if our theory is correct, it is not only the variability of fathers that contributes to their greater influence on responsibility but also the absolute level of the authority they exercise. Thus we have argued that the optimal level of discipline is different for the two sexes with boys requiring control that is firm but not harsh, and girls responding best to more moderate treatment. At the same time, our data indicate that fathers, even more than mothers, tend to treat the two sexes differently, being more strict with sons and more lenient and over-protective with daughters than mothers are. In other words, it is the fathers who are most likely to exert the degree and kind of authority which is most critical for the development of each sex. Thus, as our data indicate, it is the father more often than the mother who achieves the firm level of discipline which is associated with high levels of responsibility in boys; similarly it is he who accounts primarily for the high *nurturance, affection, power,* and *protectiveness* which are deleterious for the girl. At the same time, the greater variability among fathers in these critical variables means that they are more likely to deviate around optimal levels. Hence the substantive explanation for their greater diversifying influence on the development of both boys and girls.

As we have already noted, the above effects reach their maximum at the lower-educational levels. It is the poorly educated fathers who are most likely to be strict with their sons, to over-protect their daughters, and at the same time to show the greatest individual differences in disciplinary behavior. Accordingly, it is in the lower middle class that paternal behavior shows its greatest differential effect. Analogously, mothers become more influential at the upper-educational levels since here they show the higher means and variances in the sphere of discipline with corresponding effects on the child of each sex.

The Differential Influence of Fathers and Mothers: Some Implications in the Light of Existing Knowledge

To what extent do our findings on the differential influence of fathers and mothers on boys and girls find support in the research of others? To begin with, there is a substantial body of evidence, reviewed by Brim (1957), confirming the fact that each parent tends to be relatively more strict with the child of the same sex, this tendency becoming more marked as children grow older (Kagan, 1956). As for the effects of such differential treatment on the child, existing studies are almost entirely limited to boys. These, by and large, give support to our own findings on the special importance of the father. We have already cited the work of Bandura and Walters (1959), who found the relationship with the father particularly crucial in the prevention of boys' antisocial behavior. An even closer fit to our findings appears in the recent study of Mussen and Distler (1959) on the effects of parental identification on masculinity in a sample of 38 "predominantly middle class" five-year-old boys. Significant relationships were found for fathers only. The more masculine boys viewed their fathers both as more rewarding and nurturant and as more powerful sources of punishment. Unfortunately for our purposes both the independent and dependent variables in this study were assessed through projective techniques, parent-child relationships being inferred from responses in doll play.

Further corroborative evidence appears in the growing series of studies of effects of parental absence (Sears, Pintler, and Sears, 1946; Bach, 1946; Stolz, 1954; Tiller, 1958; Lynn and Sawrey, 1959), a number of which include female subjects as well as male. The research of Tiller, which includes controls for social class, is especially illuminating since it shows that the absence of the father not only affects the behavior of the child directly but also influences the mother in the direction of greater over-protectiveness. As all of the above studies indicate, the effect of both these tendencies is critical for male children; boys from father-absent homes tend to be markedly more submissive and dependent. Our own results are consistent in this respect since, as shown in Tables 4 and 6, father absence is negatively related to the development of both responsibility and leadership in boys. Moreover, our findings suggest a possible explanation for the almost negligible effects of father absence reported for girls. Given the fact that it is the parent of the opposite sex who is likely to be relatively more affectionate and over-solicitous toward the child, it follows that girls, in contrast to boys, are in greater risk of over-protection from fathers than from mothers. In line with this fact, our data show (Table 4, Column 3) that it is paternal presence rather than absence that correlates negatively with the development of responsibility in girls, and it is absence of the mother (Table 6, Column 4) rather than the father which impairs the leadership status of the girl.

Taken together, the findings on the effects of paternal absence give a new perspective to our understanding of the differential effect of the father's authority on the development of responsibility in the two sexes. Perhaps, where the father's power is relatively strong, the mother's tendency to overprotect the son is held in check. At the same time the strong father tends, as we have seen, to overprotect his daughter, thus keeping her more dependent. Hence firm paternal authority is associated with high responsibility in boys but low responsibility in girls.

Toward a Social-structural Hypothesis

If we follow through the logic suggested by the above train of thought, we are led from a psychological to a sociological or structural level of explanation for our findings. Specifically, the reasoning suggests that we should view our results not solely in terms of the absolute level of authority exercised by a single parent but in terms of the relative power of the two parents taken together. In fact, it is this very "difference" score that is involved in the interaction effects reported in Column 8 of Tables 4 and 6. From this point of view, the entries in both tables give complementary results. Specifically, they indicate that both responsibility and leadership are fostered by the relatively greater salience of the parent of the same sex. An examination of the actual differences themselves confirms this interpretation. Boys tend to be more responsible when the father rather than the mother is the principal disciplinarian; girls are more dependable when the mother is the major authority figure. A complementary trend in the affective sphere appears in the data on parental antecedents of leadership. Here it is relative role abdication by the same sex parent that becomes crucial. Lowest leadership ratings are obtained by *boys* from families in which the *father* exceeds the mother in absence, neglect, and withdrawal of love. Correspondingly, the most dependent *girls* come from families in which the *mother* is more often out of the home, neglects the child, and withholds her affection. In short, boys thrive in a patriarchal context, girls in a matriarchal.

But what if roles are undifferentiated so that both parents share equal responsibility for discipline and control? Our data are not in the form best suited to answer this question. They do indicate, however, that the groups classified as Low in either responsibility or leadership tend to show the smallest absolute differences between parents' scores in discipline and power. In other words, the most dependent and least dependable adolescents describe family arrangements which are neither patriarchal nor matriarchal, but equalitarian. To state the issue in a more provocative form, our data suggest that the democratic family, which for so many years has been held up and aspired to as a model by professionals and enlightened laymen, tends to produce young people who "do not take initiative," "look to others for direction and decision," and "cannot be counted on to fulfill obligations."

In the wake of so sweeping a conclusion, it seems especially appropriate to remind the reader of the tentative, if not tenuous, character of these results. As was stated at the outset, the findings are subject to bias from numerous sources—errors of omission and distortion in subjective reports of parental behavior by adolescents, the questionable validity of teachers' ratings of responsibility and leadership, and the susceptibility of conclusions to errors of Type I, Type II, and, above all, Type III—in the form of misguided interpretations by the author. The fact that many findings make theoretical sense is reassuring, but given the capacity of the human mind to perceive patterns even in the most random arrangements, it offers no guarantee against unwarranted conclusions. It is true that it has been possible to support many of the inferences with corroborative results from the work of many researchers. Nevertheless, the bulk of the findings remain *post hoc*. No apologies are made, for they were intended to be so. The purpose of this empirical study was not to confirm hypotheses but to create them. It is in the form of hypotheses that the results are summarized.

SUMMARY AND CONCLUSION

The major hypotheses emerging from this research can be conveniently summarized under three headings.

Joint familial antecedents of responsibility and leadership

1. Parental rejection and neglect impede the development of responsibility and leadership in both boys and girls.
2. The emergence of effective behavior is a function of an optimal balance of affection and control which is different for the two sexes and entails different risks in the process of socialization. Specifically,
   a. In American middle-class culture, the major obstacle to the development of responsibility and leadership in boys stems from inadequate levels of parental support and authority.
   b. For girls, the principal danger lies in the possibility of oversocialization through an overdose of parental affection and control.
3. The precise nature of the above relationships varies as a function of the sex of the parent. In general,
   a. Fathers show greater individual differences in parental behavior than do mothers and thus account for more of the variations in the behavior of their children.
   b. Relative lack of involvement in child rearing by the parent of the same sex impedes the development of responsibility and leadership in both sons and daughters.
4. The magnitude of the above effects varies systematically with social class, some relationships being reduced and others enhanced at higher-educational levels.

Familial antecedents specific to the development of leadership

5. The affectional relationship between parent and child is especially critical for the adolescent's acceptance as a leader by his peers. Extremes of parental indifference or rejection, on one hand, or over-protection, on the other, are inimical to the development of leadership in both sexes. Relative deprivation of affection from the parent of the same sex is especially deleterious.
6. Within the middle range, parental affection has sharply contrasting

effects on sons and daughters. Warmth and companionship facilitate the development of leadership in boys but impede its emergence in girls.

7. The differential effects of emotional support on the two sexes are enhanced in the higher socioeconomic strata, this increase being a function of the greater variance in affectional variables among better educated parents.

Familial antecedents specific to the development of responsibility

8. In the absence of extreme rejection or neglect, both parental affection and authority have differential effects on the development of responsibility in sons and daughters. For boys, it is the absence of sufficient warmth or discipline which more frequently impairs dependability; for girls, it is an overdose of either variable that has deleterious effects.

9. The behavior of the father, especially in the matter of discipline, is particularly crucial for the differential influence of socialization techniques on the two sexes.

10. The differential effects of parental authority on the two sexes are most marked at the lower-educational levels, where both parents, and especially the father, show greatest variability in severity of discipline.

11. Level of responsibility for both sexes varies directly with the extent to which one parent exercises greater authority over the child than the other. Specifically,

    a. Boys tend to be most responsible when the father is the principal agent of discipline; girls when the mother has relatively greater power.

    b. Both sexes are least responsible when both parents wield equal authority over the child.

These, then, are the principal emergents from this exploratory study. They should be evaluated with due regard for the acknowledged limitations of the concepts and methods chosen to be employed. The limitations are there and cannot be dismissed. An exploratory study stands or falls not on its theoretical elegance or methodological rigor, but on the fruitfulness and utility of the ideas which it generates—these are submitted here for evaluation and testing.

REFERENCES

BACH, G. R. Father fantasies and father-typing in father-separated children. *Child Develpm.*, 1946, *17*, 63–79.

BANDURA, A. AND WALTERS, R. H. *Adolescent aggression; a study of the influence of child-training practices and family interrelations.* New York: Ronald, 1959.

BRIM, O. G. The parent-child relation as a social system: I. Parent and child roles. *Child Develpm.*, 1957, *28*, 343–364.

BRONFENBRENNER, U. Socialization and social class through time and space. In MACCOBY, E. E., NEWCOMB, T. M., AND HARTLEY, E. L., *Readings in social psychology.* New York: Holt, Rinehart and Winston, 1958. Pp. 400–424. (a)

BRONFENBRENNER, U. The study of identification through interpersonal perception. In TAGIURI, R. AND PETRULLO, L., *Person perception and interpersonal behavior.* Stanford, Cal.: Stanford, 1958. Pp. 110–130. (b)

BRONFENBRENNER, U. Some Freudian theories of identification and their derivatives. *Child Develpm.*, 1960, *31*, 15–40.

BRONFENBRENNER, U., DEVEREUX, E., AND HARDING, J. Leadership and participation in a rural community. *J. soc. Issues*, 1960.

FREUD, S. Some psychological consequences of the anatomical distinction between the sexes. In *Collected papers*, Vol. V, London: Hogarth Press, 1950, 186–197.

GLUECK, S. AND GLUECK, E. *Physique and delinquency.* New York: Harper, 1956.

HARRIS, D. B., ROSE, A. M., CLARK, K. E., AND VALASEK, F. Personality differences between responsible and less responsible children. *J. gen. Psychol.*, 1955, *87*, 103–109.

HOFFMAN, L., ROSEN, S., AND LIPPITT, R. Parental coerciveness, child autonomy, and peer group role at school. Paper presented at Sixty-Sixth Annual Convention, APA, Washington, Sept., 1958.

KAGAN, J. The child's perception of the parent. *J. abnorm. soc. Psychol.*, 1956, *53*, 257–258.

KOHN, M. L. Social class and parental values. *Amer. J. Sociol.*, 1959, *44*, 337–351.

KOHN, M. L. AND CLAUSEN, J. A. Parental authority behavior and schizophrenia. *Amer. J. Orthopsychiat.*, 1956, *26*, 297–313.

LEIDERMAN, G. Effects of parental relationships and child-training practices on boys' interaction with peers. Paper read at XV International Congress of Psychology, Brussels, Belgium, July, 1957.

LYNN, D. B. AND SAWREY, W. L. The effects of father-absence on Norwegian boys and girls. *J. abnorm. soc. Psychol.*, 1959, *59*, 258–262.

MARTIN, W. E., GROSS, N., AND DARLEY, J. G. Studies of group behavior: leaders, followers and isolates in small organized groups. *J. abnorm. soc. Psychol.*, 1952, *47*, 838–842.

MERTON, R. K. *Social theory and social structure.* Glencoe, Ill.: Free Press, 1957.

MILLER, D. R. AND SWANSON, G. E. *The changing American parent.* New York: Wiley, 1958.

MILLER, D. R. AND SWANSON, G. E. *Inner conflict and defense.* New York: Holt, Rinehart and Winston, 1959.

MUSSEN, P. AND DISTLER, L. Masculinity, identification, and father-son relationships. *J. abnorm. soc. Psychol.,* 1959, *59,* 350–356.

PARSONS, T. AND BALES, R. F. *Family, socialization and interaction process.* Glencoe, Ill.: Free Press, 1955.

RYAN, T. A. Multiple comparisons in psychological research. *Psychol. Bull.,* 1959, *56,* 26–47.

SCHACHTER, S. *The psychology of affiliation.* Stanford, Cal.: Stanford, 1959.

SEARS, R., MACCOBY, E., AND LEVIN, H. *Patterns of child rearing.* Evanston, Ill.: Row, Peterson, 1957.

SEARS, R. R., PINTLER, M. H., AND SEARS, P. S. Effects of father-separation on preschool children's doll play aggression. *Child Develpm.,* 1946, *17,* 219–243.

SEARS, R. R., WHITING, J. W. M., NOWLIS, V., AND SEARS, P. S. Some child-rearing antecedents of aggression and dependency in young children. *Genet. Psychol. Monogr.,* 1953, *47,* 135–234.

STOLZ, L. M. *Father relations of war-born children.* Stanford, Cal.: Stanford, 1954.

TERMAN, L. M. AND TYLER, L. E. Psychological sex differences. In CARMICHAEL, L., *Manual of child psychology.* New York: Wiley, 1954. Pp. 1064–1114.

TILLER, P. O. Father absence and personality development of children in sailor families. *Nordisk Psykologi's Monograph Serieam,* 1958, No. 9.

TRYON, C. M. Evaluation of adolescent personality by adolescents. *Monogr. Soc. Res. Child Develpm.* 1939, *4,* No. 4.

PART **III**

Leadership
and Interpersonal Behavior
in the Large Organization

16

Leadership Skills: Their Identification, Development, and Evaluation

John C. Flanagan

American Institute for Research

Effective leadership, in this discussion, will refer to the activities of a designated leader of an organized group with respect to setting and achieving goals. Such a statement excludes emergent leadership, informal leadership, and leadership which is not goal-directed. Although it is not restricted to leaders in business, government, and education, it is clearly focused on the type of leadership typical in such organizations.

Leadership skills will be discussed in terms of three principal topics: defining effective leadership behavior, developing leadership skills, and evaluating leadership skills.

The orientation throughout will be toward practical leadership skills in important life settings. Where laboratory experiments are included, they represent an effort to reproduce important practical leadership situations revealing all essential dimensions in the laboratory setting.

DEFINING EFFECTIVE LEADERSHIP BEHAVIOR

In obtaining a detailed operational definition of effective leadership behavior, three procedures will be discussed:

1. The first of these represents the experience, opinions, and judgments of successful leaders. Lists of this type are constantly being prepared; because of their subjectivity, however, no two of them are alike. A recent tabulation of twenty-one such lists showed only one behavior—"being fair"—mentioned on as many as half of the various lists. Only four behaviors—"showing courage," "controlling emotions," "demonstrating initiative," and "making sound decisions"—were included on as many as a third of these lists. Unfortunately, such lists of leadership behaviors lack both the objectivity and the specificity necessary for a satisfactory definition.

2. The second procedure utilizes the same sources, but includes the application of such principles as sampling, objectivity, specificity, directed observations, and detailed reports. Thus, in this procedure, the experiences, judgments, and observations are collected following a formal set of rules. Such observations provide systematic data which may be analyzed and studied. It is possible with this type of data to apply tests to determine whether the sample is sufficiently large to provide comprehensive coverage of the leadership skills studied.

The critical incident technique is a procedure of this second type. In collecting critical incidents, the researcher makes a systematic effort to obtain a representative sample of data comprised of specific observations reported objectively with a minimum of interpretation. To insure representativeness of the sample, observation is directed toward a specified class of behaviors which meet a given set of criteria. A series of questions is used to provide detailed information regarding the situation in which the incident occurred and its consequences.

3. In most situations, the formulation of a precise definition of leadership behavior requires controlled experimentation regarding the relative effectiveness of various possible behaviors. Such experimentation makes it possible not only to confirm tentative hypotheses obtained from the other two procedures, but also to evaluate new types of leadership behavior not presently utilized.

Such a method of defining effective leadership behavior is much more expensive in terms of cost of experimentation. It necessarily represents, however, the ultimate test of hypotheses and ideas developed from other procedures. The effectiveness of such experimentation depends greatly on the ingenuity, imagination, and insight of the experimenter.

During the past ten years, a number of studies of leadership in business, government, and education have made use of the critical incident technique. An analysis of the effective leadership behaviors in various types of activities indicates that certain behaviors are common to effective leadership at all levels and in all types of organizations. However, even within the same organization, there is usually a marked change in emphasis in terms of the effective leadership behaviors going from the lowest to the highest levels of management.

For example, the following list of ten effective leadership behaviors has been found representative of the important behaviors in first-line management in a variety of industrial organizations:

Dealing with Subordinates:
1. Developing responsibility and teamwork in employees.
2. Helping employees improve their job performance.
3. Giving employees reasons and explanations for actions.
4. Alertness to employees' special problems.
5. Seeing that employees are treated fairly.

Performing Management Functions:
6. Planning and scheduling work.
7. Showing judgment and resourcefulness in getting work done.
8. Checking quantity and quality of work done.
9. Taking responsibility and initiative.
10. Cooperating with staff and others in higher management.

This list does not provide a satisfactory statement of the requirements in terms of effective leadership on the part of the organization's president. Similarly, a study of infantry units in Korea indicated that there was less than fifty percent overlap between the effective leadership behaviors in the lower levels of supervision and the higher levels in an infantry company.

In all of these studies, effective leadership behavior seemed to consist essentially of two main types of activity: *planning* and *motivating*. Planning is regarded as including goal setting, organizational structure, the distribution of functions, and development of programs and operating procedures to achieve the goal. Motivating is defined as including the activities of integrating the individual's needs and goals with those of the organization and carrying out a maximally effective program of individual reinforcement toward attaining these goals.

Few organizations operate without explicit aims. In many cases the aim is only a general one and the facts have not been collected and their implications analyzed to provide satisfactory guidance in forming policies and operating procedures. Although there is ample evidence to show that organizational planning has been important in the past, it is evident that accelerating technological developments will make planning the central factor in future organizational survival. This planning must include maximal adaptability to new information-gathering and data-processing equipment. The models of organizational structure which have been accepted in the past may prove inadequate in the future. With improved control and accounting methods made possible by various advances, including electronic computers, management may be able to distinguish improved structure and distribution of functions from trends and fads in administration which represent merely change rather than progress.

In the future, ideas such as those on which Alfred P. Sloane, Jr., based the reorganization of the General Motors Corporation more than twenty-five years ago can be more rapidly and more precisely evaluated before they are applied to specific organizations. His basic idea that "the process of administration should be decentralized but review or control should be centralized" is not nearly so universally accepted at the present time as it was a few years ago. Management theory is in danger of oversimplification and of becoming too firmly attached to fixed models. The application of the systems concept and decision theory methods to organizational planning offers substantial promise for increased effectiveness.

The systems approach results in the examination of the organization as a complete system, including its aims, functions, inputs, and outputs. The most effective organizational structure, distribution of functions and personnel, operating procedures, and program will depend on many factors specific to the situation. Management's problem is to determine the combination of these in the particular situation which will maximize gains in the direction of its aims. The mathematical model for solving such problems is provided by decision theory. This development in mathematical statistics by Wald and others provides a precise solution if costs and results can be estimated for various possible decisions.

It is unlikely that precise solutions to management's planning problems can be obtained using decision theory methods in the immediate future. However, the combination of improved comprehensive cost accounting and control, and high-speed, large-capacity electronic computers should make it possible to approximate solutions of this type, and it is therefore important that planning be based on the systems approach using the basic framework of decision theory.

The effective leadership behaviors in the future can therefore be anticipated to place even greater emphasis on planning, based on an analysis of aims and systematic study of facts regarding costs and outcomes. It should not be concluded that this planning will be entirely mechanical and deductive. The opportunities to create new and more effective programs, procedures, and combinations will be increased when the planners consistently use the whole system as their frame of reference in studying any specific problem.

Like planning, the other main component of effective leadership—

motivating—is a very complex activity. In this case, the complexities are not in the field of estimating costs and outcomes and processing large masses of data; they deal with the complexities of the human being.

Many factors have been reported as important for motivating personnel. Most of the studies have been based primarily on subjective opinion regarding the relationship of attitudes to the job. The very comprehensive review of Herzberg, Mausner, Peterson, and Capwell (1957) indicates there is much disagreement, in past studies, regarding what factors are related to job attitude and what the effect of job attitude is on work performance. Much of this difficulty seems to come from the unstable nature of the subjective data on which the studies are based.

As a result of this survey, Herzberg and associates concluded that the primary need was for an investigation of job attitudes in toto, a study in which factors, attitudes, and effects would be investigated simultaneously. They therefore undertook a new study using a semistructured interview in which people were asked to tell stories about times when they felt exceptionally enthusiastic or exceptionally depressed about their jobs. A group of 200 engineers and accountants in nine companies in the Pittsburgh area provided 476 such stories. The procedures of content analysis were used to identify and classify "thought units."

Using this content analysis of stories or sequences of both high and low morale periods of either long or short duration, the relevant job factors, resulting attitudes, and effects or consequences of these attitudes were studied. Herzberg, Mausner, and Snyderman (1959) conclude that only a small number of highly interrelated factors are responsible for good feelings about jobs. The key to an understanding of positive job feelings is to be found in a sense of personal growth and of self-actualization resulting from the following group of factors: *achievement, responsibility, work itself,* and *advancement.*

They further conclude that whereas these job satisfiers deal with factors involved in doing the job, the job dissatisfiers deal with factors defining the job context including poor working conditions, bad company policies and administration, and bad supervision. But, good working conditions, good company policies and administration, and good supervision were not found to lead to positive job attitudes.

The interpretation placed on this analysis by Herzberg and his associates is that jobs must be restructured to increase the proportion of workers who can derive positive motivation from doing their jobs. The other side of the job situation is regarded as primarily a *hygiene* situation, analogous to medical hygiene in which certain conditions are established to *prevent* job dissatisfaction, but which have little positive effect in developing high motivation. Specifically, recognition from the supervisor is seen as a motivator only when it is related to aspects of job achievement leading to feelings of personal growth and increasing responsibility.

The Herzberg study appears important both in terms of its methodological innovations in collecting experiences, judgments, and observations; and in using principles of sampling, directed observations, and detailed reports. Although the sampling of the individual's experience was not such as to insure representativeness, and the objectivity and specificity of the data were sacrificed in favor of other qualities, the study represents a thorough analysis of a large sample of systematically collected data regarding individual experiences. This analysis has yielded interesting and potentially very important hypotheses regarding the nature and method of operation of job satisfiers and job dissatisfiers. The ideas and analysis of the authors should stimulate similar studies more specifically focused on resolving the apparently conflicting results from previous studies relating leadership behavior to morale and productivity.

One other recent effort to obtain a representative sample of data including specific directed observations following a formal set of rules is Hahn's (1959) study of Air Force officers. This study was conducted as a part of a larger project to collect critical incidents regarding job experiences from a sample of 2200 Air Force officers. Several types of incidents were included to collect data to be used in connection with the educational program of the Air Academy. Three questions were included relating to motivation and morale. One asked for a report on the most recent time they felt especially notable personal satisfaction from the day's activities. The second question asked for the most recent time they felt sufficiently frustrated to question the value of an Air Force career for them. The third asked for the most recent situation which influenced their thinking about whether or not to remain in the Air Force.

In each case they were told to describe the incident in detail, to indicate why it made them feel this way, and to comment on the effects of such an experience. A preliminary analysis was made involving 756 statements of an action, situation, or generalized feeling associated with a factor involved in job satisfaction or motivation. This produced 23 categories. The categories were divided into two broad groups. The first included those factors dealing with some aspect of self-realization, and the second included factors related to various aspects of the general job environment. The 23 categories are listed below:

Self-Realization

1. Recognition from others for personal efforts, abilities, and potential capabilities

2. Fruition from and justification for personal actions, ideas, and recommendations
3. Sense of accomplishment
4. Personal value judgments regarding the importance of one's work
5. Convincing others regarding ideas and plans
6. Productive self-effort
7. Assumption of responsibility
8. Development and maintenance of flight skills
9. Utilization of personal skills, knowledge, and experience
10. Professionalism
11. Pride in job, unit and group performance, capability, and status
12. Teamwork and cooperative effort
13. Sense of belonging
14. Personal actions aiding other personnel

General Job Environment
15. Job assignments—the nature of and the manner in which they are made
16. Officer effectiveness, reporting and promotion procedures and systems
17. Actions and characteristics of supervisors and senior personnel
18. Personal characteristics and caliber of peers, associates, and colleagues
19. Air Force policies, regulations, and administration
20. Safety aspects associated with an Air Force career
21. Family and personal benefits, privileges, obligations, and considerations
22. Job security—regular commission status
23. Inherent nature of the tasks performed

The statements obtained in answer to the "good day" question were classified primarily in the self-realization categories (87 percent); only 13 percent were classified in the job environment categories. In contrast to this, the job environment categories included 73 percent of the incidents obtained in answer to the "frustrating day" question, as compared with 27 percent which were classified in the self-realization categories. The statements made in answer to the third question regarding situations influencing their thinking about remaining in the Air Force were, as expected, rather similar to those from the "frustrating day" question. Job environment categories accounted for 65 percent of the answers while self-realization categories accounted for only 35 percent.

Self-realization factors are positive in nature, being involved much more frequently in happy and satisfying job situations. Job environment factors, conversely, appear to be essentially negative in nature and are more frequently involved in unpleasant job situations or incidents.

This preliminary analysis appears to support some of Herzberg's conclusions. It was based on only about 10 percent of the available incidents of this type. Subsequent analyses dividing the answer to the third question into factors favoring an Air Force career and factors cited as evidence against such a career will provide additional evidence regarding these findings. Many other hypotheses can be tested with these data, including a hypothesis such as: to what extent are "good days" ones on which the individual is active in doing something over which he has substantial control, and the "frustrating days" ones on which he is passively carrying out instructions with little opportunity for initiative or control.

As indicated above, the formulation of a precise definition of effective leadership behavior requires controlled experimentation. A recent study by Spector and Suttell (1957) provided an experimental evaluation of three patterns of leadership. The design of the study included a systematic attempt to reproduce typical field conditions in a controlled laboratory situation. Twelve types of task-oriented groups aboard Naval destroyers were studied. One task situation involving the work of a small group was designed to reproduce both the structural and functional variables found in representative work groups of these types. The variables included in the task situation were: size of group, location of members, communication structure, nature of inputs to the group, group activities, group outputs, and the types of supervisory activities influencing the work group's production.

A model task consisting of information processing of the type handled in combat information centers was presented to teams of three members and a supervisor. The score, in quantitative terms, was the number of correct responses to 200 trials of information processing. A comparison was made of the effects of three different types of supervisor behavior on group performance.

Thirty teams and three leaders comprised the experimental group in which three patterns of supervisory behavior were tried out. Each leader was given suitable training in the particular pattern of behavior. He then used this pattern to supervise several groups. This was done in turn for each of the three behavior patterns.

The three patterns of supervisory behavior tried out were designed in accordance with the following principles:

1. *Single-leadership pattern.* Based on the principle that, in a task-

oriented group, the most effective supervisory behavior is that which maximized the quality of planning and decision-making, and the effectiveness of implementing these plans and decisions, by establishing and maintaining a separation of functions between supervisors and those responsible for carrying out the assignments. This pattern is similar to what is usually called *authoritarian*.

2. *Leadership-sharing pattern.* This pattern follows the principle that, in a task-oriented group, the most effective supervisory behavior is that which maximizes the individual satisfactions of the group members by providing maximum opportunity for all members to participate in planning and decision-making and to share the responsibility of achieving the goals of the group. This pattern is similar to the one usually called *democratic*.

3. *Reinforcement pattern.* Based on the principle that, in a task-oriented group, the most effective supervisory behavior is that which maximizes positive reinforcements; that is, effective rewards are identified and programmed to increase the actions that help to achieve the goals of the group.

In this study it was found that significantly higher scores were made by groups supervised by the reinforcement pattern than by those in either the single- or shared-leadership-pattern groups. Groups supervised by the reinforcement principle achieved 15 percent greater production than the single-leadership group, and 13 percent greater production than the leadership-sharing group.

DEVELOPING LEADERSHIP SKILLS

The failure of various management-development and leadership courses to develop leadership skills has become notorious in the past few years. Superficially, the impression may easily be gained that evaluative studies indicate that such studies are worthless. Since each course given under a specific set of circumstances must be evaluated on its own merits, generalizations do not seem warranted. However, it is certainly true that it is very difficult to find definite proof of the effectiveness of such courses.

An example that appears much too typical is provided by the following incident reported in the Air Academy study cited above.

> The Major was assigned to a newly formed Wing. There were numerous details to be accomplished in forming into an effective intelligence section the 25 people under him—one 1st Lt., two 2nd Lts., and 22 enlisted men. The officer failed to see any further than duty requirements. He employed no techniques whatsoever in handling personnel, and encouraging them to accomplish their assigned tasks.

The knowledge of personnel management was not employed. He had the course several times—but hardly ever employed it. This is probably the hardest thing to teach officers—that this course is not mere theory and speculation, but that it must be employed if an effective *and* satisfied unit is to be commanded.

As stated above, the possession of the knowledge was there, the employment of the knowledge was lacking and therefore every single man in the section was endeavoring to get transferred.

A similar incident began:

The officer concerned has a M.S. degree in personnel management from one of the best universities. BUT—he has never, to this date, practiced those principles taught and required in supervision.

Or to take a third example, another report said:

The officer had taken over a tactical squadron rated the highest within the Wing. With no appreciable personnel change the squadron became the least effective in hours flown, highest abort rate, and lowest training accomplished within six months.

Officer failed to exercise strict enough supervision in crew flight planning and close enough monitoring of crew pre-flight and mission preparation.

I feel this officer had the knowledge, but failed to use it.

A substantial number of similar incidents were reported. These incidents appear to point to the need for practical experience in using leadership skills in the training courses and also to the need for close supervision in using these skills in the job situation immediately following such instructions.

One procedure which appears to have substantial promise for providing practical experience in the training courses is typified by two closely related procedures called *role playing* and *situational problems*. Maier (1952) has been one of the most active psychologists in contributing to the development and use of role-playing procedures as an aid to training in human relations and supervisory skills. The practical experience of acting out personnel situations with the opportunity to apply the principles learned at a verbal level in the training courses appears to fill an important need in such training.

A more structured and supervised type of role-playing experience is provided by the situational problems illustrated in a series of projects carried out by the American Institute for Research (Sivy, Lange, and Jacobs, 1952; Suttell, 1954; Flanagan, 1954; Suttell and Richlin, 1954; Hahn, 1956; Glaser, Schwarz, and Flanagan, 1958).

In developing situational problems the first step is to determine the leadership behaviors to be included. In the series of studies just mentioned this was done by collecting and analyzing critical incidents. In this way, a list of 30 or 40 critical behaviors is developed. Typical forms of activity are then selected to provide a realistic setting. There is considerable evidence that persons performing on such situational problems behave spontaneously and naturally. Each problem is structured to include as many opportunities to exhibit the leadership behaviors included on the list as possible. During a period of an hour it is usually possible to include as many as 100 specific points to be checked as showing effective or ineffective leadership behavior. Immediate discussion of why a particular behavior is regarded as effective or ineffective provides early confirmation or correction of the trainee's actions.

In carrying out the experimental comparison of the effectiveness of patterns of leadership behavior as described above, Spector and Suttell (1957) used a novel procedure for providing training in actual performance. It was found that in the limited time available, it was not possible to ensure that the leader's behaviors were precisely those intended in the training prior to the experimental comparison trials. To secure as much standardization in training as possible, the leader was prompted by the experimenter through an earphone whenever necessary during the final training period. This type of prompting from an external source in an actual face-to-face leadership situation has the advantage of enabling the individual to be subtly guided and corrected as much or as little as necessary to perform in a relatively effective manner.

Other uses of audio-visual aids in leadership training such as those of the Human Resources Research Office suggest that such aids may prove very helpful in providing the necessary realism and practice.

EVALUATING LEADERSHIP SKILLS

The problem of evaluating the leadership skills of an individual is a complex and difficult one. The three approaches which are discussed will illustrate various compromises, each of which has important advantages and disadvantages.

The first approach is through the use of a standardized proficiency test. This test, called a situational performance test, has the advantages that it is the same for all, it provides a comparatively reliable measure in a period of only a few hours of testing; it provides systematic, comprehensive coverage of the important leadership skills in a situation which involves interaction with other people; and it supplies detailed information concerning which skills are used effectively and which are not. The primary disadvantage is that it affords a measure of what the individual can do when he knows he is being tested, which may not be the same as what he typically does in a real supervisory situation.

The situational performance test is developed in just about the same way as the situational performance training problems mentioned above. The test usually consists of a number of situations for each of which an introductory script, one or more actors, and a score sheet are provided. Tests consisting of 15 or 20 situational performance problems of this type and including 200–300 scored items usually have fairly good consistency between independently administered and scored problems (reliability coefficients about .50—see Sivy *et al.,* 1952; Suttell, 1954; Suttell and Richlin, 1954; Hahn, 1956; Glaser *et al.,* 1958). Such tests have also been shown in these same studies to have relatively low but statistically significant agreement with ratings of on-the-job leadership performance and with amount of leadership experience. In view of the notoriously low consistency of ratings of leadership performance which are not spuriously inflated by reputation and other factors specific to a particular work situation, the significant agreements found appear very promising.

The second approach is through observational or performance records of typical leadership performance. One procedure which has been successfully used to improve the practicality of such an observational procedure is to record only the leadership behaviors observed which are especially effective or ineffective. This is further simplified by a prepared performance record which contains a classified list of effective and ineffective leadership behaviors. The supervisor is required only to place a check in the appropriate box. In some situations he adds the date and a word or two which identify the incident. The advantages of this procedure are that in this way the supervisor can maintain a precise record of everything he observes which is significantly better or worse than average performance and the incidents provide a record which is very useful in assisting the supervisor to plan improvements in relevant job management or supervisory skills. The disadvantage of this approach is that it requires an additional set of records. Even though it has been shown that only a few minutes a day will save time and improve supervision in the long run, without close and authoritative monitoring most supervisors will not continue to maintain such records. Thus, the procedure has only been effective when top management regarded it as of sufficient value to them to provide effective monitoring.

The third approach is the evaluation of the production of the group working for a particular supervisor. This is clearly the most immediately relevant of any of these evaluation procedures. Its advantages are objectivity and meaningful scores in terms of profits or gains with respect to the group assignments. Its disadvantages are the lack of comparability of the scores, the difficulties of obtaining accurate records of costs and products, and the omission of the many other aspects of the supervisor's job having to do with developing subordinates, cooperating with other supervisors and with management, and special contributions in terms of ideas, motivation, and public relations.

More specifically, these disadvantages are, first, with respect to comparability of scores, supervisors are usually asked to perform different tasks with different materials, equipment, and personnel. Similarly, it is very difficult to compare the productivity of their groups in a meaningful way. In collecting data regarding production, it is difficult to know whether spoilage is the result of defects in the materials, the mistakes of other groups, or specific errors on the part of this supervisor's group. Also, costs and expected productivity are hard to estimate. The remaining disadvantage is in some ways the greatest shortcoming of current procedures of this type. There are many supervisors who "get out the work" but at the same time do the organization serious damage and interfere with effective operations considered from a long-range point of view.

All three of the approaches presented above are believed to have promise. The most precise measures for research and evaluation purposes can be obtained from situational performance tests. In the long run it seems likely that a combination of the second and third procedures can be developed which will yield a useful estimate of the effectiveness of the supervisor. This would be a combination of immediate production figures and figures representing the potential value of specific actions such as personnel development conferences. The aim would be to develop an index which included all aspects of the supervisor's job, each weighted in accordance with management's best estimate of its importance to the organization's over-all goals. Enough preliminary work has been done along this line by the American Institute for Research so that it appears both feasible and desirable.

SUMMARY AND CONCLUSIONS

In this discussion of effective leadership by a designated leader of an organized group, effective leadership has been defined as including those actions having to do with setting and achieving group goals. In discussing the development of a detailed list of effective leadership behaviors the increasing importance of two types of activities, *planning* and *motivating*, has been pointed out.

Planning, including the use of decision theory models and new information-gathering and data-processing equipment will probably result in less use of general patterns of organizational structure and distribution of functions. The best specific solution for a particular situation will be determined with relative precision and continuously modified to meet changing conditions.

It is also believed that planning and flexibility will be the key factors in motivating personnel in organizations. The distinction between motivators and satisfiers as suggested by Herzberg needs to be refined and analyzed in greater detail.

This general discussion suggests that the application of the research approach to management problems will produce a management science consisting of principles, procedures, and models. It appears to follow that in the typical organization, any reasonably competent member of management could carry out the leadership function by learning and applying the indicated principles and procedures. Although it seems clear that management *is* becoming more of a science and less of an art, the concept of the leader as a manipulator of a set of fixed routines and procedures is an erroneous one. Outstanding organizations develop because of some dynamic personal quality in their leaders which transcends the deductive process and leaps ahead to solutions and conclusions which cannot logically be inferred from available data. In addition to skills, effective leadership requires intuition and inspiration.

REFERENCES

FLANAGAN, J. C. Some considerations in the development of situation tests. *Personnel Psychol.,* 1954, 7, 461–464.
GLASER, R., SCHWARZ, P. A. AND FLANAGAN, J. C. The contribution of interview and situational performance procedures to the selection of supervisory personnel. *J. appl. Psychol.,* 1958, 42, 69–73.
HAHN, C. P. *Collection of data for utilization in curriculum planning of the U. S. Air Force Academy.* Washington, D. C.: American Institute for Research. March, 1959.
HAHN, C. P. *The development and validation of situational problems for training in those leadership behaviors essential for effective performance as a junior officer.* Washington, D. C.: American Institute for Research, 1956.
HERZBERG, F. MAUSNER, B., PETERSON, R. O., AND CAPWELL, DORA F. *Job*

attitudes: Review of research and opinion. Pittsburgh: Psychological Services of Pittsburgh, 1957.

HERZBERG, F., MAUSNER, B., AND SNYDERMAN, BARBARA. *The motivation to work.* New York: Wiley, 1959.

MAIER, N. R. F. *Principles of human relations.* New York: Wiley, 1952.

SIVY, J. LANGE, C. J., AND JACOBS, O. *Development of an objective form of the Leaders Reaction Test.* Pittsburgh: American Institute for Research, 1952.

SPECTOR, P. AND SUTTELL, BARBARA J. *An experimental comparison of the effectiveness of three patterns of leadership behavior.* Washington, D. C.: American Institute for Research, 1957.

SUTTELL, BARBARA J. *The development of a situation test to measure nonintellectual officer qualities.* Washington, D. C.: American Institute for Research, 1954.

SUTTELL, BARBARA J. AND RICHLIN, M. *Development of situational performance problems for evaluating and training potential Navy junior officers.* Officer Personnel Research Program Research Memorandum No. 29. Washington, D. C.: American Institute for Research, 1954.

WEISLOGEL, R. L. Development of situational tests for military personnel. *Personnel Psychol.,* 1954, 7, 492–497.

17

An Emerging Theory
of Organization, Leadership,
and Management[1]

Rensis Likert

Director, Institute for Social Research
The University of Michigan

In 1947 the Survey Research Center received the first of a series of grants from the Office of Naval Research to support "A Program of Research on the Fundamental Problems of Organizing Human Behavior." The proposal submitted to ONR outlined a ten-year program of studies and experimentation. ONR provided the very valuable and essential support needed to get this research program underway and continued its support for many years. Since the second year several industrial organizations have provided substantial support as have some foundations.

I shall summarize very briefly the pattern of findings emerging from this research, suggest a theoretical integration, and then examine the extent

[1] Condensation of a paper presented at the Symposium on Leadership and Interpersonal Behavior sponsored by Louisiana State University and the Office of Naval Research, March 3–5, 1959, at Baton Rouge, Louisiana. Some of this material was incorporated in the author's article on "A Motivational Approach to a Modified Theory of Organization and Management" in *Modern Organizational Theory,* edited by Mason Haire, John Wiley & Sons, Inc., 1959, and in his chapter on "Influence and National Sovereignty" in *Festschrift for Gardner Murphy,* edited by John G. Peatman and Eugene L. Hartley, Harper & Brothers, 1960. It is reprinted with permission of both publishers.

to which available data seem to support the proposed theory. The research findings are based on over twenty-five studies conducted by the Institute for Social Research[2] in such industries as: automotive, chemical, delivery service, electronics and electrical instruments, electric appliances and equipment, food, heavy machinery, insurance, petroleum, public utilities, railroads, and textiles. Studies have also been made in government agencies. Data were obtained from managers and supervisors as well as from tens of thousands of employees doing jobs requiring a large range of skill, from operations involving unskilled workers to laboratories doing highly specialized scientific research.

In carrying forward this research, several criteria have been used to evaluate organization effectiveness. These include:

1. Productivity per man hour or some similar measure of the organization's success in achieving its productivity goals.

2. Job satisfaction and other satisfactions derived by members of the organization.

3. Turnover, absence, and similar occurrences.

4. Costs.

5. Employee and managerial motivation.

The results of these studies point to an important conclusion: the traditional or classical theories of management (e. g., Gulick and Urwick, 1937; Taylor, 1911, 1947) upon which most companies and governmental agencies base their organizational policies and administrative actions have important inadequacies. These inadequacies are demonstrated by the fact that the most effective managers and supervisors are using procedures and practices which differ in important ways from those advocated by their companies.

Most companies and government agencies, for example, presently use standard operating procedures and prevailing practices which stem primarily from the classical task-oriented and authority-oriented conception of organization. These concepts specify that management should follow such procedures as the following:

1. Break the total operation to be performed into its simple, component parts or tasks.

2. Develop the best way to perform each of the component parts.

3. Hire people with appropriate aptitudes and skills to perform each of these component tasks.

---

[2] The Institute for Social Research includes both the Survey Research Center and the Research Center for Group Dynamics.

4. Train these people to do their respective tasks in the specified best way.

5. Provide supervision of such a kind that these employees perform their designated tasks using the specified procedure at an acceptable rate as determined by timing the job.

6. Where feasible, also, use incentives in the form of individual or group piece rates.

The implications of such a restrictive conception of the objectives and means of management are many. It is implied that any diversion of the manager or supervisor from task-centered activities is to be avoided; that immediate goals and work procedures should be specified in detail for each position; that pressure for performance of specified tasks and close control over performance are desirable; that influence over activities should be primarily at levels above the individual member.

A rather large amount of research is yielding results which raise questions as to the validity of some of these propositions. The results of this research have been reported fully elsewhere and will not be detailed here, except to mention some typical conclusions and to give representative sources in the literature:

1. Supervisors and managers who are "employee-centered" rather than exclusively "job-centered" tend to get better results (Kahn and Katz, 1953; Katz, Maccoby, and Morse, 1950; Katz, Maccoby, Gurin, and Floor, 1951).

2. Employees working under strong pressure for higher productivity, or strong pressure for acceptance of specified tasks, tend to perform less well (Jackson, 1953; Likert, 1952).

3. Close supervision tends to accompany poor performance rather than good performance (Katz and Kahn, 1951, 1952; Morse, 1953).

4. Freedom to set one's own work methods and work pace, within broad limits, is connected with good performance (Kahn, 1958; Meltzer, 1956; Pelz, 1957).

5. A high degree of mutual, rather than one-way, influence is associated with good performance (Pelz, 1952; Tannenbaum and Georgopoulos, 1957; Tannenbaum and Kahn, 1958).

6. Organizations with greater diffusion downward of control and influence, and wider participation in decisions, tend to show better results (Kahn and Tannenbaum, 1957; Tannenbaum and Kahn, 1958).

7. Better and poorer supervisors and managers are relatively undifferentiated with respect to fulfilling the task-centered aspects of their responsibilities but are differentiated a great deal with respect to activities

representing concern for subordinates' well-being, training and development, self-confidence, security, encouragement of free communication (Katz and Kahn, 1951; Likert, 1952; Likert and Willits, 1940; Mann and Dent, 1954).

8. Supervisors and managers who are aware of and utilize group processes tend to achieve better results (Georgopoulos, 1957; Likert, 1953; Mann, 1957; Mann and Baumgartel, 1953; Mann and Dent, 1954).

Research findings, such as referred to briefly in these statements, show that there are important inadequacies in the organizational and managerial theories upon which most American business organizations and government agencies base their present operating procedures. These inadequacies are clearly evident when the procedures used by the highest producing managers and supervisors are compared with the procedures called for by the standard practices of their organization. When this comparison is made, it becomes clear that the high-producing managers and supervisors are deviating in important and systematic ways from those advocated by their company and from the underlying theory upon which these procedures are based.

It is becoming increasingly clear, consequently, that a modified theory of organization and management, based upon the principles and practices used by the more successful managers, can help all managers and supervisors to achieve better results. An attempt will be made in this paper to summarize briefly the over-all characteristics of such a modified theory of management.

A MODIFIED THEORY OF MANAGEMENT

This modified theory seeks to build upon all that works best in existing practices. It uses fully the tools, but not the philosophy, of scientific management, cost accounting and similar technologies and developments, such as:

1. Elimination of waste and inefficiency through functionalization, work simplification and related processes;
2. Establishment of specific work goals where feasible;
3. Measurement of work accomplished and the continual examination of the extent to which the specified goals are being achieved;
4. Budgeting, cost accounting, and controls over costs.

Under the modified theory, however, these resources are used in a different manner, based on a different set of motivational assumptions and with a different logic or philosophy from those upon which the traditional or classical theories are based.

The modified theory emphasizes, as its second major concept, the necessity of a high level of motivation throughout the organization directed toward achieving the objectives of the organization. To obtain a high level of coordinated motivation, the goals of the organization must satisfactorily incorporate the needs of its members. Moreover, those motivational forces which are most powerful and most likely to be reinforcing and cumulative should be used. Procedures which produce conflicting motivational forces and which thereby reduce the level of effective motivation are to be avoided. The theory specifies, consequently, that the operating procedures for performing all such functions as supervision, communication, training, compensation, and decision-making should be of such a nature as to tap powerful motivational forces in an additive and reinforcing manner.

The major motivational forces which can be used in such a reinforcing manner include those that spring from:

1. Economic motives.
2. Ego motives (including the desire for growth and significant achievement in terms of individual values and goals as well as the desire for status, recognition, approval, acceptance, and so on).
3. Security motives.
4. Curiosity, creativity, and the desire for new experiences.

In addition to using the most powerful resources of existing theories and, insofar as possible, having all members of the organization highly motivated to achieve the organization's objectives, there is a third requirement. No matter how highly motivated are its members nor how good its procedures, an organization will not be effective unless the efforts of its members are coordinated and focused. There needs to be an efficient interaction or mutual influence system which provides the mechanism through which the goals and activities of the organization are integrated and coordinated. The character of this mutual interaction system has to be such that the following are provided:

1. Full and efficient communication of all relevant information between the various levels of the organization and across them: up, down, and sideways.
2. A distribution of influence, comparable to the information flow, which will assure that all of the experience, knowledge, and needs of members of the organization are reflected adequately in the decisions and actions taken by the organization. There should be, consequently, an

opportunity for members to exert appropriate and adequate influence on other members of the organization.

3. Decision-making processes which use fully the information and experience available in the organization and which function in such a way that the members of the organization are highly motivated to carry out these decisions.

The fourth major concept of the modified theory relates to the use of measurements. Not only should production, costs, waste, earnings be measured regularly but, in addition, measurements should be obtained of those human dimensions which affect the organization's resources and capacity to produce: the motivations of its members and the effectiveness with which such processes as communication and decision-making are carried out. Measurements of these human organizational variables need to be obtained regularly in order to build and maintain an organization capable of functioning at all times in a manner geared to achieve its objectives (Likert, 1958, 1959).

These four aspects of the modified theory are all suggested by the research dealing with the patterns of supervisory behavior displayed by the high-producing managers and supervisors in contrast to those superiors who achieve mediocre or poor results. The kind of direct treatment of subordinates by supervisors which tends to result in the highest productivity, highest motivation, and highest satisfaction shows a consistent pattern having the following general characteristics:

1. Attitude and behavior of superior toward the subordinate as a person (as perceived by the subordinate):

(a) He is supportive, friendly and helpful rather than hostile. He is kind but firm, never threatening, genuinely interested in the well-being of subordinates and their families and endeavors to treat people in a sensitive, considerate way. He is just, if not generous.

(b) He has confidence in the integrity, ability and motivations of subordinates rather than being suspicious and distrustful.

(c) His confidence in subordinates leads him to have high expectations as to the level of performance by subordinates. With confidence that he will not be disappointed, he expects much, not little, from subordinates. His expectation as to their performance level is sufficiently high to stretch them and help them grow but not so high as to break them. (This is fundamentally a supportive rather than a critical or hostile relationship.)

(d) He sees that each subordinate is well-trained for his particular job. He also endeavors to help subordinates to obtain promotion by training them for the next level job. This includes giving them relevant experience and coaching whenever the opportunity offers.

(e) He coaches and assists employees whose performance is below standard. In the case of a subordinate who is clearly misplaced and unable to do his job satisfactorily, he endeavors to find a position well-suited to that employee's abilities and arranges to have the employee transferred to it.

(f) He helps subordinates to grow by giving them freedom to participate in decisions and to make decisions, and he is supportive rather than punitive when they make mistakes.

(g) He seeks to know and use their "ideas" and to draw upon their experience. To facilitate this flow of ideas and influence, he seeks to develop an atmosphere of confidence and trust and a group form of organization.

2. Behavior of superior in organizing and directing work:

(a) He engages in such activities as planning and organizing the work to be done, training subordinates, supplying them with material and tools of satisfactory quality, initiating work activity.

(b) He has adequate technical competence, particularly in those situations where the work has not been highly standardized.

3. Behavior of superior in developing subordinates into a good working team:

(a) He creates a good working team which has a friendly, cooperative atmosphere with high group loyalty. He seems to build this high group loyalty through using participation and other recognized methods of group leadership. Moreover, the work group under his leadership exercises influence upward upon organizational objectives and methods, and in turn accepts as group goals those objectives which must be achieved if the group is to do its part of the total task effectively and at a high performance level. The work group sets specific goals and checks its progress toward these goals regularly.

These interpretations of research results from many sources strongly support the general proposition that subordinates react favorably to experiences which they feel are supportive and contribute to their sense of importance and personal worth, and react unfavorably to experiences which are threatening and decrease or minimize their sense of personal worth. Such a proposition is supported also by research on personality development and group behavior. Each of us as an individual, as a human being, wants to achieve and maintain appreciation, recognition, a feeling of accomplishment, and a feeling that people who are important to us respect us.

This general pattern of reaction appears to be universal and provides the basis for a general formula to derive operating procedures likely to yield high and cumulative motivation and an effective interaction system. Motivational forces, such as economics and ego, acting in each member of an organization are most likely to be cumulative and reinforcing when the interactions between each individual and the others in the organization convey to the individual a feeling of support and a recognition of his importance and worth as a person.

A second factor, however, is also very important: an individual's reaction to any situation is always a function, not of the objective character of the interaction but of his perception of it. It is how he sees things that counts, not objective reality. Consequently, an individual will always interpret an interaction between himself and the organization in terms of his background and culture, his experience and expectations. A subordinate tends also to expect his superior to behave in ways consistent with the personality of the superior. This means that each of us, as a subordinate or as peer or superior, reacts in terms of his own particular background, experience and expectations. In order, therefore, for an interaction to be viewed as supportive, it is essential that the interaction be of such a character that the individual *in the light of his experience and expectations* sees it as supportive. This provides the second factor needed for stating the general formula that is required to derive operating procedures, for applying the modified theory in any particular situation. The general formulation consequently is: *The structure of the organization and the manner in which the organization functions should be such that there is a maximum probability that in all interactions each of the individuals involved will, in the light of his background, experience, and expectations, view the interaction as supportive and one which contributes to his sense of personal worth.*

This general formulation provides the basis for deriving standard operating procedures which will tap fully and in a reinforcing manner economic and other powerful motives in addition to the motives associated with the sense of importance and personal worth. There is impressive evidence, for example, that economic motivations will be tapped more effectively when the conditions specified by the general formula are met rather than violated (Katz and Kahn, 1951, 1952; Whyte, 1955; Lesieur, 1959). The positive motivational forces which flow from economic rewards tend to be greater when there is acceptance and a favorable orientation toward the plan or methods of compensation rather than the converse. The level and forms of economic reward are highly important but so are the decision processes by means of which these levels and the form of compensation are established.

The manner in which the proposed general formula can be used to derive operating procedures can be illustrated by a theoretical derivation. This derivation is based directly on the desire for a sense of personal worth which is a central concept of the formula. Each of us seeks to achieve and maintain a sense of personal worth and importance primarily from the people we are close to, in whom we are interested, and whose approval and support we are eager to have. The face-to-face groups with whom we spend the bulk of our time are, consequently, the most important to us. The work group is usually one of the most important of the face-to-face groups. It is one in which we spend much of our time and one from which we are particularly eager to derive a sense of personal worth. As a consequence, most persons are highly motivated to behave in ways consistent with the goals and values of their work group in order to obtain recognition, support, and favorable reactions from this group. It can be concluded, therefore, that *management will make full use of the potential capacities of its human resources only when each person in an organization is a member of one or more well-knit, effectively functioning work groups which have high skills of interaction and high performance goals.*

The full significance of this derivation becomes more evident when we examine the research findings that show how groups function when they are well-knit and have high interaction skills. Research[3] shows, for example, that the greater the attraction and loyalty to the group, the more the individual is motivated (a) to accept the goals and decisions of the group; (b) to seek to influence these goals and decisions so that they are consistent with his own experience and his own goals; (c) to communicate fully to fellow members; (d) to welcome communication and influence from other members; (e) to behave so as to help implement group goals and decisions, especially those which are seen as most important to the group and (g) to behave in ways calculated to receive support and favorable recognition from those members the individual feels are more powerful and of higher status. Groups which display a high level of member attraction to the group and high levels of the above characteristics will be referred to in this paper as effective (high mutual influence) groups.

As our theoretical derivation has indicated, an organization will function best when it is made up of groups of people who are loyal, effective workers with high performance goals. Consequently, management should deliberately endeavor to build effective teams linking them into an over-all

---

[3] Part of this research on small groups has been conducted by the Research Center for Group Dynamics under contract with the Office of Naval Research. (See Cartwright and Zander, 1953).

organization through the aid of individuals who hold overlapping group memberships in which the superior in the bottom group is a subordinate in the next group and so on up through the organization. If the work groups at each hierarchical level are well-knit and effective, the linking process will be accomplished easily. Staff as well as line should be characterized by this group pattern of functioning.

In most organizations it will be desirable also to have various committees, both ad hoc and continuing, as well as other staff activities set up on a group or team pattern. These groups and committees, if they function well, can also help further to tie many parts of the organization together. These links are in addition to the linking provided by the overlapping members in the line organization and strengthen further the interaction-influence system. Throughout the organization the supervisory processes should develop and strengthen group spirit and group functioning. This theoretically ideal organizational structure when properly used provides the interaction-influence system called for by the modified theory. If the theory is valid, this form of organizational structure will result in a high capacity for efficient, full communication in all directions, high loyalty and trust, and high motivation to achieve goals.

TESTING THE THEORY

It is possible to test whether the group form of organizational structure, when used effectively, does or does not achieve better performance in such matters as greater productivity, better communication, and higher motivation to achieve organizational goals. Ideally this test should be made by conducting experiments in field situations. Such tests probably will require three or more years at least and should be done in several different situations. A simpler but partial test was made using data collected in 1955 in a study conducted by the Institute for Social Research. The data are from 31 geographically separated stations (from a company which operates nationally) which perform essentially identical operations and for which extensive productivity and cost figures are available continuously. These stations vary in size from about 15 to over 50 employees.

A single score was computed for the manager in charge of each of the 31 stations. The scores are based on seven items in a questionnaire and are intended to represent a crude approximation of the extent to which the managers have supportive attitudes toward their men and the extent to which the managers endeavor to use group methods of supervision. These scores, labeled for convenient reference *attitude toward men,* are based on the managers' own answers to the questionnaire and, consequently, reflect their own concept of their job. Their actual behavior in some instances may not be fully in accord with their expressions of point of view.

The relationship between the *attitude toward men* scores of the managers and the productivity of the stations is shown in Table 1.

Table I

RELATIONSHIP BETWEEN MANAGERS' "ATTITUDE TOWARD MEN" SCORE AND STATION PRODUCTIVITY

	MANAGER'S ATTITUDE TOWARD MEN SCORE		
Station Productivity	*Unfavorable*	*Medium*	*Favorable*
High	0	5	3
Medium	2	7	5
Low	7	1	1

Figures show number of stations in each segment of the field. The point correlation for these data is +.64.

As these data show, those managers who have a favorable *attitude toward men* score achieve significantly higher performance than those managers who have an unfavorable score. Managers who have a supportive attitude toward their men and endeavor to build them into well-knit groups obtain appreciably higher productivity than managers who have a threatening attitude and rely more on man-to-man patterns of supervision.

An additional series of tests of the group form of organizational structure were made using data from these same 31 stations. These more extensive tests examined data obtained not only from managers but from the men as well.

One such additional test involved classifying the 31 stations on the basis of the extent to which there existed effective group-based interaction. An estimate of this variable was based on the extent to which the manager and the men agreed that there were worthwhile group discussions involving the supervisors and the men. Data on the usefulness of group meetings were obtained through the following questions, asked of managers and men, respectively:

> Are there any *group meetings* in which the nonsupervisory people in your station or department can discuss things with the supervisors? (Check one.)
>
> _____ Yes, and they are always worthwhile.
> _____ Yes, and they are usually worthwhile.
> _____ Yes, but usually nothing much is accomplished.

_____   Yes, but they are just a waste of time.

_____   No, we never have such group meetings.

Are there any *group meetings* in which the people you work with can discuss things with the supervisors? (Check one.)

(The same five response categories used in the managers' questionnaire were repeated).

The responses to these questions were used to classify the stations into the following groups or clusters:

Cluster A included all 10 stations in which managers said meetings were held and were always or usually worthwhile and where the men's points of view were substantially the same.

Cluster B included all stations, a total of 7, in which managers stated group meetings were never held.

Cluster C consisted of 14 stations in which meetings were held but the men had felt that "nothing much was accomplished" or that the meetings were "just a waste of time," or both the men and the managers had felt the meetings were not worthwhile.

The term *group meetings* means not only formal meetings but informal discussions and spontaneous work sessions. The formality of group meetings is not the significant dimension. The important dimension is the willingness of the manager in formal or informal setting to discuss problems fully with the men as well as his interest in their ideas, his use of their ideas, experience and recommendations, and his desire to stimulate constructive interaction among them.

The group form of organizational structure called for by the modified theory predicts that Cluster A should show better results than the other two clusters on all such variables as production, communication and coordination, the exercise of influence, the degree of confidence and trust, attitudes toward supervision, and employee satisfaction.

The poorest results were expected, theoretically, in Cluster C both because the group meetings were not developing effective work groups and also because meetings called to no purpose imply a disregard for the value of men's time and ideas. This violates dealing with people in such a way as to contribute to their sense of personal worth. As we shall see, the results proved that it is better to hold no group meetings at all than to conduct meetings seen by the men as accomplishing nothing.

When the average productivity of the stations in the different clusters was examined, the productivity results conformed to expectations. There were substantial differences in productivity between the clusters of stations.

Cluster A showed the highest productivity, with 64 percent of these stations showing above average productivity compared with 54 percent for stations in Cluster B and only 32 percent for stations in Cluster C.

When the ratings of top management as to relative effectiveness of stations are used as a criterion, results very similar to those found for productivity are obtained. This is not surprising since management takes productivity very much into consideration in making judgments of station effectiveness. The two different methods of evaluating station performance, productivity and management's rating of station effectiveness, both yield results which conform to expectations based on the modified theory.

It would be expected from the theory that the effectiveness of inter-personal communication processes would be best in Cluster A and poorest in Cluster C, and this turned out to be the case. There were large differences between the three clusters of stations with regard to the proportion of men in the stations who took their complaints first to their supervisor or manager. The stations in Cluster A had an effective group structure, as measured by the presence and quality of group meetings. Among these stations in Cluster A, 96 percent of the men took their complaints and grievances first to their supervisor or manager. Among the men in Cluster B, where there were no meetings, 62 percent said they would do so, but among the stations in Cluster C where the meetings were considered largely a waste of time, only 29 percent would do so. As would be expected, there are substantial barriers in the Cluster C stations which block communication. Several different measures of communication showed the same pattern: communication is best in Cluster A and poorest in Cluster C.

The effect of group meetings upon the efficiency of communication throughout the organization is both marked and important. Not only do the results support the modified theory, but they add evidence that the traditional man-to-man pattern of organization does not achieve the levels of efficient communication required by the complex, highly interdependent human organization necessary to our present-day technologies. The research findings indicate that the achievement of satisfactory efficiency in the communication process requires a relatively high level of effective group functioning in every work group in the organization. Whenever a work group is ineffective, communication at and through that point in the organization is likely to break down. Some managers, recognizing the possibility of this breakdown, periodically hold meetings across two levels of supervision so as to detect any breakdowns and to be able to take steps to correct them.

The modified theory places emphasis not only upon efficient communication but also upon organizational structure and processes through which influence can be effectively exercised. The overlapping group form of organization theoretically should be more effective both with regard to the influence processes and with regard to communication.

The data show that the results conform to the expected pattern. For example, the men in Cluster A stations felt to a greater extent than did the men in the Cluster C stations that they exercised an influence on what goes in their station. Cluster B falls in an intermediate position. (See Figure 1.) These results were obtained from the men's response to the question: "In general, how much say or influence do you feel each of the following groups *has* on what goes on in your station?"

The results in Figure 1 show that the men in the Cluster A stations felt to a greater extent than did the men in the other stations that their station manager exercised appreciable influence on what goes on in station activities. In addition, these men felt that higher management exercised more influence on their station than did the men in the other clusters of stations. The men in Cluster A, in fact, saw *every* level of the organization as exercising more influence on what went on in the station than did the men in the other stations. They saw themselves as exercising more influence, and they saw a greater total amount of influence throughout this part of the organization. There was more reciprocal influence, more coordination, and more influence by management in the Cluster A stations than in the other stations and less in the stations in Cluster C. Here again the results conform to theoretical predictions. In stations where the greatest amount of effective group functioning exists, management and men have more influence upon what goes on in the station. *The group form of organization increases the total amount of influence being exerted and increases in turn the amount of real influence which management can exert.*

When managers' estimates of the situation are used, the same pattern of results is obtained. The managers in the stations in Cluster A saw themselves and their men as exercising more influence than did the managers of the stations in the other clusters. Because of the small number of managers involved, these differences based on the managers' estimates of the situation were not statistically significant. The results corresponded, however, to the men's estimates of the situation.

The data from these stations help to shed light on the kinds of supervisory and managerial behavior which characterize the leadership of the different station clusters. The findings conform to the pattern which the modified theory predicts. The leadership in Cluster A stations, as seen by the men, was more supportive and more likely to use participation than was the leadership in the other stations. Thus, for example, the men in

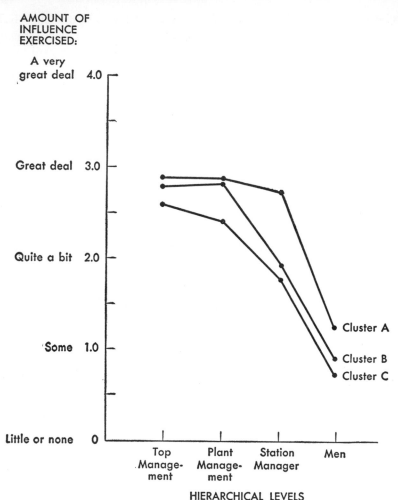

Fig. I. THE RELATIVE AMOUNT OF INFLUENCE EXERCISED BY THE DIFFERENT HIERARCHICAL LEVELS AS SEEN BY THE MEN IN STATIONS DIFFERING IN DEGREE OF GROUP-BASED INTERACTIONS

Cluster A stations were less likely than the men in the other stations to feel that the following modes of behavior described their boss: "Quick to criticize," "blames men," "treats employees like inferiors," "stubborn," "looks out for himself first."

Instead of this threatening and rejecting behavior, the men in Cluster A were more apt than the men in Clusters B or C to see their superior as interested in their welfare. They also saw their supervisor behaving more supportively in other ways. They more often believed that their supervisor would go to bat for them, and consequently they felt freer to discuss their personal problems with him. They also saw their superior as more often asking their opinions when a problem came up involving their work than did the men in Clusters B or C. As might be expected, the men in the stations in Cluster A more often thought than did men in the other stations that their manager handled people well. (Tables and charts representing these results are omitted here but will appear elsewhere in a more complete account of this research.)

There is not space here, unfortunately, to present the data on all the different tests made using the three clusters of stations. Results were obtained, however, demonstrating that the stations in the three clusters did differ in a manner corresponding to theoretical expectations. In summary, Cluster A stations displayed to the greatest extent and Cluster C to the least extent the following:

1. Higher productivity.

2. Fuller, more candid communication throughout the organization (communication upward, downward, and sideward).

3. Higher levels of influence and interaction, including greater amounts of influence by subordinates upon superiors as well as influence by superiors upon subordinates. There was also more influence exerted by the men upon their own colleagues. That is, there was more influence exercised by each person as well as more influence felt by each person.

4. Greater decentralization of the decision-making process with decisions made at lower levels. This was reflected not only in a greater feeling by subordinates that they could exercise influence upon decisions but also that they had sufficient authority and that they were free to make important decisions affecting their work, such as setting their own work pace.

5. More ready acceptance of the goals of the organization. There were more favorable attitudes toward the company and a greater feeling that what was expected of them was reasonable.

6. Higher motivation and evidence of more cumulative and reinforcing motivation and less conflict in motivations and less conflict between personnel.

As a further test of the effectiveness of the group form of organization, a different grouping of the stations into clusters was also used. This second approach to arranging the stations in clusters involved classifying them on the basis of their level of work-group loyalty. Loyalty to the work group was measured not only in terms of loyalty among peers in a group but also included the degree of loyalty to the superior. Moreover, it included the extent to which the superior, himself, showed loyalty to the work group. The 31 stations were divided into four clusters based on these concepts. The two methods—the group-meeting method and the group-loyalty method—used for arranging the stations in clusters yielded somewhat different groups of stations.

When the data were examined for the four clusters of stations based on the degree of group loyalty, the results were comparable to those obtained from the clusters of stations based on whether group meetings were held and were worthwhile. In general, however, the four clusters based on the degree of group loyalty in the stations yielded larger and more marked differences than did the clusters based on group meetings.

The preceding pages have been devoted to examining the performance and operating characteristics of clusters of stations when arranged so as to differ in the extent to which they reflect the group form of organization. In spite of the fact that quite crude measurements of limited reliability were used to classify stations into clusters, impressive results emerged. Equally important differences were obtained from both methods of classification. With both methods, the more a station approached the group form of organization, the greater was the productivity, the better the communication and, in general, the more it approached conformance with the management theory we have proposed.

This test of only one aspect of the modified theory—the group form of organization—yielded sizable differences in performance and operating characteristics. These findings suggest that an effective, full-scale application of the modified theory would achieve a substantial improvement in performance over results now being obtained from more traditional methods of organization and management. Full-scale field tests are needed, of course, to test the amount of improvement which can be obtained. Such tests are being conducted.

The experimental application of the findings emerging from the research done thus far indicates that appreciable improvement in productivity, costs, and human satisfaction can be achieved (Coch and French, 1948; French, Ross, Kirby, Nelson, and Smyth, 1958; Havron, 1960; Hood, 1956; Likert, 1956; McAnly, 1956; Mann and Sparling, 1956; Morse and Reimer, 1956; Rose, 1956). These results, coupled with the promise which research on leadership, organizations, and organizational theory holds for substantial improvement in performance, suggest an important conclusion: there is need for a significant increase in research efforts on these problems. In the United States at present we are devoting less than one-quarter of one percent of our research and development funds, and less than 1/400 of one percent of our total payroll, to basic research in this area. In relation to the importance of this kind of research politically and economically, as well as in terms of world conflict and the rate of growth of our economy, it is evident that we are devoting a seriously inadequate amount of resources and energy to it.

Research needs to be carried on in a substantial and sustained manner; problems are too complex to be solved efficiently by piecemeal attempts. Long-range, programmatic research supported by longevity funds is needed in addition to individual research projects.

REFERENCES

CARTWRIGHT, D. AND ZANDER, A. (Eds.) *Group dynamics: research and theory.* Evanston, Ill.: Row, Peterson, 1953.

COCH, L. AND FRENCH, J. R. P., JR. Overcoming resistance to change. *Human Relations,* 1948, *1,* 512–532.

FRENCH, J. R. P., JR., ROSS, I. C., KIRBY, S., NELSON, J. R., AND SMYTH, P. Employee participation in a program of industrial change. *Personnel,* Nov.-Dec., 1958.

GEORGOPOULOS, B. S. The normative structure of social systems: a study of organizational effectiveness. Unpublished doctoral dissertation, Univ. of Michigan, 1957.

GEORGOPOULOS, B. S. AND TANNENBAUM, A. S. A study of organizational effectiveness. *Amer. Soc. Rev.,* 1957, *22,* 534–540.

GULICK, L. AND URWICK, L. (Eds.) *Papers on the science of administration.* New York: Institute of Public Administration, Columbia Univ., 1937.

HAVRON, M. D. *The contribution of the leader to the effectiveness of small military groups.* See Chapter 10.

HOOD, R. C. Concern for cost: a participative approach. American Management Association *Manufacturing Series No. 221,* 1956, 24–40.

JACKSON, J. M. The effect of changing the leadership of small work groups. *Human Relations,* 1953, 6 (1), 25–44.

JACOBSON, E., KAHN, R. L., MANN, F. C., AND MORSE, N. (Eds.) Human relations research in large organizations. *J. soc. Issues,* 1951, 7 (3), 1–74.

KAHN, R. L. Human relations on the shop floor. In E. M. HUGH-JONES (Ed.), *Human relations and modern management.* Amsterdam, Holland: North Holland Publishing Co., 1958. Pp. 43–74.

KAHN, R. L. AND KATZ, D. Leadership practices in relation to productivity and morale. In D. CARTWRIGHT AND A. ZANDER (Eds.), *Group dynamics: research and theory.* Evanston, Ill.: Row, Peterson, 1953.

KAHN, R. L. AND TANNENBAUM, A. S. Union practices and member participation. *Personnel Psychol.,* 1957, *10,* 277–292.

KATZ, D. AND KAHN, R. L. Human organization and worker motivation. In

L. R. Tripp (Ed.), *Industrial productivity.* Madison, Wis.: Industrial Relations Research Association, 1951. Pp. 146–171.

KATZ, D. AND KAHN, R. L. Some recent findings in human relations research. In SWANSON, E., NEWCOMB, T., AND HARTLEY, E. (Eds.), *Readings in social psychology.* New York: Holt, Rinehart and Winston, 1952. Pp. 650–665.

KATZ, D., MACCOBY, N., GURIN, G., AND FLOOR, L. G. *Productivity, supervision and morale among railroad workers.* Ann Arbor, Mich.: Institute for Social Research, 1951.

KATZ, D., MACCOBY, N., AND MORSE, E. *Productivity, supervision and morale in an office situation: Part I.* Ann Arbor, Mich.: Institute for Social Research, 1950.

LESIEUR, F. G. *The Scanlon plan.* New York: Wiley, 1959.

LIKERT, R. Motivational dimensions of administration. In *America's Manpower Crisis.* Chicago: Public Administration Service, 1952. Pp. 89–117.

LIKERT, R. Motivation: the core of management. American Management Association *Personnel Series A155,* 1953, 3–21.

LIKERT, R. Developing patterns of management, I and II. American Management Association *General Management Series No. 178,* 1955, 1–20 and *General Management Series No. 182,* 1956, 3–29.

LIKERT, R. Measuring organizational performance. *Harvard Business Review,* 1958, *36* (2), 41–50.

LIKERT, R. Motivational approach to management development. *Harvard Business Review,* 1959, 37 (4), 75–82.

LIKERT, R. AND WILLITS, J. M. *Morale and agency management.* Hartford: Life Insurance Agency Management Ass., 1940.

MCANLY, L. C. Maytag's program of expense reduction. American Management Association *Manufacturing Series No. 221,* 1956, 24–40.

MANN, F. C. Studying and creating change: a means to understanding social organization. *Research in Industrial Human Relations,* IRRA Series, Pub. 17. New York: Harper, 1957. Pp. 146–167.

MANN, F. C. AND BAUMGARTEL, H. *Absences and employee attitudes in an electric power company.* Ann Arbor, Mich.: Institute for Social Research, 1953.

MANN, F. C. AND DENT, J. *Appraisals of supervisors and attitudes of their employees in an electric power company.* Ann Arbor, Mich.: Institute for Social Research, 1954.

MANN, F. C. AND SPARLING, J. E. Changing absence rates: an application of research findings. *Personnel,* Jan., 1956, 3–19.

MELTZER, L. Scientific productivity in organizational settings. *J. soc. Issues,* 1956, *12* (2), 32–40.

MORSE, N. *Satisfactions in the white-collar job.* Ann Arbor, Mich.: Institute for Social Research, 1953.

MORSE, N. AND REIMER, E. The experimental change of a major organizational variable. *J. abnorm. soc. Psychol.,* 1956, *52* (1), 120–129.

PELZ, D. C. Influence: a key to effective leadership in the first line supervisor. *Personnel,* Nov., 1952, 3–11.

PELZ, D. C. Motivation of the engineering and research specialist. American Management Association *General Management Series No. 186,* 1957, 25–46.

ROSE, I. A. Discussion. American Management Association *General Management Series No. 182,* 1956, 18–29.

SEASHORE, S. E. *Group cohesiveness in the industrial work group.* Ann Arbor, Mich.: Institute for Social Research, 1955.

TANNENBAUM, A. S. AND GEORGOPOULOS, B. S. The distribution of control in formal organizations. *Social Forces,* 1957, *36* (1), 44–50.

TANNENBAUM, A. S. AND KAHN, R. L. *Participation in union locals.* Evanston, Ill.: Row, Peterson, 1958.

TAYLOR, F. W. *The principles of scientific management.* New York: Harper, 1911.

TAYLOR, F. W. *Scientific management.* New York: Harper, 1947.

WHYTE, W. F. (Ed.) *Money and motivation.* New York: Harper, 1955.

18

Leadership and Organizational Behavior

Carroll L. Shartle

The Ohio State University

A paradigm for the study of leadership (R. T. Morris and Seeman, 1950) formed the framework for a series of studies at Ohio State over a 12-year period. Concepts developed (including method of measurement) were: group dimensions (Hemphill, 1956; Rush, 1957); responsibility, authority, and delegation scales, and administrative work patterns (Stogdill and Shartle, 1955); goal and achievement (Browne, 1950); leader behavior dimensions (Hemphill and Coons, 1957; Halpin, 1957; Fleishman, 1957); and criteria (D. T. Campbell, 1956). Leader behavior change (Fleishman, Harris, and Burtt, 1955) was also studied. An over-all summary from the practitioner point of view was presented (Shartle, 1956), and a new theoretical model has been developed (Stogdill, 1959).

This paper describes an interdisciplinary, descriptive model. It developed from the Ohio State Leadership Studies and places new emphasis on the situation, the environment of organizations, and organizational values. Earlier versions have appeared (Shartle, 1958 a; 1958 b).

ENERGY CHANGE, EVENTS, AND BEHAVIOR

In exploring human behavior, it is necessary to have a certain commonality. We shall use energy change as the basic activity. Energy change in many situations can be perceived, it can be described, and it can be recorded. Furthermore, even though it is not perceived, described, or recorded, it can be inferred as having occurred; or it can be predicted as something that will or will not occur.

Energy change has wide applicability for both theory and empirical research. Kinetic energy, potential energy, and entropy concepts may be used. Miller, in his theory (1955), has developed system levels of the cell, organ, individual, group, and society.

Energy changes can be counted, and their extent and frequency can be estimated and measured in accordance with various standards. Energy changes are also called *events*. When the events are concerned with human beings, they may be called *acts*. Acts singly, or multiple, are human performance or behavior. Organizations also can be described as acts, performance, and behavior. In this paper an organization is considered an arrangement of related functions in which persons perform tasks that contribute to one or more common objectives.

In studying the behavior of persons in organizations, events with various reference points are considered. These include:

1. Individual behavior (acts of a particular person).
2. Organizational behavior (events occurring within the organization).
3. Environmental events (events outside the organization).
4. Interactions of 1, 2, and 3.

No clear and absolute differentiation can be made between these three categories of events; however, it is possible to deal more specifically with one category than with another. For example, the behavior of one person can be studied, but it must be realized that such behavior has a past or present relationship to events in an organization and outside of it. Likewise, events within or without organizations involve acts by individual persons. Also, an observed event is not an energy change in isolation, but it is an observed instance in a complex of many other events.

Figure 1 illustrates relationships. The individual, for example person I_1 among persons I_2 ----n, performs in an organization A. He interacts with events within this organization. He also interacts with events outside the organization which also represent the environment of the organization. This environment B might be a community, for example. A larger environment C could be the state, D could represent the nation, and E outside the nation. Events in A, B, C, D, and E can have an effect on I_1. In attempting to predict the behavior of I_1 in A, it would seem advisable to include events of probable significance in B, C, D, and E.

For example, in predicting whether or not I_1 will remain a member of

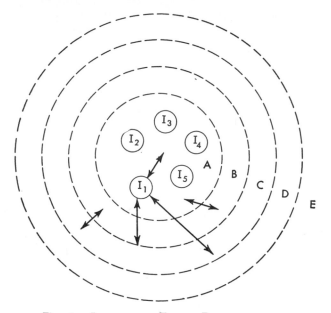

Fig. I. INDIVIDUAL–EVENT RELATIONSHIPS

organization *A* for a specified period of time, events in *B, C,* or *D* may be as significant as events in *A.*

A rise in living costs or new opportunities for employment in *B, C,* or *E* may be important events in such a prediction; yet, in attempting to predict the behavior of persons in an organization, such events are often excluded. Furthermore, we may attempt to predict events in *B, C,* or *D* and fail because events within one or more of the other environmental areas were not included.

ACTS

Human behavior, as mentioned earlier, can be described in terms of energy changes called *acts.* Acts may be described orally or in writing; they may be photographed, predicted, recorded, measured, and evaluated. An act may be the reporting on another act. This is called a *reported act.* Two or more persons may state having seen John Jones enter a specific room at ten o'clock in the morning. Such a reported act (from the standpoint of the reporter) is called a fact. It is simply relating the occurrence of an act or event. In this instance the person, the location, and the time were given.

Whether or not an event occurred, is frequently unclear. One person may report it did occur, another may state that it did not. There also are problems of perception and language involved in reporting an event. The same event may be described differently by various observers; also, instruments used in recording an event may show variations.

An act that is an evaluation of another act, a series of acts, or of an object may be called a *value act.* A person may perform value acts in written or oral form, such as in a questionnaire or an interview. He may report his evaluation in such personal criterion terms as good, poor, worthwhile, beautiful, correct, approved, disapproved.

An observer may infer value acts of a person by observing him directly or by studying his recorded acts; thus, an observer may report that individual I_1 places a high value on hard work for its own sake, or that he thinks working for a large organization is better than working for a small one.

Value acts can be classified according to various scientific concepts. Groups of value acts may be scaled and called *value dimensions.* A combination of value dimensions is called a *pattern.* An individual may be described in terms of his value pattern. An organization, a nation, or a culture can also be described quantitatively in terms of value patterns. The studies of C. Morris and Jones (1955) and of Carter (1951) are illustrations.

The subject matter areas for the study and classification of both *reported acts* and *value acts* are varied. They include:

1. *Historical.* Acts may be noted or inferred in a time setting from documents and other data. They may be classified, and they may be studied as hypothetical dimensions and patterns. Their derivations can be analyzed and their development related to other events and to concepts. The "frontier hypothesis" as an explanation of American values is an example. Methods of content analysis have also been developed (White, 1951).

2. *Socioeconomic.* Acts may be described and grouped within the framework of sociological concepts, economic theory, class structure, stratification, utility theory, culture, group dimensions, organizational behavior, and the like. Kluckhohn (1952), for example, uses a social action theory and presents several dimensions of values including content, intent, generality, intensity, explicitness, and extent. Hyman (1953) mentions class differences in values, and Boulding (1956) uses values in his theory of "Eiconics." Hickman and Kuhn (1956) point out the necessity of knowing the over-all values in American society, for they consider satisfactions as results of achieving group-held values.

3. *Psychological.* Acts may be described and classified in terms of psychological concepts, such as ability, aptitude, interests, needs, personality, self, learning, leadership goals, and motivation. There are many studies in this area. Dimensions of ability, aptitude, interests, and personality have been developed empirically. The Allport-Vernon-Lindzey study of values has been related to interests (Getzels and Guba, 1956; Sarbin and Berdie, 1940) and to perception (Postman, Bruner and McGinnies, 1948).

LEADERSHIP ACTS

Acts which result in others acting in a shared direction we may call *leadership acts.* If they are reports of other acts, they may be either reported acts or value acts.

Within an organization we may define a "leader" in terms of a given proportion of his acts in a span of time that are rated by an observer as leadership acts. Such concepts as "democratic leadership," "good leadership," or "poor leadership" can be defined in terms of such acts; and observed, counted, and recorded.

ACTS AS PREDICTORS

It is well known that persons show individual differences in leader behavior in organizations. It is assumed that part of individual behavior can be accounted for by the more stable or more repetitious events that occur in the organization. For example, if the organization performs in a highly structured fashion, it may be assumed that, other things being equal, a person would perform in a fashion to conform to this organizational characteristic. It is also known that individual performance patterns exist (Stogdill, Shartle, and Associates, 1956). Work habits are formed which tend to be repeated; thus, there is some stability in both organizational behavior and individual behavior.

The Situation

The difficulty in prediction comes, however, when the situation changes. No two days, no two problems, and no two issues are exactly alike. Events are continually occurring which change the picture and throw off the prediction. It is therefore necessary to study, describe, and classify various situations and develop a rationale that will include these new or changed situations.

A situation may be defined as a complex of events occurring at any given time. The events are thus components of the situation. No two situations are exactly alike. Two persons placed in the same physical environment, say an office, may agree on certain events that form the situation, and disagree on others. An observer may present a third picture, describing the situation that both persons are in. In predicting the behavior of a person, certain events in a situation may be useful, independent variables; while others may have no significance in prediction.

Situations can be described and studied as dependent variables. The events which form them can be classified and the dimensions of situations can be developed. These may be shown in patterns and treated quantitatively in research.

Value Patterns

One may assume that an individual will tend to perform acts that he considers worthwhile or more worthwhile than other acts that he could perform at a given time. He acts within his framework of values and modifies his behavior in the light of the situation at hand. For example, an administrator may consider bigness valuable. If asked if he would like his personnel budget increased, he would gladly accept; however, the situation in the organization might be such that to accept would create a serious morale problem in his division. He values the personal job satisfaction of his staff highly and turns down the offer to increase the size of his unit.

Other Measures

While it is assumed that value patterns and situational patterns are important in understanding and predicting leader behavior, it is likewise necessary to have measures of human skill, capacity, interest, and personality to aid in predicting the behavior of the individual person or the organization. The diagram in Figure 2 illustrates the model for behavior prediction in organizations.

While predictions are indeed difficult, encouraging results in predicting individual work performance of persons in nonsupervisory roles in military and civilian organizations can be found in the personnel psychology literature. For persons in supervisory or administrative roles the evidence is slight. Stogdill, Shartle, Scott, Coons, and Jaynes (1956) made a study in predicting the behavior of naval officers by studying the situations to which they were being transferred. Some of the predictions were significant.

In predicting organizational behavior, the results outside of laboratory studies are very rare.

Independent Antecedent Variables	Dependent Variables
1. Value patterns 2. Situational patterns 3. Measures of aptitude, knowledge, and skill 4. Measures of personality and interest 5. Measures of physical energy and capacity 6. Past individual and organizational performance 7. The task or problem assigned	Performance in the organization, including: 1. Decisions made 2. Ratings of performance 3. Measures of attitude change 4. Objective measures of performance 5. Tenure and mobility 6. Work patterns 7. Leader behavior dimensions 8. Sociometric ratings 9. Learning behavior

Fig. 2. ILLUSTRATIVE VARIABLES IN A MODEL FOR PREDICTING ORGANIZATIONAL BEHAVIOR

ORGANIZATIONAL VALUES

Now let us return to a more specific discussion of values. In studying value acts in organizational behavior, a number of methods may be used. It seems appropriate that the organization should provide the framework for measuring individual values. In this method the individual describes his ideal of organizational behavior. This method has the advantage of some degree of indirectness. It allows for the projection of personal values in a particular setting. Also, in the Ohio State Leadership Studies it appeared that there were fewer stereotype responses in describing group behavior than in describing self-behavior or the behavior of individual persons.

Another advantage in using the organization as the frame of reference is that in this method the value patterns of organizations can be indicated as well as those of the individuals in it. Both the desired and the actual value pattern of the organization can be measured in terms of the responses of its members and of outside observers. Also, a person may describe the ideal organization in which he might serve before he becomes affiliated with it. He may also describe what he would expect to find if he did join, and later he could describe the actual values of this organization as he perceives them; thus, a school system, a military service, an industry, or an educational organization can be described and compared with other organizations.

In studying the behavior of small groups, value patterns for each member may be compared, and predictions made concerning the behavior of each individual and of the group when confronted with a specific problem. Bipolar groups can be created, and their behavior likewise studied. In one unpublished study at Ohio State bipolar and unipolar groups were established on a single-value scale. Predictions were made concerning the length of time to reach consensus. A significant relationship was found between actual and predicted time. In decision making, the individual value patterns of participants can be arranged to form a part of the situational framework which should represent a significant factor in predicting the outcome.

In developing the measures for determining value patterns, a large number of statements describing organizational performance have been prepared. Source materials from several disciplines were utilized as well as data from industrial and military organizations.

Certain tentative dimensions of value acts have been considered. Some of the hypothesized dimensions are the following:

1. *Achievement.* It is better to accomplish, to get somewhere, to show progress.

2. *Efficiency.* The more efficient organization is a better one.

3. *Satisfaction.* It is better to be happy than unhappy. The happy organization is a better one. The play that ends happily is the better play.

4. *Changefulness.* Frequent changes are better than infrequent ones.

5. *Competition.* It is good to compete against others.

6. *Newness.* New ideas and things are better than older ones; the newer office, for example, is the better one.

7. *Quality.* Higher quality is better than lower quality. It is best to give high-quality service. A school with higher standards is a better school.

8. *Independence.* It is better to be self-sufficient and independent than dependent. To be able to go it alone, if necessary, is important.

9. *Effort.* Effort for its own sake is good. It is good to try.

10. *Security.* It is better for an individual or an organization to be secure in its existence.

11. *Size.* A bigger organization is a better one. Larger budgets are better than smaller ones.

12. *Rate.* It is better to be fast than slow. To reach a decision in one hour is better than to do it in two hours.

These dimensions have been expressed in positive terms, but it is hypothesized that individual differences can be shown by proper item construction and scaling; in fact, such differences have already been shown, although the hypothesized dimensions which emerged in a preliminary study varied somewhat from the foregoing list.[1] The principal criterion for a value dimension is its worth in predicting behavior.

Some of the specific items are as follows:

> The organization expands at every opportunity.
> The organization emphasizes high standards of work.
> Promoting happiness among employees most important.
> The organization will give a staff member a break in spite of high financial cost.
> The organization meets its objectives regardless of cost.
> Getting things done quickly is strongly emphasized.
> The organization stresses the importance of competition.

In describing an ideal organization, each item is rated according to a criterion of value. It seems wise to have a large number of short statements rather than a smaller number of longer ones as was used, for example, by Morris and Jones. Items can be selected according to the value concepts as proposed by representatives of several disciplines. Some items will fit more than one concept. For example, economic utility concepts may utilize many of the same items as a selection based upon social status or needs.

It is hypothesized that the value patterns of individual persons will show both harmony and conflict in relation to perceived organizational value patterns. A person gains as well as loses something when he becomes a part of an organization. Persons performing leadership acts of wide significance should show greater value agreement with the organization than persons with less influence.

SITUATIONS

The development of dimensions of situations is a difficult task, but there have been sufficient studies of organizations so that a large number of events can be listed and classified. The classifications can be used in describing a number of situations, and the results analyzed to develop dimensions that are relatively unique.

Situations present a challenging problem for theory and for empirical test. The term is often mentioned in the literature, however, and also in day-to-day administration. Cattell (1950) has suggested factorial analysis of situations. Rotter (1955) has emphasized the importance of psychological situations within a social learning theory. R. F. Campbell (1957)

---

[1] The project on value acts and situational variables in organizational behavior is supported by the Office of Scientific Research, U.S. Air Force.

has described its importance in administration. In common dictionary usage situation means *place, location,* or *site.* Within the framework of this paper the situation has a location in time and space, and is describable in terms of objects and events which are assumed to be relevant to predicting the behavior of an organization, or one or more individuals in it. Situations may be described by the persons involved, or by outside observers. Situations may be described in physical, psychological, and social terms. Let us examine several possible *components of situations:*

1. *Distance.* What is the physical distance of *I* (the person whose behavior is being predicted) from the problem that will be acted upon? Is it a problem, for example, in his own office or one in a distant office? It is hypothesized that a decision given by *I,* involving a problem far away, will result in less consideration for the persons concerned than similar decisions in which the members involved are close at hand.

2. *Duration.* (a) How long has *I* been in this described situation, and (b) how long has the situation lasted whether *I* has been in it or not?

3. *Frequency.* (a) How many times has *I* been in this or similar situations, and (b) how many times has this same situation occurred in this organizational setting whether *I* has been a part of it or not?

4. *Social structure.* How structured, in terms of group dimensions, is the situation in which *I* finds himself? It is hypothesized that a person whose value pattern is low on structure will have shorter tenure in highly structured situations than in lower ones.

5. *Status.* How high in status is the individual in the setting in which he will perform? Higher status may result in greater personal independence of action in performance and will more closely resemble the value pattern than in lower status positions.

6. *Leadership climate.* What are the dimensions of leadership climate (as described by an observer or by superiors) in which performance takes place? It is hypothesized that in a climate high in a particular dimension, initiating structure, for example, performance is more likely to be high than low in the dimension.

7. *Value climate.* What is the prevailing value climate in the situation? It is probable that behavior of an individual will tend to show positive relationships with the dominant group patterns in the setting in which performance takes place.

8. *Supply-demand ratio in the occupational field.* It is hypothesized that a low S-D ratio in the occupational area of which the individual is a member will be related to decisions more likely to favor the individual than the organization.

9. *Threat.* How threatening is the situation (as rated by an observer) to the person or the organization whose performance is being predicted? It is hypothesized that in situations of considerable threat, performance is more likely to be structured to minimize the threat.

These examples represent a very incomplete list of possibilities. Within each tentative dimension relevant statements of specific behavior can be prepared. These can be tried out later in "live situations" to determine empirically the uniqueness of the measures and their power to discriminate among situations reliably. Revisions must be made to improve the measures for later use in prediction studies.

LEADERSHIP

Now let us return to the phenomenon of leadership in the organization. We shall consider an organization as an arrangement of related functions performed by persons. The persons perform tasks which are related to a stated purpose of the organization. The organization can be described in three ways:

Physical resources
1. Personnel including their number, training, experience, and potentialities.
2. Equipment such as machines, tools, and weapons.
3. Facilities including plant, buildings, layout; and their location and environment.
4. Monetary resources including reserves, operating funds, and debts.

Structure or *officially intended performance*
1. Stated purpose and goals as found in constitutions, bylaws, policy statements, annual reports.
2. Stated required functions of segments of the organization and their relationships as found in organizational manuals, memoranda.
3. Stated duties of persons; that is, what is required performance as found in job descriptions, operational instructions, task assignments, etc.

Performance, which includes reported and value acts regarding
1. Over-all activity of the organization.
2. Activities of various segments such as departments, divisions, and work groups.
3. Performance of individual persons, their tenure and relationships.

If we assume that a leadership act is an influence act, and we wish to predict both the occurrence of the leadership act and its immediate consequences, we must select and utilize variables from all three of the previous categories. These include:

1. Variables concerning the leader, himself, such as abilities, aptitudes, values, personality measures, education, job experience, social status, previous decisions made, and the like.

2. Variables concerning the dimensions of the situation.

3. The problem, or assigned task within the purpose of the organization.

4. Leadership acts; and behavior in the organization that can be ascribed to the acts.

Suppose we take a hypothetical example: In organization O we have 30 persons assigned to administrative positions. The positions they will occupy are described in the organization structure, and we note that the duties appear to have relatively high-leadership potential in both frequency and power (extent of the influence in terms of number of persons affected).

Within the model previously described, we would predict occurrence of selected events within a specified time span. These might include turnover of personnel, sociometric pattern, job satisfaction of personnel, ratings given administrator by superior, work-pattern profile, rating of productivity of the units under each administrator, tenure of the administrator, size of budget request, and proportion of allocated funds spent. The predictions would be tests of hypotheses of behavior in natural organizations. For each prediction a corollary prediction could be made to indicate the proportion of variance that might be ascribed to the leader behavior of the administrator.

IDEAL LEADERSHIP

Many concepts are found in the literature and in practice which relate to ideal leadership. Much of the variation seems to be in terms of degree, or relative emphasis of leadership styles and outcomes. For example, Halpin (1955) found that the same dimensions of leader behavior seemed to apply to both Air Force and school organization, but the ideal as described by educational administrators and airplane commanders differed significantly in degree within the dimensions. Browne (1957) emphasized "set," or a readiness for the leader to make quick adjustments as the situation and task demand.

Evaluation of leadership is a relative matter regardless of how objective it is claimed to be. The variables selected and the criteria used in selecting the variables are related to several classes of events or characteristics.

First, the purpose of the organization is important. The variables selected for evaluating leadership must be relative to the organization's purpose. General purpose is usually easy to obtain, but to define it specifically may be highly subjective revealing disagreements among persons most familiar with the organization. A second aspect is the task in which the person in a leadership role is concerned in the organization. The task has various characteristics, and within this framework we select variables that seem to be pertinent to the task in which the leader and his group, or a segment of the organization, find themselves. A third factor in evaluation appears in terms of the point of view of the investigator himself. An engineer will perceive certain performances as important in the framework of his evaluation whereas a psychologist will have another point of view that is related to his background and training, and the kinds of performance that he considers important in leadership.

The point of view of the investigator is interesting to observe. For example, Selznick (1957) indicates that the institutional leader is primarily an expert in the promotion and protection of values, and perceives that leadership declines in importance as formal structure increases. In a study in which Selznick's point of view is dominant, we would expect a different set of variables to be considered in the evaluation from those of someone who is oriented toward the small groups approach and who looks upon the leadership effectiveness as primarily one of first-level performers.

March, Simon, and Guetzkow (1958) have a clear preference for propositions that assume that members bring to their organizations attitudes, values, and goals. The propositions they dislike most are those that look upon employees as "passive instruments." The rational man who at one time received a great deal of attention seems to have lost favor but is still highly respected in the literature. Research on small groups seems to have had an influence in diminishing the importance of rationality as a factor in organizational worth and in the appraising of leader performance.

A fourth aspect of evaluation is related to the cultural influences of the time. Evaluating a leader twenty years ago would involve somewhat different variables from those we have in our present cultural influences. In recent years there has been greater importance placed on the "morale" and so-called "human relations" aspects of organization, whereas formerly production and output in specific units of productivity received more emphasis. Taylor's (1911) concepts in scientific management have lost relative importance because of cultural change; yet, one could subscribe that efficiency is still a leading component of both leadership and organizational worth in our present culture. If we define efficiency in terms of input-output ratio, even the social psychologist and the client-centered counseling psychologist are trying to make individuals and organizations more efficient. Tension and conflicts are symptoms of maladjustment. The relaxed person is the one who is physiologically and psychologically efficient. In terms of an organization, we may say that an unhappy individual, or a maladjusted individual, will take up more time of administrators and supervisors and therefore reduce the output of the particular units over which an individual has influence.

These foregoing aspects which one should consider in appraising leadership, or in understanding reports in the literature regarding leadership, necessarily increase the number of variables involved. When one observes the great complexity of leadership and organizational performance, he realizes that at least a sampling of variables from a number of aspects is necessary if one is to have a relatively complete picture. Technological development in statistical analysis and the speed of analysis offset increasing the number of variables and finding relationships among all the variables. The future of research on leadership will involve increased complexity of research design, and a utilization of variables that are often transient. Evaluation is transitory and events in the culture, events in the structure, or changes in task may put quite different emphasis on what one considers ideal leadership. The time factor makes it necessary to have more studies and to accumulate results of such studies in longitudinal experiments that give one a greater perspective.

REFERENCES

BOULDING, K. *The image.* Ann Arbor: Univ. of Michigan, 1956.

BROWNE, C. G. Study of executive leadership in business: III. goal and achievement index. *J. appl. Psychol.,* 1950, *34,* 82–87.

BROWNE, C. G. Leadership and change. *Personnel Admin.,* 1957, *20,* 43–47.

CAMPBELL, D. T. *Leadership and its effects upon the group.* Bur. Business Res. Monogr. No. 83. Columbus: Ohio State Univ., 1956.

CAMPBELL, R. F. Situational factors in educational administration. In R. F. CAMPBELL AND R. T. GREGG (Eds.), *Administrative behavior in education.* New York: Harper, 1957. Pp. 228–269.

CARTER, R. E., JR. An experiment in value measurement. *Amer. sociol. Rev.,* 1951, *21,* 156–163.

CATTELL, R. B. *Personality: a systematic and factual study.* New York: McGraw-Hill, 1950.

FLEISHMAN, E. A. A leader behavior description for industry. In R. M. STOGDILL AND A. E. COONS (Eds.), *Leader behavior: its description and measurement.* Bur. Business Res. Monogr. No. 88. Columbus: Ohio State Univ., 1957. Pp. 103–119.

FLEISHMAN, E. A., HARRIS, E. F., AND BURTT, H. E. *Leadership and supervision in industry: an evaluation of a supervisory training program.* Bur. Educ. Res. Monogr. No. 33. Columbus: Ohio State Univ., 1955.

GETZELS, J. W. AND GUBA, E. G. Interests and value patterns of Air Force officers. *Educ. psychol. Measmt.,* 1956, *16,* 465–470.

HALPIN, A. W. A factorial study of the leader behavior descriptions. In R. M. STOGDILL AND A. E. COONS (Eds.), *Leader behavior: its description and measurement.* Bur. Business Res. Monogr. No. 88. Columbus: Ohio State Univ., 1957.

HALPIN, A. W. The leader behavior and leadership ideology of educational administrators and aircraft commanders. *Harvard educ. Rev.,* 1955, *25,* 18–32.

HEMPHILL, J. K. *Group dimensions: a manual for their measurement.* Bur. Business Res. Monogr. No. 87. Columbus: Ohio State Univ., 1956.

HEMPHILL, J. K. AND COONS, A. E. Development of the leader behavior description questionnaire. In R. M. STOGDILL AND A. E. COONS (Eds.), *Leader behavior: its description and measurement.* Bur. Business Res. Monogr. No. 88. Columbus: Ohio State Univ., 1957. Pp. 6–38.

HICKMAN, C. A. AND KUHN, M. H. *Individuals, groups, and economic behavior.* New York: Holt, Rinehart and Winston, 1956.

HYMAN, H. H. The value systems of different classes: a social psychological contribution to the analysis of stratification. In R. BENDIX AND S. M. LIPSET (Eds.), *Class, status, and power.* Glencoe, Ill.: Free Press, 1953. Pp. 426–442.

KLUCKHOHN, C., *et al.* Values and value-orientations in the theory of action. In T. PARSONS AND E. A. SHILS (Eds.), *Toward a general theory of action.* Cambridge, Mass.: Harvard, 1952. Pp. 388–433.

MARCH, J. G., SIMON, H., AND GUETZKOW, H. *Organizations.* New York: Wiley, 1958.

MILLER, J. G. Toward a general theory for behavioral sciences. *Amer. Psychologist,* 1955, *10,* 513–531.

MORRIS, C. AND JONES, L. V. Value scales and dimensions. *J. abnorm. soc. Psychol.,* 1955, *51,* 523–535.

MORRIS, R. T. AND SEEMAN, M. The problem of leadership: an interdisciplinary approach. *Amer. J. Sociol.,* 1950, *56,* 149–155.

POSTMAN, L., BRUNER, J. S., AND McGINNIES, E. Personal values as selective factors in perception. *J. abnorm. soc. Psychol.,* 1948, *43,* 142–154.

ROTTER, J. B. The role of the psychological situation in determining the direction of human behavior. In M. R. JONES (Ed.), *Nebraska Symposium on motivation.* Lincoln: Univ. of Nebraska, 1955. Pp. 245–268.

RUSH, C. H., JR. Leader behavior and group characteristics. In R. M. STOGDILL AND A. E. COONS (Eds.), *Leader behavior: its description and measurement.* Bur. Business Res. Monogr. No. 88. Columbus: Ohio State Univ., 1957. Pp. 69–73.

SARBIN, T. R. AND BERDIE, R. F. Relation of measured interests to the Allport-Vernon study of values. *J. appl. Psychol.*, 1940, *24,* 287–296. Reprinted in D. C. MCCLELLAND (Ed.), *Studies in motivation.* New York: Appleton, 1955. Pp. 89–101.

SELZNICK, P. *Leadership in administration.* Evanston, Ill.: Row, Peterson, 1957.

SHARTLE, C. L. *Executive performance and leadership.* Englewood Cliffs, N. J.: Prentice-Hall, 1956.

SHARTLE, C. L. A theoretical framework for the study of behavior in organizations. In A. W. Halpin (Ed.), *Administrative theory in education.* Chicago: Univ. of Chicago, Midwest Administration Center, 1958. Pp. 73–88. (a)

SHARTLE, C. L. Value dimensions and situational dimensions in organizational behavior. Proc. Tenth Annu. Meeting Ind. Relat. Res. Assoc., New York, 1958. Pp. 303–313. (b)

STOGDILL, R. M. *Individual behavior and group achievement.* New York: Oxford, 1959.

STOGDILL, R. M. AND SHARTLE, C. L. *Methods in the study of administrative leadership.* Bur. Business Res. Monogr. No. 80. Columbus: Ohio State Univ., 1955.

STOGDILL, R. M., SHARTLE, C. L., AND ASSOCIATES. *Patterns of administrative performance.* Bur. Business Res. Monogr. No. 81. Columbus: Ohio State Univ., 1956.

STOGDILL, R. M., SHARTLE, C. L., SCOTT, E. L., COONS, A. E., AND JAYNES, W. E. *A predictive study of administrative work patterns.* Bur. Business Res. Monogr. No. 85. Columbus: Ohio State Univ., 1956.

TAYLOR, F. W. *Shop management.* New York: Harper, 1911. Pp. 22, 123–124.

WHITE, R. K. *Value-analysis: the nature and use of the method.* New York: Society for the Psychol. Study of Soc. Issues, Association Press, 1951.

19

*Organizational Leadership**

Chris Argyris

Department of Industrial Administration
Yale University

In my early studies of leadership, I believed that organizational leadership was not much different, on a conceptual level, from other types of leadership and was interested in arriving at generalizations about leadership in any situation. For example, although I conducted a study of the leadership pattern of a particular plant manager within an industrial organization, I paid little attention to the organization. As carefully as I could (and as much as the situation permitted) I studied (a) the impact of the plant manager upon his subordinates, (b) the subordinates' adaptation to the leader, and (c) their adaptation to each other (Argyris, 1953a). The results of this field study confirmed the results of such experimental studies as those of Lewin (1948), Lippitt, and White (1957); namely, that an autocratic leader's impact leads the subordinates to become dependent, submissive, and leader-centered; to be in competition against one another which at times results in interpersonal rivalry and hostility; to be productive when the leader is present; to lose a high degree of productiveness when the leader departs.

During the feedback stage of this study, the "subjects" agreed that many of the conclusions such as those listed above mirrored reality as they

---

* The ideas in this article are dealt with in more detail in a forthcoming publication entitled, *The Integration of the Individual and the Organization.*

perceived and experienced it. However, after further discussions it became painfully clear that such phenomena as the managerial controls (for example, budgets, production bogeys), performance ratings, and the formal policies and practices tended to have basically similar impact upon the subordinates as that attributed to the autocratic leadership of their superior. After repeated discussions with the subordinates it became uncomfortably clear that it was impossible for them to separate the impact of the leader from the impact of the organization's controls, and formal policies. Many of the subordinates even spent long hours trying to help construct questionnaires and other research instruments which would effectively control the other relevant variables except the leadership pattern. But, as one man remarked, formal policies and managerial controls were, for him, so integrated with the leadership pattern that when he tried to focus *only* on the boss' leadership pattern, "it just didn't make sense."

Let it be clear that the research team had no difficulty in differentiating between the leadership pattern and formal policies and managerial controls. Consequently, it was hoped that some research instruments could be created that would permit the subjects to make the same differentiations. At one point, the indications were that we were succeeding. It seemed as if accurate instruments had been constructed that truly measured the impact of the leadership pattern alone. However, after careful analysis leading to an agonizing reappraisal, it became evident and was confirmed later by the subjects, that the data did not represent how the subjects truly felt as much as how they knew we wanted them to feel. As one man put it, "After getting to know you so well and watching you struggle to study leadership, what the hell, I tried to give you all the information about leadership in this plant as possible. But now that you pin me down, sure some of the same answers hold for the budgets and the company policies."

LEADERSHIP THEORY AS A SPECIAL CASE OF ORGANIZATIONAL THEORY

After a number of similar failures, I concluded that reality *for the subjects* being studied in an *organizational setting* was a pattern of variables (leadership, managerial controls, and so on) so inextricably inter-related that it was impossible for the subjects to separate them and still speak of reality.

The next step was to conduct a research project in an organization where such variables as controls, formal policies and practices and technology were similar in two units (departments) while the leadership pattern was different. Such an organization was found and a study begun. Shortly, it became obvious that even in such a controlled situation the variables were so interrelated that they critically influenced each other. Thus, in the two departments the same controls and policies were *not* the same for the subjects. The differences in leadership pattern within each department made the same budgets and policies different in the eyes of the subjects.

The more I studied human behavior in an organizational context, the greater became my frustration at the difficulty in controlling variables. Unlike the experimental situations, variables relatively independent of one another seemed nonexistent. As I learned later, it is the very nature of organization not to have independent variables. *An organization is a pattern of variables and to dissect the pattern even analytically is no longer a study of the organization.* I was, therefore, forced to conclude that organizational leadership must be studied not with the major emphasis on leadership, but on the organization.

Leadership theory became a special case of organizational theory. *How does one study leadership through organization?* One important clue related to studying organization (and eventually organizational leadership) came from some early clinical-field-theoretical leadership studies by McGregor and Knickerbocker. They proposed that leadership is a set of functions required by all groups and that a leader in a group free to choose its leadership will tend to be that person who is viewed by the group members as best capable of fulfilling their needs. They also hypothesized that the person selected to lead must need to be a leader if he accepts the group's "call" (McGregor, Knickerbocker, Haire, and Bavelas, 1948).

If this logic is valid, then why would not organizational leadership represent those functions that are necessary for an organization to fulfill its needs? This immediately raises the question, what are the needs of an organization? In order to ascertain these needs we need to know first the properties of organization.

There are a number of ways one can go about defining the properties of organization. One is to develop the properties by conducting empirical research. Another way, and the one I chose, is to define what one believes to be the nature of organization by reviewing the available literature.

The task of reviewing the literature in organizational behavior and developing a theoretical framework was completed. A summary outline of the main propositions which will serve here as the guide for discussion follows. (For greater detail see Argyris, 1957.)

ORGANIZATION VIEWED AS STRATEGY

Personality research suggests that the personality of an individual represents his best attempts to integrate himself internally and with the environment in which he is embedded. It represents his strategy for living. May not the same be hypothesized for an organization? The makeup of an organization becomes simply its strategy to achieve its objectives. These are postulated to be achieving its goals (intended consequences), maintaining itself internally, and adapting to its external environment.

Who chooses the strategy that the organization will follow? At the outset, those signing the legal charter to create the organization have much to say as to how it shall be organized. They plan an organizational structure which they assume represents the best strategy for the organization. Because of historical reasons too complex to discuss here, the basic characteristics of the structure are usually defined by generalizations from economics, scientific management, public administration, and traditional formal organization theory. This strategy is crystallized, "photographed" and represented as a typical organizational chart.

Let us look more closely at the nature of the phenomena depicted by the organizational chart.

THE INTENDED RATIONALITY OF FORMAL ORGANIZATION

The first requirement (or the first characteristic of the strategy) is for the organization to be rational and to make rational demands upon employees. Thus the initial or formal structure represents the intended rational strategy of the organization. Urwick (1953), one of the pioneers in formal organizational theory describes the property of intended rationality eloquently. He insists that the creation of a formal organization requires a logical approach. Although he admits that "nine times out of ten it is impossible to start with a clean sheet," the organizer should sit down and in a "cold-blooded, detached spirit . . . draw an ideal structure." The task of the organizer, therefore, is to create a logically ordered world where, as Fayol suggests, there is a "proper order" and a "place for everything (everyone)" (Koontz and O'Donnell, 1955).

The possibility that the formal organization can be altered by personalities, as found by Arensberg and McGregor (1942) and Stodgill and Koehler (1952), is not denied by formal organizational experts. Urwick, for example, states that the planner must take into account the human element. But he perceives these adjustments as "temporary deviations from the pattern in order to deal with idiosyncrasy of personality." If possible, these deviations should be minimized by careful prior planning.

SOME BASIC PRINCIPLES OF FORMAL ORGANIZATION [1]

Along with the emphasis upon rationality is the emphasis on specialization of tasks, power, and conformity to and loyalty for company objectives. These emphases are embodied in four principles—more accurately assumptions—of scientific management theories represented by the work of men like Urwick (1944), Mooney (1947), Holden, et al (1951), Fayol (1949), Dennison (1931), Brown (1947), Gulick (1927), White (1939), Gauss (1936), Stene (1940), Hopf (1935), and Taylor (1948). Anyone wishing to understand the nature of present formal organization should become well acquainted with the work of these men.

Briefly these principles may be stated as follows:

Task (Work) Specialization. If concentrating effort on a limited field of endeavor increases the quality and quantity of output, organizational and administrative efficiency is increased by specialization of tasks assigned to the participants of the organization.

Chain of Command. The principle of task specialization creates a plurality of parts, each performing a highly specialized task. However, a plurality of parts busily performing their particular objective does not form an organization. A pattern of parts must be formed so that the interrelationship among parts creates the organization. Following the logic of specialization, the planners create a new function—leadership—whose primary responsibility is the control, direction, and coordination of the interrelationships of parts and to make certain that each part performs its objectives adequately. Thus the assumption is made that administrative and organizational efficiency is increased by arranging the parts in a determinate hierarchy of authority where the part on top can direct and control the part on the bottom.

If the parts being considered are individuals, then they must be motivated to accept direction, control, and coordination of their behavior. The leader is therefore assigned formal power to hire, discharge, reward, and penalize the individuals in order that their behavior be molded toward the organization's objectives.

Unity of Direction. If the tasks of every person in a unit are specialized, the objective or purpose of the unit must be specialized. The

---

[1] For a more detailed discussion see Argyris, C., *Personality and Organization,* New York: Harper, 1957, Chapter III.

principle of unity of direction states that administrative and organizational efficiency increases if each unity has a single activity (or homogeneous set of activities) that is planned and directed by the leader.

Span of Control.[2] The principle of control states that administration efficiency is increased by limiting the span of control of a leader to no more than five or six subordinates whose work interlocks.

THE IMPACT OF THE FORMAL ORGANIZATION UPON THE INDIVIDUAL[3]

The impact of the principles above is to place employees in work situations where (1) they are provided minimal control over their workaday world, (2) they are expected to be passive, dependent, and subordinate, (3) they are expected to have a short time perspective, (4) they are induced to perfect and value the frequent use of a few skin-surface shallow abilities and (5) they are expected to produce under conditions leading to psychological failure.

All these characteristics can be shown to be incongruent to the ones *healthy* human beings in our culture are postulated to desire. They are much more congruent with the needs of infants in our culture. In effect, therefore, organizations adapt an initial strategy where they are willing to pay high wages and provide adequate seniority if mature adults will, for eight hours a day, behave in a less than mature manner.

Stating the findings up to this point about the nature of organization in terms of propositions they are:

Proposition I. *There is a lack of congruency between the needs of healthy individuals and the demands of the formal organization.*

If one uses the traditional formal principles of organization (that is, traditional chain of command or task specialization) to create a social organization, and if one uses, as input, agents who tend toward a mature state of psychological development they are predisposed toward relative independence, activeness, use of their important abilities, control over their immediate work world),[4] then a disturbance is created because the needs of healthy individuals listed above are not congruent with the requirements of formal organization which tends to require the agents to work in

---

[2] First defined by V. A. Graicunas (1927).

[3] For a detailed discussion of these principles plus their impact upon the individual *see* Argyris, C., *loc. cit.*

[4] A model for understanding healthy personality is presented in Chapter II, Argyris, C., *op. cit.*

situations where they are dependent, passive, and use few and unimportant abilities.

Corollary 1. The disturbance will vary in proportion to the degree of incongruency between the needs of the individuals and the requirements of the formal organization.

An administrator, therefore, is faced always with an inherent tendency toward continual disturbance.

Drawing on the existing knowledge of the human personality, a second proposition can be stated.

Proposition II. *The resultants of this disturbance are frustration, failure, short-time perspective, and conflict.*

If the participants in the organization desire a healthy, more mature self-actualization, they will tend to experience:

1. Frustration because their self-expression will be blocked (Barker, Dembo, and Lewin (1941); Dollard (1939).

2. Failure because they will not be permitted to define their own goals in relation to central needs or the paths to these goals (Lewin *et al* (1944); Lippitt and Bradford (1945).

3. Short time perspective because they have no control over the clarity and stability of their future (Lewin, 1948).

4. Conflict because, as healthy agents, they will dislike frustration, failure, and short-time perspective which is characteristic of the present job. However, if they leave they may not find a new job easily and, even if a new job is found, it may not be different (Newcomb, 1950).

Based upon analysis of the nature of formal organization, one may state a third proposition.

Proposition III. *Under certain conditions the degree of frustration, failure, short-time perspective and conflict will tend to increase.*

The resultants of the disturbance in the organization will tend to increase (in degree):

1. As individual agents increase in degree of maturity.

2. As the degree of dependence, subordination, passivity increases. This in turn tends to occur: (a) as one goes down the chain of command; (b) as directive leadership increases; (c) as management controls are increased; (d) as human-relations programs are undertaken but improperly implemented.

3. As the jobs become more specialized.

4. As the exactness with which the traditional formal principles are used increases.

Proposition IV. *The nature of the formal principles of organization cause the subordinates, at any given level, to experience competition, rivalry, intersubordinate hostility and to develop a focus toward the parts rather than the whole.*

1. Because of the degree of dependence or subordination of the subordinates toward the leader, and because the number of positions above any given level always tend to decrease, the subordinates aspiring to perform effectively and to advance will tend to find themselves in competition with and receiving hostility from each other.[5]

2. Because, according to formal principles, subordinates are directed towards and rewarded for performing their own task well, subordinates tend to develop an orientation toward their own particular part rather than towards the whole.

3. This part-orientation increases the need for the leader to coordinate activity among the parts in order to maintain the whole. This need for the leader, in turn increases subordinates' degree of dependence or subordination, creating a circular process whose impact maintains or increases the degree of dependence and subordination plus the rivalry and competition for the leader's favor.

Proposition V. *Employees react to the formal organization by creating informal activities.*

Continuing from proposition II, it can be shown that under conflict, frustration, failure, and short-time perspective, employees will tend to maintain self-integration by creating specific adaptive (informal) behavior such as:[6]

1. Leaving the organization.

2. Climbing the organizational ladder.

3. Manifesting defense reactions (day dreaming, aggression, ambivalence, regression, projection).

4. Becoming apathetic and disinterested toward the organization, its make-up and goals. This leads to such phenomena as: (a) Employees reduce the number and potency of the needs they expect to fulfill while at work; (b) Employees goldbrick, set rates, restrict quotas, make errors, cheat, slow down.

5. Creating informal groups to sanction defense reactions, apathy, disinterest, and lack of self-involvement.

---

[5] These problems may not arise for the subordinate who decides to become apathetic or disinterested.

[6] Adaptive activities numbered one to nine become major categories under which much empirical research can be included.

6. Forming informal groups.

7. Evolving group norms that perpetuate the behavior outline in 3, 4, 5, and 6 above.

8. Evolving a psychological set that human or nonmaterial factors are becoming increasingly unimportant while material factors become increasingly important.

9. Acculturating the youth to accept the norms discussed in 7 and 8. Comparing the informal organization, we may state:

Proposition VI: *Employee adaptive behavior maintains individual self-integration and simultaneously impedes integration with the formal organization.*

Proposition VII: *Adaptive behavior of employees has a cumulative effect, feeds back into the formal organization, and further entrenches itself.*

1. Adaptive reactions reinforce each other so that they not only have their individual impact on the system, but they also have a cumulative impact. Their total impact increases the degree of dependence and submissiveness, and also increases the resulting turnover, apathy, disinterest. Thus a feedback process exists where the adaptive mechanisms become self-maintaining.

2. The continual existence of these adaptive mechanisms tends to make them norms or codes which, in turn, act to maintain adaptive behavior and to make it the proper behavior for the system.

3. If the above is valid, then employees who may desire to behave differently from the norms will tend to feel deviant, different, not part of the work community (for example, rate busters).

The individual and cumulative impact of defense mechanisms is to influence the output-input ratio in such a way that greater input (energy, money, machines) will be required to maintain a constant output.

Proposition VIII. *Certain management reactions tend to increase the antagonisms underlying adaptive behavior.*

1. Those managements that base their judgment on the logics of formal organization will tend to dislike the employee. It follows, therefore, that these managements should tend to take those "corrective" actions that are congruent with the logics of formal organization. These actions tend to be: (a) Increasing the degree of directive leadership; (b) Increasing the degree of management controls; (c) Increasing the number of pseudo-human relations programs.

The first two modes of reaction tend to compound, reinforce and maintain the basic disturbance outlined in Proposition I. It follows, therefore, that the behavior included in Propositions IV, VI, and VII will also be reinforced. (This is the behavior management desires to change in the first place.) The third mode of reaction tends to increase the distance and mistrust between employee and management because it does not jibe with the realities of the system within which the employee works.

One must conclude that the management behavior described in Proposition VIII primarily acts to influence the output-input ratio so that a much greater input is required to obtain the same constant output, or that a disproportionately higher input will be necessary for a given increment of increased output.

A word about the propositions outlined above: it is possible for a physical scientist to make such predictions as, if one passes electricity through wire, heat will result. However, he cannot predict a priori *how much* heat will result. The amount of heat can be predicted only by ascertaining the values of such variables as the length and type of wire, the capacity of the battery, the milieu in which the experiment is conducted.

The propositions presented above are on a similar level of generalization. They make such predictions as that the dependence and submissiveness, that people will experience will tend to be caused by formal organization, directive leadership, and managerial controls—to list three major variables. They predict that dependence and submissiveness will frustrate people and place them in conflict *if* people aspire toward the mature ends of the continua listed above. They predict further that people will tend to react by creating informal activities (apathy, indifference, goldbricking, rate-setting). Nothing is said however about *how much* dependence, submissiveness, conflict, frustration, apathy, and indifference is caused. This is a matter of empirical research. The value of theoretical propositions is that they guide the researcher in his choice of relevant variables and the probable relationships among these variables.

For example one can predict that conflict and frustration will tend to be high when the formal organizational structure, the directive leadership and the controls require (a) "maturity-directed" people to be directed toward infancy[7] and (b) "infancy-directed" people to be directed toward maturity. One can predict therefore that absenteeism, turnover, and apathy will be as high when "mature" people are frustrated by being required to be immature as when "immature" people are frustrated by being required to be mature. Furthermore, one can predict that the conflict, frustration, and so on will tend to be minimal when (c) "infancy-

---

[7] The "amount" of conflict, frustration, etc. must be empirically ascertained by measuring the "maturity-directiveness" of employees and the degree to which the organization requires that they be "infancy-directed."

directed" employees are required to behave immaturely, and (d) when "maturity-directed" employees are required to behave maturely.[8]

The predictions above assume that the *amount* of impact of the formal organization structure, leadership, and managerial controls is the same. This may not be the case in actual practice. One might find that the directive leadership, in a given organization, causes more dependence than do the formal organizational structure or the controls. In another organization, the controls may be the major cause of dependence. In short, in the actual world many different combinations are possible. The predictions above also assume that the *direction* of impact for all three variables is the same. Thus, the theory hypothesizes that if the formal structure is defined according to such principles as unity of command or task specialization and if the leadership is directive, and if the controls are defined as they are in scientific management, then employees will tend to experience dependence and submissiveness.[9] Thus the theory hypothesized a priori that these three variables (as defined in the theory) will always lead toward dependence, submissiveness, and so on.[10]

RECAPITULATION

The main points that I have tried to communicate so far are:

1. It may not be possible to study leadership phenomena in an organizational setting without studying the nature of the organization. An organization is a patterning of variables, one of which is leadership. Consequently, to study organizational leadership without relating it to the other variables is futile.

2. Broadly defined, leadership within the organization will function to fulfill the organization's demands in its attempt to achieve its objectives,

---

[8] Case (a) was chosen to be illustrated in *Personality and Organization* because most of the research literature that the writer is aware of supports the view. This does *not* imply that *all* organizations can be so categorized. Organizations will differ and the same organization may differ at different periods of time. In *Personality and Organization* job enlargement and role enlargement are cited as two activities that work against the trend predicted above.

[9] Readers and especially practitioners should be reminded that the model purports to understand all organizations who use, at the outset, a pyramidal structure and people. Thus, for example, churches, families, schools and scout troops tend to coerce dependency long before people become employees of industrial organizations.

[10] Again the problem of ascertaining *how much* dependence or submissiveness is an empirical one that requires research. Also, the impact or effect of dependence submissiveness upon the individuals and in turn upon the organization cannot be predicted without knowing the needs of the individuals. If they desire to be dependent, the effect will be different than if they desire to be independent.

maintain itself internally, and adapt to the sociocultural milieu in which it is imbedded. It follows that to understand the basic functions of organizational leadership we need to understand the nature of organization.

3. Organizations are grand strategies individuals create to achieve objectives that require the effort of many. For historical reasons, most social organizations follow a particular initial or formal strategy whose roots may be found in military theory, industrial economics, scientific management, or public administration.

4. The strategy derived from these roots leads to a pyramid-shaped formal organization defined by such principles as chain of command, unity of direction, span of control, and task specialization. If this formal strategy works as intended, then the analysis could end here. Unfortunately, the formal organizational strategy hits some snags: the primary one being the individual human being.

5. Mutual adaptions take place where the organization modifies the individual's personality and the individual, through informal activities, modifies the formal organization. These modifications become part of the organization.

6. A total organization therefore is more than the formal organization. Conceptualizing it as a behavioral system we may conclude that an organization is a composite of four different but interrelated subsystems resulting in the following kinds of behavior: (a) The behavior that results from the formal organizational demands. (b) The behavior that results from the demands of informal activities. (c) The behavior that results from each individual's attempt to fulfill his idiosyncratic needs. (d) The behavior that is a resultant of the unique patterning for each organization of the preceding three levels.

THE NEED FOR A NEW THEORY OF ORGANIZATION

These four levels of behavior as just described do not exist in real life as separate categories. They are highly interrelated and inseparable.

It now becomes clear that organizational leadership must concern itself with all levels of behavior and not simply with the needs of formal organization. To be sure most administrators (industrial, governmental, etc.) view the leader as being the guardian of formal activities. According to our analysis, however, informal activities and idiosyncratic activities are not only an integral part of the organization, but they assist the organization to achieve its formal objectives (Argyris, 1957, pp. 229–232).

Viewing the formal and informal as inextricably interrelated, points up the difficult position of the organizational leader. For example, if he follows the logic of formal organization, he would not reward employee apathy, indifference, rate-setting, and goldbricking. Yet, these behaviors may be necessary if employees are to maintain mental stability. He could overcome some of these "undesirable" states by becoming a more directive leader and by tightening managerial controls. This may well increase production but it will also increase the dependence and submissiveness of employees which in turn will increase employee apathy, indifference, and so on (Likert, 1958), the very "states" he wants to overcome. Moreover, if directive leadership becomes the rewarded and accepted leadership pattern—and this *is* the most prevalent in industry today (McMurry, 1952, p. 47)—it will tend to inhibit the development of management. The directive, aggressive, upwardly mobile executive tends to have little patience, and even less capability, to develop a cohesive executive *peer* group (Argyris, 1955).

How is the organizational leader to function effectively if he is responsible for administering an organization whose formal and informal subsystems require acts that may run the gamut from being congruent to interfering to being completely incompatible with one another?[11] Which demands shall receive priority? For example should he, for the sake of the formal goals, emphasize dependent, submissive subordination? What informal activities are in the interests of formal organization? Are apathy, indifference, goldbricking, rate-setting acceptable? Are absenteeism, turnover, grievances and conflict necessarily unhealthy? If some conflict is healthy, how much should be permitted and under what conditions? How much idiosyncratic behavior is helpful to the total organization? If there is fear of the organization-man (Whyte, 1956), the opposite extreme of organizational chaos may be even more deadly.

These questions cannot be answered by traditional formal theories of organization because they do not take into account sufficiently the needs of healthy human beings. The informal system or human relations theories of organization are also inadequate because they have little to say about the importance of the achievement of formal goals.

In short, the formal and informal subsystems, although part of the total organization, actually emphasize different values. The differences may be illustrated in the following model. The model represents a series of dimensions each of which is a continuum. On one end is the subsystem whose focus is on individual needs (informal); on the other, the subsystem whose focus is on attainment of the formal objective.

[11] The problems that arise when subsystems of the whole require antagonistic behavior. See Barker, Wright, and Gonick, 1946.

Formal Organization	Informal Organization
1a. At the outset interpersonal relations are *prescribed,* and they reflect the *organization's* idea of the most effective structure within which to achieve the *organization's goals.*	1a. At the outset interpersonal relations *arise* from members' interaction and reflect the *need* of *members* to interact with each other in order to fulfill their needs.
1b. The *leadership* role is assigned to the person the *organization* feels can best perform *organizationally* defined duties.	1b. The leadership role is delegated to the individual the *members* believe will best fulfill their needs.
2a. The formal behavior in organization manifested by an individual is "caused" by the individual's acceptance of *organizationally* defined reward and penalty (sanctions).	2a. All behavior of individual members in the group is caused by the attempts of individual members to *fulfill their needs.*
2b. The dependency of members upon the leader is *accepted* by members because of the existing organizational sanctions.	2b. *Dependency* of members upon the leader is created and accepted by members because they believe it will fulfill their *needs.*

A theory of organization is required which will provide a framework broad enough to include formal and informal behavior as part of a larger more inclusive system. The theory should stipulate the objectives and the internal structure of the organization as well as the relationships it would have with the environment in which it is embedded.[12]

Such a complete theory is not only unavailable, it requires research much of which at this time is not even possible to envision. Has any reader tried to create (even on paper) an organization that changes fundamentally the basic concepts of power, control, and task specialization it may use? Nevertheless a first step must be taken even if it is to be tentative and requires early revision. Some point of departure is needed. What should it be?

One possible *first step* in the development of a more inclusive theory is to define a series of dimensions "external to" or "independent of" the formal and informal activities. They could be used to ascertain quantitatively the present "mix" of these activities and serve as a basis for the selection of the "proper mix" desired for the organization. To put this another way formal and informal activities are strategies. Each is a

---

[12] The relationships between the organization and the environment are represented by strategies not even considered in this paper. However, they must be taken into account if the final theory is to be truly comprehensive.

strategy designed to organize human effort in such a way as to maximize certain values. Formal activities based on scientific management strive to maximize the formal objectives of the organization. Informal activities based on human relations focus on the actualization of the individuals. *Neither activity (alone or combined) is adequate because it cannot specify the proper mix that is required of both.* A new strategy needs to be developed for this purpose.

How is this new and more inclusive strategy to be evolved? Neither of the strategies above is based upon knowledge about the *nature* (properties) of organization. Would it not be possible to develop a more basic strategy by deriving it from what is presently known about the properties of organization? Instead of relating our strategy to the nature of human personality, why not relate it to the nature of organization *per se*? Could not a set of criteria be inferred from the existing literature of organization that can provide the conceptual tools to select the "proper mix" of formal and informal organizational strategies?

Such an approach assumes that we know the properties of organization. Clearly, complete knowledge about the properties of organization does not exist. However, there is an increasing number of scholars in many different fields dedicated toward understanding organization. Part of the impetus stems from a group of scholars interested in unity of knowledge. They believe that the concept of organization may provide the conceptual link among the many levels of analysis that exist today. Another impetus stems from an increasing number of physical scientists (chemist, physicists, and especially biologists) who are beginning to view "organization" as the basis of life—if not life itself.

The writer decided to attempt to develop from readings such as those listed below a first approximation definition of the nature of the organization.[13] The hypothesis was that if some properties of organization could be defined, even if they were very tentative, they might form the basis for defining dimensions of the new more inclusive organizational framework being sought.

A search of the literature revealed that some ideas about the nature of organization keep recurring in the writings of people representing many diverse disciplines. The writer kept an inventory of these basic propositions, which eventually formed the basis for a conceptual definition of the nature of organization. Some examples of propositions that the writer

[13] Gerard, 1958; Redfield, 1942; Feibleman, 1954; Nadel, 1951; Boulding, 1956; Klein, 1953; Szasz, 1955; Bertalanffy, 1952, 1956; Sinnott, 1950; Schneirla, 1951; Goldstein, 1939; Margenau, 1950; Allport, 1955; Mace, 1953; Sinnott, 1952; Cameron, 1950.

found useful were: An organization is characterized by an arrangement of parts that form a unity or whole which feeds back to help maintain the parts (Wiener, 1950). A part of an organization is actually an "organic" part in that it exists by virtue of its position in the pattern that is the whole (Kluckhohn, 1955). The whole, in turn, may be differentiated from the parts along two dimensions. First, the whole has a different boundary than any given part (or subset of parts) (Herbst, 1957; Simon, 1952). Second, the functional unity of the whole displays properties only revealed in the actual process of full operation of the whole (Kurtz, 1956).

These propositions have led the writer to form a tentative conceptual definition of organization. An organization is (1) a plurality of parts, (2) co-existing and interrelated in such a manner that, (3) the parts exist because of their interrelatedness, and (4) simultaneously these parts achieve specific objectives and (5) while accomplishing 3 and 4 adapt to the external environment, thereby (6) maintaining the interrelated state of the parts.

We may now hypothesize that the present "mix" of formal and informal activities of a given organization may be understood and quantified by using a model that incorporates as dimensions the properties implied in the definition above. The properties are: (1) The organization is a pattern of parts. (2) The parts maintain the whole through their inter-relatedness. No one part (or sub set of parts) controls or dominates the whole. (3) The parts change their interrelationships to cope with, and adapt to, new stimuli threatening the organization. (4) The whole is able to control the environment up to the point that is necessary for main-tenance of itself.

The next question that arises is how to use these dimensions? In attempting to answer this question an assumption is made that each of these dimensions does not represent a clear-cut state of affairs. For example, considering the dimension of control (4) we are not implying that one should view it as "no control" versus "control" over the environ-ment. The real world, it is assumed, is not organized in such a "black or white" manner. It is assumed that if the dimensions are to represent the empirical world accurately each should be stated in terms of degrees (more or less control). In other words, the dimensions that are being evolved will be used to measure the *degree* to which an organization has control over its internal make-up, the environment, and other factors.

Each represents a process of minimum to maximum degree of expres-sion. (Minimum and maximum are theoretically rather than empirically definable points.) A process is defined as a sequence of behavior leading to an intended consequence. Each process is assumed to be reversible.

It may seem that an implicit value judgment in the theoretical viewpoint being proposed is that it is "good" to maximize dimensions such as the organization's control over its internal make-up and its environment. If such a dimension could be considered independent of the others, then such a value judgment would indeed be made. However, the position taken here is that organization exists when *all* the properties exist *simultaneously*. It follows, therefore, that *all* the properties ought to be maximized simultaneously. An examination of these properties, however, will show that by their very nature they are not all maximizable at the same time. For example, control over the environment could be maximized if one part (or subset of parts) dominates the whole. If this occurs then the dimension of "the whole being created through the patterning of the parts," is greatly inhibited.

The hypothesis *is* made that every organization should find that *state of optimization* where *all* the dimensions are obtaining maximum possible expression (that is, each dimension is *optimized* in relation to the other dimensions). It is the hypothesis of the writer that no one state of optimization will be "best" for all conditions. Rather, there may be different states of optimization depending upon the conditions being considered at a given time.

The value of the model being proposed lies in its providing the participants of any organization with a systematic methodology by which to determine the degree of expression of each dimension at a given time and to consider the probable outcomes of other states of optimization. By "probable outcomes" one means simply the effect of a change in any one (or more) dimensions on the remaining dimensions. It is assumed that there are not any other relevant outputs for an organization. This suggests another value of the model, namely that it alerts its user to the number of dimensions (and their interrelationships) to be taken into account in considering what is the "proper mix" of the human, formal organizational and environmental activities, in the organization.

A TENTATIVE MODEL FOR UNDERSTANDING THE ORGANIZATIONAL MIX

By using the four basic properties of organization listed above, the following model to understand the mix may be offered for consideration (see Table 1). Four of these dimensions are simply direct copies of the four dimensions discussed above. The other three are inferred from the first four. They are listed as separate dimensions in order to evolve a more differentiated model with greater potential in the empirical world.

Table I

DIMENSIONS FOR UNDERSTANDING THE ORGANIZATIONAL MIX

1. awareness of self as plurality of parts	awareness of wholeness
2. domination of whole by one or subset of parts	maintenance of whole by interrelationships of parts
3. inability to influence internal make-up	influencing internal make-up as desired by participants (parts)
4. few and limited abilities in problem solving	many and deeper abilities in problem solving
5. dependent upon and controlled by environment	controlling own environment and being master of own fate
6. short time perspective	longer time perspective
7. achieving its objectives	achieving objectives so that it can continue to achieve its objectives

I. Awareness Dimension

From an awareness of itself as a plurality of parts to an increasing awareness of itself as a pattern of parts (that is, an awareness of the nature of its internal wholeness).

The first dimension is for the organization to become aware of what it is (its wholeness). Obvious as this dimension may be, few organizations take it seriously. Many managers, in fact, find it easier to treat the organization as if it were a series of discrete parts.[14] They continually make decisions about one department, fully expecting it not to affect the total organization. The fundamental philosophy of managerial controls compounds this practice. Budgets, for example, split an organization into a plurality of discrete parts. The unity, if it is to exist, is to be found in the office of the top official. Such a situation leads to very few people in the organization being aware of, and feeling responsibility for, the pattern (the whole organization). Moreover, if top management performs its coordination function well it can be shown that this will tend to inhibit the expression of the next dimension which will be discussed below (Argyris, 1953b).

Being aware of the uniqueness of the organization is also important

---

[14] For example, see the work of E. W. Bakke, Ernest Dale, Robert Dubin, Mason Haire, Douglas McGregor, William Newman, and William F. Whyte.

because it provides a manageable (conceptual) picture for participants enabling them to identify with the organization. At the same time, the uniqueness of the organization (its organizational charter), to quote Bakke, is valuable for communicating to the outside world the "personality" of the organization (Bakke, 1954). Such knowledge can significantly influence the type of person attracted to the organization as an employee. It also influences customers (individuals or other organizations) to decide if they wish to conduct business with the organization.

2. Control Dimension

From domination of the whole by any part or subset of parts to the maintenance of the whole by the interrelationships of all the parts.

This dimension focuses on the extent to which the organization is controlled or dominated by a particular part. The traditional domination, of course, is that of management over employees. However, this is by no means the only example. In some organizations "sales," in others manufacturing or research and development dominate.

The reader may be interested to learn of a pioneering experiment being conducted in a plant where the traditional concepts of power are being seriously questioned. In this organization any individual is given organizational power as a function of what the individual contributes to decision-making. If he is capable of providing much help for a particular decision, the concomitant organizational power will be given to him. The amount of organizational power an individual (or department) is given varies from decision to decision depending upon the role he (or it) plays in that decision.

In this experiment thought is now being given to changing the financial-rewards system along similar lines. In the traditional scheme organizational power is fixed and static. Mr. A. is assigned a particular responsibility and given a particular scope of authority. Mr. A's wages tend to correlate with the authority and responsibility assigned to him. In the example cited above, the organization is conceived as a series of problem-solving processes, some very simple and some highly complex. Following the first and third dimension, as many parts are included in a decision as is necessary. A given individual, Mr. A, receives organizational power as a function of his contributions to a particular decision. Similarly, his wages might also be computed as a function of his contribution in that decision-making process.

3. The Internal-Influence Dimension

From an inability to influence its internal make-up to influencing the internal make-up as the participants deem desirable.

If we assume that internal adjustments and modifications will be necessary if the internal equilibrium is to be maintained, then it follows that the organization should be able to change itself as it desires. Considering the dimensions Awareness and Control one would also say that as the number of parts that are capable of instituting, participating, and completing changes increases, the organization's effectiveness along this dimension (3) also increases.

One may also hypothesize that any organizational activity the participants desire to change but cannot is a sign of the participants' being controlled by the organization's defenses. Organizational activity that continues against the desires and is beyond the control of the participants is a sign of compulsive activity. It may also be hypothesized that as the participants increase their control over the organizational activity, they will also tend to increase their feelings of success and subsequently feelings of self-worth. These feelings of success, it may be further hypothesized, will tend to lead to organizations developing a "climate" of success.

4. The Problem-solving Dimension

From a few and limited abilities in problem solving to many and deeper abilities. Deeper abilities are those that lead to an analysis of problems in their full complexity and wholeness. Limited abilities are those that lead to analysis of partial aspects of the problem (oversimplification).

In this dimension the properties of "wholeness" and the participation of all the relevant parts to a particular decision-making process are imputed to the problem-solving process per se. Not only must an organization become aware of its wholeness, but it must strive to become aware of the wholeness of the problems that it faces. The more an organization is aware of, or willing to become aware of, its problems, the greater are its chances of solving these problems. Those problems and activities that are kept from conscious awareness and discussion tend to be more rigid, compulsive and uncontrollable. The more the discussion of these problems and activities is suppressed or inhibited the greater the rigidity and uncontrollability of these activities.[15]

Modern organizations have tended to try to maximize this dimension by delegating the more complex decision-analysis or decision-making to high-level staff or line groups. Although such groups could theoretically maximize the expression of this dimension, to the extent that they succeed they will tend to inhibit the achievement of the dimensions Awareness, Control, and Internal Influence. This paradox emphasizes that problem

---

[15] For a stimulating discussion of awareness and therapy see Rex Collier (1956 and 1957).

solving per se is a crucial catalyst with which to achieve the expression of the other dimension or organizational health. To use an example, it may be that an organization can facilitate its influence over the environment (dimension 5) if an expert operations research team finds ways of solving complex marketing problems that traditionally take much time and much effort of many people throughout the entire organization. It can, however, also inhibit the dimensions of Control and Internal Influence because (1) fewer people become aware of the wholeness of the organization, and (2) a few people dominate the decision-making thereby emphasizing a power structure where power resides in the few.

5. The External-Influence Dimension

From being highly dependent upon and controlled by the environment to controlling the environment to the extent that the organization becomes master of its own fate (relative independence).

Organization must be capable of modifying or adapting to the environment so that it can maintain itself. If the organization exists in competition with others then it must find appropriate strategies in order to survive. Research and development, marketing and finance tend to play crucial roles in this dimension. So much has been given this dimension by administrators in the past that further discussion seems unnecessary.

6. The Time Perspective Dimension

From a short-time perspective where the present largely determines the organization's behavior to a longer-time perspective where the behavior is increasingly affected by considerations including the past and future.

An organization that wishes not to be dominated by its environment and that wishes to develop deeper problem-solving abilities characteristically may plan ahead to foresee as much of the future as is possible. The longer the perspective the greater the opportunity to discover new analyses and to make the necessary internal changes in order to adapt to the external environment.

7. The Organizational-Objective Dimension

From achieving its objectives to achieving them in such a way that the organization will be permitted to continue to achieve them.

This dimension is inferred from the fact that the organization exists in an environment where legal, economic, ethical demands may be made of it. An organization that does not take into account the demands of the cultural milieu within which it is embedded, may well find that it is jeopardizing its existence. For example, years ago when many managements operated without thinking of the cultural milieu, laws were passed regulating their behavior. In short, the organization can be facilitated or inhibited by the socioeconomic-political matrix in which it is embedded.

The dimensions above provide only the barest and most tentative outline for measuring the impact of the organizational formal and informal activities mix. They are not offered as definitive but as suggestive of possible fruitful directions. Clearly much research needs to be done to learn if the proposed concept is meaningful and empirically fruitful. Research especially is needed to specify the interrelationships among dimensions. Some dimensions (for example, Awareness and Control) seem to be congruent. Some are congruent at certain points along the continua but become antagonistic at other points. Thus Internal Influence may increase its degree of congruency with Awareness and Control as the number of participants involved increases. It may decrease its degree of congruency as the opposite trend occurs.

Along with the study of the interrelationships among dimensions much research is needed to determine the resultants of a given pattern of dimensions. An organization may wish to know what the "outputs" would be for different combinations or patterns of expression of these dimensions. What would the difference be, for example, if one decreased the expression of awareness, control, and internal influence and increased the expression of problem-solving, external influence, and time perspective? One might increase the tolerance that the organization has toward stress, but also decrease its profit-making and increase the dominance of certain parts over others. The different outputs would have to be defined for all possible patterning of the dimensions.

One final word about use of the model. In the discussion above phrases are used such as, "the organization needs," "the organization must," and "the organization strives." The question arises—as "to what does the organization refer?" Do we imply that there is a unity, independent of the parts? How is the position of "the organization" along each dimension ascertained?

No attempt is being made here to return to the old concepts of "group mind" or "organization mind." In actuality the organization is composed of a number of interdependent subunits (top management, informal groups). For certain problems the organization's position on a given dimension may be a composite score of the three levels of management and employees (the degree of awareness of the whole may increase as one goes up the line). For other problems the organization's position might be a composite of top management and the remainder of the participants (the top management may dominate everyone). In short the actual empirical referrants for the concept of "the organization" on any given dimension will be made explicit in each study. The point being made is that we are not attempting to reify the concept of organization.

SOME IMPLICATIONS OF THE MODEL FOR UNDERSTANDING PRESENT LEADERSHIP LITERATURE

It is very difficult to discuss the implications of a concept which itself has not been clearly defined. Nevertheless, there are a few implications that seem probable and may perhaps provide some idea of the usefulness of the concept.

It is interesting to note that there is nothing in the model that implies a particular leadership style (democratic or autocratic, or laissez-faire, or employee-centered or collaborative leadership style) is best. It is the writer's hypothesis that the type of leadership that will be most effective will depend upon the specific dimensions one decides to emphasize.

Evidence to support this hypothesis is obtained by comparing some of the existing leadership research with the dimensions above. For example, it may be that when a leader attempts to increase the expression of dimensions Control and Problem-solving, he may find it unnecessary to be understanding but be judgmental and critical (Fiedler, 1957). Similarly could not dimensions control and problem-solving be achieved without maintaining maximum friendly atmosphere (Torrance, 1955; Cattell, 1951; Martin, Darley, and Gross, 1952)? Is it possible that Case's (1954) and Davison's (1954) findings that an effective leader may go against public opinion could be related to the organization's attempt to decrease the environment's control over its destiny? Cannot Halpin's (1954) and Hemphill's (1955) findings that both consideration and initiating structure are important dimensions be inferred from the model? In short, the model may well provide a conceptual bridge to integrate many presently seemingly discrete and, at times, antagonistic findings that have been emerging from the leadership research.

May not the model also shed light on the old problem of leadership trait theory *versus* the situational theory. Stogdill (1948), Gouldner (1950), Krech and Crutchfield (1948), Gibb (1947), and Jennings (1943), and many others criticize the trait theory of leadership, but when faced with the task of providing a conclusion they suggest that leadership behavior depends primarily upon the situation and not upon any inherent leadership traits—although some traits may be common to all leaders. Carter typifies this middle-of-the-road conclusion when he states, "As a general statement, it would appear that leadership is neither completely general nor completely specific to the situation" (Carter, 1953).

If one focuses on a total organization one immediately notes that organizations tend to evolve a particular culture or character. This culture tends to define what is appropriate leadership. As organizational norms coerce conformity to particular types of leadership patterns, individuals soon learn how they should behave as leaders within these organizations (Argyris, 1958). Thus the nature of the organization's culture defines the accepted leadership behaviors which are then internalized by the "successful" leaders. As soon as one accepts the possibility of a feedback from the environment "into" individuals, then the trait *versus* situational argument becomes fruitless.

If the organization coerces leadership toward a narrow band of behaviors then a homogeneous list of appropriate leadership behaviors will evolve. Assuming organizational leaders follow the dictates of the organization then they make the appropriate behavior part of themselves (perhaps through unconscious processes such as identification and suppression). Under these conditions leadership traits will tend to make sense. If, on the other hand, an organization coerces a variety of leadership behaviors and rewards non-conformity then the trait theory will not tend to be particularly applicable.

SOME IMPLICATIONS OF THE MODEL ON ORGANIZATIONAL EFFECTIVENESS MEASURES

For many years the armed forces and certain large organizations have been conducting research to measure the effectiveness of a unit. The logic is that if organizational effectiveness can be understood then the tasks of organizational leadership would become evident. In these studies *formal organizational strategy* is used to obtain dimensions of effectiveness. Thus if absentee rates, grievances, turnover, work stoppages are low and production is high the organization is assumed to be healthy (Merrehue and Katzell, 1955).

The difficulty with this approach is shown in recent research conducted by the writer. A plant was studied that was evaluated as "excellent" and "the best in the system" by the top corporate staff and by the top local management of the plant. Moreover, the employees themselves reported high positive attitudes toward the company. They liked it and remained very loyal to it. As a result the grievances, turnover and absenteeism were so low that no central records were kept either at the plant level or the corporate headquarters. Production was high. By the typical indices this plant was highly effective.

However, after careful investigation it is now apparent that along with the above indices of effectiveness one also finds a very high degree of (a) emphasis on money and security by employees (b) high *non*involvement in the company's financial and organizational problems, (c) high desire *not* to interact with management or employees and (d) high degree of alienation (Argyris, 1959). These results can be made intelligible by showing that this organization's "mix" includes only a few of the dimensions defined above.

A second limitation of the majority of "organizational effectiveness" studies is that they focus on *end products* such as loyalty, morale, turnover, grievance rates, and so on. There are two basic problems that arise from this approach. First, end products as these are *symptoms* of the *internal* system. They may, but they may *not,* be accurate signs of the internal state of the organism.

In the field of medicine some symptoms (for instance, of the absence of cancer) turn out to be quite inaccurate under more careful diagnosis. Thus end products as symptoms may not necessarily represent a true picture of the internal state of the organization. Moreover, since organizations exist in an ever changing milieu no one set of symptoms can remain valid for a lengthy period of time. One way medicine attempts to increase the predictive validity of its symptoms is to pick those symptoms that are derived from research knowledge about the *mechanisms* of illness. This should provide a hint for organizational research.

It may be more useful to focus on the *processes* (mechanisms) by which effectiveness or noneffectiveness is created rather than on end results. The dimensions defined are hypothesized to be valid processes and can serve as the basis for such studies.

SOME IMPLICATIONS OF THE MODEL FOR ORGANIZATIONAL LEADERSHIP [16]

What implications are to be inferred from the model for the functions of an organizational leader?

---

[16] These dimensions are presumably valid for any kind of activity within the organization. Economic, technological and human activities should presumably strive to maximize the organization's position along each of the continua above. In the case of leadership activities within the economic and technological aspects of the organization, little can be said by this author. I can only hope that some economists and engineers might find these dimensions useful and develop operational measures for each.

First an effective organizational leader is aware that the formal organization is designed with a much simpler concept of organizational effectiveness in mind. High profits and high human loyalty to the formal organization are the primary components of the traditional theories of organization. In the model above profits have their place. For example, an organization cannot, in our culture, produce without a profit and at the same time minimize its dependence upon the environment (5) and guarantee continued production (7). But there may be much more to effectiveness than profits. The dimensions Control, Internal Influence, and Problem-solving do not deal directly with profits. On the other hand, the informal or human relations theories are also incomplete and an over emphasis on them could lead to other difficulties. Consequently, the organizational leader must find ways to optimize (not maximize) the degree to which individuals obtain self-expression and simultaneously formal organization achieves a profit.

As is mentioned before, the reason that optimization is desirable is that the organizational leader is faced with some dimensions whose maximization may lead to the minimization of another dimension.

The organizational leader functions to help departments and divisions become aware of their organizationally determined defenses and rigidities. Once awareness is obtained then the next step is to control these defenses and rigidities. Control over the organization's defenses can lead, if the participants wish, to their modification.

These examples illustrate some questions that can be raised when the model presented here is used and are adequate enough to show the theoretical and practical possibilities in studying organizational leadership by focusing on the total organization.

REFERENCES

ALLPORT, F. H. *Theories of perception and the concept of structure.* New York: Wiley, 1955.

ARENSBERG, C. M. AND MCGREGOR, D. Determination of morale in industrial company. *Applied Anthropology*, 1942, *1*, 12–34.

ARGYRIS, C. *Executive leadership.* New York: Harper, 1953 (a).

ARGYRIS, C. Human problems with budgets. *Harvard Business Review*, 1953, *31*, 97–110 (b).

ARGYRIS, C. Top management dilemma. *Personnel*, 1955, *32*, No. 2, 123–134.

ARGYRIS, C. *Personality and organization.* New York: Harper, 1957.

ARGYRIS, C. Some problems in conceptualizing organizational climate. *Administrative Science Quarterly*, 1958, *2*, 501–520.

ARGYRIS, C. The individual and organization: An empirical test. *Administrative Science Quarterly*, 1959, *4*, 145–167.

BAKKE, E. W. *The fusion process.* New Haven: Yale Labor and Management Center, 1954.

BARKER, R. G., DEMBO, T., AND LEWIN, K. *Frustration and regression.* University of Iowa, 1941.

BARKER, R. G., WRIGHT, B. A., AND GONICK, M. R. Adjustment to physical handicap and illness: A survey of the social psychology of physique and disability. *Social Science Research Council,* 1946, *55,* 8–54.

BERTALANFFY, L. V. AND RAPOPORT, A. (Eds.), *General systems.* Society for the Advancement of General Systems Theory, 1956, 1.

BERTALANFFY, L. V. *Problems of life.* New York: Wiley, 1952.

BERTALANFFY, L. V. Problems of general system theory. *Human Biology,* 1951, *23,* 302–312.

BOULDING, K. *The image.* Ann Arbor: Univ. of Michigan, 1956.

BROWN, A. *Organization of industry.* New Jersey: Prentice-Hall, 1947.

CAMERON, E. *General psychotherapy.* New York: Grune and Stratton, 1950.

CARTER, L. F. Leadership in small group behavior. In SHERIF, M. AND WILSON, M. O. (Eds.), *Group relations at the crossroads.* New York: Harper, 1953.

CASE, L. M. *French opinion on war and diplomacy during the second empire.* Philadelphia: Univ. of Pennsylvania, 1954.

CATTELL, R. B. New concepts for measuring leadership in terms of group syntality. *Human Relations,* 1951, *4,* 161 and 184.

COLLIER, R. M. Consciousness as a regulatory field: A theory of psychopathology. *Psychol. Rev.,* 1956, *63,* 360–369.

COLLIER, R. M. Consciousness as a regulatory field: A theory of psychotherapy. *J. abnorm. soc. Psychol.,* 1957, *55,* 257–282.

DAVISON, W. P. Preliminary finds reported in a paper identified as *P-851.* Santa Monica, Calif.: The Rand Corp.

DENNISON, H. S. *Organization engineering.* New York: McGraw-Hill, 1931.

DOLLARD, J. et al. *Frustration and aggression.* New Haven: Yale, 1939.

FAYOL, H. *General and industrial management.* New York: Pitman, 1949.

FEIBLEMAN, J. K. Theory of integrative levels. *Brit. J. phil. Sci.* 1954, 5 and *17,* 59–66.

FIEDLER, F. C. Non fraternization between leaders and followers and its effects on group productivity and psychological adjustment. Paper presented at Symposium on Preventive and Social Psychiatry, Walter Reed Army Institute of Research, April, 1957.

GAUSS, J. M., WHITE, L. D., AND DEMACK, M. E. (Eds.), *The frontiers of public administration.* Chicago: Univ. of Chicago, 1936.

GERARD, R. W. (Ed.) Concepts in biology. *Behav. sci.,* 1958, *3,* No. 2, entire issue.

GIBB, C. A. The principles and traits of leadership. *J. abnorm. soc. Psychol.,* 1947, *3,* 267–284.

GOLDSTEIN, K. *The organism.* New York: American Book, 1939.

GOULDNER, A. *Studies in leadership.* New York: Harper, 1950.

GRAICUNAS, V. A. Relationship in organization. In L. GULICK AND L. URWICK (Eds.), *Papers on the science of administration.* New York: Institute of Public Administration, 1927. Pp. 183–187.

GULICK, L. AND URWICK, L. (Eds.), *Papers on the science of administration.* New York: Institute of Public Administration, 1927.

HALPIN, A. W. The leadership behavior and combat performance of airplane commander. *J. abnorm. soc. Psychol.,* 1954, *49,* 19–22.

HEMPHILL, J. K. Leadership behavior associated with the administrative reputation of college departments. *J. educ. Psychol.,* 1955, *46,* No. 2, 385–402.

HERBST, P. G. Situation dynamics and the theory of behavior system. *Behav. Sci.,* 1957, *3,* 13–29.

HOLDEN, P. E., FISH, S., AND SMITH, H. L. *Top management organization and control.* New York: McGraw-Hill, 1951.

HOPF, H. A. *Management and the optimum.* Ossining, N. Y.: Hopf Institute of Management, 1935. An address before the Sixth International Congress for Scientific Management, London.

JENNINGS, H. H. *Leadership and isolation.* New York: Longmans, 1943.

KLEIN, M. J. Order, organization and entropy. *Brit. J. phil. sci.,* 1953, *4.*

KLUCKHOHN, C. Anthropology. In J. C. NEWMAN (Ed.), *What is science.* New York: Simon & Schuster, 1955. Pp. 356–357.

KOONTZ, H. AND O'DONNELL, C. *Principles of management.* New York: McGraw-Hill, 1955. P. 24.

KRECH, D. AND CRUTCHFIELD, R. S. *Theory and problems of social psychology.* New York: McGraw-Hill, 1948.

KURTZ, P. W. Human nature, homeostasis and value. *Phil. and Pheno. Res.,* 1956, *17,* 36–55.

LEWIN, K., *et al.* Level of Aspiration. In J. McV. HUNT (Ed.), *Personality and the behavior disorders.* New York: Ronald, 1944. Pp. 333–378.

LEWIN, K. Time perspective and morale. In G. W. Lewin (Ed.), *Resolving social conflicts.* New York: Harper, 1948. Pp. 103–124.

LIKERT, R. Measuring organizational performance. *Harvard Business Review,* 1958, *36,* 41–50.

LIPPITT, R. AND BRADFORD, L. Employee success in work groups. *Personnel Administration,* 1945, *5,* 6–10.

LIPPITT, R. AND WHITE, R. K. An experimental study of leadership and group life. In T. M. NEWCOMB AND E. L. HARTLEY (Eds.), *Readings in social psychology.* New York: Holt, Rinehart and Winston, 1957.

MACE, A. Homeostasis, needs and values. *Brit. J. Psychol.,* 1953, *20,* Part 3, 200–210 (General Section).

MARGENAU, H. *The nature of physical reality.* New York: McGraw-Hill, 1950.

MARTIN, W. E., DARLEY, J. G., AND GROSS, N. Studies in group behavior: II. *Educ. psychol. Measmt.,* 1952, *12,* 533–553.

McGREGOR, D., KNICKERBOCKER, I., HAIRE, M., AND BAVELAS, A. The consultant role and organizational leadership. *J. soc. Issues,* 1948, *4,* No. 3.

McMURRY, R. N. Man-hunt for top executives. *Harvard Business Review,* 1952, *32,* No. 1.

MERREHUE, W. V. AND KATZELL, R. A. ERI—Yardstick of employee relations. *Harvard Business Review,* 1955.

MOONEY, J. D. *The principles of organization.* New York: Harper, 1947.

MORLEY, R. *Bio Politics.* London: Dent.

NADEL, S. F. *The foundations of social anthropology.* London: Cohen and West, 1951. Pp. 29–30.

NEWCOMB, T. M. *Social psychology.* New York: Holt, Rinehart and Winston, 1950.

REDFIELD, R. (Ed.) *Levels of integration in biological and social systems.* Lancaster: Jacques Cattel Press, 1942.

SCHNEIRLA, T. C. The 'Levels' concept in the study of social organization in animals. In ROHRER, J. H. (Ed.), *Social psychology at the crossroads.* New York: Harper, 1951.

SIMON, H. A. Comments on the theory of organization. *Amer. pol. sci. Rev.,* 1952, *46,* 1130–1139.

SINNOTT, E. W. *Cell and psyche; the biology of purpose.* Chapel Hill, N. C.: Univ. of North Carolina Press, 1950.

SINNOTT, E. W. The biology of purpose. *Amer. J. Ortho-Psychiatry,* 1952, *22,* 457–468.

STENE, E. D. An approach to a science of administration. *Amer. pol. sci. Rev.,* 1940, 34.

STOGDILL, R. M. Personal factors associated with leadership: A survey of the literature. *J. Psychol.,* 1948, *25,* 35–71.

STOGDILL, R. M. AND KOEHLER, K. *Measures of leadership structure and organization change.* Columbus, Ohio: Personal Research Board, Ohio State Univ., 1952.

SZASZ, T. A. Entropy, organization and the problems of the economy of human relationships. *Int. J. of Psychoanalysis,* 1955, *36,* 289–297.

TAYLOR, F. W. *Scientific management.* New York: Harper, 1948.

TORRANCE, E. P. Perception of group functions as a predictor of group performance. *J. soc. Psychol.,* 1955, *24,* 271–282.

URWICK, I. *The elements of administration.* New York: Harper, 1944.

URWICK, I. *The elements of administration.* New York: Harper, 1953.

WHITE, L. D. *Introduction to the study of public administration.* New York: Macmillan, 1939.

WHYTE, W. H. *Organization man.* New York: Simon & Shuster, 1956.

WIENER, N. *The human use of human beings.* New York: Houghton, 1950.

PART **IV**

Critique

20

Critique[1]

John G. Darley[2]

University of Minnesota

In 1946, when the Office of Naval Research Advisory Panel on Human Relations was created, its members attempted to define rather broadly the areas of research for which contract support might be granted. Three of these five areas were defined as: leadership, communications, and performance of groups. Now it is compellingly clear that these three areas cannot stand as separate categories. The chapters of the current text clearly indicate the interaction of the variables within and between these three broad domains. History, again, has demonstrated that research does not remain confined in the neat and tidy pigeonholes frequently perceived from armchairs.

In a recent article (Darley, 1957), I attempted to tell the story of the first ten years of this program, which started in 1946. In 1950, at Dearborn, Michigan, the first symposium was held for the presentation of research findings to that point. The proceedings at the Dearborn symposium were later published in the volume entitled *Groups, Leadership, and Men* (Guetzkow, 1951).

There are many signs of positive progress since the earlier symposium and during the years that have passed since Jenkins wrote his review of the

---

[1] This invited critique by Dr. Darley followed the symposium presentation and discussion of papers. It is considered a valuable commentary by a person who has been associated closely with such research in both military and civilian settings for many years.

[2] Now Executive Officer, American Psychological Association, Washington, D. C.

357

field of leadership research (Jenkins, 1947). For one thing, our statistical and design sophistication has increased tremendously; we have today better statistical tools and they are more widely known among research workers. In the second place, we do our research somewhat more incisively —some of our variables are better named and better measured. In the third place, I think we do have some generalizable findings and a larger body of verifiable knowledge on group behavior, on communications, and on leadership. Finally, some of our best research places considerable emphasis on time and the flow of experience as the matrix in which group and individual interactions take place; in 1950 and earlier we were less skillful in weighing the importance of these variables. While we may still be a long way from solving all of our problems or turning over to society a technology of leadership and group behavior, we have made undeniable progress toward these goals.

Now let us consider two criterion questions that may be asked by any informed layman and must be answered, since the ultimate fruit of research in this society is application. First, this question: If we were given the job of setting up a group or an organization to attain a given set of objectives, how well could we do it on the basis of our present knowledge? This is not an unrealistic demand; the situation is often faced in a society such as ours. How would we select the members of this new group? how long would we have them together to attain maximum development? how would we train them? how would we measure their effectiveness? how would we displace them if it became necessary to do so? how long a period of infancy and adolescence would the group have to serve?

The second question is not unrelated to this. If we had to select leaders for society, could we choose them more efficiently than society now does? in how many situations would we have to see them perform before we were satisfied that they were leaders? are our earlier and unsophisticated ideas about leadership traits completely invalid? is leadership only to be perceived in specific situations? These queries reflect realistic requirements for a society that needs leaders most desperately. While much progress has been made, the over-all measure of this progress may be found in our answers.

Before reviewing specific chapters, some gaps and some pitfalls in current research may be mentioned. One of these gaps is the lack of research on power. With rare exceptions, the problem of power and its use as a central issue in the psychology of groups and individuals is ignored. In 1953 Cartwright delivered a brilliant paper on this subject as his SPSSI presidential address; French (1956) and his students have made important contributions. Many of the problems with which psychologists deal fundamentally may be treated as illustrations of the exercise of power, psychologically defined, yet it seems to me that too little attention has been given to this as a central problem in the psychology of groups and leadership.

Second, research on the problem of organization and its meaning in society must increase. A basic reference here, of course, is still Barnard's book *The Functions of the Executive* (1938). Sociologists have been more concerned with this issue than have psychologists and with telling theoretical effectiveness; Caplow on the problems of organizations (1953) is a good example. Caplow establishes three criteria for organizations: the performance of objective functions, the minimizing of internal conflict, the maximizing of personal satisfaction. He furthermore gives certain properties of organizations: identity, continuity, authority, and calendarity.

Psychologists seem to treat groups and organizations as entirely separate entities; and it may well be that a profitable area of investigation should involve the behavior of people in organizations rather than of people in what we call the "small face-to-face groups." The transition from group to organization is a gradual and possibly imperceptible one and the organization may be the scene of interaction that is more important.

In this same context, and again with reference to sociology, we fail to take account of organizational problems that can be conceptualized and treated independently of human participants. References have been made to the work of the sociologist, Philip Selznick. I should like to make an additional reference to a study by one of his students, Burton Clark (1956). Clark studied the decline of the adult education function in the Los Angeles city high schools and the parallel emergence of control of that function by junior colleges in the Los Angeles area. The concepts which he formulated can be treated independently of the human participants in the conflict situation he dealt with. These concepts have considerable relevance where a sick organizational system is doomed to death and where the social forces are operating to bring a new system into being.

Our reason for concern with these matters is the possibility of a fundamental incompatibility between the individual and the group. If we look at the domain of industrial management and work simplification, we can see at least one limiting case. If, for example, the same volume of work can be accomplished in half the present working time, why not do it in the same working time with half the working force? It is obvious that the history and the sociology of labor-management relations make this solution impossible.

This suggests that leadership studies should go beyond the use of groups uniformly made up of well-mannered, white, Anglo-Saxon, upper-middle-class youth, with IQ's above 110, found in the sophomore classes of the major state universities and colleges of the United States. More field studies of ongoing organizations should be made.

Another matter of continuing concern is the reification or definition of variables as they appear in many experiments. In the realm of definition, I think we have completely demonstrated and overdetermined two variables that first arose in the Ohio State University research on leadership: consideration and initiation of structure (Stogdill and Coons, 1957). Like the authoritarian scale, however, they were found to be somewhat multiform as we trace, through Research Monograph No. 88, the items which appear in the scales under various conditions and at various times. But again, like the authoritarian scales, these variables seem adequately defined, and they seem essentially to be the same variables that Dr. Flanagan talks about under the terms *Planning and Motivating.* They may also be the same variables that Dr. Berrien describes under the terms *formal achievement* and *group need satisfaction;* they are the same that Dr. Likert has in mind when he discusses feelings of personal worth and ways of attaining these feelings. In all these studies, research converges to give the reader greater assurance that these are true and relevant variables in understanding the behavior of individuals in either groups or organizations.

In the study reported by Dr. Fiedler, and the study by Dr. Berrien examples of reification may occur. In the Fiedler study the variable entitled "assumed similarity of opposites" (ASo) is set forth. As he makes his series of successive sorts based on his sociometric data, the correlations between assumed similarity of opposites and a good production criterion maximize. But his sortings based on sociometric scores result in increasingly tight networks of influence and relationship between key personnel: the general manager, the immediate subordinate, the most influential director who is also the formally designated Board of Director's leader. ASo may be an artifact and neither a causal nor a contingent variable, while other variables are truly producing the maximized validity coefficients. If so, the reification of ASo may be misleading in this context. Since the studies reported by Dr. Fiedler are part of a continuing and systematic program of research, these matters will be resolved as the body of results grows.

Similarly, Dr. Berrien discusses in his study the correlations among the independent and dependent variables and the reduction of the matrix to some smaller number of variables that might be more meaningful and more clearly named. The theory in this study is highly intriguing but its

CRITIQUE   ·   361

demonstration requires further evidence because of the problem of definition of the variables coordinated to the theory.

The dichotomy *democratic–authoritarian* used to define leadership behavior or group behavior should be avoided by psychologists. These terms have a legitimate and meaningful usage in the field of political science. But when they are taken out of this context and applied to laboratory research they may be misleading and may have a pejorative connotation that biases the interpretation of research findings. An article that appeared several years ago discussed these terms in their applications to the psychotherapeutic process (Meehl and McCloskey, 1947). The authors pointed out the dangers of this kind of conceptualizing and the inapplicability of these terms to interpersonal processes. This issue is raised because we perceive an immediately favorable aura surrounding any experiment that is "democratic" and we are unfavorably biased by the term "authoritarian," without a clear understanding of whether these dimensions are really applicable in studying leadership or group behavior.

Let us return for the moment to the possibility of a fundamental incompatibility between the needs of the individual and the needs of the group or organization. In the article by Caplow he points out that two of his criteria of organizational success may at times be incompatible. In the Ohio State studies, we learn that group efficiency is high only when both consideration and initiating structure are adequately high. In effect, the manager or the supervisor or the intermediate leader is trapped in the service of two masters. If he fails markedly in consideration, his subordinates will find him inadequate. Alternatively, if he fails markedly in initiating structure, his superiors may find him inadequate. This situation is dealt with by Professor Argyris.

There are two other issues to which I think we may fail to give adequate attention. Both of these are touched on in the paper by Dr. Havron. The first of these is the effect of the size variable in the study of groups or organizations; this has been a largely neglected issue. An exception to this general statement is the study showing a positive relation between size and goodness of administrative reputation of academic departments recently reported by the Ohio State series (Hemphill, 1955). Certainly with respect to organizational effectiveness our folklore about size is extensive, but true evidence about size either related to tasks or to interpersonal networks is hard to find. In our folklore, the small organization is good and the big organization is somehow bad.

The second issue, which also appears in Dr. Havron's paper, is the phoenix of leadership traits, which rises again from the ashes in which

Stogdill earlier found it entombed (Stogdill, 1948). The reader will recall that Dr. Havron reported very high correlations between intelligence-test scores of the leader and an external criterion of the effectiveness of the group. These correlations may go almost unnoticed in the discussion but they deserve far more serious consideration since it has become fashionable to define leadership as related to situations and as relatively uninfluenced by individual traits. We cannot, I think, brush under the rug the problem of leadership traits as easily as we have seemed to do in recent years. Two examples come fairly quickly to mind. In Thurstone's 1944 factorial studies of perception, in which he used very small samples of administrators and nonadministrators, he found that the variable which he named "speed of closure" gave rather clear differentiation between his two samples. In another study, done in our laboratory, Hochbaum found that the group was able to exert less influence on a deviant member if the deviant member was convinced of his own ability to deal successfully with the task facing the group. Conversely, when the deviant member was made to feel that he had no competence in the group task, he was easily influenced by the group (Hochbaum, 1954).

More attention in our studies of group behavior and leadership should be given to the interaction of individual traits and situational factors. This in part is the contribution I find in Bronfenbrenner's chapter, when he tries to analyze patterns of family development as these may relate to external criteria when the individual is studied later in his role as group member. If asked about our ability to select leaders better than society presently does, would we not in answering be obliged to use trait names or individual variables as well as situational variables?

Toward the end of World War II in a conference on military psychology (Kelly, 1947), an argument was made for dropping the word "morale" from our vocabulary as a psychological construct or as an intervening variable because we could not clearly arrive at its components or the behavioral criteria for it. In the report of the 1950 ONR symposium (Guetzkow, 1951) a point quite similar to this was made by Katz in describing some of the results of the Michigan ONR projects. I wonder what would happen today if we dropped the word "leadership" from our vocabulary for essentially the same reasons and focused our attention primarily on differential behaviors or leading behaviors in groups or organizations. With respect to this problem of the global concept of morale or leadership, a review by Brayfield and Crockett shows low relations between morale and productivity (1955). The authors conclude that the various global terms—morale, satisfaction, and so on—are surprisingly unrelated to individual or group performance.

With respect to the individual chapters, I used a criterion that may not be satisfying to some, but it has meaning to me and it can be simply stated: which research has been most helpful to me as a psychologist serving as an administrator in higher education? Admittedly, this is a highly personalized criterion and is unacceptable for other situations. Additional criteria should be used to evaluate research in a comprehensive manner. The following examples illustrate some research related to such a practical purpose.

Dr. Roby's work meets this applied criterion because it embodies a new theoretical framework for the function of the power group in the executive group and shows how this functioning can aid in the definition of the leader's role and responsibility. In general, this conceptualization opens a new window on the executive function and permits it to be viewed in a meaningful way.

Dr. Back's study is unusual in that it deals with definable and replicable processes for exercising power. Influence is brought to bear for the attainment of stated ends, and differential influence forms are clearly analyzed. Dr. Back's research, while it goes beyond the earlier article by French, has its origins in the same kind of theoretical framework.

The series of studies reported by Dr. Hemphill provides the greatest utility in the outcomes of the third and fourth experiments. The relations that he establishes between motivation for the group task and expectancy of accomplishing it and between expertness and task accomplishment are meaningful and useful findings in the area of attempted leadership.

The chapter by Dr. Hollander not only clears away some of the confusion surrounding the relations between leaders and followers and "popularity" nominations, but importantly provides the developmental concepts of idiosyncrasy credit and status emergence, as these variables operate over time, to give clearer insight than we have had in the past on the interaction between situations and individual traits.

In the report by Dr. Flanagan, particularly in his summary of the Herzberg study, we have a formulation that accounts for many of the findings of limited correlations between job attitudes, management policies, and productivity. Here the job situation is first defined in terms of its power to prevent dissatisfactions; beyond this job situations may or may not be so arranged as to lead to positive motivations for workers. This, schematically, might be represented by a truncated or J-shaped distribution of the variables.

Dr. Guetzkow, as I have pointed out earlier, comes to grips with the group and organization problem; I was fascinated by the fact that some form of organization did emerge in 14 of his 41 groups. His treatment of learning and of personal variables as part of the contingent nature of leadership emergence gives a new emphasis for consideration of these factors. Perhaps he should further analyze the origins of the decisions that led certain groups to take on organizational structure whereas other groups failed to do so.

Out of the long-continuing history of concern with problems of leadership behavior, Dr. Shartle and his colleagues now project pragmatic means for scaling the situations and value patterns to be found in organizations. This would appear to be a development as fruitful as the earlier Ohio State research on leadership behavior and also happens to be quite comparable to the very crucial research now under way at Syracuse University by Pace and Stern in their studies of college environments and student needs and the congruence or lack of congruence between these two domains. Thus Dr. Shartle's report has a pragmatic utility in this series of papers.

In Dr. Torrance's work, based on studies of behavior under stress, he carries, as no one else has done, the fate of the group to its ultimate dissolution or death under certain conditions of stress. This phenomenon is more frequent than we may realize in the great variety of groups that spring up in any community. If they do not actually die or dissolve, they achieve a moribund state and their effectiveness and membership appeal sink almost to the vanishing point. The variables which he names are not always clearly distinguishable: power, communication, goal linkages—but these can be classified and the major importance of the presentation lies in its emphasis on time and on the interaction of personal and situational variables.

I have already commented upon the chapter by Professor Argyris, and I believe that this contribution most clearly faces us with the issue of the conflict between individual needs and group needs in the organizational setting.

I cannot deny a sense of urgency that motivates me, in using such a criterion, to urge psychology to move ahead as rapidly as possible in practical realms and as significantly as it is capable of doing. It may be later than we think in a society that needs our services, and we may have less time than we might hope for in a less disturbed world.

Much more should be said about the theories underlying the research reported in this volume. New leadership theories are emerging as illustrated in various chapters. Some are in fairly advanced stages. In contrast to older theories, they are buttressed by an accumulating body of experimental data. This is the crucial distinction between current psychological work on leadership and most of the previous writing. Some of the studies follow the epistemological method of deduction from prior theoretical positions; others represent an approach through observational studies in a more natural setting. Both approaches are useful in the present state of our knowledge.

In 1950, when summarizing the results of the Dearborn symposium, I identified certain issues which, I felt, had received too little attention in research projects. Let me mention these briefly, since I think they are pertinent here also.

First, we had then and we have now no adequate taxonomy of groups. We have no good classification scheme accompanied by defining and distinguishing characteristics of groups. We are not entirely clear how they come into being, what their types and functions may be, and how they grow and die.

Second, and I believe this follows from our lack of taxonomy, we had in 1950 and we have now no clear sampling characteristics of the universes of groups with which we deal. Since we have no idea of the parameters, we have also no idea of the samples and our generalizations are, therefore, in some degree indeterminate.

In the third place, in 1950 and again today, we are too quickly willing to reason by analogy from the domains of individual behavior to the domains of group behavior. We often use the same terminology in describing the behavior of groups that we have found to be valid in describing the behavior of individuals. This tendency may actually obscure the relevant variables and may delay the formulation of concepts that we need. Schutz's reversal of this tendency presents an intriguing, and possibly useful, direction for research.

As a fourth issue, it seems to me that we fail to do enough research on groups comprising young children, in which one might postulate that we would find purer samples of the behavior under investigation. We should show more concern with the developmental aspects of the behavior of individuals in group situations, as Bronfenbrenner has done.

Finally, now as in 1950, criteria for the effectiveness of groups need improvement. Certainly the criterion problem has a long and thorny history in psychology and this history haunts us today when we must concern ourselves with the performance of groups.

This symposium has been another step in the long development of military support of psychological research. This support imposes an obligation upon us that is in no way incompatible with our freedom as scientists to explore new pathways. The obligation that we cannot avoid, however, is to produce at the highest level of excellence of which psychology is capable.

REFERENCES

BARNARD, C. I. *The functions of the executive.* Cambridge: Harvard, 1938.

BRAYFIELD, A. H. AND CROCKETT, W. H. Employee attitudes and employee performance. *Psychol. Bull.,* 1955, *52,* 396–424.

CAPLOW, T. The criteria of organizational success. *Social Forces,* 1953, *32,* 1–9.

CARTWRIGHT, D. Toward a social psychology of groups. Presidential address, SPSSI, Cleveland, Ohio, September, 1953. Mimeographed, 34 pp.

CLARK, B. R. *Adult education in transition; a study of institutional insecurity.* Univ. of California, 1956.

DARLEY, J. G. Psychology and the Office of Naval Research: a decade of development. *Amer. Psychologist,* 1957, *12,* 305–323.

FRENCH, J. R. P., JR. A formal theory of social power. *Psychol. Rev.,* 1956, *63,* 181–194.

GUETZKOW, H. (Ed.) *Groups, leadership, and men.* Pittsburgh: Carnegie Institute of Technology, 1951.

HEMPHILL, J. K. Leadership behavior associated with the administrative reputation of college departments. *J. educ. Psychol.,* 1955, *46,* 385–401.

HOCHBAUM, G. The relation between group members' self-confidence and their reactions to group pressures to uniformity. *Amer. Sociol. Rev.,* 1954, *19,* 678–687.

JENKINS, W. O. A review of leadership studies with particular reference to military problems. *Psychol. Bull.,* 1947, *44,* 54–79.

KELLY, G. A. (Ed.) *New methods in applied psychology.* Proceedings of the Maryland Conference on Military Psychology, 1947, (see especially pp. 129–135).

MEEHL, P. E. AND McCLOSKEY, H. Ethical and political aspects of applied psychology. *J. abnorm. soc. Psychol.,* 1947, *42,* 91–98.

STOGDILL, R. M. Personal factors associated with leadership: a survey of the literature. *J. Psychol.,* 1948, *25,* 35–71.

STOGDILL, R. M. AND COONS, A. E. (Eds.) *Leader behavior: its description and measurement.* Ohio Studies in Personnel, Research Monograph No. 88, Bureau of Business Research. Columbus: The Ohio State Univ., 1957.

Subject Index

Action, 139, 145
Action units, 119
Acts, 311–316
Adolescent leadership
  dependency and, 262
  differential parental influences on, 265–266
  differing antecedents of, 261–263
  father's educational level and, 242, 249–252, 263–265
  major hypotheses, summary of, 268–269
  maternal influences in, 246–249
  methodology
    design limitations, 245–246
    information gathering methods, 242–246
    post hoc evaluation of, 241, 246
  parental behavior and
    absence, 243, 251, 253, 256–257, 266
    perception of, 253, 257
    permissiveness, 239–240
  parent-child relations, dimensions of, 242–246
  responsibility, relation to, 256
  socialization practices, sex factors in, 246–249, 259–261, 265

  social-structural hypothesis, 266–268
  socioeconomic factors, 239–240
  variables affecting, 241, 243, 248
Affect linkages, 106–107, 108, 111–113
  adverse factors in, 111–113
Affiliative companionship, 252, 254
Alloplastic adaptation, 54
Ascendance, 195–196
ASo
  as psychological distance measure, 182
  reliability, 182
  sociometric aspects, 183
  studies of, 182–185
Assumed similarity between opposites, see ASo
A-system, 143–147, 158–160; see also Power
Attempted leadership; see also Leadership
  acceptance of, 205–207
  and decision making need, 212
  motivation for, 213–214
  needs, types of, 205–207, 212
  rejection of, 205–207
  task factors
    completion expectancy, 207–209
    completion motivation, 207–209, 213–214

367

evaluation of, factors in, 321–323
experimentation on, lack of, xiii–xiv
followership dichotomy, 30
formal achievement, 98
functions
  as completer, 61–62
  in conflict-free group sphere, 60–61
  executive, 119, 130–135
  FIRO view, 54
  interpersonal needs, 59–60, 62, 98–99
  outer reality factors, 58–59
  in small groups, 61–62, 199
general theory, 3–9
good squad leader, 172–173
group and
  defense level, 72; see also Defense level
  optimal size, 175–176
  need satisfactions, 98–99
  small, 199
  selection standards, 34, 38
  task orientation, 187–200
headship as distinct from, xvii–xviii
historical theories, xii
historical trends in study of, xix–xxv
homeostasis, see Homeostasis
ideal, 321–323
idiosyncracy credit in, 38–45
improvement, methods of, 109–115
influence exertion in, 162
intelligence and, 169–171, 193–195
interdependent variables in, 98
local learning, effects of, 196–198
military training for, 173–175
models of
  organizational mix, 350–351
  pyramid, 35–38
Navy participation in study of, xxv–xxvii
operational conception of, 175
opinion, types of, 158–159
and organization xvii–xviii
organizational, theory of, 327–328, 337–342
overchoosing in, 16
paradigms for study of, 310, 327–328
perceptual criteria of, see Role
personal mechanisms in, 193–196
personal, study of, 134–135
phenomenological aspects, 7
planning in, 196–198
popularity, 16–17, 32, 34, 162
power loadings in, 35
predictors of, 169–171

prior reinforcement of followers, 4
providing structure, 14, 16, 101–102, 187–200; see also Initiation-of-structure in interaction
psyche-tele attraction, 34
pyramid model, 35–38
reinforcement, 283
restricting factors, xiv–xv
role criteria, see Role
selection of, personal aspects, 34
sharing of, xvii, 283
situational factors in, xxiii
social growth promotion, 16
social process facilitation, 14, 21–22
sociometric study of, 10–29, 33–36
  criteria, 15–17, 34–35
  definitions, 14–15
socio-tele attraction, 34
status in, 5
stress factors, 100–117
  continuity under, 101, 108
  loneliness under, 110–111
  mediation of, 105–108, 112
style pattern sequence, 69–70
successful, 4–6, 14, 17, 21, 201–202
supplementary processes in, 118–121
supportive aspects, 303–330
task proficiency superiority, 169–171, 202–204
task process facilitation, 14
technical competence, 169–171, 202–204, 209–210
theory, lack of, xiii–xiv
trait approach to, xxi, xxii, 32, 179–181, 201, 361–362
  vs. situation, 181, 348
types of, 4–5
wartime studies of, xxiv–xxv
willingness to act in, 173
Leadership skills
  definitions of, 275–283
    procedures, 276
    representative behaviors, 277
  development of, 283–285
  evaluation of
    group production, 286–287
    performance records, 286
    situational performance, 285–286
Lever movements, 132
Local learning, 196–198
  and hierarchical organization, 197
  prematurity of, 197

Majority organ, 141
Maladaptive role distribution, 70–73

Author Index

378 • AUTHOR INDEX